BODIE

"THE MINES ARE LOOKING WELL . . ."

BODIE

"THE MINES ARE LOOKING WELL . . ."

―――――◦◦―――――

The History of the Bodie Mining District
Mono County, California

―――――◦◦―――――

By Michael H. Piatt

NORTH BAY BOOKS
EL SOBRANTE, CALIFORNIA

Published by
North Bay Books
P. O. Box 21234
El Sobrante, California 94820
(510) 758-4276
www.northbaybooks.com

Cover design by Judy Hicks.
Interior design and typesetting by John Strohmeier.
Maps by The Map Center, Berkeley, California (themapcenter@aol.com).
Color photography by James C. Ritchie (www.JCRitchie.com) and Bob Pilatos (rlpilatos@earthink.net).
Stock certificates reproduced with permission of the following: Addenda Gold & Silver Mining Company (1787), Roger Lauderdale; Bechtel Consolidated Mining Company (5573), Gil Schmidtmann; Bodie Bluff Consolidation Mining Company, Gil Schmidtmann; Bodie Consolidated Mining Company (14018), Gregory Bock; Bodie Consolidated Mining Company (15583), Roger Lauderdale; Bodie Tunnel and Mining Company (1257), California Historical Society; Empire Gold and Silver Mining Company (395), Ken Prag; Goodshaw Mining Company (5384), Roger Lauderdale; Jupiter Mining Company (2060), Gregory Bock; Jupiter Mining Company (939), Roger Lauderdale; Mono Gold Mining Company (8406), Roger Lauderdale; Mono Gold Mining Company (9177), Gregory Bock; Noonday Mining Company (158), Roger Lauderdale; Noonday Mining Company (425), Gregory Bock; Oro Mining Company (605), Roger Lauderdale; Standard Consolidated Mining Company (2355), Gregory Bock; Tioga Consolidatd Mining Company (1265), Roger Lauderdale.

Printed by Edwards Brothers, Ann Arbor, Michigan.
Distributed by Publishers Group West.

ISBN (Paper): 0-9725200-0-7
ISBN (Cloth): 0-9725200-5-8

Library of Congress Control Number: 2003105823

First Printing: August, 2003

Note: Abandoned mining areas pose extreme dangers.
The Bodie mining district contains many hazardous
sites that are not open to visitors. When you visit Bodie
State Historic Park, please respect all restrictions.

CONTENTS

APPENDICES

MAPS

Hard rock, hard work, and often very hard prospects, although combined with difficulty and danger, have never for a moment daunted or dismayed them. Above ground or under, by daylight or candlelight—onward—ever onward—has been their unswerving resolve—and the guiding star of hope has ever shone with cheering light upon their labors. May the reward be near.

—Hutchings' California Magazine, October 1857

I never started mining until I was six years old. I dug a hole out back by the porch, and my dad fell in it. That was the end of my mining until I was 15.

—Robert T. "Bobby" Bell, February 26, 2000

This work is dedicated to Bobby Bell and all Bodie miners who struck hammer against steel in the search for riches.

Robert T. "Bobby" Bell
1914-2003

Map 1. Bodie Locator

ACKNOWLEDGMENTS

During years of research and writing about Bodie, I have been extremely fortunate to receive assistance from many people, and I would like to express my gratitude to them. Foremost was Robert T. "Bobby" Bell, who befriended me at Bodie more than 30 years ago, and who has generously shared his mining savvy and knowledge of Bodie District. Without his constant tutoring this work would be greatly diminished. I owe a tremendous debt to Gregory Bock and Vickie Daniels, who graciously provided many photographs from their private collections. Their generosity significantly improved the book's historical value. For providing other photographs and original materials, I express sincere thanks to Daniel L. Bryant, Russell and Anne Johnson, Gill Schmidtmann, Mallory Hope Ferrell, Ken Prag, Roger G. Lauderdale, and Peter E. Palmquist. Thanks also to the institutions whose names appear in the photograph credits.

On the difficult geological and mineralogical sections, invaluable assistance was provided by California professor of geology and Bodie enthusiast, D. D. Trent. Corri Jimenez unselfishly supplied material discovered while researching her master's thesis on Bodie architecture and structural preservation. Rod MacDuff, Paul Thompson, and Larry Meeker of the Friends of Bodie Railway & Lumber Co., Inc., and David F. Myrick and Mallory Hope Ferrell shared information about Bodie's railroad.

For their kind assistance in locating information and supplying materials, my thanks to the staff of many research facilities: the Bancroft Library at the University of California–Berkeley, California State Library–California History Room, Nevada Historical Society, California Historical Society, California Department of Parks and Recreation, California State Archives, California Department of Conservation–Division of Mines and Geology Library, Boston Public Library, Society of California Pioneers, Seaver Center for Western History Research at the Natural History Museum of Los Angeles County, New York Public Library, W. E. B. Du Bois Library at the University of Massachusetts, Bernhard Kummel Library of the Geological Sciences at Harvard University, Baker Library–Harvard University Graduate School of Business Administration, the Library of Congress, and the Mono County Recorder's Office. Special thanks go to those employees of the Research Library at Old Sturbridge Village who processed countless interlibrary loan requests.

Among the historians, writers, and valued friends who generously gave me the benefit of their expertise and wisdom are Stanley W. Paher, Robert E. Stewart, Gregory Bock, Evanne Jardine, Jessica Holland, Thomas D. Kelleher, Peter Komlos-Hrobsky, H. James Nicholson, Ruth M. Lyon, Henry Peach, Peter E. Brightman, Kitty Lowenthal, and John Strohmeier. I am especially indebted to Larry Lowenthal, who took time from his own research and writing projects to read several drafts of the manuscript and who provided invaluable guidance throughout its development. Thanks also to James C. Ritchie and Bob Pilatos for permission to use their ghost town photographs of Bodie.

To my wife, Anne S. Hrobsky, who challenged me to write this book, then endured endless conversations about Bodie's mining history, I wish to express my deepest gratitude.

Finally, I wish to acknowledge my appreciation to my long-time friend, Dick Koerner, who tirelessly accompanied me on several chaotic research adventures across California and Nevada.

Michael H. Piatt
August 2003

FOREWORD

BY GARY F. KURUTZ

Bodie, in the popular mind, is best known as one of the wildest and wickedest mining camps in history, giving rise to such colorful expressions as "Goodbye, God. We are going to Bodie," and "The Bad Man From Bodie." Its photogenic weather-beaten structures annually draw multitudes of tourists eager to learn about Bodie's heyday, when its Main Street roared with drinking and gambling saloons and its earth yielded millions in gold and silver. Surviving today as part of the California State Parks System in a "state of arrested decay," the picturesque ghost town of Bodie serves as a powerful reminder of a time when much of California and the West depended on the boom and bust economy of her mines.

Bodie's relatively long history occupies a distinctive place in the annals of Western mining. While "discovered" in 1859 and thriving by the 1880s, Bodie had its roots in the California gold rush and Nevada's Comstock Lode. Once those diggings had played out or showed signs of decline, former 49ers and Comstockers headed to the barren slopes of the eastern Sierra hoping to "see the elephant" once again. Producing paying ore well into the twentieth century, Bodie witnessed the evolution of an industry from picks and shovels to highly sophisticated mechanized mining. It has thus been called "the last of the old time mining camps." In short, this ghost town out in the middle of nowhere enjoys an unmatched charisma, captivating all who wander its abandoned streets inspecting the relics of a bygone era.

With such a storied and raucous past, Bodie and its mines have attracted scores of historians, journalists, archaeologists, and enthusiasts of the Old West. It has inspired a rich literature, full-scale museum exhibitions, and multimedia productions. Not surprisingly, many of the guidebooks, narrative histories, and other productions about Bodie focus more on its glamorous and romantic side rather than the complexities of industrialized mining. Fortunately, much documentation has been carefully preserved in archives, libraries, and museums, providing the resources for the historian and curator. Bodie is also a photographer's dream with its classic Western storefronts, dusty streets, abandoned mining equipment, and barren yet magnetic landscape. This jumble of abandoned hotels, saloons, residences, and stores presents a scene straight out of a classic Hollywood shoot-em-up Western.

Michael Piatt, in this brilliantly and exhaustively researched book, has produced a history of this famous Mono County mining community like no other, combining both the lure and lore of its colorful past with a systematic and energetic account of the industry that made the town. As will be seen through the fact-filled pages of this book, he brings a unique perspective. Trained as an engineer, and later as a traditional blacksmith, he has an unmatched feel and enthusiasm for his subject. Because of his background, one senses that his keen mind can easily relate to the problems encountered by the engineers who built the machinery needed to bring out the ore and convert it into bars of bullion.

Bodie: "The Mines Are Looking Well . . ." tells the story of this mining town by providing a thorough analysis of the harsh and bitter reality of the day-to-day struggle to eke out a living digging for the elusive gold and silver hidden below the surface. Pulling together an impressive array of firsthand accounts, countless reports from newspapers and scientific journals, interviews with the town's last residents, and compelling historical photographs, he weaves an incredible narrative of how the men of Bodie tackled the daunting physical challenge of extracting its precious metals.

Bodie superbly illustrates the evolution of mining technology in the Far West and represents an amazing industrial timeline. The stereotype of the lone prospector, symbolized by the area's namesake, W. S. Bodey, gave way to a phalanx of men armed with heavy equipment directed by absentee corporate executives. Making a profit in this risky business required constant engineering inventiveness and flexibility. Skill and experience, combined with a little luck, uncovered immense deposits of mineral-bearing rock. As the decades passed, however, the high-grade ore became more and more elusive, demanding ever-increasing ingenuity. When drilling deeper and deeper failed to produce the desired result, the shafts were abandoned. Showing mulish faith, those in charge turned to mill tailings, then to the mountains of dumped rock outside mine entrances, seeing in those heaps of waste materials potential wealth by employing newer recovery techniques.

Extracting the ore, however, was more than digging, drilling, and sifting. Manipulation of mining company stocks seemingly became as important as engineering skill. Supporting complex operations such as the mines of Bodie required massive infusions of capital to sustain operations and purchase the equipment necessary to drain the shafts, build stamp mills and hoisting works, grade and maintain the supply roads, and provide the immense quantities of firewood needed to fuel the steam-powered pumps, hoists, and stamp mills. Owners of these operations consumed cash at alarming rates, and constantly turned to investors in the stock exchanges of San Francisco and New York to raise funds. Assessing stockholders became a common practice. The hint of a big strike could reap a fortune (at least on paper), and the rumor of a dead end could just as quickly cause financial ruin. Speculation was rampant.

Mining had a strong psychological element. While Bodie's mines did produce millions of dollars, the town lived on hope, hope for the next bonanza. Like all mining districts, its investors, engineers, miners, laborers, and their families pinned their futures on finding the next golden vein. Many projected that Bodie would surpass the mighty Comstock Lode. Every freighter, boilermaker, liveryman, barkeep, housewife, and prostitute associated with a mining town hoped and prayed that those toiling hundreds of feet below would continue to find paying ore. Just a few more feet of tunneling would result in hitting the big one that would sustain the town for years and pay off its owners and investors.

Inevitably, the Bodie mining district and its town died. The low productivity of the mines and a terrible inferno in the 1930s accelerated the area's demise, and souvenir-hunters threatened to desecrate what was left of this once proud bonanza town. Fortunately for history, the California Department of Parks and Recreation stepped in and took over custodial responsibility, thereby ensuring Bodie's survival. In so doing, the remnants of Bodie we see today possess a dignity not always found in former mining towns. Rather than bombarding the onlooker with curios and ersatz history, the park inspires the imagination with thoughts of grizzled miners descending into deep shafts, men pouring molten gold into molds, stagecoaches packed with passengers and baggage pulling up in front of a hotel, and weary mechanics strolling up to a bar on Saturday night and reaching for a bottle of liquid comfort.

Piatt is to be commended for presenting such a complete history of the mining district. However tempting it is to focus on its wild days, he has brought together a total package. Seemingly, no aspect is left untouched, and the chronicle of Bodie's declining years becomes as interesting and important as its glory days. Students of the West's mining history will appreciate and delight in Piatt's extensive endnotes and bibliography, and his glossary of mining terms. The inclusion of lively sidebars add glitter to an already formidable text, and quotations drawn from newspapers and mining journals preface each chapter, beautifully encapsulating contemporary opinion. Finally, the author deserves special praise for his handling of photographs. As his lucid captions bring out, these rare black and white images are not just decorations to fill a page, but serve as documents of remarkable evidentiary value. Because of Piatt's devoted research, the mines of Bodie are indeed "looking well."

MAP OF THE BODIE MINING DISTRICT.

A Birdseye View of the Mining District and the Town of Bodie, Mono County, Cal.

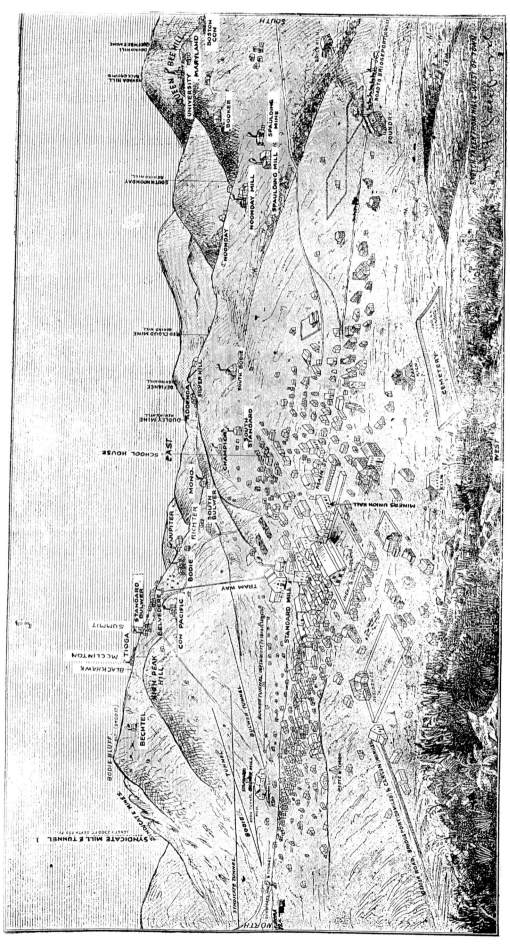

This sketch is a very accurate one, being specially drawn for The Daily Stock Report by H. F. Sanford, of Bodie, in November, 1879. It was taken from a point looking east, and shows the three or four bluffs and hills containing the ore channels of the district. These hills are topographically very distinctly defined, being almost surrounded by what was once a grassy valley, affording a fine townsite throughout the entire circuit. The town of to-day is centered in the larger valley west of High Peak and Silver Hills, and spreading both north and south. The Booker Flat, under Queen Bee Hill, is a large site in itself and is building up rapidly. The sketch shows the hoisting works and mills better than the town, which, however, is sufficiently set forth in detail to afford the reader an excellent idea of everything appertaining. The outlines of the main hills and those in the background, are nearly perfect. The Syndicate and Bodie mills cannot be shown in a side view; the first is located at the extreme north end of Bodie Bluff—the Bodie at the northeastern base of same.

PREFACE

I first saw Bodie in the summer of 1968. The old town was featured on a YMCA camping and sightseeing tour of the High Sierra. Aboard a stake bed truck, we traced Route 395 northward past Mono Lake, then turned onto a lonely dirt road. Twelve dusty miles later, the truck crested a hill and bounced to a stop. As we climbed out to enjoy the view, I gazed into a valley rich with history. There, in the distance, was a cluster of weathered buildings. At that moment, the ghost town of Bodie cast a spell on me. It has been with me ever since.

The following summer my new-found dream was fulfilled when I was employed by the California Department of Parks and Recreation as an aide at Bodie State Historic Park. I spent two summers there, making lifelong friends among fellow staff members. One of them was Bobby Bell, an old-timer who had grown up mining in Bodie. On many evenings we gathered around an old kitchen table (where a bottle of Jim Beam served as the centerpiece) to hear Bobby tell stories of Bodie. He spoke of mines, stamp mills, dynamite, and GOLD!

Long ago, the windswept hills above Bodie had echoed the scream of steam whistles and trembled under the weight of ore wagons, while men below blasted away the underpinnings of the earth to find the yellow metal. They had left behind abandoned mine shafts, a few weathered ruins, and an eerie si-lence. At the Red Cloud's hosting works, rickety floor-boards concealed a flooded shaft 870 feet deep. The Noonday's boiler shrouded a volatile box of dynamite that someone had stashed years earlier, forgotten, and left to decay. Nearby, a once-stalwart gallows frame that had lifted tons of gold-bearing rock from dark chambers below crumbled as it sank into the caving mine shaft. Bodie's ghostly hills filled me with wonder, and I understood that the mines had stories to tell.

More than three decades have passed since I first walked Bodie's hills and contemplated their mining history. Throughout those years, my interest in and respect for historical research has persisted. During an interlude in my civil engineering career I studied and applied the trade of the early nineteenth-century blacksmith at Old Sturbridge Village, a living history museum in central Massachusetts. Still, the untold story of Bodie's mines haunted me, and my fondness for the old town grew, then drove me to undertake the task of unraveling the facts concerning the mining district. The mines do have stories to tell—tales of uncertainty, high finance, drudgery, and endurance. Discovering their stories has transported me on a delightful eight-year adventure through time that has proven to be as exciting as any journey to a foreign land.

Main Street Bodie today (Courtesy, James C. Ritchie)

"THE MINES ARE LOOKING WELL . . ."

Indeed, as the Post *stated yesterday, the rise in some of these stocks is altogether premature, although the mines are looking well and will cause a greater stir in the spring. Concordia fell back to $1.80 and Oro to 50 cents. The Noondays were stronger at $1.10, however, and Bechtel and Tioga scored a slight advance. Goodshaw was active at $1.10, a decline, but orders afterwards came in which brought the price up to $1.20. Bodie sold at $5, and Addenda at 30 cents.*

  —Daily Free Press (Bodie), January 22, 1881

"The mines are looking well . . ." These words appeared in late nineteenth-century newspapers and mining journals, where they regularly championed an industry by reassuring investors who had speculated in risky, often corrupt, western gold and silver mining stocks: "The Mono shaft is down 49 feet, and the ledge at the bottom is *looking well.*" "Bodie Consolidated is *looking well* and yielding the usual quantity of high-grade ore." "Our mines are all *looking well* and give promise of soon yielding a rich reward to stockholders."[1]

Blinded by gold fever and the implied promises of overly-optimistic reporting, the speculating public gambled millions of dollars on western mines. Infused with investment capital, mining companies spent lavishly as they dug for mineral riches. Their abandon cast an air of confidence that made the future deceptively bright for burgeoning mining towns scattered throughout the American West. One such town was Bodie, California.

Today Bodie is a ghost town preserved in a state of arrested decay. Its quiet streets and abandoned buildings conjure up cherished images of the Old West. But few who visit this desolate place are aware that, beginning in 1859, gold lured men to Bodie's hills for nearly a century. For a few short years, between 1877 and 1880, there occurred at Bodie a gold mining boom, an episode of adventure and mayhem that has been glamorized in myth and legend. The town's reputation for violence during this interval nearly overshadowed the wealth contained in its mines. Saloon fights, stagecoach robberies, vigilante justice, and spontaneous exchanges of gunfire earned Bodie a well-deserved reputation for wickedness, but they obscured the real story—Bodie was a town of industry.

Disregarding approximately a hundred years of gold mining history, the current literature tends to emphasize Bodie's four boom years. This lapse is due largely to the appeal of boomtowns as settings for Wild West folklore. Supplying Bodie researchers with colorful stories, abundant local newspapers have survived from these years. Although newspapers are known to have been published in Bodie until 1912, their apparent loss after 1884 ensures that a complete history of the town has not been written, and never will be.

Of the six major books previously written about Bodie, four are well-researched histories which emphasize boomtown social history, while failing to account for the mines that were the reason for Bodie's existence. The most recent investigation, Roger D. McGrath's *Gunfighters, Highwaymen & Vigilantes* (1984), examines stories from Bodie's boomtown press to analyze frontier violence. It corrects many notions about crime in the Wild West, proving that our six-shooter heroes belong more to myth than to history. In *Bodie Bonanza: The True Story of a Flamboyant Past* (1979), Warren Loose culled newspaper articles to create a detailed, though somewhat romanticized, chronology of events through 1882, portraying Bodie during the peak of its excitement. Frank S. Wedertz rearranges much of the same material according to subject matter in *Bodie 1859-1900* (1969). Its value lies in a topical organization, but poor citations limit its usefulness as a reference source. Russ and Anne Johnson's *The Ghost Town of Bodie: As Reported in the Newspapers of the Day* (1967) is remarkable for its photographs, most of which depict Bodie during the 1890s and early twentieth century. The accompanying text, however, consists largely of quotations from boomtown-era newspapers.

By emphasizing one colorful era, these works distort our overall understanding of Bodie. Emil W. Billeb, on the other hand, presents a much different view of Bodie by focusing on a period ignored by other authors. *Mining Camp Days* (1968) is essentially his memoir of early twentieth-century Bodie. An employee of the railroad, Billeb moved to Bodie in 1908 and observed the town while its preeminent mining company struggled, then succumbed to the inevitable fate of a diminishing ore supply. Although in a position to understand the town's industry, Billeb does not give a clear account of the mines that the railroad served, nor of the wage-earning miners and their

families who presumably comprised a large segment of the town's population. Nonetheless, his recollections, enhanced by exceptional photographs, provide a highly-detailed account of life in Bodie during its declining years.

The first book to attempt a complete history was *The Story of Bodie* (1956) by Ella M. Cain. Born at Bodie in 1882, Cain returned in 1900 to teach school and collect stories from old-timers. Many of the tales she recorded have become local legends. Sadly, her writing reflects the standards of her time, characterized by a deficiency of dates and supporting research that deprives events and characters of their historical context. New information has challenged her popular story about Bodie prostitute Rosa May, raising questions about the reliability of the entire work.[2]

Particularly conspicuous in Bodie literature is a misunderstanding of extant photographs. Except for Billeb, who describes pictures from personal experience, no author has attempted to understand and clearly interpret surviving images. There is also a noticeable imbalance in the visual coverage. Bodie's colorful boom years, while generously documented, are almost devoid of photographs. After the mid-1890s the number of surviving Bodie photographs expands significantly, coinciding with advances in photography that allowed popular use of affordable roll-film cameras and mass reproduction of photographs in commercial printing. Because of the general lack of knowledge about post-boomtown Bodie, our understanding of these images is limited and often in error.

Bodie's story centers upon gold mining, uncertain as it was. Mining was Bodie's only industry, and every aspect of local life was tied to it in some way. My interest in mining led me to several underutilized sources from which to reconstruct Bodie's history. Most important were mining journals. During the late nineteenth and early twentieth centuries investors could track the activities of major western mining companies by reading several national publications. The most prominent were the *Engineering and Mining Journal* and the *Mining Record*, both published in

New York City, and San Francisco's *Mining and Scientific Press*. These weekly journals reprinted articles from newspapers, reports written by mine superintendents, and observations telegraphed by special correspondents. Clearly slanted to promote the mining industry and maintain enthusiasm among stockholders, the reports were not intended as history. Yet they are often the only surviving eyewitness accounts of Bodie after the years covered by local newspapers. By following developments in the mines, these journals also provide valuable insight into the forces that drove the town's economy.

Another important source of information for this work was the late Robert T. "Bobby" Bell, who passed away while this book was still in production. Born at Bodie in 1914, Bobby began mining at age 15 by assisting his father and grandfather with their leases in the Bulwer, Standard, and Noonday mines. He also helped operate the Standard mill until the old mill ran for the last time in 1935. His family's house and assay office are now part of Bodie State Historic Park. Miner, mill hand, prospector, and storyteller, Bobby was wonderful in answering my endless questions about the closing years of mining at Bodie. His accounts provide detailed glimpses into Bodie after 1928, a period of the town's history that has received little recognition.

A mining town's history must, of course, tell about some mines. Each has a tale, no doubt rich in successes and disappointments. Unfortunately, many mines at Bodie were abandoned so quickly that they escaped the historical record altogether. Others, such as the Hidden Treasure, Triumph, Golden Star, Bonanza, Cornucopia, Eldorado, Golden Rule, Lucky Jack, and Silver Queen, presumably given names to inspire confidence, produced little ore and even less recognition. The Hit or Miss, Double Standard, Last Chance, and Surprise seem to have tempted fate by arousing the opposite response, but fared no better. The Virginia, Savage, Crown Point, and Gould & Curry borrowed names made famous by rich mines on Nevada's Comstock Lode, then produced nothing of record.

Other Bodie mines showed promise, and their owners organized companies, issued stock, and raised working capital. The Maryland, Boston Consolidated, Spaulding, Tioga, Champion, Black Hawk, Booker, and Belvidere produced briefly, generating flurries of excitement among speculators, then quietly faded into oblivion along with their stockholders' money. Mines such as the Bechtel, Consolidated Pacific, Oro, Jupiter, Addenda, Dudley, University, Bodie Tunnel, and Syndicate also excited investors, and their stocks were traded on major exchanges. These mines were opened and closed several times, indicating some degree of success, or owner tenacity, but the surviving evidence is insufficient to derive their histories.

Only a few of the most prominent mines generated enough information to adequately tell their stories. The companies that owned them also had the most influence on the town's destiny. The saga of the Bodie mining district is essentially the rise and fall of the Noonday, North Noonday, Red Cloud, Bodie, Mono, Bulwer, and Standard mines. These mines, which once commanded local and national attention, represent the industry that made Bodie famous.

———◦◦———

1. *Bodie Weekly Standard* 11 September 1878; *Engineering and Mining Journal* 25 June 1881, 433; *Weekly Standard-News* 11 September 1880.

2. See George J. Williams, III, *Rosa May: The Search for a Mining Camp Legend* (Dayton NV: Tree By The River Publishing, 1979).

Figure 1-1: In 1864, the popular author, humorist, adventurer, illustrator, and practical mine expert, J. Ross Browne, visited Bodie to examine recently-purchased properties of the Empire Gold and Silver Mining Company. Browne sketched the tiny camp, situated on a new wagon road that connected Aurora with Sonora. Bodie Bluff, which rises to the left, and High Peak, at center, have been prospected by numerous shafts, tunnels, and placer diggings. One of the ledges purchased by the New York-based company, the Bunker Hill, outcrops the southern slope of High Peak and has a 180-foot incline shaft sunk on it. The Empire Company concentrated on driving a tunnel into Bodie Bluff's northern flank, where a 16-stamp mill was built in 1865 to process ore. (*The Bodie Bluff Mines*. Courtesy, American Antiquarian Society)

CHAPTER ONE

A PLACE CALLED BODIE:
THE SETTING

Gold is the elixir of life. All seek it—the learned as well as the illiterate, the wise as well as the foolish, the strong as well as the weak. All look forward with anxiety for its coming; all wish to delay its departure.
    —Bodie Standard, *November 7, 1877*

Speculation in mining stocks is, as a rule, disastrous financially. A broker of San Francisco . . . was asked this question; "Can an outsider, following stocks as a regular business, day by day, make money?" His candid reply was: "No; it is impossible, and my books will show it is impossible. Out of a thousand men, eight or ten may; all the rest must lose."
    —Carson Valley News (Genoa), *November 23, 1877*

The perils of operating in the Mining Share market are many, and the profits rare. This ought to be pretty well understood by this time. If people do not wish to add to their wealth rapidly, they should not take such fearful risks.
    —San Francisco Bulletin, *May 10, 1878*

Hastening to the wharf at the foot of Market Street in 1876, Colonel John F. Boyd boarded a San Francisco ferryboat. His destination: a place called Bodie in the remote, inhospitable hills immediately east of the Sierra Nevada mountains, where a couple of hardscrabble miners had a gold mine for sale. The Bullion Lode, as owners Peter Eshington and Louis Lockberg called their claim, had been yielding profitably for about a year, tempting a group of San Francisco speculators to consider purchasing it. Mindful that buying a gold mine was risky business, the prudent investors had dispatched Boyd to examine the ore body.

Only 36 years of age, Colonel Boyd was a respected mine expert. His advice on investing was highly regarded, and his knowledge of mining had made many men, including himself, very wealthy. Careful and shrewd, he represented associates who were among the most influential mine owners and stock traders on Pine Street, the metropolitan avenue that bisected San Francisco's financial district.[1]

Boyd's journey to the Bullion Mine required the better part of two days. Embarking on a late-summer's afternoon at four o'clock, the side-wheeler plied San Francisco Bay for two hours before arriving at the Central Pacific Railroad's Vallejo landing. Boyd stepped from the gangway, then boarded the *Lightning Express*, an awaiting Nevada-bound train that carried him overnight across California's Central Valley and the Sierra Mountains. At Reno he transferred to the Virginia & Truckee's 6:15 a.m. train to Carson City, where he arrived in time to book passage aboard the morning stage.

At 10:30 A.M., the stagecoach lurched past the United States Mint and the Nevada State House. Southward it sped, through the lush Carson Valley to Wellington Station and across the West Walker River into Sweetwater country. The coach bounced and jolted its way along the dusty Esmeralda Toll Road as twilight veiled a region of marginal farmland. The coach crossed the East Walker River, then traversed a nearly uninhabited wasteland. Through the night it crept over a poorly maintained road that challenged both driver and team. When daylight broke at 5:15 A.M., Boyd found himself in Aurora, Esmeralda County, Nevada. Since the previous morning, when he left the railroad's varnished coaches at Carson City, he had traveled 98 dusty, sleepless miles to this forlorn mining town among piñon pine and sagebrush.[2]

During the 1860s, Aurora had been a spirited gold and silver mining center, whose surrounding hills yielded $12,000,000 in silver and gold. When Boyd's stagecoach pulled onto Winnemucca Street, the Esmeralda County seat was nearly deserted. Its elegant, though tattered, brick Exchange Hotel registered mostly guests traveling to and from the mining towns of Columbus, Nevada, and Benton, California—or places even farther south in the mining, agricultural, and military region of the Owens River Valley.[3]

George Storey, a former mine superintendent who was now promoting mine sales, greeted Boyd as he stepped from the stagecoach. Storey was eager to show Boyd the Bullion Mine. The pair left Aurora and traveled west through Esmeralda Gulch. They passed the wrecks of five deserted stamp mills and scores of abandoned mines, relics of Aurora's former wealth. The men turned southwest into Del Monte Canyon, where three more idle mills recalled Aurora's faded glory. Flanked by arid hills, they traveled the old Sonora stage road across the state line into Mono County, California. Five miles farther, the bold, craggy outline of a ridge 8,900 feet above sea level came into view. Bodie Bluff was unremarkable in appearance except for a lone, timeworn stamp mill at its base, where men were laboring to get rusty gold-producing machinery running again.

Turning onto a road that cut through the sagebrush, the travelers drove another mile in the shadow of Bodie Bluff before ascending the treeless, wind-swept slope of High Peak. When they reached the Bullion Mine, Boyd caught sight of an unproductive, long-abandoned mine shaft, 250 feet deep, providing strong evidence of the claim's disappointing past and its doubtful future. About eight men were at work nearby, where a second, more productive shaft traced a quartz formation 200 feet into the ground. The workers were digging ore from the ledge, then bringing it to the surface in a bucket hoisted by a simple horse-powered winding device. Their rudimentary equipment handled only four or five tons of rock per day, but by selecting the richest pieces, owners Eshington and Lockberg had recovered $37,000 during the previous year. This more than covered operating expenses and piqued the curiosity of distant investors.[4]

The mine owners turned from their work to greet Storey and his San Francisco visitor. As the men shook hands, none of them could have realized that this convergence represented a turning point for the Bodie mining district. The formalities were brief, then Boyd lit a candle and climbed down a ladder into the darkness below.

———◦∞◦———

By the time John Boyd descended the incline shaft of the Bullion Mine, Bodie Bluff and its neighboring hills had accumulated 17 years of undistinguished mining history. Gold discoveries east of the Sierra had lured prospectors by the thousands from California's Mother Lode in 1859. The most remarkable migration occurred in June of that year, when fortune seekers competing to reach the Comstock Lode began the great rush to Washoe. Some 80 miles to the southeast, a smaller and less noted movement was already underway as gold hunters headed into the Mono Lake region—a bleak land that had been mined by placer and quartz miners since 1852.[5] Not until 1857 did the 100 or so placer miners working the headwaters of the East Walker River find enough gold to organize a mining district. They named their settlement Dogtown.

Two years later word spread that more extensive gold deposits had been found in a rocky ravine amid dry gulches northwest of Mono Lake.[6] Throughout the remaining months of 1859, prospectors in increasing numbers headed over mountain passes toward the new diggings, where a rudimentary town called Monoville sprang up. Among those who trekked from Tuolumne County that summer was a lowly miner whose place in history would become well-established, but whose identity remains unclear.

W. S. Bodey was among the Californians bound for the mines near Mono Lake. After reaching the developing town of Monoville, this erstwhile argonaut joined Pat Garraty, William Boyle, and an earlier acquaintance, Sonora hotel keeper Terrence Brodigan, on a prospecting expedition into the stark hills beyond the lake's northern shore. Venturing across the California state line, the four companions entered Mormon country, Utah Territory, where menacing Indians compelled them to turn back. They dug test pits along the way until their spades revealed the glimmer of gold. Gazing upon the rolling hills that surrounded them, the prospectors found themselves in a harsh, unknown country, where they tarried just long enough to determine the extent of their discovery, then proceeded to Monoville, intent upon keeping their find a secret and returning in the spring.

As winter approached, many recent arrivals, including Brodigan, Garraty, and Boyle, abandoned the dismal land, but Bodey returned to the site of the discovery with a new partner, E. S. "Black" Taylor (reportedly half Cherokee).[7] Others followed, some led by Brodigan, who had turned back after having started for Sonora. They staked claims, washed gold from the gravel, and built makeshift shelters. Although placer gold was their objective, a scarcity of water forced some to look for gold-bearing quartz veins, and at least one was unearthed. An eyewitness residing at Monoville in October 1859 recalled that Bodey and Taylor journeyed the 12 miles from their diggings, carrying sacks of dirt that made "very handsome returns."[8]

In late November Brodigan was again with a group setting out for Sonora. They met Bodey and Taylor traveling in the opposite direction after obtaining supplies at Monoville. As Brodigan recalled years later, Bodey and Taylor were on foot, with a single animal packed with provisions.[9] Winter weather was bearing down, and the men exchanged farewells, then pressed onward toward separate destinations. Bodey and Taylor proceeded toward their cabin at the mines, but before they reached it a storm buried the region in snow. The blizzard ushered in an unusually harsh winter that was recorded by Comstock chronicler Dan De Quille.

> The first snow fell on the 22nd of November; it snowed all day, and four days later again set in, when snow fell to a depth of five or six feet, cutting off all communication between Gold Hill and Virginia [City], though the two towns were but a mile apart. . . . In December . . . not only cattle, but also horses, donkeys, and animals of all kinds died of cold and hunger. Most of them starved to death.[10]

Overtaken by this memorable storm, Bodey and Taylor struggled through the howling wind until Bodey sank exhausted in the snow. Taylor carried him as far as he could, then wrapped the failing man in a blanket and fought his way to the cabin alone. Intending to help his companion to safety, he returned through the gale, but was unable to find Bodey in the blinding and deepening snow.

That winter the diggings were deserted as Taylor and other inhabitants sought refuge elsewhere. When spring broke, men began arriving to resume mining. Taylor returned in late May and found the scattered bones of his former partner. With the help of Bernhardt Staatz and Johnson King, he buried the remains where he found them—less than a mile from the cabin.[11]

Those inhabiting the area called the isolated camp "Bodey's Diggings" in honor of the fallen discoverer. Unfortunately, nobody was certain how to spell the name. When prospectors recorded their claims, "Bodey" was the most common spelling for the locale, but "Body," "Bodie," and a few other phonetic transcriptions were also employed. On July 10, 1860, the miners formally organized the "Body" mining district.[12]

The following month, on August 25, 1860, gold was found near the state line, some 12 miles northeast of the Body mining district. Within the year a town named Aurora sprang up in the newly-created Esmeralda mining district and quickly became the region's commercial and industrial hub. Its population was augmented by those who deserted Body, Dogtown, and Monoville, taking with them during the next two years the latter town's buildings. In April 1861, California created Mono County and designated Aurora its seat. The following November, shortly after Nevada Territory was severed from the western part of Utah Territory, Esmeralda County was formed. Bustling Aurora was so close to the California state line that nobody could be sure on which side of the boundary the town sat. Believing Aurora was in Nevada, the territorial governor established it as Esmeralda County's seat. For the next two years Aurora would serve as the seat of two counties: Mono County, California and Esmeralda County, Nevada Territory. The uncertainty over where Aurora was situated was not resolved until an official survey in September 1863 placed the town three miles within Nevada. Bridgeport, a crossroads agricultural community at Big Meadows, then became the seat of Mono County.[13]

Gold may be where you find it, but since it is often found in quartz, looking for a quartz ledge is a good way to get started. That is exactly what three weather-beaten prospectors did during the third season of mining at Bodey's former diggings. In mid-1861 they unearthed a quartz vein outcropping the flank of High Peak and named it the "Bunker Hill" lode.[14] Like other claims in the district, the Bunker Hill did not amount to much. Nonetheless, two men from San Francisco, James Stark, a theater star, and John Tucker, a jeweler, paid $19,500 for the Bunker Hill Mine, hoping it would feed their 10-stamp mill in Aurora. They did not have much luck, so in 1863 they sold the mill, built from a dismantled San Jose opera house, after only one run.[15] By that time "Bodie" had become the accepted spelling of the remote mining district, and the details of how gold had been discovered there, including the identity of its fallen namesake, were fading from memory.

In January 1863, while civil war raged in the East, the Bunker Hill ledge became part of an effort to attract investment capital to the Bodie mining district by pooling the resources of a number of marginally productive claims. Organized in San Francisco, the Bodie Bluff Consolidation Mining Company advertised its ownership of ledges on Bodie Bluff and High Peak, including the Bunker Hill. An Aurora newspaper endorsed the effort, exclaiming under the subtitle "Bodie Diggings" that during 1863 "a very large amount of work" had been performed by several companies. The columnist concluded:

> The Bodie Bluff Consolidation, and Bodie Bluff Consolidation No. 2, embrace a large majority of all the valuable ledges in the district, and are now taking out some of the richest ore that I have ever seen from any mine on this side of the mountains.[16]

The first consolidation's stock certificates were signed by California Governor and company president Leland Stanford, but his high-powered endorsement proved ineffectual, and the firm's real estate was sold in little more than a year and a half to a New York enterprise with abundant capital.[17]

Figure 1-2: Bodie's scattered mines were thought to be in a remote part of the Esmeralda mining district, Mono County, in 1863, when California Governor Leland Stanford signed this stock certificate representing an Aurora company owning several Bodie Bluff and High Peak ledges. The Bodie Bluff Consolidation Mining Company's property, which included the Bunker Hill Mine, was sold within a year and a half to the New York-based Empire Gold and Silver Mining Company. (Courtesy, Gil Schmidtmann)

Incorporated under the laws of the state of New York and backed by eastern investors, the Empire Gold and Silver Mining Company hired James Stark as its Aurora agent, then dispatched him to arrange the purchase of every known quartz ledge at Bodie.[18] Three nationally known scientists and mine experts, William P. Blake, Benjamin Silliman, Jr., and J. Ross Browne, were solicited to write glowing reports for the company's prospectus.

William P. Blake, soon to become professor of mineralogy and geology at the College of California and mineralogist for California's board of agriculture, was the first expert to visit the district. In November 1863, he examined several mines on Bodie Bluff. Although Blake neglected the Bunker Hill, what was important to distant investors was his general description of the district's quartz veins. "They bear gold and silver."[19]

Next of the experts to reach Bodie was professor of chemistry at Yale College, Benjamin Silliman, Jr. Well known as the editor of the *American Journal of Science*, Silliman was not above exploiting his distinguished name by adjusting his reports to suit his clients' purses.[20] While inspecting the Empire Company's proposed acquisitions, he climbed down

the 180-foot incline shaft of the Bunker Hill Mine. His report, dated April 25, 1864, reads in part: "The vein is about four feet in width, and dips westerly at an angle of about 60 degrees. . . . The stuff worked pays about forty dollars per ton, and the loss in the tailings, as I am informed by the millman, is from five to twenty dollars. About four hundred tons of this ore have been worked at the mill [in Aurora] from which this result is quoted."[21] To no one's surprise, Blake and Silliman concluded that Bodie's mines showed great promise.

Represented by James Stark, the Empire Company began acquiring property at Bodie in August 1864. Ledges belonging to the Bodie Bluff Consolidation Mining Company, which encompassed High Peak and the southerly part of Bodie Bluff, were purchased along with properties of a number of other foundering companies: the Bodie Consolidation Gold and Silver Mining Company Number Two, encompassing the northerly part of Bodie Bluff; the Isabella Gold and Silver Mining Company; the Tioga Gold and Silver Mining Company; and the Ria Vista Gold and Silver Mining Company. In all, the Empire Gold and Silver Mining Company purchased 29 ledges scattered from the northern slope of Bodie Bluff to

WHO WAS W. S. BODY, BODEY, BODIE?

In the autumn of 1859, a group of prospectors found gold at the place that would become Bodie, but 18 years elapsed before gold mining gave rise to a boomtown. In the interim, events surrounding the district's origins were nearly forgotten.

Bodie was flourishing in 1878 when Joseph Wasson became the first writer to research the story of the discovery. He sought interviews with people who had participated in the events, but because many of the key players had died, Wasson relied on memories held by two longtime area residents. Terrence Brodigan claimed to have led the four-man prospecting party into the wilderness north of Mono Lake, and recalled the Poughkeepsie, New Yorker, whose wintery death inspired the district's name.[1] Judge J. Giles McClinton, a later arrival, furnished details, such as the spelling of the doomed miner's name.

McClinton recalled that in 1861 he had found a location notice for a placer claim on the hillside east of town that appeared to have been a page torn from a diary, "folded up, and stuck in the fork of a bush." He said it bore the signature "W. S. Body."[2] Wasson accepted the spelling "Body," using it to relate the discovery story in his 1878 promotional booklet that introduced prospective investors to Bodie's mines. He repeated the spelling in an 1879 revi-

sion of the booklet, a newspaper article published in August of that year, and an interview printed in October.[3] He supported the spelling "Body" with quotations from documents written by the district's organizers: "Art. I.—This district shall be known and designated as Body District."[4]

Based on Wasson's research, Bodie's citizens and those interested in its mines believed that the man who gave the district his name called himself "W. S. Body." How the spelling came to be changed to "Bodie" was told by McClinton.

> In 1860, Prof. J. E. Clayton and the Hazlett brothers (Ben and John) located the Bodie Ranch between here and Aurora. They cut the natural growth of grass and packed it to Aurora—then a young thriving place—and built a small log stable. They then gave a verbal order for a sign, "Body Stable," but the painter, with an eye to the beautiful, which I highly commend, executed it "Bodie Stable" and the word looked so much better in that form, that the people soon adopted that style of spelling it.[5]

McClinton also remembered a pile of loose stones where the ground had settled. He had noticed the strange formation years earlier, when Bodie was sparsely inhabited, after riding from Aurora in 1871 to look after his Bodie claims. McClinton recalled that his horse had wandered away, and that he came across the

sunken spot and stones while searching for the animal in the hills southwest of the camp.

Wasson was overjoyed to hear the story, and insisted that McClinton show him the site. On Saturday, October 25, 1879, they searched the area on horseback, and within an hour McClinton had found the piled stones. The *Daily Bodie Standard* described their visit.

> They then decided to prospect the new find thoroughly, and yesterday (Sunday) morning they took a pick and shovel and "Indian Tom" to the scene. . . . The work commenced about half-past eleven A. M., and in about three-fourths of an hour a much decomposed silk necktie was unearthed. Soon followed a pretty well-preserved shoe, attached to the right foot of all that is left of W. S. Body.[6]

The next day Wasson led nine of Bodie's leading citizens and three reporters to the partially-opened grave. The group included William Irwin (superintendent of the Standard Mine), Judge F. K. Bechtel (principal owner of the Bechtel Mine), Colonel S. W. Blasdel (superintendent of the Red Cloud Mine), and Warren Loose. Taking turns shoveling, they found clothing, a blanket, and a nearly complete human skeleton. A belt encircling the skeletal waist held a leather sheath, which contained a bowie knife with a 10-inch blade. "There's his knife," exclaimed Loose, who was digging at the time. "I've heard Brodigan say he always wore it."[7]

A number of old-timers agreed that W. S. Body's last partner, E. S. Taylor, had described that exact place as the site where he had buried Body's remains. Generating widespread publicity, the staged exhumation gave townsfolk such a sense of nostalgia that the bones and artifacts were moved to Dr. Davison's downtown office and placed on public display.

Others who claimed to have known Body now came forward with stories, some of which led Wasson to believe that the man's first name had been William, and that he had been "of very slow and slouchy habits." One local resident described him as "a dirty old devil."[8] A number of the tales, however, were contradictory. While Wasson discounted conflicting accounts as brazen lies or cases of mistaken identity, some people began wondering whose bones had been unearthed.[9]

Although Wasson stood behind his findings, one former participant upset the historic record. Sylvanus B. Cobb claimed that he had been Body's partner in Sonora between the fall of 1857 and the time the latter departed on his fateful journey across the mountains. Cobb asserted that ". . . his name was William S. Bodey—not Body—and that he was a very fine man, temperate in his habits, and very neat in his personal appearance, in fact uncommonly so. He was about 5 feet 6 inches in height, light complexioned, with hair and whiskers very gray, and aged about 45 years."[10] The

"Finding Gold By Accident"

new spelling was accepted immediately, and the exhibited remains were whimsically referred to as "Bill Bodey's bones." They attracted such macabre fascination that one correspondent commented on the absurdity of the scene.

Ever since the bones of Bodey have been unearthed, they have been the subject of curiosity and comment by nearly every resident of Bodie. Yesterday afternoon, as they lay in their miniature coffin, they were closely examined by a large number of people of all classes. The skull, which had been carefully cleaned and polished up like a billiard ball, would be taken up by a miner and closely scrutinized as if it were a piece of quartz from some new discovery.[11]

On the first Sunday in November, a week after the exhumation, the Bodie chapter of the Society of Pa-

cific Coast Pioneers led a funeral procession accompanying a horse-drawn hearse carrying Bodey's bones to the cemetery.

The remains were placed in a handsome coffin about five feet long covered with black cloth, and decorated with neat ornaments. On the lid was a silver plate bearing the inscription:

> IN MEMORIAM
> W. S. BODEY
> 1879

The fire bell tolled solemn tones as mourners packed sidewalks to watch the cortege move up Main Street. Flags fluttered at half-staff and the town presented a "sorrowful appearance."

A large crowd was at the open grave, and as the procession approached an apparent feeling of woe and sorrow overcame all those present. In a buggy close to the grave sat Terrence Brodigan, old Bodey's companion in the memorable prospecting trip in which he later lost his life.[12]

Almost on the twentieth anniversary of his death, Bodey received a proper burial in the town cemetery, and an appropriate oration echoed across the valley. "Who among us can stretch imagination to compass the wild emotions of this now lifeless pioneer, as he gazed for the first time on the glittering gems of gold which studded Bodie Peak?"[13]

Already the Associated Press had telegraphed news of the archaeological discovery to Bodey's presumed hometown in New York state. The day after the remains were unearthed, a story appeared in the Poughkeepsie *Daily Eagle* headlined: "A Former Poughkeepsian's Fate— Finding the Body of Wm. S. Bodey— What Befell the Discoverer of a Famous Silver Mine."[14]

The next day the *New York Times* carried the New Yorker's biography two pages ahead of the financial column that listed Bodie mining stocks. This article claimed that the man who had left Poughkeepsie thirty years earlier and disappeared into the golden landscape of California was "Waterman" S. Bodey. Details, probably provided by his widow Sarah, were reprinted in Bodie a week later. Her lost husband, the article revealed, had been

a tinner by trade and a member of the Odd Fellows. Because of his superior skills as a workman, and his naturally energetic disposition, he was regarded by his associates as a leader. He had left his family to pursue economic gain in the California Gold Rush.

On the breaking out of the gold fever in 1848, he took passage in the sloop *Matthew Vassar*, and sailed round the Horn to California. After spending several years in prospecting and business, during a part of which time he is said to have lost heavily in the dry goods business, he finally struck the surface vein. . . . During all this time he had written regularly to his wife and sent her money for her support.

The article romanticized Bodey's struggle in the blizzard, then noted: "For twenty years, therefore, a mystery has surrounded the death of Bodey, and his wife has never given up a faint hope of seeing him again. During all these years she has resided in [Poughkeepsie], earning a scanty living as a seamstress, and enduring an accumulation of misfortunes in the successive loss of six children."[15] The New York paper naively speculated that Bodey's mining claims were still valid, and proof of his death would entitle his destitute widow to an immense fortune.

Although Bodie was a nationally-recognized gold mining town in 1879, little more than coincidence linked Sarah's missing husband to the lost prospector who gave the dis-

trict its name.

In 1961, 83 years after Wasson's investigation, Poughkeepsie genealogist Amy Ver Nooy was researching Bodey family records, when she concluded: "One thing is certain. If he was a Bodey from Poughkeepsie, his name was Wakeman, possibly Wateman, not William."[16] Her conclusions also exclude Waterman.

Thus, the identity of the lost soul evolved. W. S. Body gave way to William S. "Bill" Bodey, then to Waterman S., Wakeman S., or Wateman S. Bodey. But which name is correct? Government records provide the strongest evidence of the Poughkeepsie man's name. In 1850, when her husband was in California, Sarah Bodey told the census taker that his name was "Wakeman S. Bodey." A decade later, she reiterated "Wakeman Bodey" to an enumerator.[17] Was a 49er from Poughkeepsie the man whose 1859 discovery grew into the Bodie mining district as Joseph Wasson and Sarah Bodey believed? Was his name Wakeman S. Bodey? We may never know for certain, but he seems to be the town's most likely namesake.

With the hallowed bones safely interred in the cemetery, Bodie's chapter of the Society of Pacific Coast Pioneers began fund-raising for a stone to mark the grave. Three years later the monument stood, unpaid-for, in the stonecutter's yard, and was never erected. Once again, the site of Bodey's grave is as forgotten as it was in 1878.

the south side of High Peak.

News that the Empire Company was planning a large-scale mining operation at Bodie brought excitement to the region. A flurry of short articles in Aurora newspapers described the activity. "Business in Bodie is getting brisk," read one August 1864 item. "The demand for labor is increasing. A restaurant and saloon have recently been established there, and those who desire a square meal or 'a glass of soup,' can have either or both at short notice."[22] Another report added: "The development of the rich mines in Bodie District is going on vigorously. . . . The proximity of Bodie to Esmeralda is beneficial to both districts, as the miners of the former place depend entirely on Aurora for supplies."[23] More buildings erected at Bodie, including a hotel, enticed an Aurora paper to conclude that a gold rush was impending. "When the rich company of New York capitalists who have invested so largely in the mines of our neighbor commence developing their ledges, it will be the liveliest little place in the Territory."[24] To accommodate commuters, a semi-weekly stage line was established between Aurora and Bodie.

The 100 or so miners working Bodie prospects were expecting to be joined by 50 to 100 Empire Company employees when the third mine expert arrived.[25] J. Ross Browne spent three days studying the district's investment opportunities in September 1864. The visit was part of an extended western tour, beginning in 1863, that took Browne through Arizona, New Mexico, and Nevada territories, and Bodie. Browne stayed at Aurora for a few days enjoying the "amenities of social life," which included a badger fight and nearly witnessing a man shot to death.[26] Two years earlier, Samuel Clemens had inhabited Aurora, testing his luck in the mining camp after an unsatisfactory stint in a pro-Confederate Missouri militia company inspired a hasty journey westward. After abandoning Aurora, Clemens developed his writing skills as a Virginia City journalist.

Browne ended his Aurora sojourn by riding to Bodie in a buggy driven by local mine owner Judge F. K. Bechtel, who kept a "bottle of medicine" handy

in case of snakebites. Outside Aurora, the Real del Monte and Antelope quartz mills incited Browne's remark, "I had little expected to find in this out-of-the-way part of the world such splendid monuments of enterprise." The industrial masterpieces that Browne admired were only three years old, but working at a fraction of their capacity, a sign that ore shipments were declining and the once-booming town

of Aurora was sliding into economic decay.

Browne and Judge Bechtel proceeded up the canyon, where hay fields and cattle ranches occupied several valleys between Aurora and Bodie. Although small, the ranches produced fine grass from rich soil that was watered by springs coursing down nearby ravines. Browne observed wagons hauling hay to the Aurora market, where it sold for $40 to $60 a ton. He opined that, "Hay ranches are as good as silver mines almost anywhere on the eastern slope—better, in some respects, for they are certain to yield something for the labor expended upon them."

Browne then arrived at Bodie.

We revelled in dust along the road that skirts the Bluff; it was rich and unctuous, and penetrated us through and through, so that by the time we arrived at the Judge's cabin, where he had some workmen employed, we were permeated with the precious metals of Bodie.

INTERIOR OF THE BODIE BUNKER.

Figure 1-3: During his 1864 visit to Bodie District, J. Ross Browne examined several mines, but his report does not describe the Bunker Hill. His caption, "Interior of the Bodie Bunker," however, suggests that he entered the Bunker Hill's crude incline shaft long enough to sketch the mine which thirteen years later would become the district's leading producer. (*Harper's New Monthly Magazine* August 1865. Author's collection)

A fine spring of water, aided by a little snake-medicine, set us all right; and a good lunch prepared us for a tour of exploration over the mountains.

The 10 or 12 men the Judge employed to work his claims resided in a "frame shanty" surrounded by a "luxuriant natural garden" of weeds and sagebrush. Browne recalled:

These jolly miners were the happiest set of bachelors imaginable; had neither chick nor child, that I knew of, to trouble them; cooked their own food, did their own washing; mending their own clothes, made their own beds, and on Sundays cut their own hair, greased their own boots, and brushed their own coats; thus proving by the most direct positive evidence that woman is an unnecessary and expensive institution which ought to be abolished by law.[27]

While touring Bodie, Browne examined a number of mines purchased by the Empire Company, and described them favorably.

I descended several of the shafts, and found the veins of nearly uniform thickness; that is to say, varying from two to five feet, in gold and silver-bearing quartz, with clear and well-defined walls and casings. The work done upon them is of a very rude and imperfect character; the main object having been, apparently, to get out the ores with as little expense as possible, and without regard to the permanent development of the mines.[28]

Browne also described the scattered structures that served as a town.

There are now some fifteen or twenty small frame and adobe houses erected for the use of the workmen; a boarding-house is already established; a blacksmith's shop is in full operation; lots and streets are laid out; new houses are springing up in every direction.[29]

The Empire Company published Browne's report as a promotional pamphlet aimed at prospective investors. It reported fairly by noting that the district's yield was "probably not so high as Eastern capitalists may consider desirable," but it also compared Bodie to the famous Comstock Lode and reminded readers that the "best paying mines on this coast are those that yield a moderate average."[30]

Based on the converging angles at which the ledges pitched into the earth, Browne and the other experts believed that geologic forces had pushed molten gold- and silver-bearing quartz upward from below Bodie Bluff. The uprising liquid, after branching out near the surface, had solidified into veins. The visiting authorities reasoned that a solid core of rich ore existed deep inside the hill, where the ledges united. Here, at their source, a mother vein would be found that they called the "Veta Madre."[31] Although the premise was yet to be proven, stockholders and management bought into the theory.

About a month after Nevada Territory entered the Union as the 36th state in October 1864, the Empire Company drove three tunnels into Bodie Bluff and High Peak to find the Veta Madre. They never found it, but a few small veins prompted company

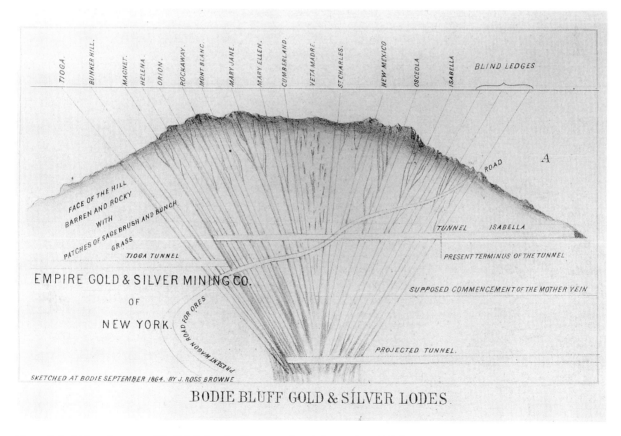

Figure 1-4: Although none of Bodie's ledges had been explored deeper than 200 feet in 1864, J. Ross Browne and other experts thought that the ore bodies grew richer as they descended toward an immense central vein called the Veta Madre. "That such a vein exists," Browne rationalized, "there can be no reasonable doubt." His report to the Empire Company contained this fanciful cross section, taken through the western flank of Bodie Bluff and High Peak. Moderating his emphatic statement and idealistic sketch, Browne conceded that his views were, "of course, based upon conjecture." Looking west, Browne's drawing shows the Bunker Hill Lode to the left, one of many ledges awaiting development. (*The Bodie Bluff Mines*. Courtesy, American Antiquarian Society)

directors to decide that profits could be improved by eliminating the cost of transporting ore to Aurora for milling. In 1865, the company built a stamp mill, the first in Bodie District. Designer B. O. Cutter of San Francisco created an attractive Gothic-styled brick structure at the northern base of Bodie Bluff. Cutter had designed a number of mills in the region including the Fogus, Durand, and Antelope mills at Aurora. He modeled the Empire mill after the Antelope. Its machinery, consisting of 16 stamps, 8 circular Washoe amalgamating pans, 3 settlers, and 4 shaking tables, was taken from the idle Fogus mill, and started running in Bodie on September 6, 1865.[32]

During the ensuing twenty months, the Empire Gold and Silver Mining Company worked various ledges on Bodie Bluff and High Peak, warranting occasional mention in a nationally-read mining journal. "The mill crushes ten tons per day, which is all that the pans can amalgamate," noted San Francisco's *Mining and Scientific Press*. "The mill is now yielding from $12,000 to $15,000 per month."[33] A later report also impressed audiences from San Francisco to New York City. "The most cheering accounts are daily received. The monthly shipment of bullion from the Empire mine shows a steady increase of the precious metals."[34]

Figure 1-5: Based on the assurances of J. Ross Browne and other experts, investors poured thousands of dollars into the Empire Gold and Silver Mining Company, which issued $1,000 bonds in 1864. During the next three years the company drove a major tunnel into Bodie Bluff and explored several ledges, but failed to find enough profitable ore to pay dividends. (Courtesy, Ken Prag)

Figure 1-6: In 1865, the Empire Company built this lavish 16-stamp mill similar to those operating at Aurora. Despite great optimism, the venture was abandoned two years later, after which Bodie was nearly deserted. Although unused during the ensuing eight years, the mill was still intact when two humble prospectors, Peter Eshington and Louis Lockberg, demonstrated that money could be made by mining gold at Bodie. San Francisco entrepreneurs purchased the mill, then renamed it the Syndicate. Bullion it produced during the last eight months of 1877 created a mining sensation. Eight more stamp mills would be built at Bodie between 1877 and 1881, but the Syndicate was the only one made of bricks. (Emil Billeb collection. Courtesy, Vickie Daniels)

The facts, however, did not live up to the reporting. After failing to make a profit, the Empire Company suspended operations at Bodie in April 1867 without declaring a dividend. The mines were abandoned along with the stamp mill, and the Bodie mining district was nearly forgotten for the next decade. Aurora had also declined, and the entire region, discredited by a staggering number of abandoned mines and neglected stamp mills, slipped into the haze of faded memory.[35] Although some mining continued, settlers arriving in the area took to farming and raising livestock. They cleared sagebrush from the best farmland, irrigated, and grew hay, alfalfa, wheat, barley, oats, potatoes, and garden vegetables. By grazing cattle, sheep, goats, horses, and mules, the settlers established an agricultural economy capable of producing surplus hay, grain, vegetables, meat, and dairy products.[36]

Among the few who persisted in mining Bodie's hills were Peter Eshington and Louis Lockberg, both of whom held office in the district. Lockberg was inspector of elections in 1868, and Eshington was elected district recorder in 1869, an office he occupied for the next six years because no miners' meetings were held to pick a replacement until 1875.[37] Another steadfast resident was William O'Harra, a black and extremely rotund cook who had been employed by the Empire Company and was kept on its payroll after 1867 to watch over the eastern company's abandoned properties. While details remain elusive, local tradition maintains that O'Harra, at some point, received the Bunker Hill Mine as payment for a defaulted loan. According to the most widely accepted version of the story, he sought to sell

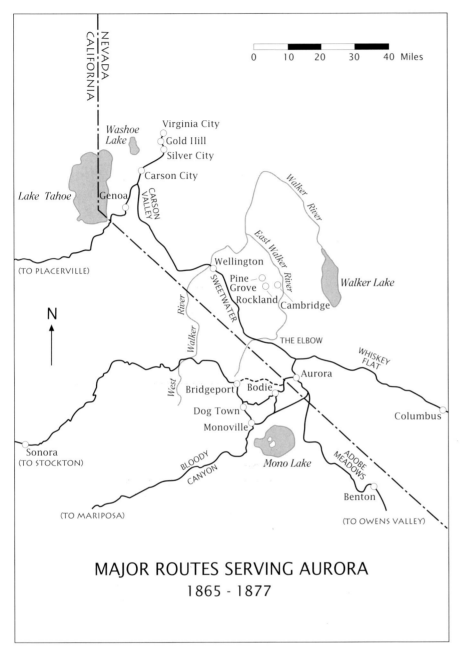

MAJOR ROUTES SERVING AURORA
1865 - 1877

Map 3: Because of the magnitude of Comstock trade during the 1860s, most freight and stage lines traversed the Sierra Nevada mountains via Placerville. East of the Sierra, roads extended south from Carson Valley through Wellington and Sweetwater to Aurora, the commercial center in the Esmeralda mining district. In late 1864, a new stage route crossed the Sierra via Sonora Pass to link Aurora with San Francisco's steamboat fleet at Stockton. Passing through Sonora, Bridgeport, and the Bodie mining district, the road offered faster travel between Aurora and San Francisco than the Placerville route. This placed Aurora on two major routes serving the trans-Sierra region, but Esmeralda's mines were in decline before the Sonora road was completed. After the Central Pacific Railroad reached Reno in 1868, and the Virginia & Truckee Railroad connected Reno to Carson City in 1872, the main route to Aurora reverted to the well-established, year-round road through Wellington and Sweetwater.

the property and recover his money, but was unable to find a buyer until Peter Eshington and Louis Lockberg agreed to work the mine and pay him an $8,000 cut of their yield.

On June 11, 1875, Eshington and Lockberg formally changed the name of their claim from the "Bunker Hill" to the "Bullion Lode."[38] For the next few months, a crew hired by the two owners worked the mine at a loss. Then, in the fall of 1875, the lonely, destitute citizens of Aurora blinked in disbelief when they saw Eshington and Lockberg arrive from Bodie with substantially more than their usual quantity of gold. After delivering the precious metal to the express office for shipment to the mint in Carson City, the two mine owners, "jubilant over the amount of bullion produced," retired to a nearby saloon. According to their often-repeated tale, they had nearly given up on their Bodie mine when it caved, exposing a rich seam of gold-bearing quartz. Even this extraordinary development did not create much interest in the region, and fundamental details, such as the discovery date, remain unknown.[39]

Eshington and Lockberg returned to their mine and, with hired hands, carried on mining and milling. Some men worked below ground, while others tended the horse and whim that slowly hoisted bucket-loads of ore to the surface. Meanwhile, yoked oxen pulled ore-laden carts 6½ miles over treeless hills to Rough Creek, where three

water-powered arrastras ground the rocky cargo to dust and removed its gold. These crude mining and milling facilities were slow, but they were practical and cheap, producing $37,000 over the ensuing year. Underground, however, miners kept running into geological formations that they called "horses," or barren spots in the ledge. Concerned that the vein was pinching out, Eshington and Lockberg decided to sell the mine.[40]

The Bodie mining district and, for that matter, the entire region had not seen a paying mine for a long time. Such a gold mine would not go unnoticed in San Francisco, especially when there were mining men like George Storey in Aurora, who, for a cut of the action, made sure word got to those with enough capital to do something about it.

The region north and east of Mono Lake, however, was remembered in San Francisco for having wasted millions of dollars during earlier excitements. Its history of squandered money discouraged investors, and only a few Pine Street speculators were adventurous enough to gamble. Two of them, Henry M. Yerington and Robert N. Graves, organized the Syndicate Mining Company in October 1875 and purchased some of the Empire Company's Bodie Bluff properties (including the 16-stamp mill) from the county for unpaid taxes.[41] The following June they

hired miners and workmen from Aurora to reopen the mine and rehabilitate the derelict mill.

A mile to the south, Eshington and Lockberg managed the Bullion Mine as George Storey worked out the details for its sale. He negotiated terms on behalf of a couple of marginal players in the clique of San Francisco mining stock operators. The bond he secured held the mine for Seth and Daniel Cook, who brought Colonel Boyd into the deal and sent him over the mountains to determine the mine's potential.[42] That anybody was interested in investing in a venture near Aurora is curious, because the odds were astronomical against this mine, or any other, turning out different from the hundreds of inconsequential holes in the ground already pockmarking the area. Nonetheless, by 1876, when Boyd passed Bodie Bluff to inspect the Bullion Mine, the Syndicate Company had its bins full of ore, and the old brick mill was nearly ready to begin treating it with ten new amalgamating pans and five new settlers.

Boyd examined the Bullion Mine on behalf of himself and his San Francisco associates, and his report was favorable. On September 9, 1876, Eshington and Lockberg received $75,000 for their claim, candles, explosives, fuse, mining and blacksmithing tools, whim, and the two horses that ran it.[43] The absentee owners hired a professional superintendent named William Irwin to manage their Bodie acquisition. Very quickly, Irwin put a crew to work. They built an office, along with bunk and boarding houses, then set up a small steam-powered hoisting engine, known as a "donkey hoist," to haul buckets of ore out of the ground.

As work progressed at the Bullion mine, the Syndicate people to the north got the mill running and started crushing their stockpiled ore. The event received recognition in mid-September, when New York's *Engineering and Mining Journal* printed an item reflecting a lingering viewpoint that Bodie was in a remote section of Aurora. Despite its errors, the column marks the first time since the 1860s that Bodie was mentioned in a national trade publication.

Nevada—The *Syndicate Gold and Silver Mining Company* of Bodey District, Esmeralda County, has just made a clean-up of their first crushing. It amounts to $5,587.94. The lead [vein] is about eight feet in width, and is gold bearing. The gold is worth only $8.67 per ounce, there being a considerable amount of silver in the ore. The company have in operation a fine mill, and their prospects are excellent, as they have only attained a depth of 200 feet.[44]

Sustained by a supply of Syndicate ore, the mill ran steadily for six weeks, until the end of October, when wagons began delivering rock from the Bullion Mine. During November and December, Superintendent Irwin sent 1,000 tons of ore, which returned $45,000 in bullion—more than Eshington and Lockberg realized in an entire year. The results so exceeded expectations that the Bullion and Syndicate outfits worked through the winter. Counting the two crews and a few individuals operating scattered claims, the population of the district reached at least 21—the approximate number of locals, according to one witness, who cast votes in the presidential election of 1876.[45]

1. Col. John F. Boyd (1840-1920). J. M. Guinn, *History of the State of California and Biographical Record* (Chicago, IL: Chapman Publishing Co., 1904), 1049-1050; John F. Parr, "Reminiscences of the Bodie Strike," *Yosemite Nature Notes* 7, no. 5 (May 1928), 33-38; Henry S. Fitch, *Pacific Coast Annual Mining Review and Stock Ledger* (San Francisco, CA: Francis & Valentine, 1878), 45.

2. Virtually nothing is known about Boyd's trip to the Bullion Mine. This scenario is based on regular travel routes of the period. Mark Wurm and Harry Demoro, "Railroad Timetable 1 May 1876," in *The Silver Short Line: A History of the Virginia and Truckee Railroad* (Glendale, CA: Trans-Anglo Books, 1983), 83; George H. Harlan, *San Francisco Bay Ferryboats* (Berkeley, CA: Howell-North Books, 1967), 16-17, 101-102, 108, 111-113; "Travelers Guide," *Carson Valley News* 2 June 1876; "The Exact Distance," *Bodie Standard* 23 January 1878; "A Trip to Bodie, Cal.," *Engineering and Mining Journal* 12 October 1878, 258-259; Herbert L. Smith, *The Bodie Era: The Chronicles of the Last of the Old Time Mining Camps* (TMs [photocopy] 1934), 1-2.

3. For more information on Aurora during the 1860s, see Robert E. Stewart, *Aurora: Ghost City of the Dawn* (Las Vegas, NV: Nevada Publications, 1996), 5-33; Roger D. McGrath, *Gunfighters, Highwaymen, and Vigilantes: Violence on the Frontier* (Berkeley, CA: University of California Press, 1984), 1-101. Clemens' wildly entertaining account of his life in Aurora is found in Mark Twain, *Roughing It* (1872; reprint, New York, NY: Penguin Books, Inc., 1980), 189-220. Excerpts of Twain's letters describing his mining experiences at Aurora are contained in George Williams III, *Mark Twain: His Adventures at Aurora and Mono Lake* (Dayton, NV: Tree By The River Publishing, 1987).

4. *Inyo Independent* 17 March 1877; *Mining and Scientific Press* 24 March 1877, 181.

5. For more information on the region's settlement, see Thomas C. Fletcher, *Paiute, Prospector, Pioneer: The Bodie-Mono Lake Area in the Nineteenth Century* (Lee Vining, CA: Artemisia Press, 1987), 1-42. Mono Lake was first seen by non-Indians in July 1852, when a detachment of U.S. infantry led by Lt. Tredwell Moore pursued a band of Yosemite Indians over the crest of the Sierra. The campaign's intent was punitive, but when Moore returned to Mariposa, he displayed specimens of placer gold found by his command. Responding to the news, Leroy Vining and others crossed the Sierra that fall and prospected the Mono Basin area. These early miners worked seasonally, returning to civilization on the western slope of the mountains each winter. (Fletcher, *Paiute, Prospector, Pioneer*, 9-27) The first recorded mining claim in Mono County was a quartz location on Mill Creek in 1854 at a place that would become known as Jordan. (*Daily Free Press* 2 April 1881; 3 April 1881)

6. One early account pinpoints the month of the Monoville discovery as July 1859. (*Daily Free Press* 18 August 1880) Other evidence indicates the excitement was already underway by then. (Fletcher, *Paiute, Prospector, Pioneer*, 31)

7. Joseph Wasson's early version of the story claims that Bodey and Taylor were delegated to hold the ground until spring. (Wasson, *Mono County Mines*, x) He later maintained that Bodey double-crossed his comrades by joining Taylor and returning to mine the discovery site. (*Daily Bodie Standard* 27 October 1879)

8. *Bodie Weekly Standard* 4 September 1878.

9. *Daily Bodie Standard* 27 October 1879.

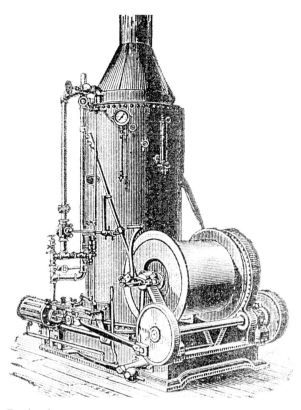

Donkey hoist

10. Dan De Quille [William Wright], *The Big Bonanza* (1876; reprint, Las Vegas, NV: Nevada Publications, 1982), 65. The storm also surprised Brodigan and his party, forcing them to abandon the Sonora trail, where they nearly lost their lives. They altered their course, reaching Sonora by way of Carson Valley and Placerville. (*Daily Bodie Standard* 27 October 1879) Joseph Wasson, acting unofficially as Bodie's first historian, initially thought that the fatal blizzard had occurred in March 1860. (Wasson, *Bodie and Esmeralda*, 5) In later versions of the tale he changed the month to November 1859, coinciding with a documented snowstorm that paralyzed the region. (Wasson, *Mono County Mines*, x-xi; *Daily Bodie Standard* 27 October 1879)

11. *Daily Bodie Standard* 10 May 1880; Joseph Wasson, *Bodie and Esmeralda* (San Francisco, CA: Spaulding, Barto & Co., 1878), 5; *Bodie Morning News* 6 November 1879. King later described the physical remains, saying that "most of the flesh had been stripped off by the coyotes and the bones were much scattered. One of the arms was never found." (*Daily Bodie Standard* 29 October 1879)

12. Wasson, *Bodie and Esmeralda*, 5-6.

13. Stewart, *Aurora*, 9-12.

14. In 1878 Joseph Wasson wrote that the Bunker Hill was first located on July 1, 1861, by O. G. Leach, E. Donahue, and L. H. Dearborn. (Wasson, *Bodie and Esmeralda*, 6) Mono County records, however, indicate the Bunker Hill lode was recorded on June 17, 1861, by J. Kerlew, J. Tucker, and S. Lamb. (Mono County, *Bodie Mining Records, Book A*, 63)

15. Wasson, *Bodie and Esmeralda*, 6-7; *Walker Lake Bulletin* 6 November 1915; *Mining and Scientific Press* 12 October 1867.

16. *Esmeralda Union* 22 April 1864.

17. Wasson, *Bodie and Esmeralda*, 7; *Esmeralda Union* 2 April 1864; 22 April 1864; 25 April 1864. In January 1863, the month the Bodie Bluff Consolidation Mining Company was organized, Stanford, along with Charles Crocker, Collis Huntington, and Mark Hopkins, broke ground in Sacramento for building the Central Pacific Railroad, the western half of the first transcontinental route.

18. *Esmeralda Union* 25 August 1864; 28 October 1864.

19. Benjamin Silliman, Jr. and William P. Blake, *Prospectus of the Empire Gold & Silver Mining Co. of New York* (New York, NY: William H. Arthur, 1864), 37.

20. *Esmeralda Union* 15 February 1865.

21. Silliman and Blake, *Prospectus*, 25-26.

22. *Esmeralda Union* 6 August 1864.

23. *Esmeralda Union* 17 August 1864.

24. *Esmeralda Union* 27 August 1864.

25. *Esmeralda Union* 27 September 1864.

26. From knowledge gathered on his trip, J. Ross Browne produced five works that contain information pertaining to Bodie. His first report was for the Empire Company. Titled *The Bodie Bluff Mines Located in Mono County, California, Belonging to the Empire Gold & Silver Mining Co. of New York* (1865), it contained specific observations intended to advise eastern investors. An amusing account of his September 1864 visit to the embryonic Bodie mining district was published in two installments in *Harper's New Monthly Magazine* as "A Trip to Bodie Bluff and the Dead Sea of the West" (1865). Much of this material reappeared in his book *Adventures in the Apache Country: A Tour Through Arizona and Sonora, With Notes on the Silver Regions of Nevada* (1869). He also wrote official reports on behalf of the federal government. *Reports Upon the Mineral Resources of the United States* (1867) and *Report of J. Ross Browne on the Mineral Resources of the States and Territories West of the Rocky Mountains* (1868) documented mining throughout the American West.

27. J. Ross Browne, *Adventures in the Apache Country: A Tour Through Arizona and Sonora, With Notes on the Silver Regions of Nevada* (New York, NY: Harper & Brothers Publishers, 1869), 393-398.

28. J. Ross Browne, *The Bodie Bluff Mines Located in Mono County, California, Belonging to the Empire Gold & Silver Mining Co. of New York* (New York: Clark & Maynard, 1865), 9.

29. Browne, *Bodie Bluff Mines*, 7-8.

30. Browne, *Bodie Bluff Mines*, 10.

31. Browne, *Bodie Bluff Mines*, 6-7. Ore bodies are defined by two angles, their strike and their pitch. The strike is

the direction of an imaginary line drawn horizontally through the stratum as if plotted on a map. The strike is often discernible by following the ledge where it out-crops the surface. The pitch, also called the dip, is the angle at which the stratum is inclined downward into the earth, measured from horizontal.

32. *Mining and Scientific Press* 23 September 1865, 178; 20 January 1866, 38; *Walker Lake Bulletin* 6 November 1915.

33. *Mining and Scientific Press* 20 January 1866, 38.

34. *Mining and Scientific Press* 7 April 1866, 214.

35. The decade following the closure of the Empire Company is one of Bodie's most difficult periods to research because of an absence of sources. Although the region was inhabited between 1868 and 1877, no newspapers were published in the area, which included the county seats of Bridgeport and Aurora. The closest newspapers to Bodie during this time period were the *Alpine Chronicle*, published some 50 miles to the northwest in Alpine County, California, and the *Borax Miner*, 60 miles eastward in Esmeralda County, Nevada.

36. *Mining and Scientific Press* 16 March 1867, 167; Fletcher, *Paiute, Prospector, Pioneer*, 29-42.

37. D. V. Goodson, *Mining Laws of Bodie Mining District Compiled from the Original Records* (Bodie, CA: Bodie Standard Printing House, 1878), 19-20.

38. *Bodie Weekly Standard* 4 September 1878; Wasson, *Bodie and Esmeralda*, 9-10; *Daily Bodie Standard* 9 April 1880. On June 10, 1875, Eshington and Lockberg located the Bunker Hill lode. On the same day they recorded the identical piece of ground as the Bullion lode: "Commencing at the lower Bunker Hill Shaft and running North and South each way from said shaft Seven Hundred and fifty (750) feet . . ." (Mono County, *Mining Locations, Book A*, 90; Mono County, *Bodie Mining Records, Book D*, 91; *Inyo Independent* 12 February 1876)

39. Parr, "Reminiscences," 34. Though history does not pinpoint the date of this momentous mishap, John F. Parr, who was in Aurora at the time, states that bullion from the ore exposed by the cave-in was brought to Aurora in the fall of 1875. His remembrances, recorded 50 years later, contain the only known eyewitness account of these crucial events. (Parr, "Reminiscences," 33-38) A possible clue to the date of the accident is found in a Columbus, Nevada, newspaper, which reported that a worker died in Columbus of injuries received on October 30, 1875, "from a cave in the mine of Eshington & Co., at Bodie." The clip does not mention a rich discovery. (*Borax Miner* 20 November 1875)

40. *Inyo Independent* 17 March 1877; *Mining and Scientific Press* 24 March 1877, 181. "Horse" is a Cornish word meaning "a mass of country-rock inclosed in an ore-deposit." (Rossiter W. Raymond, "A Glossary of Mining and Metallurgical Terms," *Transactions of the American Institute of Mining Engineers*, 9 (Easton, PA: A. I. M. E., 1881), 146, s.v. "horse.")

41. Fitch, *Pacific Coast Mining*, 249-250; Wasson, *Bodie and Esmeralda*, 25.

42. In a letter recounting the district's early history, Wasson wrote: "In September, 1876, George W. Story [sic] took a bond on the old Bunker Hill Bullion property to Seth and Dan Cook, who sent John F. Boyd out to report on the ground." (*Bodie Standard* 17 April 1878) The verb, "bond" means "to give or secure an option upon, as a mine or other property, by a bond tying up the property till the option has expired." (*Webster's New International Dictionary of the English Language*, 2d ed, Unabridged, s.v. "bond.") Other sources indicate that a bond is simply a written agreement binding the owners of a property to sell it when specific conditions are met.

43. Parr, "Reminiscences," 34; Official documents record the selling price at $75,000. (Mono County, *Bodie Mining Records, Book L*, 586, 620) If George Storey received a 10% commission, the two miners actually got $67,500, as stated in other sources. (Wasson, *Bodie and Esmeralda*, 27)

44. *Engineering and Mining Journal* 16 September 1876, 189.

45. *Engineering and Mining Journal* 26 October 1878, 296; Parr, "Reminiscences," 35.

Who Was W. S. Body, Bodey, Bodie?

1. The unlucky miner's last partner, E. S. Taylor, was also dead. After burying his fallen partner's bones in the spring of 1860, Taylor was employed grazing livestock in southeastern Mono County in 1862. There he was killed by warring Paiute Indians, near Blind Springs Hill, a place destined to become the mining community of Benton.

2. *Daily Bodie Standard* 27 October 1879.

3. Joseph Wasson, *Bodie and Esmeralda* (San Francisco, CA: Spaulding, Barto & Co., 1878), 5-6; Joseph Wasson, *Com-*

plete Guide to the Mono County Mines (San Francisco, CA: Spaulding, Barto & Co., 1879), x-xi; "Bodie's Discoverer," *Daily Bodie Standard* 4 August 1879; "The End—The Question Settled as to Body's Grave," *Daily Bodie Standard* 27 October 1879. In *Bodie Bonanza*, Loose quotes these and other sources, but changes the spelling of "Body" to "Bodey" where it was advantageous. In *The Ghost Town of Bodie*, the Johnsons also rely on quotations to tell the discovery story, but conveniently change the spelling of "Bodey" to "Body."

4. Wasson, *Bodie and Esmeralda*, 6. Wasson was more than Bodie's first historian. He had been elected on September 6, 1879, to the California State Assembly as a representative from Mono County.

5. "Cold History Condensed," *Daily Bodie Standard* 29 October 1879.

6. *Daily Bodie Standard* 27 October 1879.

7. *Daily Bodie Standard* 27 October 1879. Later writers have suggested that a pistol was found in the grave, but eyewitness accounts do not mention a firearm.

8. *Daily Bodie Standard* 27 October 1879.

9. *Daily Bodie Standard* 4 August 1879.

10. "The Remains of W. S. Bodey," *Bodie Chronicle* 1 November 1879.

11. "Bill Bodey's Bones," *Daily Free Press* 3 November 1879; "The Last of All—W. S. Bodey's Remains Re-interred Yesterday," *Daily Free Press* 3 November 1879.

12. *Daily Free Press* 3 November 1879.

13. *Daily Free Press* 3 November 1879.

14. "A Former Poughkeepsian's Fate," *Poughkeepsie Daily Eagle* 28 October 1879. The article notes that: "While here he followed the trade of a tinsmith, working for the firm of J. H. & J. E. Allen, who carried on business for a long time on the corner of Main and Academy Streets. . . . His widow is now living in this city, and resides at No. 9 Mansion Street."

15. "The Fate of Bodie's Discoverer," *New York Times* 29 October 1879; "Body's Family," *Daily Bodie Standard* 7 November 1879.

16. "Specter of City Man Lives Again as California Revives Ghost of Wild, Wicked Bodie," *Poughkeepsie Journal* 5 February 1961.

17. That her husband was entered in census records for Dutchess County, New York, at a time when Sarah later claimed he was in California has raised doubts about whether he could be the man for whom the mining district of Bodie was named. Listing family members who were not at home, however, was common among nineteenth-century census takers. Sailors, for example, are often found enumerated as "heads of households" when they were away on long sea voyages.

Figure 2-1: The Standard Gold Mining Company completed this 20-stamp mill in July 1877, when Bodie's population was only about 300. The mill utilized machinery from the Del Monte mill near Aurora, and was capable of crushing 45 tons of ore per day. Five months later, an aerial cable tramway would be built to transport ore directly from the mine. Cordwood, stacked at right, fueled the mill's steam-powered machinery. (Harry M. Gorham collection. Courtesy, California Historical Society, San Francisco)

CHAPTER TWO

BONANZA!
1877-1878

The Californians pride themselves on being a pre-eminently smart people, yet it can safely be said that no other community would allow itself to be fleeced so unmercifully, or would take stock in concerns managed as the majority of the mines here are in the interest of inside rings.
   — Engineering and Mining Journal, *January 20, 1877*

The California stocks are, as a rule, wisely let alone, and are thrown about among the brokers on washed sales in the endeavor to entrap some unwary outsider into parting with his money.
   — Engineering and Mining Journal *in* Mining and Scientific Press, *March 31, 1877*

At the present time there is not a single dividend paying mine on the whole length of the Comstock, while the assessments are steadily increasing. . . . When we turn to look at Bodie, a brighter picture meets our gaze. We see the Standard and Bodie making regular disbursements, . . . and a big demand is springing up for Bodie stocks, not alone in San Francisco but in the Atlantic cities.
   — Bodie Weekly Standard, *November 27, 1878*

The Standard and Bulwer Mines

By the spring of 1877, the Bullion shaft had been driven 400 feet into the lode. A 10,000-ton winter's accumulation of ore—10 times the quantity already milled—awaited transportation to the Syndicate mill. Impressed by the ore exposed, the Bullion's owners hired a San Francisco contractor to construct a 20-stamp mill at the foot of High Peak. He began grading its foundation in March. Immediately downhill from the mine, the new mill would use machinery from the neglected Del Monte mill near Aurora.[1]

"We also have quite a town started here," wrote a visitor from Inyo County. "We have already two stores, and considerable preparations for numerous whisky mills and hash houses. . . . Jumping of town lots and watching mining claims that might be jumped, has commenced. Scalping knives and six-shooters are kept in [working] order in case they might be needed." The visitor also noticed numerous properties being prospected, and that "all the claims are looking well and have plenty of good ore."[2]

Bodie was growing. By the end of March 1877, it had been enhanced by the addition of a saloon and a hotel, and the population reached 150.[3]

A month after initiating construction of their mill at Bodie, the Bullion Mine's owners organized the Standard Gold Mining Company, incorporated on April 11, 1877, with a capitalization of $5,000,000, represented by 50,000 shares of stock.[4] Seth and Daniel Cook owned half of the stock. Dan Cook was elected president of the company, and John F. Boyd its vice president. George Storey, who had acted as intermediary in the purchase, earned a commission of 10% of the selling price. He also received 1,000 shares of stock, ranking him among the company's principal shareholders. Thereafter, the Bullion property was known as the Standard Mine.[5] It would prove to be the richest mine in Bodie District, a designation challenged only twice in the next 36 years.

The Standard Company's business offices were in San Francisco's Nevada Block, in the heart of the city's business district. This elegant new edifice had been built in 1875 by the Comstock's Bonanza Kings to house the Nevada Bank, a financial institution they had established explicitly to compete with the mighty Bank of California.[6] Containing banking and business offices, the Nevada Block stood at the corner of Pine and Montgomery streets, where it was conveniently located diagonally across the intersection from the San Francisco Stock and Exchange Board.[7]

A week after the Standard Company was organized, ore shipments recommenced and the Syndicate mill's 16 stamps started hammering away on the second run of ore from the Standard's Bullion lode. Meanwhile, Standard directors sought to expand their Bodie holdings. In June they purchased a controlling interest in a mine owned by Henry Goode Blasdel, who had been Nevada's first state governor.[8] The Homestake was situated west of the Standard and included a shaft and a horse whim. Of particular interest were the Homestake's three ledges: the Homestake, Ralston, and Stonewall. The Ralston ledge had been named for William C. Ralston, once president of the powerful Bank of California and known as "the man who built San Francisco." Ralston

had sold the mine to Blasdel in the mid-1860s, after losing thousands of dollars while working it. The Standard people purchased the property, renamed it the Bulwer (pronounced "Bulver"), and organized a company to mine it. The Bulwer Mining Company was formed on June 29, 1877, with 60,000 shares of stock and a capitalization of $6,000,000.[9] The two companies, the Bulwer and Standard, had the same corporate directors and shared the same San Francisco offices.

The Standard Company, rich with ore from Eshington and Lockberg's former mine shaft, drove deeper into the Bullion lode. As the shaft approached the 600-foot level, construction of the Standard mill neared completion. On July 20, 1877, the pounding of its 20 stamps, complemented by 10 Washoe amalgamating pans, 5 settlers, 2 agitators, and 200 feet of blanket sluices, joined a din from the Syndicate mill as the two mills crushed the Standard's ore. Keeping pace with 36 thundering stamps, miners below doubled their rate of ore extraction. Newspapers in nearby towns listed bullion shipments and reported that people were "flocking" to the region in "great numbers."[10]

During the autumn of 1877, Bodie became "an excitement" with the potential to rival the Comstock.[11] Overlooking the growing town, four hills that comprised the Bodie mining district churned with activity, as miners located claims and blasted their way into the earth in search of hidden treasure. Bodie Bluff, High Peak, Silver Hill, and Queen Bee Hill were invaded by individual and corporate fortune seekers. On the slightest chance that rich lodes would be struck, companies were organized, stock sold, hoisting equipment purchased, and shafts sunk.

Bodie's allure in late 1877 was strong enough to overcome the difficulties of getting there. A visitor described his September journey from the Comstock in unforgettable terms.

A trip to Bodie involves a deal of personal discomfort, annoying dust, heat, and extreme cold, especially while passing through the Sweetwater country. The stage line is abominable, consisting of rackety [sic] old coaches, mud wagons, and half-starved stock, and prices high enough to bankrupt a man of ordinary means. . . . If my trip is an average specimen, their fastest time does not exceed six miles an hour. Passengers are only an annoyance, and are carried under protest. The shotgun messengers are the feature of the trip, and the line is run for their benefit, they being the guardians of the weekly shipment of treasure from this place, which averages about two bars of $21,000 each, or $42,000 and they of course imagine passengers only a secondary consideration. . . . We saw the remains of [a stage] coach lying in the canyon about fifteen feet below the road, about three miles from Aurora, where the passengers were taken to have their wounds dressed.[12]

"Bodie is improving very fast," read another traveler's letter, documenting the town's rapid growth.

There is [sic] about one hundred and ten houses, and two quartz mills running thirty-six stamps night and day. We have a population of about six hundred—and lots of Piutes. Two stores, one kept by Bryant, of Bridgeport, and the other by S. B. Smith, of Aurora; seven saloons; five eating houses; two lodging houses; two barber shops; one tin shop; one shoemaker shop; two meat markets; three lumber yards (and not able to supply the demand); from three to six houses are started every day, besides quite a number of tents and mud cabins. People are taking up and jumping lots in every direction. I must not forget to mention that we have a Postoffice, F. K. Bechtel, Postmaster, and Wells Fargo's Express, which is at S. B. Smith's store, he being the agent. The mail and express arrive and depart daily. . . . The prospects are now quite favorable for the establishing of a school district and the building of a school house . . . A wholesale and retail grocery and liquor store is about to be erected. The 16th of September is to be celebrated in style by the Mexicans, of which there are a large number in this vicinity. . . . Yesterday being pay day, the boys have plenty of pocket change, and anyone seeing the amount of coin in circulation would readily presume that the mines of Bodie district were in a decidedly healthy condition, of which there is no doubt.[13]

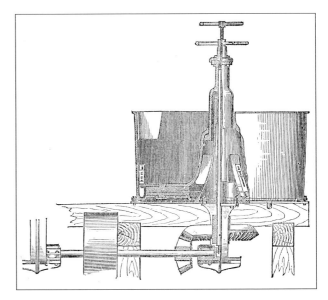

Washoe amalgamating pan

In September, exactly one year after the Bullion Mine's purchase and just five months after the Standard Company was formed, company directors declared a dividend of $1 per share, disbursing $50,000 among shareholders.[14] A second $1 dividend was declared in October, the month that Bodie's first newspaper, the *Bodie Standard*, began telling the world about the wonders of the district. Every week its columns tabulated the bars of gold bullion leaving the Standard and Syndicate mills for the U.S. mints in Carson City and San Francisco. Wells, Fargo & Company, possessing the duty of seeing to it that the precious cargo reached its destination, protected each stage with a guard of armed messengers.[15] In case guns were not enough to discourage holdups, other measures were taken. "They play now a very mean trick on the road agents by making the bars 120 pounds each, which makes them very awkward to handle so that the stage robberies are not likely to be profitable."[16] While deterrents were needed to prevent robberies on the open road, Bodie, as yet, remained relatively free of violence. "A man named Lockwood dropped his pistol yesterday evening and shot himself. . . . This is the only shooting we have had, and there is very little amusement in town."[17]

The Standard declared yet another $1 dividend

in November. To develop the lode and remove its ore more efficiently, the company purchased a hoisting engine, said to be the largest steam hoist in the district. It was needed to sink a second shaft. The new shaft would be vertical, unlike the former Eshington and Lockberg incline shaft that pursued the Bullion lode on an angle. It would also contain three compartments, so that men, tools, rock, and timbers could be hoisted in two compartments, reserving the third for pumping machinery.[18] At intervals along the shaft, chambers called "stations" would be blasted out. From these underground workrooms, which would also serve as staging areas, horizontal crosscuts would be driven to intersect the ledge on various levels. Known as the "Standard new shaft" or the "Standard main shaft," it was positioned between the Standard and Bulwer properties in an old claim called the "West Bullion."[19] Its central location, 675 feet west of the incline shaft, was considered excellent for bisecting the included angle between the converging Standard and Bulwer ore bodies and reaching the Veta Madre, if such a thing actually existed.

By the time the Standard Company declared its fourth $1 dividend in December, Andrew. S. Hallidie, famed as the inventor of San Francisco's cable car system, was building one of his "Endless Wire Ropeways" (an aerial cable tramway) to bring ore from the two Standard shafts to the mill. Fifty buckets, dangling from a moving steel cable, would deliver a steady stream of ore to the Standard mill 2,500 feet below the mine.[20]

On December 3, 1877, the Syndicate mill finished crushing the 10,000-ton stockpile of Standard ore mined the previous winter. The milling had started in April, requiring eight months. During this period, the rock that went through the batteries yielded $428,000. This mill run reportedly returned the purchase price of the mine and the costs of building the Standard mill, the aerial tramway, and a new steam-powered hoisting works at the incline shaft. It also paid the company's first dividend in September, and there was still $40,000 left in the treasury.[21]

While golden treasure streamed from the Syndicate mill, the Standard mill had been hammering out even more. The Bullion ledge surpassed all expectations, and the rapid success of the Standard Gold Mining Company stunned the mining world. Even Professor Silliman, reassured by the confirmed (more likely accidental) accuracy of his 14-year-old report to the Empire Gold and Silver Mining Company, piped up with newfound conviction, "I have always stoutly maintained that outside of the Comstock, there was no mining district in California or Nevada, known to me, which embraced so many elements of a great future as Bodie."[22]

At year's end the Standard Gold Mining Company had paid dividends in September, October, November, and December. The Bullion lode was opened to a depth of 850 feet, where the incline shaft encountered water. From stations on the 200-, 300-, 450-, 550-, and 650-foot levels, north and south drifts probed the vein. Ore from the drifts was delivered to all five stations, where it was loaded onto a skip that ran up and down the incline and transported it to the surface.

The Bullion lode, dipping to the west at an angle of 78 degrees, was big, measuring 15 feet wide in places. Gold deposits worth $2,000,000—enough to pay steady dividends for the next two years—were already exposed.[23] Furthermore, no one could tell how far pay rock extended below the water. The full size of the ore body would not be known until the vertical main shaft reached the water and pumps were installed. The advancing shaft was still only 100 feet deep. It would be some time before it began clearing water from the mine.

The Standard Gold Mining Company's success was astonishing. The California State Mineralogist placed the mine's 1877 production at an incredible $784,523. In comparison, the combined product of a dozen other newly-formed Bodie companies was only about $10,500.[24] These figures, however, are somewhat misleading. The apparent lack of production by numerous surrounding mines was due more to a deficiency in milling facilities than to an absence of ore. So far, the district's two mills had worked almost exclusively on Standard ore.

The swift rise to prominence of the Standard Mine was almost as remarkable as how quickly a few scattered bunkhouses and cabins were transformed into a scruffy ramshackle municipality. When the output of two sawmills near Bridgeport proved insufficient to construct the town and develop its mines, lumber was hauled more than 100 miles from Carson City.[25] In less than a year, Bodie had grown from a gathering of hired hands into a bustling community of more than 1,200 people. Reflecting on the amazing events of 1877, the editor of the *Bodie Standard* titled his column "GOLD" and scribbled philosophically:

> But a few short months ago Bodie was an insignificant little place, now she is rapidly growing in size and importance and people are crowding in upon her from far and near, and why? Because of the rich discoveries of gold, "yellow, glittering, precious gold," the bane of man and yet his antidote; his blessing and his curse; his happiness and his misery.[26]

In San Francisco, the economic, manufacturing, and cultural capital of the West, the phenomenon was summed up by the cry, "Ho! for Bodie!"[27]

During 1877, 13 companies had been incorporated to work claims in the Bodie mining district: the Standard, Bulwer, Bodie, Red Cloud, Bodie Tunnel, Bechtel, McClinton, Summit, Belvidere, Black Hawk, South Standard, Spaulding, and Booker.[28] Including the Syndicate, incorporated in 1875, they all paid wages. But because few of these companies had milled any ore, salaries came from the sale of shares or through assessments. An assessment required stockholders to pony up additional money or forfeit their shares. Outlawed in many states, the practice of levying assessments was customary in California and Nevada, where investors, as part owners of a company, were expected to contribute to a mine's operation as well as benefit from its profits. The system was defended as a means of developing a mine by raising capital when it was needed. In some cases,

RED CLOUD CONSOLIDATED MINing Company—Location of principal place of business, San Francisco, California—Location of works, Bodie Mining District, Mono county, California.— Notice is hereby given, that at a meeting of the Board of Directors, held on the Fifth day of August, 1879, an assessment (No. 6) of Twenty (20) Cents per share was levied on the capital stock of the corporation, payable immediately in United States gold coin, to the Secretary, at the office of the company, Room No. 58, Nevada Block, northwest corner Pine and Montgomery streets, San Francisco, California.

Any stock upon which this assessment shall remain unpaid on the tenth day of September, 1879, will be delinquent and advertised for sale at public auction, and unless payment is made before, will be sold on TUESDAY, the Seventh day of October, 1879, to pay the delinquent assessment, together with costs of advertising and expenses of sale.

JOEL F. LIGHTNER, Secretary.
Office—Room No. 58, Nevada Block, northwest corner Pine and Montgomery streets, San Francisco, California.   au8td

Figure 2-2: An August 1879 notice in the *Bodie Morning News* advises stockholders that the Red Cloud Consolidated Mining Company had levied a 20-cent per share assessment. This was the company's sixth assessment. Nationally read mining journals also published lists of assessment notices. (*Bodie Morning News* 28 August 1879)

advocates argued, systematic assessments provided enough funds to keep an unprofitable mine open until pay ore was found.

Each assessment afforded investors an opportunity to reevaluate the mine's potential and decide whether or not to continue funding it. If the assessment was not paid by a specified date, the delinquent stock automatically reverted to the company. Accumulated stock could be resold to raise working capital when there was public interest, otherwise it languished in the company's treasury. The system's major drawback was the ease with which stock prices could be manipulated with opportune assessments. There were also pervasive suspicions that company directors plundered stockholders by levying assessments to pay extravagant salaries instead of develop-

MINING ON THE ASSESSMENT PLAN

During a long and colorful journalistic career on the eastern slope of the Sierra Nevada mountains, James W. E. Townsend enlivened the columns of numerous newspapers with whimsical yarns. He began writing for Virginia City's *Territorial Enterprise*, whose readers had been entertained by young Samuel Clemens (Mark Twain) and William Wright (Dan De Quille).

In January 1881, Townsend moved to Lundy, Mono County, California, where he took over the *Homer Mining Index*. Within the year he sold that paper to become local editor for the Reno *Gazette*. There "his talents made the paper one of the most popular in the state." After a few months at the Carson City *Index*, he returned to Mono County, where he resurrected the *Homer Mining Index* in 1894. In 1895, he took his printing press to Bodie and pro-

duced the *Bodie Mining Index*. The following year it merged with the *Evening Miner* and became the *Bodie Miner-Index*, continuing until 1908.[1]

Better known as "Lying Jim Townsend," he filled the pages of his papers with amusing tales. Sadly, few issues survive. Lying Jim, who enjoyed criticizing others, became the subject of a yarn that pokes fun at the evil side of stock assessments. The tale appeared in an 1890 *Carson Appeal* column that was reprinted in Hawthorne's *Walker Lake Bulletin*.

While Jim Townsend was [in Carson City] a few weeks ago, he was sitting by the Arlington House stove talking in his usual exaggerated vein.

"If you want to see mining on a big scale, go to Mono county."

"How big?" said a little man close by.

"Why, the Big Hole Mine, that I am connected with, has the deep-

est shaft and the biggest workings in the world."

"How deep?" said the little man.

"You can't measure it, because if we stopped work long enough to see how deep the shaft was, it would materially interfere with bullion production. We dropped a line down once and reeled it out until it broke with its own weight. When a boy falls down the shaft, he strikes the bottom a grandfather."

"Must have a big payroll?"

"We used to send the money down to the hands in cages until the workings got so deep that we didn't get the winter account settled until a way along in the spring. So we started a bank and telegraphed the money orders. That system saved us an awful wear and tear on the cages. The miners live down there and rear their families. They got an underground city bigger'n Carson, with a regular charter and municipal elections twice a year. They publish two daily papers and a literary magazine."

ing their mines.

It mattered little to newcomers whether wages at Bodie derived from bullion or from assessments. The expectation of regular paydays brought a flood of humanity. "Main Street has presented a lively sight during the past week," wrote one reporter in December, observing the developing economy awash in cash. "The stores, shops and saloons have been doing a big trade, especially in the last five days, with nearly seventy thousand dollars in miners wages circulating around."[29]

The giddy economy took a sobering turn when

the winter of 1877-78 brought layoffs, as mines with unsheltered hoisting equipment had to close for the season. The growing number of unemployed prompted concern, and the local newspaper alerted new arrivals about Bodie's lack of jobs and insufficient lodging. The warnings did no good, and the influx of humanity continued through the dead of winter. A reporter writing for a February 1878 Reno daily was struck by the large number of idlers among able-bodied men. "Bodie has a population of 1,500, about 600 of whom are out of employment, and of which . . . not over 250 would work could they find

"I never heard of the magazine," said the stranger.

"Of course not, it would be a year old when it got to you. Besides they hold a fair there annually and racing every Saturday. Finest four mile track in the world, lit with electric light. No mud, no dust, always in the same condition. Perfect paradise for sports. What do you think of that for a mine?"

Here the stranger, who was a Californian, threw his leg carelessly over the arm of a chair, and lighting a cigar, replied in a deep earnest tone:

"I don't think much of your mine. You work too much for small results. When your mine plays out you have a lot of old truck on your hands, and where are you? You mine after primitive methods, like all new countries. It takes experience and hard work to tackle the industry in the proper shape. With your mine you must be on the ground in person and have any amount of men to look after this department or that. Now, I have a bigger mine than yours. It is located in Storey county, somewhere in the northern part I believe, and I run it quite up to the handle with one or two assistants."

"How deep might the shaft be?"

"It might be pretty deep if I al-lowed the men to rush forward and overdo the thing, but at present there is no shaft at all."

"Hoisting works up?"

"No, no hoisting works—not if I know it. You can fool away a great deal of good hard coin on hoisting works."

"How in thunder do you run your mine?"

"On the assessment plan, sir. That's the latest and most improved method. We have a big map of the mine hung up in the company's office, made by one of the most competent artists on the Coast. Now when we have a good map of the lower workings we don't need any works to speak of. We photographed the Savage hoisting works from the top of the Hale & Norcross trestleworks—an entirely new view—and call it by our name; the Bullion Brick. I keep a man in Virginia [City] at $60 a month to superintend the location and write weekly letters, and I stay in San Francisco in my office on Pine street and levy the assessments every 60 days; that's as often as the law allows. I'm the president, board of trustees, secretary, treasurer and everything—more especially the treasurer. Of course, I draw the salary for all the offic-ers, and when I get through drawing salaries, I turn the rest over to the agent in Virginia to pay off the hands. By not employing any hands he saves enough to pay himself. My regular income from the mine is $200,000 a year, and never a pick struck the ground. This is what I consider scientific mining, sir. You get the silver out of the pockets of the stock holders and leave the vast argentiferous and auriferous deposits in your claim for your children, who can go right ahead and develop the mine just as soon as the people quit putting up, which isn't at all likely to occur. As soon as a man drops on the game he dies, and the newcomers have to learn for themselves. As long as people are being born in Nevada and California, my mine will run on like a chronometer clock."

"But," said Townsend, "my style of mining keeps a lot of men at work."

"So does mine," quoth the Golden Gate chap. "Thousands of men are working night and day to pay the assessments. It keeps the country as busy as a beehive," and the speaker sauntered to the telegraph office to order assessment No. 36.[2]

work to do." He also provided a description of the town which suggests that over the course of the winter the number of saloons increased from seven to seventeen. His count of "fifteen houses of ill fame" was a strong indication that Bodie was taking on attributes of a real boomtown. The reporter closed with a cautionary remark. "Many persons in Bodie are elated over the prospects of the camp, while others in speaking of it use language wholly unbecoming a Christian."[30]

The future of Bodie as a mining center depended on wood, both for fuel and for timbers to support the underground workings. Seeing this need, three principal owners of the Standard Mine, the two Cook brothers and Robert N. Graves, along with two associates, acquired a large stand of Jeffrey pine south of Mono Lake. One of the five, H. M. Yerington, had invested heavily with Graves in the Syndicate Mine. The men organized the Bodie Wood and Lumber Company and received permission from the state in January 1878 to harvest timber. Their holdings, in the largest California forest area on the eastern side of the Sierra, amounted to 11,000 acres or more.[31] In four years, this wooded tract would become the reason for building a railroad northward to supply Bodie with lumber.

Month after month, dividends from the Standard Gold Mining Company continued uninterrupted, into the spring of 1878. On the 850-foot level, a station was blasted out in the incline shaft, from which drifts were started north and south along the Bullion lode. Meanwhile, the Standard main shaft reached a depth of 400 feet, slicing through four new ledges during its descent. The Standard mill ran around the clock, fed by a string of ore-laden buckets moving continuously from the mine. "There is no music so inspiring to go to bed to now a days," wrote Joseph Wasson, "as a quartz mill turning out a regular and healthy stream of bullion."[32]

Instead of declaring dividends, the Bulwer Company had levied a 50-cent per share assessment on stockholders to continue developing its mine. At the foot of High Peak, near the mouth of Bodie Canyon, the company reopened one of Governor Blasdel's abandoned tunnels. Already extending 480 feet into the hill, the tunnel received new timbering and was driven eastward toward the three known ledges in the Bulwer Company's ground.[33] The tunnel reached a length of 600 feet in late April 1878. Another 1,200 feet beyond its advancing face lay the Standard main shaft, where a station was blasted out 365 feet below the surface of High Peak. From this station, two crosscuts were started, one westward to meet the approaching tunnel and the other eastward to intersect the Standard's inclined workings at the Bullion ledge. Once these passageways were connected, the artery they formed would play a key part in the future prosperity of the district. The major horizontal segment, extending from the base of High Peak to the Standard shaft, would come to be known as the "Bulwer Tunnel." Its importance came not from any great wealth in the Bulwer Mine, but from greatly reducing the expense of removing ore and waste rock from the Standard Mine.[34]

Anticipating the Standard Mine's prosperity, management initiated improvements to their mill in May. The building's north side was extended to house six additional amalgamating pans and three more settlers. The new machinery increased the mill's capacity from 45 to 75 tons per day by capturing the precious metals at pace with the stamps. On the flat below, the tailings pond was enlarged so that the mill's muddy effluent would not flood the lower end of Main Street.[35]

Warm spring weather brought a mining and prospecting frenzy to Bodie in 1878, as numerous mines reopened and more were started. Joseph Wasson, gathering information for a promotional pamphlet, toured the district and evaluated its investment opportunities. He calculated that there were about 400 men who received $4 per day, including those working in and about the mines, teamsters, and woodcutters. The Standard Company employed about 75 men; the Bechtel, 40; the Syndicate, 30; the McClinton, 20; the Red Cloud, 20; the Bodie, Bulwer, Belvidere, from 15 to 20 each; and the Black Hawk, 10. A score of other mines employed from 5 to 10 men each. Wasson also estimated the town's population at about 2,000.[36]

Developments in the mines were faithfully reported by the town's most loyal advocate: the local press. Tailored for outside consumption, their articles were reprinted by far-flung newspapers, including national mining journals. Through these widely-disseminated reports, it seemed, the desiderata of Bodie and the nation merged, both relishing stories of gold and adventure. When Bodie's telegraph was completed, it was immediately used to promote the district's virtues. The first dispatch read: "Bodie (Cal.) May 7—Bodie sends greetings and proclaims to the mining world that her gold mines are the most wonderful yet discovered."[37] At least one local journalist recognized the value of the new communication link to exploit the public's insatiable appetite for mining news. "The future of Bodie never looked more encouraging than at present," exclaimed an editorial titled "Bright Prospects." "The completion of the telegraph will put us in a position to make known to the outside world the rich strikes which are almost daily being made in our mines and on the hills surrounding our town."[38]

As the Bulwer Tunnel inched eastward, the crosscut from the Standard main shaft advanced toward it in the opposite direction, passing through the Bulwer's old workings. The Bulwer, whose ledges were now connected to the Standard main shaft, abandoned its own shaft and horse whim and took advantage of the Standard's powerful steam hoist. Soon the dump at the mouth of the Standard main shaft was brimming with Bulwer ore.[39]

Unfortunately, no mill could be found to crush it. An acute shortage of milling facilities impeded bullion production throughout the district. The Syndicate had added four stamps to its mill, but the only mill built since the Standard's was a little 4-stamp concern called the "Miners mill," whose machinery had been moved from the Humphrey mill at Silver City, Nevada. Its new location in Bodie Canyon, about five miles below town, forever hindered its usefulness because of the cost of transporting ore to it.[40] These eight stamps, added to the district's milling capacity in May, fell short of the number needed. With no stamp mill of its own, the Bulwer Company was unable to produce any bullion.

The Standard main shaft reached a depth of 700 feet in early October as more people and capital poured into Bodie. Throughout the remainder of 1878, the frenzy continued on the hills above town. "The past week has been distinguished for remarkable activity," reported a local mining columnist. "One can stand on Main Street and watch the erection of machinery and buildings, and the gradual increase of dump piles from the various mines being worked. . . . Before winter sets in there will be a small city of houses covering hoisting engines all along the hill"[41] The Bodie correspondent for the nationally read *Engineering and Mining Journal* counted 22 steam-powered hoisting works and said that more were under construction.[42]

Ignoring the district's milling deficiency, many mines had ordered steam-powered machinery, even though most of them had not revealed ore of suffi-

cient value to warrant such a costly investment. Until the machinery arrived, ore and waste rock were brought to the surface with either a horse-powered whim or a hand-cranked windlass. Raising buckets of broken rock from a hole in the ground with a horse that walked in circles to turn a winding mechanism may seem primitive, but the horse-powered machine was a welcome replacement to the miner's backbreaking chore of reeling heavily-laden buckets to the top of a mine shaft with a windlass. A steam hoist was even better. "From our office window we can look out upon the many steam hoisting works extending from Bodie Bluff on the north to Queen Bee Hill on

the south. We know they are all steadily at work as the steam issuing from the various pipes gives us evidence."[43] It was stated that the shriek of the steam whistles could be heard all the way to Aurora.

Bodie's hills are arid. Water to feed the boilers for the hoisting engines had to be hauled in barrels by wagon from springs near town.[44] A scarcity of water also meant that a mill site was carefully selected to ensure the availability of a spring capable of supplying enough water for the milling process. Despite a mill owner's best efforts, additional measures were often needed to provide ample water for ore reduction. At the Standard mill, particulates were settled in the tailings ponds, and the water was reused. After the mines encountered water, machinery raised it to supply surface facilities, where a parched landscape belied an abundance of groundwater that impeded downward expansion. On one occasion, a stream of water 30 feet long gushed from the face of a crosscut

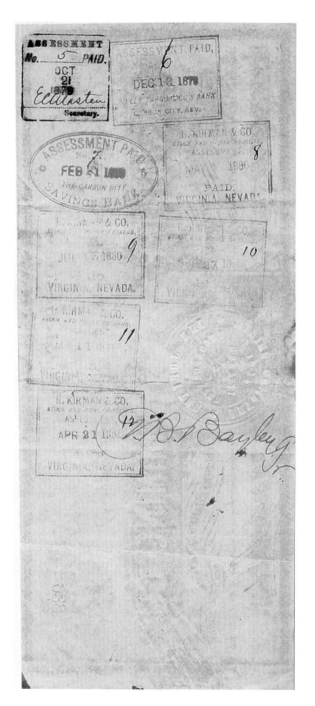

Figure 2-3: Faced with an assessment, shareholders wishing to maintain their investment were required to pay the specified amount at a nearby financial institution. The stock was then validated by stamping the certificate. If the assessment was not paid before the due date, the stock was forfeited to the company. Displaying proof that the owner paid eight assessments, this Jupiter Consolidated Mining Company stock certificate bears "assessment paid" stamps from the Bank of Wells, Fargo & Co., the Carson City Savings Bank, and the brokerage house of R. Kirman & Co in Virginia City. (Courtesy, Roger Lauderdale)

another passageway, 112 feet east of the Bullion ledge, they found a parallel vein that came to be called the "East Standard ledge." It gave every indication of being as large as the Bullion. Initial interpretations were wrong, but just off a drift near the claim's southern boundary a more important ore body was found lying parallel to the Bullion. It was named the "West Standard ledge."[46]

In December 1878, miners tunneling eastward from the Standard main shaft to the Bullion lode struck yet another ledge. Between the vertical and incline shafts they stumbled upon the greatest ore body in Bodie's history—a mineral formation that would determine the town's destiny. But because the crosscut passed immediately into a horse, the true size of the ledge was disguised. Since it appeared inconsequential, initial reports were understated. The first account emphasized progress in the crosscut, but attached no particular importance to the discovery. "The east crosscut from the main shaft, 400-foot level has been advanced during the past week 20 feet; total length 105 feet. At 90 feet from the shaft a fine ledge 12 feet wide was passed through."[47] That "fine ledge" would prove to be huge, the district's largest exploitable geologic formation.

From just below the surface, the ledge extended on a westward pitch of about 70 degrees to the 300-foot level. There it nearly leveled off before descending gradually to the 500-foot level. It was immense near the Standard's southern boundary, and even larger to the north, where it diminished somewhat in value, but reached widths of 90 feet. Averaging 20 feet in width, the "Main Standard ledge," as it came to be called, contained several hundred thousand tons

on the Standard Mine's 700-foot level, driving the miners to higher ground.[45]

As the Standard main shaft made its final descent to the water level, the mine continued yielding pay rock. Meanwhile, additional ore bodies had been discovered. Miners crosscutting eastward from the vertical shaft to the inclined workings discovered a vein that they named the "Cook ledge." In of ore assaying at about $60 per ton. The bullion it produced was 92½ percent gold and 7½ percent silver, and it continued to yield profitably into the twentieth century.[48]

The Standard's ore bodies, including the Main Standard ledge, were seldom noted for richness. Unlike the sensationally rich veins in the adjacent Bodie Mine, those in the Standard were remarkable for their large size. Based on quantity of ore, the Standard was often compared to the great Comstock mines. Such comparisons were exaggerated, but because the Standard yielded mostly gold, its ore was richer than that from the enormous silver-producing Comstock ledges.[49]

As 1878 ended, the vertical Standard main shaft was stalled at the water line 780 feet below the surface. Four hundred feet above, the Bulwer Tunnel penetrated 1,000 feet into High Peak, progressing 20 feet per week to meet the westward advancing crosscut. Rising to envelop the shaft's mouth was the timber frame for a building that would house the hoist and a powerful new pumping engine.

During the year, the Standard Company had paid 12 monthly dividends like clockwork, enabling the mine to be true to its newly coined nickname, "Old Reliable." With a stunning production of $1,025,383 for 1878, the Standard Mine had already become distinguished as one of California's greatest gold mines. Its keen management inspired elation. "We must, right here, accord unlimited praise to Superintendent William Irwin for the masterly manner in which he has opened up the greatest gold mine the world has ever seen."[50]

The Bulwer Company, still waiting to turn its stockpiled ore into bullion, had at last contracted with a stamp mill and was shipping its best rock down the long road to the recently-constructed Bodie mill, where difficulty in locating a reliable water supply would delay crushing until March 1879.[51] Because the Bulwer Company milled no ore during 1878, it produced no bullion. As a result, dividends could not be declared. Bulwer stockholders waited and wondered which would come first, a dividend or another dreaded assessment.

The Bodie and Mono Mines

The nation's investing community was infected with gold fever after the Standard Gold Mining Company paid four consecutive monthly dividends during the last third of 1877. Everyone interested in mining stocks was amazed by Bodie's growth. But nothing prepared them for the stampede that took place in 1878, when a second company began paying dividends. These were the result of two rich strikes in the Bodie Mine that sent shock waves across the country. As gold seekers and the unemployed streamed into town, the population of Bodie swelled five times over in less than a year.

The Bodie Mine's story began in September 1876, when prospector Edwin Loose staked a claim adjacent to Peter Eshington and Louis Lockberg's Bullion Mine on the south slope of High Peak. He called his ground the "Bodie Mine." Unlike most prospectors, who located their claims based on evidence of a quartz outcropping, Loose had yet to find any indications. He chose the site believing that the Bullion lode crossed the boundary into his ground. The concept seemed sensible, as demonstrated by at least two other individuals who had the same idea. One was William M. Lent, a shrewd, well-known San Francisco stock trader who had become wealthy investing in Comstock mines.[52] Another was Col. John F. Boyd, who teamed up with Lent in 1876 to acquire Bodie mining properties, including the Bodie Mine.

Lent was fresh from an 1872 financial setback in which a couple of crafty prospectors with a bag of low-grade diamonds and a cleverly staged scheme had duped a number of San Francisco's most prominent mining financiers. Among the victims was William C. Ralston, president of the then-ubiquitous Bank of California. Lent, who had been elected president of the company formed to mine the imaginary gems, was swindled out of at least $100,000 in the fiasco known as the Great Diamond Hoax.[53]

Anxious to achieve control of the Bodie Mine, Lent, according to legend, hired a San Francisco gunman and a couple of drifters to intimidate Loose into selling. The plan failed when Loose became fearful of claim jumpers and recruited his brothers, Warren and William, as reinforcements. Well-armed and determined to defend the mine (consisting of a 60-foot hole in the ground, a hand crank windlass, an ore bucket, and a shack), Will mistook a tripod and transit for a long-range artillery piece, and fired at a survey party. "He saw a cloud of dust," his wife recalled years later. "The contraption was thrown down the hill several yards and landed broadside. Three men were scattering wide apart and rolling and scrambling on hands and knees down the hill."[54]

The skillfully-aimed rifle shot convinced Lent that nobody, including his hired thugs, could ever take the Bodie Mine by force, so he offered Ed Loose generous terms. Visions of wealth have ways of clouding rational judgment, but Loose knew that developing a gold mine required machinery and expertise. Most of all, he rationalized, it required large doses of capital. Reaching the Bodie Mine's uncertain ore body was likely to be costly, so he took the offer and sold the claim to Lent and his San Francisco associates.[55]

The general north-south strike of the district's ledges was a strong indication that the Standard's revenue-producing lode extended into Bodie ground. Further titillating observers was the knowledge that the ore body grew richer near the Bodie boundary. The problem facing the Bodie's new owners was financing an operation needed to find the ledge. From his office in San Francisco's Nevada Block, Lent incorporated the Bodie Gold Mining Company on August 22, 1877, with a capitalization of $5,000,000, divided into 50,000 shares of stock.[56] To no one's surprise, Lent was elected company president, and his eldest son, William H. Lent, was given the position of secretary. John Boyd became a trustee.

The Bodie Gold Mining Company hired a crew of miners to find the lode. With a horse and whim they sank Loose's old shaft deeper into High Peak. Then they installed a steam-powered donkey hoist to expedite the work. In November, the workers reached the 240-foot level, from which a crosscut was started westward toward the anticipated extension of the Bullion lode.[57] Through the winter of 1877-78 the crosscut advanced with no results. As the mine expanded, the little engine brought up load after load of worthless rock. Acutely low on funds by February 1878, the company levied a 50-cent per share assessment to raise more money.

Sure that a golden treasure was waiting below, the miners accepted company stock in lieu of wages.[58] Weekly reports, however, varied little: "The main west cross-cut is now in a distance of 425 feet . . . there has been no change in the character of the ground."[59] By May the crosscut extended 300 feet beyond the point where it had been expected to intersect the ledge, and still there was no ore.[60]

At the base of High Peak, Bodie bustled in the spring of 1878.

On entering Bodie for the first time a stranger would be struck with the business air which characterizes the movements of all. Men walking fast; job wagons running up and down the streets; large freight wagons unloading, etc. In short, it is a lively, pushing place; fine commodious buildings going up; eligible lots commanding a good price, and the place generally wearing a look of prosperity and permanency, for the citizens seem plainly to say we have come to stay.[61]

This exuberance, expressed by the local press, was not always shared. A traveler returning to Reno in April was more restrained.

There are about 200 men in employment there, and between 700 and 800 out of work, with no present prospect of getting any. In fact, it is not likely the camp will support its present population for a long time to come to say nothing of the crowds daily rushing in. The road is populous with men with their blankets on their backs, making their way back as best they can. The streets of the town are full of penniless hungry men, who are anxiously waiting for any kind of work to get them grub. Prices are high—one dollar a night for a bed, but many think bar-room floors good enough to spread their blankets on.[62]

The visitor, who the article said was familiar with other mining camps, declared that "Bodie is the roughest one he ever saw—fighting, shooting, and cutting being an important industry."

Preoccupied with building a town and evaluating developments in the Standard, Bodie's restless population paid scant attention to the Bodie Mine. That changed early in June 1878, when rumors began swirling around streets and saloons that the Bodie Mine had struck it rich. Its stock jumped from $1 to $3.50 per share in just one week. On June 5, the headlines proclaimed: "OUR SECOND WIND—BIG STRIKE IN 'BODIE'—A Remarkably Rich Ledge."[63]

Miners working in the crosscut on the 240-foot level, some 528 feet west of the shaft, had cut into an unbelievably rich vein. They named it the "Bruce ledge." It was a bonanza!

As excitement swept the camp, a reporter from Virginia City entered the mine and examined the lode.

> The face of the drift in this ledge shows ore of almost fabulous richness. The quartz sparkles with coarse gold, and when pulverized in a mortar and horned out, a single handful of the rock will show a return calculated to stagger an ordinary prospector and make him doubtful of his own eyes.[64]

Bodie's telegraph had been operating only one month when the click, click, click of the key told the world about the wonders of the Bodie Mine. As speculators scrambled to buy, stock in the Bodie Gold Mining Company climbed to $5 per share. Miners drilled and blasted westward another 125 feet, where they cut yet another rich vein. This they named after company trustee C. A. Burgess. Still more veins were found: the Mollie, Bodie, Gildea, Edith, and Granger. Assays were sensational. The superintendent calculated that in some places the ore would yield $1,000 per ton.[65] The news electrified the country, and headlines compared the Bodie Mine to the Comstock's Big Bonanza.

The discoveries made such an impact in San Francisco that Pine Street stock traders later recounted the precise moment when they realized something was up in Bodie. Jaws dropped in disbelief when William M. Lent "waltzed" into the lobby of the stock exchange with extraordinary exuberance. "He wore salmon colored kid gloves, his mustache was elegantly waxed, and he had a telegram in his vest pocket from Colonel Boyd." Lent's dazzling display of sartorial splendor evoked such assurance that startled speculators rushed to buy, and Bodie Company stock shot from $10 to $18 per share.[66]

Such stories were contagious and inspired even more people to head for Bodie. Doctor D. M. Geiger, builder of the famous Geiger Grade at Virginia City, arrived in June to construct a road between Bodie and Bridgeport that would be more direct than the old Sonora stage road. His grade, west of Bodie, proved to be too steep for heavy freight wagons, but his professional opinion about geology added to the excitement by endorsing the old Veta Madre theory. "The ledges on the west side of the hill are pitching east," Geiger asserted, "and those on the east pitching west, and . . . they must come together somewhere below."[67] Given such misinformed proclamations, there were few who disagreed that John F. Boyd, William M. Lent, Dan and Seth Cook, Henry M. Yerington, and Robert N. Graves were destined to become the world's next Bonanza Kings.

Once the rich ore was taken from the ground, the Bodie Company would need a stamp mill to crush it and recover the gold and silver. But in June 1878, there were only three mills in Bodie, with one more under construction. Nearby, the 20-stamp Standard mill only processed ore from the Standard Mine. The Syndicate mill, 1½ miles down Bodie Canyon, had been renovated after completing the previous year's 10,000-ton run of Standard ore. Increased from 16 to 20 stamps in May, it was now doing a brisk business crushing ore from a number of other mines.[68] Farther down the canyon a 10-stamp mill was being built for the Bechtel Company. Finally, even farther away, the 4-stamp Miners mill also processed ore under contract.

The owners of the old brick Syndicate mill

agreed to crush the Bodie Mine's ore. The first ship-ments were hauled to the mill under armed guard on June 20, 1878. Two more gunmen were stationed at the mill to protect the growing stockpile of rocks. On July 12, the Syndicate mill started crushing. It was a remarkable run, lasting 31 days.[69] The mill's superintendent later recalled the first run of ore from the Bodie Mine.

> We have had the amalgam accumulate in the pans, not once, but frequently, so that it would stop the en-gine. . . . I have had the gold accumulate in the battery until recognizing, by the sound that the stamps were no longer crushing rock, that they were not striking iron. I would take off the screen to find that the gold had accumulated in the bottom of the mortar until it was flush with the die, and I have taken out of a single mortar with an ordinary iron fire shovel, such as we used in cleaning up, free gold enough to fill a Wells Fargo express box.[70]

The first bars of bullion from the Bodie Mine were shipped to the U.S. mint in Carson City on July 30, 1878. The younger Lent boasted about the high price he paid Wells, Fargo & Company to trans-port the precious cargo. The cost included insurance, seven armed guards, and compensation to the stage company for lost revenue when passengers, afraid of robbers, refused to travel with the gold. He also claimed that it cost more to ship the bullion than it did to mine it.[71]

Stock in the Bodie Gold Mining Company surged to $46 and kept rising. Trading was frantic, and the residents of Bodie were in a frenzy. Miners and merchants who had accepted Bodie Gold Min-ing Company stock in lieu of cash suddenly found themselves wealthy. From San Francisco, William M. Lent watched his fortune grow, and his good luck was trumpeted nationwide. "The recent rise in the stock of the Bodie Company is a marked example of profitable mining investment," affirmed New York's *Engineering and Mining Journal.* "The gentleman who is now President of the company bought 30,000 shares at 50 cents; he can now realize a profit, if he chooses,

of $1,365,000."[72]

Lent was not the only shareholder getting rich. Groups of miners who had received stock as pay would bring their certificates to the Wells Fargo office and give orders to sell at market price. About three days later, the stage from Carson City would deliver the earnings in $20 gold pieces.

> If you can visualize this crowd of men receiving piles of gold coin, filling pockets, and in some instances us-ing their hats, wild with excitement and then going down the line of saloons and resorts to celebrate, you will have some idea why men will flock to a prosper-ous mining camp. This hilarity was a daily occurrence for much of the time during the rise in the stock.[73]

A misplaced Bodie stock certificate brought panic to one Comstock family. The story was reported from Virginia City.

> A few months ago, a man owing a saloon keeper in this city $30 for liquor offered him 100 shares of Bodie stock in payment remarking that it was the best he could do. The saloon keeper "scowled" considerably, but took the stock, valued then at 40 cents a share, and gave it to his wife. On the 12th of June he noticed that Bodie was quoted at $3 per share and concluded to sell. He asked his wife about the stock and she looked over a lot of old papers, but was unable to find it. Mean-while, the price went up every day and when it reached $25 the husband and wife were nearly crazy because they couldn't find the stock. And still it went up, a dollar or two, and the higher it went the madder the unhappy pair grew. One day the husband noticed his little boy working on a new kite. He had finished past-ing the paper over the frame, and was about to paste some "pretty pictures" on the face of the kite, when his father came along. A hasty glance showed the old man that the pretty pictures were his lost Bodie stock. He sold his one hundred shares that very day and cleaned up $3,500.[74]

As these and similar appraisals heralded Bodie's riches, more ore wagons, pulled by 16-mule teams, rumbled down the hill to the Syndicate mill. Any lingering doubts about the wealth in the Bodie Mine were erased in August, when the Bodie Gold Mining Company declared three dividends: $1, $2, and $5 per share, and its stock hit $52. Mill foreman John Parr later recalled: "The Bodie mill run of 1,000 tons . . . sent a thrill through the mining world. It was like a blinding flash. Many people would not believe it was true."[75] But it *was* true, and the old mill proved it by pounding out $601,104 in bullion. According to one mining journal, 1,050 tons of Bodie ore went through the Syndicate mill in August 1878 averaging almost $600 per ton. Someone claimed it was "the greatest monthly yield of any gold mine in the world." Another said it was "unprecedented in California quartz mining."[76]

Such wealth permitted unimaginable excesses. Miry tailings from the Syndicate mill were known to have value, but were of no concern.

It is a well-known fact that the slimes, which ran down Bodie creek from the Syndicate mill during the crushing of the ore, contained nearly as much gold as was saved . . . Those slimes are known to have contained over one hundred dollars a ton, and yet this golden stream was allowed to flow away day after day, week after week.[77]

Bodie's success inspired trading in mining stocks, and prices for other California and Nevada shares climbed whether the mines were paying or not. "Speculative fever" had taken hold, and everyone was said to be "wild—drunk with the excitement of making millions."[78]

Since Bodie's economy was based on mining, it was difficult for anyone living there to be distressed. The discovery in the Bodie Mine had instilled more life and vigor into the district. The hills were alive with activity as gold hunters poured into town. Claims were located, hoisting works constructed, and rich strikes reported throughout the district. Unemployed workers from distant places, especially the Comstock, arrived daily in search of work. Specula-

tors and mine owners traveled from San Francisco to examine their properties and investigate the possibilities of new investments. Downtown residences and business establishments sprang up as if by magic, while storekeepers and hotel owners brought buildings with them from towns depopulated by those heading for Bodie.[79]

Amidst the excitement, the Bodie Gold Min-

ing Company divided its ground into two equal claims. The southern half was used to organize a new company, the Mono Gold Mining Company, with young William H. Lent as its president. The county recorder's office filed the location on August 23, 1878.[80] Each holder of Bodie stock received an equal number of shares in Mono stock. Listed on the San Francisco exchange in mid-October, "Mono" began trading at $4 per share.

Almost immediately, the Mono Gold Mining Company began sinking a two-compartment shaft. Its fancy new hoisting works was said to be the "most

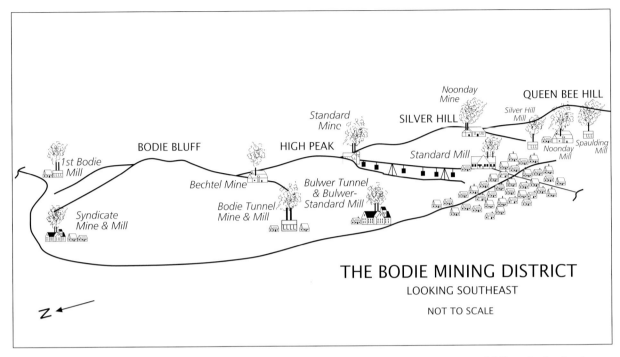

Noonday
Mine

QUEEN BEE HILL

Standard
Mine

SILVER HILL

Silver Hill
Mill

BODIE BLUFF

HIGH PEAK

Standard Mill

1st Bodie
Mill

Noonday
Mill

Spaulding
Mill

Bechtel Mine

Bulwer Tunnel
& Bulwer-
Standard Mill

Bodie Tunnel
Mine & Mill

Syndicate
Mine & Mill

THE BODIE MINING DISTRICT

LOOKING SOUTHEAST

NOT TO SCALE

N

Map 4: Approaching from Aurora, the road to Bodie skirts Bodie Bluff as it ascends the canyon and follows Bodie Creek into town. Most nineteenth-century travelers reached Bodie on this road, which passed the Miners, Bodie, Syndicate, Bodie Tunnel, and Bulwer-Standard mills. Viewed from Main Street, the four hills comprising Bodie's mining district present something of an illusion. Although Bodie Bluff and High Peak are the largest hills, they rise above the *lower* end of town. To the south, Silver Hill and Queen Bee Hill constitute the district's south end and overlook the *upper* end of town.

extensive and perfectly arranged" in Bodie District, with machinery capable of sinking a shaft to an "indefinite depth." To finance its mine shaft and equipment, the Mono levied a 50-cent assessment on stockholders.[81]

The unexpected assessment, and, for that matter, the very existence of the new company, drew immediate accusations that investors had been swindled. In New York, the ever-cynical *Mining Record* challenged Lent's ring of insiders. "This subdivision," the newspaper alleged, "was manipulated chiefly by operators whose names are, probably, sufficient warranty that no mercy was intended to any outsiders so luckless as to fall into their net."

The paper exposed deceptions that had been specifically designed to dupe Mono investors.

Telegrams containing flagrantly untruthful descriptions of "wonderful developments" in Mono, were sent to and fro, hither and thither, between the members of

the inside ring, marked "confidential," which were purposely left lying around, as if inadvertently, that all might read the wonderful secrets, and so snap at the bait thus cunningly laid out. In this, and similarly crooked ways, Mono stock was quickly "boosted" up to nine and ten dollars a share, though there never was, and never has been, the first thing discovered on the Mono property that would warrant the stock bringing even one dollar a share.[82]

The creation of the Mono Company doubled the number of shares controlled by the Bodie management. Dividing the property also reduced the price per share, making the stock more accessible to the "poor" and "laboring" classes. "The object is not at first apparent," forewarned New York's *Engineering and Mining Journal*, "but it is in reality to reach . . . a larger *clientele* to unload stocks through, and who are less likely to know when a new deal is to be made, and are, consequently, less on their guard than the knowing ones who hold large quantities of stock."[83] Often incapable of making deposits on margin calls, victims of modest means were expected to "sell out at any price" when a so-called "deal," or stock swindle, drove prices down. The poor also played into the hands of heartless insiders by forfeiting their shares instead of paying assessments. Their losses were deplorable, imposing hardship upon those who were least able to recover.

Among this class of investor were many citizens of Bodie who gambled in local mining stocks. "STOCK SPECULATIONS!" read a San Francisco brokerage firm's advertisement in a Bodie newspaper. "Fortunes made in one deal by our new and popular system of Stock Privileges! . . . Money can be remitted by Post, Money Order, Registered Letter, Bank Draft or Express . . ."[84] Many of the investors in Bodie were the miners themselves. Possessing direct information regarding developments in a mine and having a clear understanding of the business should have given locals an advantage in stock trading. Yet the San Francisco rings so masterfully manipulated prices independent of actual conditions, that even firsthand knowledge was of little value in avoiding unmerciful stock swindles. Grant H. Smith, Bodie resident between 1879 and 1881, was a casualty of the Mono Mine. He vividly recalled his sad experience.

> To illustrate the methods of the men who manipulated mining stocks in those days, I will recount my own experience as a purchaser of stock in the Mono mine. The Mono adjoined the Bodie, and the hoisting works were within a stone's throw of each other. Everybody believed that the rich ore of the Bodie would extend into the Mono; the stock was purchased freely and was very active, the price being based wholly on hope. The work of developing the mine was expensive, no ore was found, and assessment after assessment was levied on the stock until over $600,000 had been poured in by the stockholders. In 1881, when the stock was $12 a share, the stock-manipulators decided that the rich Bodie veins did not extend into the Mono. To save themselves, the whisper was spread, "Mono has struck

it." Hundreds of people who thought they alone had received this "inside information," eagerly bought the stock. My mother heard the rumor, eagerly invested her savings account of $1,500, and advised me to do likewise with the $600 that I had saved for my education. As soon as "the insiders" had unloaded all the stock they could on the public, the shares began to fall rapidly in price; they dropped from $12 to practically nothing in a short time. My mother and I never realized a penny from our gamble.[85]

For the remaining life of the mine, the managers of the Mono Gold Mining Company repeatedly upheld their reputations for chicanery.

While the Mono Mine was attracting ridicule, the Bruce and Burgess veins in the Bodie Mine continued to yield inconceivable riches as the little donkey hoist chugged away, pulling bucket loads of gold- and silver-laden rock out of the ground. A specimen sent to Virginia City was assayed at the Consolidated Virginia Mine. The results defied credibility. A ton of the rock would impart $102,926 in gold and $4,827 in silver. Comstock mine owner and millionaire James G. Fair said it was the highest assay ever made in that office.[86] In September 1878, the Bodie management rewarded investors with a $3 dividend.

Impatient to amass wealth sooner rather than later, the Bodie Company began sinking a two-compartment shaft directly over the rich ore bodies. Often called the "Bodie new shaft," it was equipped with a powerful, 50-horsepower steam hoisting engine.[87] The wooden structure that enclosed it stood on the slope between the Standard and Mono mines, where 3,000 people admired it from town. Riding the crest of his good fortune in San Francisco, William M. Lent moved his corporate offices to the newly-completed, pretentious San Francisco Stock Exchange Building at 327 Pine Street. There he joined a number of other Bodie mining companies, including the Bechtel Gold Mining Company, the Tioga Consolidated Mining Company, the McClinton Mining Company, and the Goodshaw Mining Company.[88] Lent then traveled to the East Coast to pitch stock in his Bodie companies.

While the Bodie Mine delivered rich ore to the Syndicate mill, the new shaft drew closer to the Bruce ledge. It reached the 180-foot level in late October, just as the Bodie Gold Mining Company declared another $2 per share dividend. November brought a $1 dividend. Descending 13 feet per week, the new shaft reached the 250-foot level in December, when another $1 dividend was declared. Still more rich ore was brought to the surface, and January 1879 saw another $1 dividend. The town went wild.

As high-grade ore from the Bruce/Burgess bo-

nanza streamed from the Bodie Mine the company realized it needed long-term milling arrangements, and sought to procure a stamp mill of its own. Just off the road to Aurora was a recently completed 10-stamp mill located ¾ of a mile beyond the Syndicate mill and at least 2¼ miles from town. Moved to Bodie Canyon from the Comstock, where it had been known as the "Sherman mill," Bodie's fourth stamp mill was built by E. Detrick, who expected to hire it to the Bechtel Company, one of many Bodie entities sporting William M. Lent among its corporate officials.

The mill's first contract was to process 8,000 tons of Bechtel ore for $12 per ton. As expected, the price of Bechtel stock went up with news that its ore was about to be converted into gold bullion. The advance allowed Lent and his associates to sell their Bechtel shares at a substantial profit, after which the mill proved incapable of recovering more than $9 per ton. Feigning surprise that the ore cost more to treat than it yielded, Lent's organization accused the mill's staff

of incompetence and halted ore shipments, allegedly to prevent the loss of more good rock. Later, however, assays disclosed that the ore never was rich enough to turn a profit. Throughout this well-choreographed flim-flam, the facility was referred to as the "Bechtel mill." It was less than five months old when it was purchased in December at a greatly reduced price by Lent's ring of insiders and renamed the "Bodie mill." [89]

Unfortunately, there was a problem with the Bodie Company's new mill. Quartz milling is profoundly dependent upon water, and the lack of a reliable source at the Bodie mill was a problem that required large sums of money to correct. The company first tried digging a well—actually a 35-foot mine shaft with a 150-foot crosscut. When the well failed to sustain the mill, the company built dams across Bodie Creek to impound water from the Syndicate and other upstream mills. The reservoirs would also capture water that had been bailed from mines and dumped into Bodie Canyon and Taylor Gulch. Even water from the Bodie mill's tailings would be reused after the solids had settled. [90]

The Bodie mill would not become operational until the reservoirs were completed in early 1879. Until then, the Bodie Company continued shipping its bonanza ore to the Syndicate mill, where the last month of 1878 was spent turning out even more golden bars.

Triggered by discoveries in the Bodie Mine, a population explosion during 1878 had enlarged the town from 150 buildings to somewhere between 600 and 800. [91] A visiting Sacramento reporter described the growth.

> From one end of Main Street to the other, on both sides, as well as on the back streets, the morning sun rises on workmen engaged in putting up buildings, and the sound of the hammer and the saw is heard until night closes over all, darkness only preventing the prosecution of the work. The cry for lumber! lumber! goes up from hundreds of people waiting to commence or finish their respective houses or stores. [92]

Just as Edwin Loose had predicted, the Bodie Mine's bonanza veins extended from the Standard. The Bruce ledge was a continuation of the West Standard. The Burgess, said to be the vein that produced the "richest ore ever found in Bodie District," was, in fact, an extension of the Cook ledge.[93] The great wealth of these two geological formations had made Bodie's most flamboyant absentee mine owner something of a celebrity.

Lent, much to his own surprise, I fancy, struck it rich in the Bodie mine proper, and now he is wealthy and a highly respectable mine manager. Mr. Lent's other mines in Bodie, such as [the] Mono, Richer, Summit, and Booker, are as yet unproductive. . . . No mine ever opened here has paid so large a proportion of its yield in dividends as has [the] Bodie. Out of the million or so produced $800,000 have been paid in dividends.[94]

The $800,000 distributed to Bodie Mine investors had been paid through eight dividends during the six months between that incredible August in 1878 and January 1879, yet the company had levied only $25,000 in assessments. For 1878, the California State Mineralogist placed the total production of the Bodie Mine at $1,042,237. It was the largest annual production of any mine at Bodie and almost $17,000 more than the Standard Mine had produced during the same year. The Bruce and Burgess ledges made 1878 the biggest year that the Bodie Mine would ever see, and their richness brought nationwide prominence to the town. Meanwhile, the neighboring Mono Mine produced no ore whatsoever.

The Red Cloud Mine

The district's south end had played a decisive role in Bodie's early development, beginning at the base of Silver Hill where the glint of gold caught the attention of a passing group of prospectors in 1859. Within weeks, Bodie's first quartz claim was located nearby, in August, and named the "Montauk."[95] But attention quickly shifted northward, where discoveries on High Peak and Bodie Bluff gave rise to flashy corpo-rations, such as the Bodie Bluff Consolidation Mining Company and the Empire Gold and Silver Mining Company. During the 1860s and early 1870s, Silver Hill was quiet, until Eshington and Lockberg's success in the Bunker Hill Mine on High Peak spread gold fever. Interest returned quickly to the south end, where the Red Cloud claim was staked on the southeastern slope of Silver Hill. The mine entered the historic record on October 5, 1876, when the "Red Cloud Lode" was recorded in the district's ledger book.[96]

Silver Hill is an unusual name for a prominent geological formation in a gold mining district, but its quartz ledges contained a higher percentage of silver than any others in the area. Silver is a complicated metal. Unlike gold, which occurs in a metallic state as nuggets, dust, and minuscule particles embedded in rock formations, near-pure silver rarely occurs in nature. Instead, it tends to form compounds that mask its identity. The Comstock's silver-rich minerals confounded early placer miners, who were trying to mine gold from the nation's richest silver lode. It defied recognition because it was combined chemically with elements that form sulfides. These sulfur compounds had scientific names, but the raw discoverers of the Comstock Lode referred to the bothersome material obstructing gold extraction as "blasted blue stuff."[97] Sophisticated mining men called them "sulphurets." At Bodie, it was inside Silver Hill where sulphurets were most concentrated. Silver Hill was also known for placer gold, and throughout most of Bodie's life miners washed the yellow metal from gravel on the hill's eastern slope and from Taylor Gulch, the shallow valley below it, where W. S. Bodey and his companions first panned gold.

When the Red Cloud ledge was encountered 17 years later, in 1876, San Francisco was in a depression that had begun with the Panic of 1873. Losses were heavy, and scores of factories and retail establishments closed their doors. Financial difficulties intensified when several Comstock mines shut down in 1877. The streets of Virginia City, Gold Hill, and Silver City were crowded with unemployed men when stories about Bodie shifted attention toward the distant mining camp. The first sketchy accounts emanated from Genoa, where stagecoaches paused with bullion from the Syndicate mill. Hastily printed in March 1877, a published account appeared in Carson Valley's newspaper. "Joe Lupton has been to Bodie; returned Tuesday; reports these particulars, as follows, namely, to wit: Bullion the principal mine; got hoisting works up and shaft down about 400 feet; ledge from 3 to 6 feet wide; claim that the rock will average $100 per ton in gold." Turning to the Red Cloud, Lupton remarked: "Down 40 to 50 feet; got good milling ore; some stratas assay as high as $500 per ton; commenced work taking out ore last Monday."[98]

Although little more than a hole in the ground, the Red Cloud shaft pierced a vein that offered further proof that there were rich ledges to be found at Bodie. In August 1877, after an Aurora mill finished crushing a run of Red Cloud rock, the mine's owners were rewarded with $9,000 in bullion. Considered a rousing success, the mine was purchased in September by Gov. Henry Blasdel, who headed a group of San Francisco investors.[99] At a time when many Bodie mines had produced no bullion at all, and only a few showed evidence of pay ore, the Red Cloud appeared destined to be a big producer.

Blasdel and his colleagues acquired a group of small contiguous claims surrounding the Red Cloud, and in October 1877 they incorporated the Red Cloud Consolidated Mining Company, capitalized at $5,000,000. Company business offices were in San Francisco's posh Nevada Block. After appointing himself company secretary, the Governor placed his son, Colonel S. W. "Weaver" Blasdel, in charge of the mine as superintendent.[100]

Fortified by new capital, the Red Cloud Consolidated Mining Company dug deeper into the Red Cloud vein. "Gold was plainly to be seen," revealed a local reporter who visited the mine, "and blue sulphurets of silver [were] in almost every piece of ore." Approximately 93 feet below the surface, the ledge disclosed an unusually rich streak in December. San Francisco's foremost mining journal reported assays as high as $31,861 per ton in gold and $5,321 in silver.[101]

Based upon these and other sensational specimens, the company purchased a steam-powered donkey hoist and began sinking a more substantial vertical shaft immediately west of the ledge. When the new shaft struck another vein only 82 feet below the surface, investors were ecstatic. The vein was named the "Packard & Morton," after two claims in the consolidation. Downward the shaft went. In December, miners reached the 126-foot level and started an eastward crosscut toward the Red Cloud vein.[102] Crosscutting and drifting, miners worked day and night to uncover a golden treasure, while others drove the shaft downward to explore the lode at greater depths.

Desperate to transform these magnificent ore bodies into spendable cash, the company needed a stamp mill. But during early 1878, the old Syndicate mill was undergoing repairs to expand the number of its stamps from 16 to 20, and the Standard Company's new 20-stamp mill was running exclusively on Standard ore. The Red Cloud Company would have to wait.

On February 28, 1878, with funds running low, the Red Cloud Consolidated Mining Company levied its first assessment to raise enough capital to continue work in the vertical shaft. At the 250-foot level more crosscuts were driven, one east to intersect the Red Cloud vein, and another west toward the Packard & Morton. Working around the clock, miners reached the 400-foot level in June, then started another crosscut eastward toward the Red Cloud vein.[103]

Meanwhile, Red Cloud managers had finally arranged to have their ore milled by the recently-completed 4-stamp Miners mill. Superintendent Blasdel gave the order, and miners began stoping ore. Some rocks reportedly contained so much gold and silver that they were gathered in sacks to prevent the loss or theft of a single piece. Soon the surface bin was overflowing and ore was piled around it in heaps. On June 27, teams began hauling Red Cloud ore down the dusty road to the little mill.[104]

A week later, the citizens of Bodie paused from their toil to celebrate Independence Day. In a flag-adorned procession, Grand Marshal S. W. Blasdel rode a "coal black" horse behind the Carson City marching band. As part of the holiday observances, nine Red Cloud employees accepted a challenge from the redoubtable Bodie Baseball Club, and lost 20 to 5 in a game cut to two innings by other scheduled events. The ensuing patriotic festivities included a barbecue, a war dance performed by local Paiute Indians, a reading of the Declaration of Independence, and an evening ball at the Miners Union hall.[105]

When the holiday ceremonies ended, one intolerant wit complained about the celebration having detracted from mining gold, "but now that it is happily over we can all turn our attention again to getting rich."[106] The Red Cloud's defeat on the baseball diamond was forgotten a week later, when the first new bar of bullion emerged from the Miners mill. Valued at $1,190, this gleaming specimen of metallic wealth guaranteed the Red Cloud's place among the handful of Bodie mines that were yielding bullion. More significantly, it was produced by a mine in the district's south end, where it confirmed that pay ore reached a mile or more beyond the Standard.

Flush with excitement, mining men from San Francisco to New York City were certain that Bodie's rich lode began at the Syndicate Mine on Bodie Bluff, extended southward through the Standard and Bodie mines on High Peak, passed directly through the Red Cloud on Silver Hill, then continued on to Queen Bee Hill. A few lofty thinkers even believed that Bodie's ledges were part of an enormous mineral belt that extended all the way from the Comstock Lode.[107]

The little Miners mill pounded away through July and August as jubilant Red Cloud investors rejoiced in anticipation of prosperity. The results, however, proved disastrous. Only one more bar of bullion was produced, worth a meager $737.50. So far, the Red Cloud had produced only $10,928.[108] To make matters worse, the Bodie Gold Mining Company had delivered a staggering August 1878 yield of $601,104. While news of the Bodie Mine's bonanza electrified the country, the Red Cloud Company stunned its stockholders by levying another assessment.

Work in the Red Cloud Mine continued as assessment money trickled in. Miners on the 400-foot level drilled and blasted their way eastward toward the Red Cloud vein, where they hoped that the ledge would again yield high-grade ore. The crosscut had advanced only 40 feet when water began pouring in at the face. The hoist removed 25,000 gallons per day with the ore bucket, but the little engine could barely keep ahead of the flow. Using hand drills and dynamite, the miners drove onward toward the Red Cloud vein. They advanced only 40 more feet before incoming water stopped work.

As water flooded the 400-foot level and miners retreated to the upper levels, the company added another drum to the steam hoist and purchased larger buckets. With two big buckets, one in each compartment of the shaft, 86,000 gallons were raised daily, but it was not enough. Hopes of exploring the lower levels had to be abandoned until more powerful equipment could be purchased. In October, a third assessment was levied, and soon new machinery began to arrive.[109]

During the second week of November 1878, miners on the 250-foot level made an encouraging find. Initial reports said that the Packard & Morton vein had been found 115 feet west of the shaft. In the words of a visiting reporter, ". . . we broke down from the vein a candle box full of clay and quartz which we took to the surface. With the facilities at hand we transformed ourselves into placer miners and washed out a pan-full of dirt from which we obtained many colors of coarse gold."[110] The story spread that Superintendent Blasdel was so happy that he rewarded each of the four discoverers with a suit of new clothes. One of the recipients "celebrated the event by getting gloriously drunk" and ended up in the town lockup. He was released after paying a small fine.[111]

The Red Cloud's new hoisting engine was impressive. Built in San Francisco by Prescott, Scott & Company, it was identical in size and capacity to the

Hoisting with a windlass

largest hoist in the district, the one at the Standard Mine. The mighty machine was positioned upon a massive masonry foundation near the Red Cloud shaft.[112] The new equipment also included two 400-gallon bailing tanks, each weighing 4,600 pounds when full. The boiler was fired up, the steam whistle gave a toot, and on Friday the 13th of December, 1878, the Red Cloud's big engine started raising water from the bottom of the mine and dumping it at the surface. The powerful new hoist lifted the "enormous weight with perfect ease," reported one observer.[113] By the end of the year, the mine had been cleared of water.

With the water problem solved, work on the 400-foot level resumed, and the crosscut was driven onward toward the Red Cloud vein.[114] When the ledge was reached, some 155 feet from the shaft, it proved to be impoverished. A crosscut was driven in the opposite direction, to the west, in hopes that the Packard & Morton vein would be richer there than

above. The vein was found 114 feet from the shaft. It too, was barren of profitable ore.

The Noonday Mine

On the ridge above the Red Cloud another south end mine was attracting attention in 1878. Like most Bodie mines, it had been abandoned by prospectors in the 1860s. A decade or so later, in November 1875, the "Noonday Lode" was located, but it was forfeited within the year "for want of work."[115] It was relocated, or recorded again, in November 1876 by Judge F. K. Bechtel, the chief stockholder in a number of Bodie companies. Bechtel, who had been mining in Bodie since 1862, was distinguished as one of the region's pioneers. He rose to prominence in boomtown Bodie mostly on the perceived wealth of the Bechtel Mine. The mine's exceptional location in the saddle between Bodie Bluff and High Peak made it one of the district's most desirable properties, and belief in its potential solidified early. Favored among speculators, Bechtel stock rocketed to $12 per share in December 1877, before the mine produced any bullion. Flagrantly overrated, the property produced sporadically through 1881 without paying dividends.[116]

The Noonday Mining Company entered the game late. It was incorporated on March 6, 1878, when Bodie's boom was in full swing and the Red Cloud Consolidated Mining Company had already levied its first assessment.[117] Judge Bechtel served on the Noonday's board of trustees, and the company president was William Morris Stewart, president of the Bechtel Mining Company. Stewart had been an accomplished California gold rush attorney in the 1850s. After 1861, he earned acclaim around Virginia City by arguing Comstock mining cases. Stewart was appointed one of Nevada's first two U.S. senators when the territory became a state in 1864. One of his early accomplishments in Washington, D. C. was the Federal Mining Act known as the "Law of 1866." He was later recognized as the father of a more comprehensive federal land law, the "General Mining Law of 1872." This legislation was designed to open the West's public lands to prospecting and mining. It was the law under which Bodie's mining boom was adjudicated, and, though it contained a complex concept known as the "Law of the Apex," which granted extensive rights to a ledge's discoverer, much of it survives to this day.[118]

Retiring in 1874 after his second senatorial term, Stewart returned to San Francisco to manage his mining investments. He opened the Noonday Mining Company's office in the heart of the financial district at 310 Pine Street, a five-story edifice where scores of western mining companies, including the Belvidere and Maybelle at Bodie, maintained their corporate headquarters. Within a short walk, other Bodie companies occupied suites in the Nevada Block and San Francisco Stock Exchange.

Overshadowing the Noonday Mine during the first eight months of 1878, several other south end mines were receiving extraordinary acclaim in the national press despite scanty yields. Based on the flimsiest of evidence, the Red Cloud, Booker, Spaulding (owned by Boston speculators led by Boston-born Bodie merchant, A. F. Bryant), Maryland (owned by New York speculators), Maybelle, Goodshaw (site of the first quartz ledge discovered in Bodie in 1859), and the Old Dan were popular among investors, who had been swept up by gold fever and more than a touch of journalistic hyperbole.

Ignoring the Red Cloud's disastrous August 1878 showing and the south end's discernible deficiency of ore, the Noonday upheld the West Coast's reputation for risk taking (especially in gold and silver mining) by defiantly sinking a vertical two-compartment shaft into the flank of Silver Hill. "The average Californian is a confirmed gambler," mused a New York-based mining journal.

It makes no difference how often he may have "speculated" in mining stocks and lost his money, the passion, like that of the opium-eater or the drunkard, is all but incurable, and with the first sign of a "rise," he becomes frantic and launches his all upon another throw of the dice.[119]

Begun in September 1878 with the aid of a horse and whim, the Noonday's shaft was positioned to cut through a quartz vein that had been revealed in the 1860s by an early prospect shaft. Named the "Keystone ledge" by the previous owner, the vein dipped at an angle of about 80 degrees toward the east, where the Noonday Company expected to intersect it at a depth of about 100 feet. Instead, at 20 feet the shaft entered an unknown vein that assayed at $30 to $40 per ton. It was named the "Noonday ledge." What surprised everyone even more was that after the miners resumed sinking toward the Keystone, they did not break through the bottom of the Noonday ledge until they reached a depth of 115 feet.[120]

The discovery of a vein 95 feet wide in Silver Hill added significantly to the town's acclaim. Ignoring the onset of winter, 30 people were arriving daily, and enthusiasts believed that anyone leaving probably intended to return. Main Street was said to be a mile in length, with lots staked in all directions. A local reporter described Bodie in a December 1878 column titled "Roundabout Town," which provided details of great importance to certain individuals.

There are now probably not less than forty saloons, and two or three more building. To a dozen or fifteen of these are attached gambling rooms, in which are dealt faro, roulette, rouge et noir, twenty-one, and all the other games known to the profession. . . . Everybody coming here can find what they want. If they are looking for a fight, they can . . . get gloriously whipped within three minutes of entering town. If they wish to behave themselves, they will be as safe and as little interfered with as they would be in the streets of New York or Boston.[121]

Few mining camps had piercing winter winds, deep snow, and subzero temperatures comparable to those of Bodie. Inclement weather at an elevation of 8,400 feet was an unparalleled burden.

The approach of winter is beginning to make itself felt in Bodie. A good many of the smaller claims, which during the summer months were worked with a windlass, are now closed down, in consequence of the severity of the weather, and, as a natural result, there are more idle men about town than there were formerly. . . . A trip through the saloons discloses a large number of men in the vicinity of the stoves, most of whom have no other place to go to. Then there are not a few "tough citizens" who never do work, and who are always attracted to a live camp. This combination leads to frequent brawls—knock-downs and drag-outs—and occasionally to a shooting scrape.[122]

Grant Smith recalled that during the winter of 1878-79 "accommodations were of the poorest sort; consequently the winter found thousands of people poorly housed, poorly fed, with little employment, and nothing to do but hang around the saloons and gamble and fight and get drunk and lie out in the snow and die."[123]

<hr>

1. *Mining and Scientific Press* 24 March 1877, 181; Joseph Wasson, *Bodie and Esmeralda* (San Francisco, CA: Spaulding, Barto & Co., 1878), 27-28; *Bodie Standard* 17 April 1878; Henry S. Fitch, *Pacific Coast Annual Mining Review and Stock Ledger* (San Francisco, CA: Francis & Valentine, 1878), 247-248; *Bodie Weekly Standard* 2 October 1878.

2. *Inyo Independent* 17 March 1877.

3. John F. Parr, "Reminiscences of the Bodie Strike," *Yosemite Nature Notes* 7, no. 5 (May 1928), 33-36; *Engineering and Mining Journal* 26 October 1878, 296; *Inyo Independent* 7 April 1877.

4. Joseph Wasson, *Bodie and Esmeralda*, 25.

5. *Mining and Scientific Press* 19 July 1879, 34.

6. "The Nevada Bank," *Borax Miner* 25 September 1875.

7. There were few stock exchanges in 1850s America. Then, spawned by rapid industrial growth during the Civil War, they became popular financial institutions. Speculation in securities spread across social classes. Two subsequent decades witnessed mining companies develop into the largest number of stock issuances, giving rise to a proliferation of exchanges that specialized in them. By 1880 mining stock exchanges dotted the country, with the most influential located in the competing financial centers of San Francisco and New York City. San Francisco's prominent exchanges during Bodie's boom era were the San Francisco Stock and Exchange Board (1862), the California Stock and Exchange Board (1872), and the Pacific Stock Exchange (1875). New York hosted, among others, a revival of the New York Mining Stock Board (1864) renamed the New York Mining Stock Exchange (1875), and the American Mining Stock Exchange (1880). Exchanges specializing in mining stocks were also found in Denver, Salt Lake City, St. Louis, New Orleans, Chicago, Cincinnati, Boston, Philadelphia, Providence, Baltimore, and other cities. For an overview, see Marian V. Sears, *Mining Stock Exchanges, 1860-1930: An Historical Survey* (Missoula, MT: University of Montana Press, 1973), 3-59 and appendixes.

8. Henry Goode Blasdel (1825-1900).

9. Wasson, *Bodie and Esmeralda*, 25; Fitch, *Pacific Coast Mining*, 178.

10. *Bodie Weekly Standard* 15 May 1878; 11 September 1878; *Inyo Independent* 25 August 1877; Wasson, *Bodie and Esmeralda*, 28-29; *Mining and Scientific Press* 18 August 1877, 107.

11. *Bodie Chronicle* 5 June 1880.

12. *Gold Hill Daily News* 28 September 1877.

13. *Inyo Independent* 15 September 1877.

14. Dividends and assessments in this text are inventoried by calendar year. Because the Standard Company's reporting period was from February to February, a two-month shift will be noticed when compared to contemporary reports.

15. *Inyo Independent* 13 October 1877; *Bodie Standard* 14 November 1877; *Gold Hill Daily News* 23 August 1877.

16. *Mining and Scientific Press* 13 October 1877, 231.

17. *Gold Hill Daily News* 25 October 1877.

18. *Bodie Standard* 14 November 1877; 28 November 1877; *Bodie Weekly Standard* 27 November 1878.

19. *Weekly Bodie Standard* 15 February 1879.

20. *Bodie Standard* 12 December 1877; 19 December 1877.

21. Wasson, *Bodie and Esmeralda*, 27-28; *Bodie Standard* 17 April 1878.

22. *Bodie Standard* 26 December 1877.

23. Wasson, *Bodie and Esmeralda*, 29-30; *Engineering and Mining Journal* 23 February 1878, 130; Fitch, *Pacific Coast Mining*, 247-248.

24. California State Mining Bureau, *Eighth Annual Report of the State Mineralogist, for the Year Ending October 1, 1888* (Sacramento, CA: Superintendent of State Printing, 1888), 396. One would expect to find reasonably accurate reports of annual production for individual mines. Knowing what a mine produced during a given year would seem to be fundamental to investment. Oddly, no such figures exist. The Bodie newspapers listed production levels only haphazardly, and few annual reports from mining companies survive. The national mining journals tabulated dividends and assessments without considering a thing so crucial as a mine's production. The California State Mineralogist published reasonably accurate

yields for several Bodie mines between 1877 and 1888, then reported infrequently thereafter. Though the statistics differ somewhat from other sources, the most comprehensive tabulation of annual yields for the Standard Company through 1913, and the entire district through 1941, is found in Charles W. Chesterman, Rodger H. Chapman, and Cliffton H. Gray, Jr, *Geology and Ore Deposits of the Bodie Mining District, Mono County, California (Bulletin 206)* (Sacramento, CA: Division of Mines and Geology, 1986), 32, 33.

25. *Inyo Independent* 20 October 1877.

26. *Bodie Standard* 7 November 1877.

27. *Inyo Independent* 1 December 1877.

28. The frequency of corporate organizations can be surmised by noting the chronology through 1877: Syndicate, October 1875; Standard, April 1877; Bulwer, June 1877; Bodie, August 1877; South Standard and Bechtel, September 1877; Black Hawk and Red Cloud, October 1877; Belvidere, McClinton, Bodie Tunnel, Spaulding, and Summit, November 1877; Booker, December 1877. (Wasson, *Bodie and Esmeralda*, 25-27; Fitch, *Pacific Coast Mining*, 172-259) Though they carried similar names, the Bodie Tunnel Mine, owned by the Bodie Tunnel and Mining Company, should not be confused with the Bodie Mine, which was owned by the Bodie Consolidated Mining Company. The Bodie Tunnel Mine was located about a half mile northwest of the Bodie Mine. The Bodie Tunnel's primary feature was a tunnel driven more than 2,100 feet into the base of Bodie Bluff. The Bodie Mine, in contrast, pierced High Peak with a shaft.

29. *Bodie Standard* 12 December 1877.

30. *Reno Gazette* 26 February 1878 in *Bodie Standard* 6 March 1878.

31. Karen Colbourne McAbeer, "The Bodie Railroad" (Master of Arts Thesis, California State College, Sonoma, CA, 1973), 70-73; Wasson, *Bodie and Esmeralda*, 42; *Daily Free Press* 27 August 1880.

32. *Bodie Standard* 17 April 1878.

33. *Bodie Standard* 13 March 1878.

34. *Weekly Bodie Standard* 15 February 1879; *Engineering and Mining Journal* 29 March 1879, 220; *Mining Record* 28 June 1879, 550.

35. *Bodie Weekly Standard* 15 May 1878; Wasson, *Bodie and Esmeralda*, 29; *Bodie Morning News* 21 August 1879.

36. Wasson, *Bodie and Esmeralda*, 23-24.

37. Wasson, *Bodie and Esmeralda*, 23.

38. *Bodie Standard* 1 May 1878.

39. *Bodie Weekly Standard* 30 October 1878.

40. *Bodie Standard* 23 January 1878; *Bodie Weekly Standard* 25 December 1878.

41. *Bodie Weekly Standard* 11 September 1878.

42. *Engineering and Mining Journal* 9 November 1878, 333.

43. *Bodie Weekly Standard* 13 November 1878.

44. *Daily Bodie Standard* 8 February 1879; *Mining and Scientific Press* 8 February 1879, 85; *Mining Record* 14 June 1879, 501.

45. *Daily Bodie Standard* 28 June 1879; 6 August 1879.

46. *Weekly Bodie Standard* 29 March 1879; William Irwin, *First Annual Report of the Standard Consolidated Mining Co. for the Year Ending February 1, 1880* (San Francisco, CA: Bunker & Hiester, 1880), 7-12; William Irwin, *Second Annual Report of the Standard Consolidated Mining Company for the Year Ending February 1, 1881* (San Francisco, CA: Bunker & Hiester, 1881), 35-42 and sketches.

47. *Daily Bodie Standard* 30 December 1878.

48. Chesterman, et.al., *Geology and Ore Deposits of the Bodie Mining District*, 26; California, *Eighth Annual Report*, 389; U.S. Bureau of the Mint, *Report of the Director of the Mint upon the Statistics of the Production of the Precious Metals in the United States [for 1882]* (Washington, DC: Government Printing Office, 1883), 66-68; William R. Balch, *Mines, Miners, and Mining Interests of the United States in 1882* (Philadelphia, PA: The Mining Industrial Publishing Bureau, 1882), 1145-1146.

49. The vein system in the Standard Mine contained several parallel ledges that comprised what later became known as the "Incline Series." The deposit was a system that old-time miners called "gash-veins," or parallel quartz deposits that showed no outcrop. Few of these veins extended below the 500-foot level. At about the 300-foot level, they were often very wide and sometimes fairly rich. Detailed descriptions of Bodie's geology are found in: Chesterman, et.al., *Geology and Ore Deposits of the Bodie Mining District*, 26-27; Robert Gilman Brown, "The Vein-System of the Standard Mine, Bodie, CA," *Transaction of the American Institute of Mining Engineers* 38 (New York, NY: A. I. M. E., 1908), 343-357; H. A. Whiting, "Bodie District," in California, *Eighth Annual Report*, 382-401.

50. *Daily Bodie Standard* 17 December 1878.

51. *Weekly Bodie Standard* 8 March 1879; 15 March 1879.

52. William M. Lent (1818-1904).

53. For the story of the Great Diamond Hoax, see Asbury Harpending, *The Great Diamond Hoax and Other Stirring Incidents in the Life of Ashbury Harpending* (Norman, OK: University of Oklahoma Press, 1958); T. A. Rickard, "The Great Diamond Hoax: How A Colorado Desert was Salted With Gems in 1872," *Engineering and Mining Journal* 30 May 1925, 884-888.

54. Warren Loose, *Bodie Bonanza: The True Story of a Flamboyant Past*, (Las Vegas, NV: Nevada Publications, 1979), 40-47; "Bodie: Archangel of the Mining Camps," *True West* 23, no. 2 (November/December 1975): 8-13, 30, 44-47; Parr, "Reminiscences," 36-37.

55. Edwin, also known as C. E. Loose, remained in Bodie several years before joining his brothers in Utah. Warren, known as W. A. R. Loose, returned to Bodie in 1894, rich from his Utah mining investments. Later the brothers pur-

chased the Syndicate Mine and mill, and became prominent in Bodie early in the twentieth century. Warren is buried on the hilltop west of town. (Loose, "Archangel of the Mining Camps," 9-13)

56. Wasson, *Bodie and Esmeralda*, 250.

57. *Bodie Standard* 7 November 1877.

58. Herbert L. Smith, *The Bodie Era: The Chronicles of the Last of the Old Time Mining Camps* (TMs [photocopy] 1934), 29.

59. *Bodie Weekly Standard* 22 May 1878.

60. *Bodie Standard* 28 November 1877; *Bodie Weekly Standard* 22 May 1878.

61. *Bodie Standard* 24 April 1878.

62. *Daily Territorial Enterprise* 6 April 1878.

63. *Bodie Weekly Standard* 5 June 1878.

64. *Bodie Tri-Weekly Standard* 31 July 1878 in Loose 1979, 62.

65. *Bodie Weekly Standard* 31 July 1878; *Bodie Weekly Standard* 5 June 1878.

66. *Bodie Weekly Standard* 7 August 1878.

67. *Bodie Weekly Standard* 5 June 1878.

68. *Bodie Standard* 8 May 1878.

69. Parr, "Reminiscences," 36-37.

70. *Mining and Scientific Press* 16 August 1902, 92-93.

71. *Mining and Scientific Press* 5 July 1879, 12; *Bodie Weekly Standard* 18 September 1878.

72. *Engineering and Mining Journal* 24 August 1878, 143.

73. Smith, *The Bodie Era*, 52.

74. *Bodie Weekly Standard* 28 August 1878.

75. Parr, "Reminiscences," 37.

76. *Bodie Weekly Standard* 4 September 1878; *Engineering and Mining Journal* 14 September 1878, 191; *Daily Stock Report* 5 August 1880, 1; Fitch, *Pacific Coast Mining*, 176.

77. *Mining Record* 4 September 1880, 222.

78. *Engineering and Mining Journal* 14 September 1878, 182-183.

79. *Engineering and Mining Journal* 17 August 1878, 118; 31 August 1878, 155; *Bodie Weekly Standard* 28 August 1878; *Mining and Scientific Press* 31 August 1878, 132; Smith, *The Bodie Era*, 30; *Alpine Chronicle* 12 October 1878.

80. Parr, "Reminiscences," 36-37; Mono County, *Mining Locations*, Book A, 274; Fitch, *Pacific Coast Mining*, 220.

81. *Engineering and Mining Journal* 21 September 1878, 204; 7 December 1878, 406.

82. *Mining Record* 23 October 1880, 392.

83. *Engineering and Mining Journal* 17 February 1877, 103.

84. *Bodie Morning News* 25 May 1879.

85. Grant H. Smith, "Bodie, Last of the Old Time Mining Camps," *California Historical Quarterly* 4 (1925), 77-78.

86. *Daily Territorial Enterprise* 19 September 1878.

87. *Mining and Scientific Press* 14 September 1878, 164; 29 May 1880, 340.

88. *Bodie Weekly Standard* 18 September 1878; 20 November 1878; *Mining and Scientific Press* 6 October 1877, 209.

89. *Bodie Standard* 8 May 1878; *Bodie Weekly Standard* 5 June 1878; 26 June 1878; 10 July 1878; 31 July 1878; *Mining Record* 28 August 1880, 200-201; *Bodie Standard-News* 11 October 1880.

90. *Bodie Weekly Standard* 4 December 1878; *Daily Bodie Standard* 11 December 1878; *Weekly Bodie Standard* 22 February 1879; 8 March 1879; *Mining Record* 15 March 1879, 208; 16 August 1879, 131. The ruins of Ed Gray's 7-stamp mill, built in 1927, stand on the stone foundation of the Bodie mill.

91. *Sacramento Union* 12 December 1878.

92. *Sacramento Union* 15 October 1878.

93. Irwin, *First Annual Report of the Standard*, 9.

94. *Engineering and Mining Journal* 22 February 1879, 128.

95. The ledge claimed in 1859 as the Montauk was abandoned soon thereafter, then re-located in July 1877 as the Goodshaw lode. (Wasson, *Bodie and Esmeralda*, 5, 26, 38; Mono County, *Mine Locations*, Book A, 167; Fitch, *Pacific Coast Mining*, 200)

96. Mono County, *Mine Locations*, Book A, 388.

97. Dan De Quille [William Wright], *The Big Bonanza* (1876; reprint, Las Vegas, NV: Nevada Publications, 1982), 19, 27.

98. *Carson Valley News* 30 March 1877.

99. *Borax Miner* 18 August 1877; *Inyo Independent* 25 August 1877; 8 September 1877; *Daily Stock Report* 5 August 1880.

100. Wasson, *Bodie and Esmeralda*, 26; Fitch, *Pacific Coast Mining*, 234. Most Bodie mines were consolidations of small claims. Federal law set the maximum length of a claim at 1,500 feet along the lode's strike with a maximum width of 600 feet, unless overridden by local rules. The early prospectors who organized the Bodie mining district accepted the 1,500 foot maximum length, but adopted a slender 100 foot width. Instead of separate companies mining narrow strips of land, expenses could be reduced by grouping several properties and operating them as one. See "Why Not Consolidate," *Daily Free Press* 3 December 1879.

101. *Bodie Standard* 7 November 1877; 14 November 1877; *Gold Hill Daily News* 5 December 1877; *Mining and Scientific Press* 15 December 1877, 373.

102. *Bodie Standard* 5 December 1877; 19 December 1877; 26 December 1877.

103. *Bodie Standard* 3 April 1878; *Bodie Weekly Standard* 26 June 1878.

104. *Bodie Weekly Standard* 5 June 1878; 3 July 1878.

105. Smith, *The Bodie Era*, 36; *Bodie Weekly Standard* 10 July 1878.

106. Smith, *The Bodie Era*, 34.

107. *Bodie Weekly Standard* 10 July 1878; *Mining and Scientific Press* 14 June 1879, 381; 27 December 1879, 414.

108. *Bodie Weekly Standard* 17 July 1878; *Engineering and Mining Journal* 29 March 1879, 220; California, *Eighth Annual Report*, 396.

109. *Bodie Weekly Standard* 31 July 1878; 13 November 1878.

110. *Bodie Weekly Standard* 13 November 1878.

111. *Bodie Weekly Standard* 13 November 1878.

112. *Bodie Weekly Standard* 27 November 1878; 11 December 1878; *Daily Bodie Standard* 12 December 1878; 16 December 1878. Prescott, Scott & Company later built two locomotives for the Bodie Railway and Lumber Company. Locomotives No. 2 (*Inyo*) and No. 3 (*Mono*) were built and delivered in 1881. Two Prescott, Scott & Company steam hoists are displayed at Bodie State Historic Park.

113. *Daily Bodie Standard* 16 December 1878.

114. *Bodie Weekly Standard* 25 December 1878; 25 January 1879.

115. Mono County, *Mine Locations, Book A*, 388.

116. *Bodie Standard* 28 November 1877; Smith, *The Bodie Era*, 83; Wasson, *Bodie and Esmeralda*, 32-33.

117. Wasson, *Bodie and Esmeralda*, 26; Fitch, *Pacific Coast Mining*, 224.

118. William Morris Stewart (1827-1909). Fitch, *Pacific Coast Mining*, 30-31; Grant H. Smith, *The History of the Comstock Lode 1850-1920*, University of Nevada Bulletin 37,

No. 3 (1 July 1943) (Reno, NV: Nevada Bureau of Mines and Geology, 1980), 52-53. The apex law assumed that a lode closely resembled an inclined plane and allowed many claims to be staked, end to end along its length. The law presumed that each claim possessed parallel *end lines* and allowed each claim holder to mine his section of the lode by following it between extended end lines. Ore could be taken from all "dips, spurs, and angles" as far as they went—even if they passed beyond the *side lines* of the claim and into ground claimed by another. Legal problems arose because it could not be known whether a surface outcropping represented an individual lode, or a branch of one claimed by someone else. Encroachment disputes were complex as mineral formations usually snaked through a crazy quilt of claims, and the extended end lines, which were theoretically perpendicular to the outcropping, often crossed each other.

119. *Engineering and Mining Journal* 14 September 1878, 182-183.

120. *Bodie Weekly Standard* 30 October 1878; 18 September 1878; *Weekly Bodie Standard* 18 January 1879.

121. *Bodie Weekly Standard* 25 December 1878.

122. *Bodie Weekly Standard* 25 December 1878.

123. Smith, "Last of the Old Time Mining Camps," 68.

Mining on the Assessment Plan

1. Richard E. Lingenfelter and Karen Rix Gash, *The Newspapers of Nevada: A History and Bibliography, 1854-1979* (Reno, NV: University of Nevada Press, 1984), 42, 177, 253; Alan H. Patera, *Lundy* (Lake Grove, OR: Western Places, 2000), 7-8, 12.

2. *Walker Lake Bulletin* 8 January 1890.

Figure 3-1: As Bodie's population surpassed 4,000 in early 1879, the demand for lumber, cordwood, and mine timbers was met by large-scale logging operations in the Sierra. Bodie photographer J. C. Kemp recorded this May 1879 view of a water-powered sawmill as a big team departs with a load of lumber. Two-and-a-half years would pass before Bodie was connected by railroad to timberlands south of Mono Lake. (J. C. Kemp & Co., Great Flying Photograph Gallery, Bodie. Courtesy, Peter E. Palmquist)

Figure 3-2: A stock certificate issued by the Standard Consolidated Mining Company. (Courtesy, Gregory Bock)

CHAPTER THREE

"GREAT SCOTT! WHAT A MINE!"
1879

Our peace officers report everything quiet about town; in fact, no arrests have been made for several nights, and . . . our winter is likely to roll around with disgusting sameness as regards matters riotous. However, we do not despair, as any day may bring forth some new cause of grievance which will induce the cheerful sound of the pistol to reverberate through our at present quiet streets.
    —Daily Bodie Standard, *January 21, 1879*

Every day the work of opening up and developing our mines is continued with the most encouraging results. Of course it must not be expected that every shaft will prove a mine, yet there can be but little question that those lying on the great mineral belt will prove valuable properties.
    —Mining and Scientific Press, *December 27, 1879*

The Noonday Mine

By January 1879, anyone speculating in western mining shares had heard about Bodie and knew that its mines were producing. This was good news around Virginia City, where a discernible decline in profitable ore had resulted in a large number of discharged workers. Hundreds departed in search of opportunities elsewhere, and Bodie became the primary destination. A Comstock reporter described the desperate scramble to board a departing stagecoach in late January.

> There was a regular old-time excitement in Virginia today when the Bodie stage got ready to start. When it drew up in front of Wells, Fargo & Co.'s office a crowd of about two hundred congregated around and made things appear lively there for a time. Every seat in the vehicle held its complement of three persons, and five besides the driver were on top.[1]

Two weeks later another Bodie-bound stage was surrounded by "a crowd of about 500 men, many of whom wished to go also." Those who managed to climb aboard left behind about a ton and a half of their baggage. The clamor to reach Bodie compelled the stage company to increase the frequency of its departures from every other day to daily.[2] Augmented by people from Virginia City, Bodie's population approached 5,000 by the spring of 1879.

The Noonday shaft in Bodie's south end finally reached the Keystone ledge at a depth of 129 feet, where the ore assayed $75 per ton. At 152 feet, the ledge yielded rock valued at $90 per ton. In

February, at a depth of 160 feet, assays had increased to $462 per ton. Surrounded by ore, the shaft reached the 200-foot level, where stations were opened and drifts started to follow the vein north and south.[3] Most of Bodie's mine dumps contained waste rock, the result of miners blasting through barren ground to find a vein. At the Noonday, however, the dump was heaped with high-grade that grew richer as the miners dug deeper. The amazing rock pile at the shaft's mouth drew the admiration of onlookers, but the company needed the services of a mill to turn it into bars of bullion.

On March 14, 1879, ponderous wagons began hauling Noonday ore through town to the 20-stamp Syndicate mill. The first load, halted on Main Street while the team rested, attracted considerable attention, and people crowded around to examine the cargo. "The universal opinion was that the ore would

Sinking a shaft using air-powered rock drills

work well, and many expressed surprise to see such fine rock from a point a mile and a half south of the main bluff."[4] Responding to the anticipated mill run, stock in the Noonday Mining Company doubled in price, climbing to $2 per share.

The Syndicate mill began crushing Noonday ore in late April. At the same time, the Noonday Company started sinking a second shaft. Jointly owned by the Noonday Mining Company and its neighbor, the North Noonday Mining Company, the new vertical shaft straddled the boundary between the two claims and was advantageously positioned 450 feet northeast of the existing shaft to intersect the Noonday and Keystone ledges as they pitched eastward.

The jointly-owned shaft would be of first-class construction, fully timbered, and it would contain three compartments: two for hoisting, one for pumping. It was initially called the Noonday "combination shaft," "joint shaft," or "main shaft," but after a while, most people just referred to it as the "Noonday shaft."[5] To sink it, miners began by drilling and blasting, then shoveling the broken rock into an ore bucket, which was raised and dumped on the surface by men at a windlass. Around them carpenters were busy constructing a building in which powerful steam hoisting machinery would be placed.

The Syndicate mill delivered the Noonday's first bar of bullion in the middle of May. Representing the proceeds of the mill run, the bar was worth $12,981. It contained $11,241 in gold, the rest silver. Then, through a new contract, the little Miners mill took over crushing the Noonday's rock.[6]

Sinking three-compartment shafts and erecting steam-powered hoisting works are endeavors that consume capital at alarming rates. To fund them, the steady steed plodded a circular route at the old Noonday shaft, slowly winding riches up from the 200-foot level. This crude hoisting method would continue supplying ore for the Miners mill until the new shaft reached the ore bodies.

The jointly-owned, three-compartment shaft was 90 feet deep when its new hoisting engine received a boiler and smokestack in late June. Manufactured in San Francisco by Prescott, Scott & Company, the hoist could raise rock from a depth of 2,000 feet. The new machinery was of splendid workmanship, capable of handling double-decker cages and self-dumping skips. A compressor ran air-powered rock drills that would expedite the work taking place below. After the windlass was removed, the boiler was fired up, and sinking commenced under steam power.

Stock in the two companies climbed to $3.50 per share as the shaft descended toward the veins. Meanwhile, miners drifting northward on the 200-

Figure 3-3: "If you can whack a sixteen-bull team, hit a drill, engineer a wheelbarrow, or deal faro and shoot with some degree of accuracy, then we advise you to come right along; otherwise stay where you are." The *Daily Bodie Standard*'s August 1879 warning did little good, and more people crowded into Bodie, where mining companies reported rich strikes almost daily. Prospect shafts dominate the foreground of a panorama photographed between June 1878, when the Miners Union Hall was completed, and October 1879, when a brick post office was built on the south Main Street lot occupied by a stable. Inhabitants could not escape the incessant clatter of stamps and the periodic shriek of a steam whistle from the Standard mill, at right. (J. C. Kemp photograph. Courtesy, Special Collections, University of Nevada-Reno Library)

foot level continued delivering ore to the old shaft, where the horse and whim raised it to the surface. Following the Keystone ledge, the drift yielded ore along its increasing length. After a second horse was added to the whim, the four stamps in the Miners mill could not keep pace.[7] Once again, a growing pile of ore demonstrated that no mills had been built since late 1878, when the Bodie mill was completed. Frustrated by the district's inadequate milling capacity, managers announced that the Noonday and North Noonday companies would build their own stamp mill.

The Noonday mill would be magnificent. Its 30 stamps would make it the largest in the district. To build it, the Noonday and North Noonday companies reincorporated, increasing each company's capitalization to $10,000,000. Selling more stock and levying assessments raised the necessary capital. By late July, a contractor had been selected, crews were grading a site for the mill, and wagons were delivering stone and lumber for its construction.[8]

In early August, the joint shaft reached the 212-foot level, where a crosscut started toward the west would rendezvous with the drift advancing northward along the Keystone ledge. They connected during the first week of September. Meanwhile, the big shaft was pushed deeper, reaching the 312-foot level the same week. From there, a crosscut ran eastward along the boundary line between the two properties to intersect the Keystone ledge. The vein was cut 30 feet from the shaft. Another 80 feet and the larger Noonday ledge was pierced. From these two intersections, drifts were run north and south along the veins.[9]

The local press rejected subtlety, producing sensational reports that fit the mood of a mining town in its heyday. One reporter toured the Noonday Mine's 312-foot level and described the Keystone ledge. "All the way the drift follows a vein of glittering white quartz from 20 inches to 2 feet in width which assays well in gold and gives a small return in silver." The reporter proceeded through the dank passages until he reached the Noonday ledge. There he waxed creative. "At this point the ledge is about 5 feet wide, of shining white quartz that flashed back the light from the candles in a thousand brilliant sparkles. Overhead the drift looked as if studded with gems."[10]

These and other seductive stories of wealth attracted even more people. "Bodie is improving wonderfully," wrote a local reporter.

> The noise of the saw and hammer resounds from daylight till dark, telling the story of improvement. All over town the work is going on. Mills, hoisting works, stores and dwelling houses are going up on every hand with the greatest rapidity. The growth of Bodie heretofore has been remarkable, and it continues to grow.[11]

Another column celebrated a stream of street-congesting commerce.

> Few people properly appreciate the vast amount of freight coming into Bodie. The quantity is simply enormous. The number of teams freighting between Bodie, Carson and other places, is almost countless. The roads leading into Bodie are lined with them. Prairie schooners, loaded with goods, merchandise and machinery, and big teams loaded with lumber, pour into our town continually, and keep the streets blocked up during the daytime unloading.[12]

Every kind of conveyance crowded Bodie's streets. Cumbersome big-team freighting outfits delivered staples for sustenance, lumber to build a community, and machinery for mining. Their wagons, coupled in tandem and pulled by 16-, 18-, or 20-mule and horse teams, required nearly a week to travel between Bodie and the railroad at Carson City. Fast freight companies made the trip in three days on fixed schedules, charging elevated rates for swifter service. One fast freight company cut the time to only 24 hours by changing teams in relays, like stagecoaches. Main Street was also travelled by heavily-laden ore wagons that rumbled towards the mills, while wood wagons brought fuel to warm Bodie's inhabitants, cook their meals, and sustain the fires of their industry. Hay wagons delivered feed for the beasts of burden. There were also stagecoaches, drawn by four- or six-horse teams, bringing more people and carrying away bars of gold and silver bullion. Six stage lines served Bodie: two to Carson City that carried parcels, including bullion, shipped by express; one to Virginia City; one to Sonora; another to Mammoth; and a local that dashed between Bodie and Aurora.[13]

As the town expanded, so did its mining district. Swarming over the hills, gold seekers advanced southward beyond Silver Hill, staking claims and sinking shafts on any spot of ground that they thought might be on the lode.

> It is but a few months ago that the Red Cloud hoisting works were the last in that direction, and beyond that point there was nothing except a few prospect holes, none of them exceeding 100 feet in depth. We now have some of the heaviest machinery in the district at work far south of what was considered then the south end.[14]

In October, the Noonday joint shaft reached the 412-foot level, where another crosscut was run eastward along the property line to intersect the two ledges. North and south drifts followed the ore from those intersections. As the miners descended toward the 512-foot level, water began seeping into the shaft.[15]

At year's end, crosscuts and drifts extended from the three-compartment joint shaft's 212-, 312-, 412-, and 512-foot levels. The Noonday companies had consumed nine months sinking their main shaft, developing its underground, and building the region's finest hoisting works and stamp mill. Nearby, the horse and whim had steadily hoisted most of 1879's pay ore through the old shaft, delivering $36,532. The yield placed the combined Noonday companies fourth in district bullion production and established their enterprise as the south end's most prolific. "For a mine worked by a whim and one horse," a local newspaper noted, "the Noonday certainly has done wonders."[16]

Amid popping champagne corks, the Noonday's marvelous new mill started up on Christmas Day, 1879. Its whistle sounded and the ponderous machinery started moving "like the works of the most delicate watch."[17] With that, the citizens of Bodie welcomed their fifth and largest stamp mill. The engine, meticulously built by the Harris Corliss Engine Works of Providence, Rhode Island, powered 30 stamps weighing 800 pounds each. The stamps would crush ore into particles finer than sand, after which 24 circular amalgamating pans and 12 settlers would extract the gold and silver. Toasts were drunk, but the noise of the pounding stamp batteries made conversation impossible. The mill was divided into two sections with 15 stamps each, so that either Noonday company could run its half independently. A trestle from the hoisting works would bring mine cars directly from the main shaft, eliminating costly contracts to transport ore by wagon and permitting ore deliveries in foul weather.

District-wide, five mills now dropped 84 stamps on Bodie's ore, and two more mills were under construction. This was where a great many people hoped to find their fortunes, especially those from the Comstock, where mine closures and alluring reports about rich deposits at Bodie were compelling. Among the arrivals, many were out of work miners and tradesmen seeking employment. Some were also prospec-

tors, hoping to discover bonanzas of their own. Prior to January 1876, only 18 claims had been recorded in the district, when it was inhabited by a modest gathering of intrepid individuals. From that date until January 1878, about 206 new claims were located. During 1878, 360 were recorded, and 374 claims the following year. Although few had yielded more than promises, 958 locations had been recorded by the end of 1879.

Those citing the number of claims while trumpeting the district's bright future found unexpected support in the federal mining law of 1872. Although not necessarily followed to the letter, it decreed that "no location of a mining claim shall be made until the discovery of the vein or lode." While few Bodie claims exhibited pay ore in profitable quantities, and most claims showed no indications at all, the law was used to perpetuate the illusion that countless ore bodies had been discovered. "As no claim can be located without a ledge having been struck, they all, at least, may be said to have a vein."[18]

Bodie had taken on a decidedly industrial demeanor. "The shrill shriek of the whistle is heard at intervals during the day and night, calling the hundreds of miners and laborers to their work," one observer reported. "The incessant buzz of machinery makes music to the ears of all interested in our prosperity and advancement."[19] Twenty-five mines flaunted steam-powered hoisting works: the Standard, Bodie, Mono, Noonday, Red Cloud, Bechtel, Black Hawk, Tioga, Summit, McClinton, Consolidated Pacific, Butler, South Bulwer, South Standard, South Bodie, Goodshaw, Addenda, Oro, Maryland, University, Queen Bee, Jupiter, Champion, Spaulding, and Booker.[20] The state mineralogist, however, reported that only four of these mines were producing. Whether the others were stymied by a shortage of milling facilities or by a scarcity of pay ore, expensive hoisting machines on so many ineffectual mines proved that speculators were willing to buy stock and pay assessments on the outside chance that developments would eventually return profits.

The Bodie and Mono Mines

The two Noonday companies widened public awareness of Silver Hill, and the town sprawled southward in response to developments there. To the north, however, the Bodie Mine was delivering surprises of its own. While the Bodie Company groped for water to supply its new mill, the main shaft was driven past the 350-foot level toward the fabulous Bruce and Burgess veins. Stockholders were joyful. But the celebration did not last long. By the end of January 1879, the high-grade ore was exhausted.[21]

The Bodie Mine's bonanza had lasted only eight months. Stock tumbled in value when the company failed to pay the anticipated February dividend. Re-

HERCULES POWDER

fusing to acknowledge that the district's two richest ore bodies were depleted, New York's outspoken *Mining Record* accused the Bodie's management of withholding the dividend to manipulate stock prices. The journal contended that stockholders with inside information could have sold out early, then profited by buying again at lower prices before a dividend drove stocks upward. The paper condemned Lent's ring of insiders. "These are the things which are so constantly

happening in connection with San Francisco mining corporations as to engender the deepest distrust of all mining enterprises having their management in that city."[22]

As businessmen schemed in distant cities, miners toiled by dim candlelight deep within High Peak. Occasionally one would die. Early on the frosty morning of February 6, 1879, Rodger Ryon was helping to dump the ore bucket at the top of the Bodie new shaft when tragedy struck. The bucket, used earlier for bailing, had spilled water around the shaft's collar. When ice formed, the footing became unsafe. About two o'clock in the morning, Ryon opened the trapdoor to allow the bucket to pass. Reaching to untangle the trip rope, he slipped and fell 420 feet to the bottom of the shaft, glancing off timbers on his way down. Witnesses heard him call out "Clear the shaft," to warn those working below. The engineer sent the bucket down after him. It returned with his lifeless body. The following Sunday Ryon was given a hero's burial by the Bodie Miners Union.[23]

Mine shaft accidents were the industry's most common cause of death, a fact well known in Bodie. "The shaft of a mine is a locality fraught with danger," affirmed a *Daily Free Press* editorial titled "Life and Death in the Shaft."

A misstep on the surface sends a human being through the bowels of the earth hundreds of feet, and his mutilated remains, scarcely recognizable, are brought up from the bottom of the shaft. Another, by some mischance, becomes wedged between the "cage" and the side of the shaft, and in a moment life and all semblance of humanity is crushed out from him. A shift of men are working in the bottom of the shaft and through the carelessness of the engineer, or a misunderstanding of signals, a heavy iron cage, weighing several hundred pounds, is lowered on them, and they are either killed instantly, or are left to linger a few days suffering indescribable tortures.

The most prolific cause of death, the paper noted, was "running a cage into the sheaves." Instead of stopping an ascending cage at the surface, the engineer would accidently raise it until it crashed into the gallows frame, which supported the wheel over which the hoisting cable passed.

> Then ensues a scene of terror and death. . . . The time is so short—but a second or two—after the surface is reached before the cage is in the sheaves, that men can not act. Some jump, only to fall back in the shaft. Some meet death in one way, and some in another.[24]

Injuries also resulted from cages dropping with men aboard, objects falling down shafts and striking personnel, and mishaps with the hoist and equipment. Of Comstock mining fatalities between 1863 and 1880, 61% were related to shafts or the hoisting machinery. Calculating the lives lost in other Comstock mining accidents, 17% resulted from subterranean fires, 7% from accidental detonation of explosives, and 6% from cave-ins.[25]

Eight months after Ryon's unfortunate death, Bodie's second-worst industrial disaster, measured in terms of mortality, occurred in a mine shaft. At six o'clock on October 3, 1879, nine men on the evening shift crowded aboard the "safety cage" at the Tioga Mine and prepared to descend. The cage suddenly plummeted hopelessly out of control, falling more than 500 feet to the shaft's bottom. The grisly results were poignantly tabulated by the morning paper: Henry Richards, native of Cornwall, England, age about 45 years, "killed outright." James Cassidy, native of Canada, age about 40 years, "both legs broken; not expected to live." Samuel Martin, native of Maine, age about 45 years, "both legs broken; cannot live." Manuel Alves Garcia, native of Portugal, age about 28 years, "injured internally; will die." Joseph Brodeur, native of Canada, age about 33 years,

"injured seriously."[26] By nightfall Cassidy, Martin, Garcia, and Brodeur had joined Richards in death. Flags fluttered at half-staff on the hill as the five bodies lay in state at the Miners Union hall. Pat Brannon, whose condition was initially listed as "arm fractured and injured internally; now dying," lingered fitfully until death took him eight days later. Bodie rallied to aid orphans and widows of the tragedy by raising relief funds through a benefit play, dance, and supper held at the Miners Union hall.

Investigating the accident, a coroner's jury headed by Joseph Wasson concluded that the six were killed and their three companions injured because the hoisting engineer had relied solely on the hoist's brake to check the cage's descent. Contrary to the custom of "clutching" the cable reel to the steam engine, the brake alone was used, and proved insufficient to hold the weight of the cage and its nine passengers. The jury concluded that "in no case should the use of breaks [sic] be permitted, except as auxiliaries to the steam power, and that all hoisting and lowering should be done with the engine."[27] Realizing the extent of his error, the engineer had left the mine after the accident and was observed walking down the hill toward his house. He changed clothes, then left town.

Safety cages were designed to stop automatically if the supporting cable broke. At the moment the cable went slack, spring-loaded eccentrics would bite into the wooden guide rails. These toothed devices were universally employed on the Comstock by 1876 and were widely available during Bodie's boom period.[28] At the Tioga, however, the hoisting cable did not break. It was held taut by the engine's resisting brake, and the tension was sufficient to prevent the safety mechanism from engaging.

Responding to the tragedy, Tioga superintendent Charles H. Golding developed an improved safety cage and received a patent for it. The cage of his invention could be stopped "in any part of the shaft by the men on the cage, and is entirely independent of the engineer in charge." When ascending, it would ring a bell about 100 feet from the sur-

REMINISCENCES OF GEORGE MONTROSE

George Montrose, a Gardnerville, Nevada, attorney and former editor of the Bridgeport *Chronicle-Union*, spent his boyhood in the booming mining camp of Bodie. His reminiscences, printed in 1921, recall the lifelong torment experienced by a survivor of the Tioga disaster.

On October 3, 1879, the cage in the Tioga shaft in Bodie, through the unpardonable, if not criminal, negligence of the engineer, John Boynton, went crashing to the bottom of the shaft, a distance of 631 feet, laden with nine men. Boynton took to the hills immediately after the accident and was never heard of in that section again.

Harry Richards, Manuel Alvaras [sic], Samuel Martin, Joseph Brothers [sic], John Cassidy [sic] and Pat Brannan were killed; Peter Bluff and John French were seriously injured and were crippled for the remainder of their lives, while Thomas Moran was slightly bruised.

It was the wonder of the time how Moran escaped such a fall with scarcely a bruise, but this was cleared up when Bluff and French told of the awful fall. The nine men standing on the cage, three in a row, holding the cross-bar above, were quick to recognize that something had gone wrong with the engine and knew that only by a miracle could they be saved. Moran raised himself by his arms off the floor of the cage and threw his legs around the waist of Samuel Martin, thus serving as a bumper for the shock. When the cage struck the bottom of the shaft, Martin was mashed into an unrecognizable mass and Moran thrown free with barely a scratch.

From that time on, Tommy Moran was a marked man in the camp. Miners refused to work underground with him and he was ostracized and took to the consolation of drink. After a couple of years he left Bodie and went to the Copper Mountain section, about eighteen miles away, where he was known as a drunken prospector. His wife and two children made a precarious living by doing the washing for the miners and chores around the camp.

Moran's luck seemed to change for a day and he located a claim which he was able to sell for a few thousand dollars. The wife got most of the money, and with her children, went to San Francisco to live. One of the boys became a somewhat famous jockey around the Bay District and after a few years sent for his father to come to the Coast and live with them. Life, however, could not have been very sweet to Tommy, as one morning his lifeless body was found swinging from a branch of a tree in Golden Gate park.[1]

face "so as to guard against accident by the running of the cage into the sheaves."[29] Several Bodie mining companies, including the Tioga and Bechtel, had cages built using Golding's design.

Other calamities beset the district during the early months of 1879. In February, a district-wide four-day labor dispute initiated by the Mechanics Union on behalf of the hoisting engineers succeeded in shutting down nearly every mine in the district. When stock prices rose contrary to reason, one smart aleck suggested that the advance was probably caused by "the assurance that if the mines are closed down there will be no more assessments."[30]

While controversy discredited the mining district, miners in the Bodie Mine unearthed another bonanza. Unlike the Bruce/Burgess bonanza, the second big discovery did not create an immediate stir. The vein had been cut 346 feet below the surface in January 1879 by the Bodie new shaft, when the objective was to reach the Bruce and Burgess ore bodies. Because the vein was impoverished at that point, the formation went unreported. It was cut again in the spring, this time in a crosscut on the 433-foot level, 144 feet east of the shaft. Here its wealth was immediately recognized, but insiders so successfully cloaked the new bonanza in secrecy that the discovery date is not known. Suspicions were aroused when Bodie's citizens noticed that the Bodie Mine, which they had been told was depleted, resumed ore shipments. Soon, stories of extraordinary values raced through town. In the middle of March 1879, stock in the Bodie Gold Mining Company began advancing. The mining world held its breath. Then in April, defying all expectations, an *assessment* was announced! Extraordinarily high at a dollar per share, it was the Bodie Company's first assessment since February 1878.[31]

Mining companies of this era were unregulated, and deceptions were prevalent. The Bodie management's plan was to keep the discovery secret and enhance the illusion that the mine was in decline by levying an assessment. This was expected to drive stock prices down and trick unwary shareholders into selling or forfeiting. After the insiders had bought the stock at low prices, the rich discovery would be announced. Stock prices would rise, and the inside clique would profit by selling at inflated prices.

Instead, persistent rumors about the ore's great wealth upset the scheme's intended effect, and stock prices advanced instead of falling.[32] Official silence lingered until late in May, when the *Engineering and Mining Journal* in New York was first to verify the strike in print.

> The strike in the Bodie mine, which, according to telegraphic information, continues to develop very richly, caused quite an excitement in that stock. The price of that stock had reached $23 last Friday. On Tuesday, when the transactions amounted to 870 shares, the range was from $30 to $31. Since then, the business has fallen off a little, but the price has steadily advanced, reaching $50 this afternoon [May 29, 1879]. Very much higher prices are still predicted.[33]

The second bonanza in the Bodie Mine was now confirmed. It was named the "Fortuna lode."

The word "Fortuna" echoes through the history of Bodie and is woven into the fabric of fact and folklore alike. In Spanish, the word means "wealth" and "fortune," and its three syllables conjure up seemingly endless riches. Although the vein's average width was no more than two feet, it was so rich that it became the primary source of revenue for the Bodie Company through the next 17 years.[34] Miners would follow it 1,200 feet into the earth.

A newspaperman representing the *Bodie Morning News* toured the mine with a group led by superintendent D. H. Fogus and foreman J. Showers. The visitors were taken to the 433-foot level, where they entered a winze—an exploratory shaft started from an underground level—to behold the ore.

> Mr. Showers planted his guests on the cage, each with his heart in his throat and a candle in his hand; then with a wave of his hand, and a "Bill, send her to the bottom" to the engineer, the cage shot down into the void, and all was as black as night . . .
>
> Col. Fogus led the way into a drift to the south, and in a second the visitors got the first sight of the new bonanza. . . . Mr. Showers jammed his candle up against a narrow, grayish seam, running along the side of the drift at an angle of about 20 degrees, and said, "Look at that!" There it was, a beautiful, gray and yellowish streak, flecked with shining particles of pure gold. Below that a streak of decomposed rock, so thick with gold that a handful seemed to weigh a pound. Then another streak of spotted quartz and yellowish matter fairly alive with glittering specks, and then a streak of brownish clay. "Here's where we find the nuggets," said Mr. Showers, and with that he poked the end of his candlestick into the brownish streak. A little shining lump fell down and in a moment it lay glittering in the writer's hand—a beautiful lump of gold as big as a white bean. The writer sat down on a golden boulder, pressed the little lump in his hand, and said, "Great Scott! What a mine." "Hump! That's nothing," remarked the sturdy miner, "come down into the winze."
>
> Down ladders Mr. Showers led his guests, Col. Fogus with a big candle bringing up the rear. Reaching the bottom of the winze the Colonel remarked, "Now you are at the lowest point in the Bodie mine, 470 feet from the surface. I want you to have some specimens from the very bottom." . . . Here the whole

bottom of the winze seemed to blaze with the precious metal. Flecks, specks, nuggets, scales, and the rich black sulphurets lay so thickly embedded in the grayish quartz as to give the idea of a solid, golden mass.[35]

Robert T. Bell, who worked in Bodie's mines during the 1920s and 30s, adds more details.

The Fortuna was only found in the Bodie Mine, nowhere else. Quartz veins at Bodie tended to be nearly vertical at about 75 to 85 degrees. . . . The Fortuna was a different vein system altogether; it pitched toward the east at an angle of about 30 degrees. It predated all the others because they all cut it. It kept faulting and was never found between the 300-foot level and the surface. There must still be a 300-foot piece of it in the hill.[36]

The Fortuna was the only vein system where argentite, the silver sulphuret known on the Comstock as "blasted blue stuff," was found in Bodie. It was rich, but the Fortuna never outproduced the immense ore bodies in the Standard Mine, which consistently yielded 10 times the volume of ore and between two and five times the amount of bullion of the Bodie Mine.

The Fortuna lode lay deep within High Peak. To remove ore from the ledge as it pitched away from the shaft, a hoist was installed below ground, in a remote drift on the 433-foot level. Inside a large man-made cavern, hoisting equipment was run with compressed air piped from a compressor on the surface. An incline shaft, started from the subterranean hoisting works, would follow the Fortuna as it coursed downward toward the east.

In June 1879 the Bodie Gold Mining Company consolidated a group of surrounding claims, changed its name to the more formidable and fashionable Bodie Consolidated Mining Company, and doubled its capitalization to $10,000,000. The elder William Lent, acting unofficially as the district's emissary, opened a branch office at 137 Broadway in New York City. It soon became the eastern headquarters for mining speculation and dealing in Bodie stocks.

Dressed in a "faultless suit of light clothes, white necktie, nobby straw hat, and daintily trimmed moustache," Lent enjoyed hosting tea parties for prospective investors. His office suite was "constantly crowded by people who . . . had made up their minds that it is safer to deal in solid mining securities than in high-priced railroad fancies."[37] When asked about the latest news from the mine, Lent's customary reply was an assured, "The outlook for the future is decidedly brilliant." Then he would add, "My reports from Bodie are all favorable."[38]

Because of delays in finding water, the Bodie Company's new mill did not become operational until after the Bruce/Burgess bonanza was exhausted. Dams completed in March 1879 impounded enough water from Bodie Canyon and Taylor Gulch for milling, but winter weather complicated matters when the reservoirs froze.[39] A water supply wholly dependent upon the discharge from upstream mines and mills was only one of the Bodie mill's imperfections. Another was its distance from the mine. The shortest route was a 1½ mile wagon road following Taylor Gulch around the east side of Bodie Bluff. Ore wagons were limited to hauling on days when the road was passable. Winter snow and spring mud often brought ore shipments to a standstill, and sometimes halted milling. Ore-freighting contracts were also a constant drain on company finances, cutting heavily into profits. Only ore rich enough to cover the cost of transportation could be selected, and low- or marginal-grade ore was passed over.[40]

Despite these nagging disadvantages, the Bodie mill began thundering away on ore from the Fortuna lode in July 1879.[41] Calculated to infect the reader with an acute case of gold fever, the company reported that "the result of a two days' run in the batteries of the Bodie mill was . . . a collection of gold nuggets worth $15,000."[42]

Based largely on reports from the Bodie Mine, unrealistic stories of the district's wealth spread, and the town experienced a population surge during 1879 that eclipsed the boom of 1878. From 1,200 inhabitants estimated in the fall of 1878, the number of people in Bodie had increased to more than 7,000 during 1879. A local newspaper remarked:

> The town is full of strangers. Men from the Comstock, from Pioche, White Pine, Eureka, Elko, and everywhere in the State of Nevada; residents of San Francisco, San Jose, Oakland, San Diego, and Los Angeles; natives of England, Ireland, Scotland, Germany, France, Spain, Mexico, and every portion of the habitable globe are mixed up promiscuously on our streets. And still they come.[43]

The number gainfully employed in mines and mills, however, was only 1,000 to 1,300. Bodie also employed a large force of carpenters, teamsters, blacksmiths, bricklayers, stonemasons, painters, woodchoppers, lumbermen, shopkeepers, and clerks. Still, a large percentage of the arrivals could not find work, and the number of idle men in August 1879 was estimated at about 1,500.[44] In a rare note of disparagement, the local press published a letter mailed from Bodie that stressed many hardships of frontier life.

> There are hundreds of good men ready to leave, but they can't, as they haven't got the money. There is a great deal of sickness here, as we have no sewers, and the water is awful. . . . There isn't an air tight house in all of Bodie. The wind whistles through every shanty in the camp. How can a pneumonia patient get well if he is not protected against the cold blasts which have already set in? For a rich camp this is the poorest one I've seen.[45]

Mining gold is thirsty work, and the reckless consumption of alcohol kept the slippery path toward homicide well lubricated. A population of men that outnumbered women "nine or ten to one," a bewildering number of saloons, and a willingness to exchange gunfire over a careless remark earned Bodie a reputation as a mining camp that was both unruly and bloody.[46] Saloons were the most popular social institutions. Gaming rooms provided additional manly amusements. People with money spent it in riotous excess, drinking, gambling, swearing, and fighting to their heart's content, while fresh oysters and champagne gave the town an air of refinement.

An explosive mix of rough-and-tumble men crowding abundant saloons led to trouble. Particularly perilous was their tendency to discharge firearms. Whether resulting from confrontations between drunken adversaries or gleeful target practice, the gunfire disturbed at least one editorialist. "Every night we can hear the reports of pistol shots coming from various portions of the town. . . . Such playfully disposed individuals should be taught a severe lesson when captured, and be made acquainted with the inside of the jail."[47] When the *Gold Hill News* asked, "Why can't a man get along in Bodie without fighting?" Bodie's press thought it might be the high altitude. "There is some irresistible power in Bodie which impels us to cut and shoot each other to pieces [and] the clashing of knives and the cracking of revolvers up and down Main Street can be constantly heard." The correspondent joked that "scarcely a man in town wears a suit of clothes" without knife slashes or bullet holes in it. "Yes," the article concluded, "it is sad, but only too true, that everybody must fight that comes to Bodie."[48] More than one local columnist employed the popular nineteenth-century expression "having a man for breakfast" when reporting the previous night's fatalities.[49]

Bodie was among several western boomtowns that were gaining infamy during the late 1870s for frontier violence. Noteworthy among its contemporaries were the mining towns of Tombstone, Arizona Territory, and Deadwood, Dakota Territory. Dodge City, a Kansas cattle town, was also earning legendary status. Bodie relished its standing among hard places, and competed grandiloquently for prominence. "There has not been an arrest for fighting or drunkenness, not even a man killed for as much as two days," complained a local editor. "This sort of thing won't do. Bodie has a reputation at stake."[50]

Contributing to Bodie's violent image were two highly-publicized 1879 armed altercations that involved the Mono Mine's feisty superintendent, George Daly. The first incident, showcasing a quick draw, had taken place in February, when the labor

Figure 3-4: After mid-1879, several Bodie companies installed "steam pumps" to remove water from their lengthening shafts. Versatility and low initial cost made these self-contained pumps an attractive alternative to Cornish pumping systems. Steam pumps could be installed any place in a mine where water presented a problem. They were also employed on the surface to fill boilers and fight fires. (*Engineering and Mining Journal* 27 January 1877. Courtesy, Engineering and Mining Journal)

HARRIS STEAM PUMP

strike by hoisting engineers aroused Daly's ire. Nobody was hurt in that confrontation. Six months later, another Daly quarrel deteriorated into a Wild West claim-jumping gunfight that took the life of one man before it ended in a standoff. (See pages 79, 82).

Besides stock swindles, assessments, and gunfire, the Mono Gold Mining Company was known for its mine, which was located immediately downhill from the Bodie Mine and was expected to strike it rich at any moment. Rich strikes, however, were not forthcoming. Instead, the Mono had an abundance of underground water—down on the 420-foot level. Initially a 300-gallon bailing tank solved the problem, and the Mono's hoist raised 19,000 gallons per day, permitting the shaft to be dug deeper. Then managers, most of whom were directors and principal owners of the Bodie Company, realized that the neighboring Bodie Mine could be drained at the expense of Mono shareholders. Because the collar of the Mono shaft was some 56 feet lower in elevation than that of the Bodie, water from both mines could be raised to the surface more economically through the Mono. As the Mono shaft descended, bailing increased to 40,000 gallons per day so the winze at the bottom of the Bodie Mine could probe its rich

ore.[51] Still, incoming water hampered progress, and the miners descended only a few more feet.

To remove more water, a steam pump was placed in the Mono shaft in June 1879, followed by others in July and August. The pumps raised 300,000 gallons per day, permitting both mines to go deeper, but more steam was needed. While ore from the Fortuna allowed the Bodie Company to resume dividend payments, Mono stockholders paid assessments from which two additional boilers were purchased. Still, water impeded progress. When a pump in the Mono shaft clogged with sand, both mines flooded again. Another pump, shipped from New York, drained the water so the plugged pump could be reached for repairs.[52] This, and a pump placed in the winze, finally overcame the setbacks, and work areas remained dry.

Removing water from the bottom of a mine required huge outlays of capital. Pumping, initiated at the Mono Mine in June 1879, marked a turning point for the district.[53] Many companies had shafts deep enough to strike water and had been confined to working levels above the water line and those that could be drained with bailing tanks. The tremendous cost of pumping machinery, however, was surpassed by the expense of running it. Pumping could easily

THE MECHANICS UNION STRIKE

Two events in 1879 contributed greatly to Bodie's "Wild West" image. Both involved George Daly, a headstrong, articulate superintendent at the Mono Mine. The first incident was an armed street confrontation, in February. The second was a shootout concerning mine ownership in August.

In addition to the Miners Union, organized in December 1877, Bodie was home to a 125-member Mechanics Union, organized in November 1878 and composed of about 50 hoisting engineers and a number of other non-mining tradesmen, such as firemen, blacksmiths, machinists, boilermakers, pipefitters, millwrights, masons, and carpenters.

The Mechanics Union felt that engineers, who were stationed at the controls of the hoisting machinery that raised and lowered men in the mine shafts, held the lives of many in their hands. Union leaders argued that a 12-hour workday exhausted the engineers and thus endangered the miners. Demands placed on hoist operators, the union asserted, also called for higher pay. The organization therefore demanded that the shift for hoisting engineers be reduced to eight hours, and that their pay be increased from $4.50 to $5.00 a day.[1] Mine managers, most of whose mines had yet to produce profitable ore, countered that few of the engineers had served apprenticeships, and most of the engines were small donkey hoists that required no particular skill to operate. They stressed that only two Bodie companies were paying dividends, and complying with these demands would be prohibitively expensive.

On Wednesday morning, February 12, members of the Mechanics Union met downtown and voted to strike. They filed from the meeting hall and marched up the hill. Beginning at the south end, they advanced northward, visiting each hoisting works and conferring with its superintendent. When the procession reached the Mono Mine, however, Superintendent George Daly locked the doors and placed himself in a state of defense. A spokesman for the union threatened to forcibly enter the works and carry away its engineers. No action was taken, and the spurned mechanics eventually moved on.

Mine superintendents discussed the matter and consulted with their directors in San Francisco. By noon the following day, most companies had closed down operations rather than submit to the union.[2] The only mines still being worked were the Standard and the Mono. The Standard Company, having recently listed its stock in New York, was reluctant to interrupt production. It accepted terms that preserved operations at its incline shaft. The Mono, however, conceded nothing and kept running, while its engineers remained at their posts under Daly's orders. Further provoking the strikers, Daly raised an American flag over the works. Fluttering patriotically from the Mono's flagpole, the banner symbolized a common nineteenth-century viewpoint that organized challenges to big business were un-American. Clearly visible from town, where the population contained a large percentage of working-class citizens, the flag inflamed ill will toward the confrontational superintendent and his spirited resentment of strikers.[3]

With all but two mines idled by the Mechanics Union, about 1,000 miners were locked out of work. These men sympathized to some extent with the strikers, but as members of the Miners Union, they were taking no part in the protest. An eyewitness, noticing the inactive smokestacks on the hill, chronicled the downtown scene. "The crowds of idle men thronging our sidewalks this morning, slowly passing to and fro, earnestly discussing some question of evident importance, . . . attest to the fact that we were in the midst of a 'strike'."[4]

George Daly, fractious and defiantly anti-union, neither closed the Mono Mine nor accepted terms demanded by the mechanics. After placing the Mono hoisting works under Old Glory's noble fold, the brassy superintendent further antagonized the opposition by declining to participate in negotiations. On February 14, the third day of the strike, Daly had finished breakfast and was walking up Main Street from a downtown restaurant when he noticed several men had gathered around him. Suddenly, he was tapped on the shoulder. It was Phil Maher, a spokesman for the striking mechanics. A curt discussion ensued, during which Daly refused to attend an ongoing union meeting. Daly was grabbed by members of the crowd and forced toward the parley taking place at the Miners Union hall. He wrestled free. "I jumped into the street," recalled Daly, "and drew my revolver, covering Maher." Daly exclaimed that he would "kill the first man who attempted to lay his hands" on him.[5] At this, most of the men ran up King Street.

The incident, though somewhat anticlimactic in comparison to the seemingly endless confrontations and assaults taking place in Bodie's streets and saloons, caught the interest of the local press. One editor opined, "The demonstration on the streets this morning, in which an attempt was made to force Mr. George Daly to go where he did not wish to go, was unlawful and illegitimate, and no organization can afford to defend it."[6]

The mechanics' strike, resisted by the mine owners and unsupported by the miners, lost momentum quickly, and the miners and mechanics returned to work the next day. Without the active participation of the Miners Union, the strike had faltered after just four days. That group's leadership realized that since most of the local mining companies had not found any ore, complying with the strikers' demands would further deplete dwindling funds and reduce the district's chances of developing more ore bodies.[7] George Daly, however, appeared to many as the compelling anti-union force behind the strike's failure. His antagonistic, uncompromising stance earned him many enemies.

Some months later, the brunt of their resentment would be directed toward him when he became embroiled in another, more bloody, conflict.[8]

consume 24 cords of wood per day, and fuel at Bodie was expensive. Firewood had to be hauled great distances by wagon. Furthermore, once the pumps were started they had to operate day and night or levels below the water line would flood again. Nonetheless, over the ensuing 12 months a dozen companies installed pumping machinery. Seven mines chose compact steam pumps: the Mono, Bodie, Noonday, Dudley, Goodshaw, South Bulwer, and South Bodie. Five others purchased cumbersome Cornish pumping systems: the Standard, Booker, Champion, South Standard, and Jupiter.

However inspired, most of the companies installing pumps had yet to mill any ore. Prior to the completion of the Noonday in late December, there were only four mills in Bodie during 1879: the Syndicate, Standard, Bodie, and Miners, and their 54 stamps were regularly tied up by seven major firms: the Standard, Bulwer, Bodie, Noonday, North Noonday, Syndicate, and Bechtel.

Most other mines had nothing to show in the way of bullion, and their stock sold for less than four bits per share. Yet managers wagered dwindling resources and pressed stockholders for more money, gambling that pumps would let them reach the next Big Bonanza. On the strength of overoptimistic reports, susceptible stockholders thought that their investments would make them millionaires if only the mines went deeper. Meanwhile, the discharged water from pumps and bailing tanks at quartz mines stimulated another aspect of Bodie's economy. Placer miners, using sluice boxes and rockers, thrived amid newly dug ditches that channelled wastewater to previously seasonal gravel diggings.[54]

The Bodie Mine was connected to the Mono shaft at the 400-foot level by an underground passage in December 1879.[55] This passage put both mines in compliance with California law, which required that mines of this depth have a means of escape other than the main shaft. The connection also improved ventilation. By joining two mine shafts, natural updrafts and downdrafts were created. The moment a connection was made, air from the surface descended one shaft and ascended the other. Strategically-placed underground doors distributed air through the drifts and crosscuts. A tunnel driven from the foot of a hill would also provide a natural draft when connected to a shaft.

Companies that cooperated by joining their workings avoided the expense of power-driven blowers to force fresh air to their workers. Natural drafts were rudimentary but effective in ventilating mines, especially when enhanced by ductwork. Such a system was described in the Bodie Mine. "An air-pipe runs from the surface down all through the mine and the draft in the winze, which connects with the Standard, will blow out a candle." By clever application of the shaft's hoisting machinery, "Every time the bucket is raised or lowered fresh air is puffed into the various drifts of the mine."[56]

Although the Fortuna produced steadily through the remaining months of 1879, traders of Bodie Company stock were not enraptured by the mine's crooked managers. Disputing sensational reports, speculators who scrutinized bullion shipments calculated the mine's production at $784,057, significantly less than the previous record-breaking year, when the Bruce/ Burgess bonanza was exploited. After May 29, 1879, when Bodie Company stock had soared to $50 per share (based on mere rumors of the Fortuna), prices fell to $6. Midway through this long decline an editorial reached Bodie that probed New York's fascination with Lent and his artful enthusiasm for the Bodie Mine. "Strange as it may seem . . ." wrote the eastern correspondent,

the stock . . . began to drop, and never stopped until it had tumbled from $25 to $10½, and the praises of the mine are now sung by the same sweet voice, but in a *minor key.* This seemed remarkably strange—almost unaccountable—to those who had acted upon advice

given with the utmost frankness and candor, and yet there are those here now—so thoughtless, perhaps even so unkind, as to suggest that Mr. Lent is buying back from his friends at from $10 to $11 per share— stock which he so strongly recommended them to buy at $20 to $25 per share less than three months ago.

Contemptuous of Lent's stock-swindling antics, the writer predicted that, after insiders had purchased ample shares of Bodie Mine stock at deflated prices:

The mine will then again assume its magnificent appearance, will glitter as of old with its fabulous wealth. That large additions will be made to its milling facilities, that a solo, in a *major key,* this time will be sung by our good friend Mr. Lent himself; that the stock will go flying up to higher figures than ever before, and that as usual the public will then frantically rush in and buy the shares.[57]

Another article confirmed investor distrust. "So many were burnt with this stock on the late decline, that it is difficult to reestablish confidence."[58]

Controversy notwithstanding, the Fortuna's richness could not be ignored. "The bullion shipments are increasing, and the reports from the developments are again encouraging."[59] Following the unexpected April assessment, dividends were declared in July, August, October, and November— though the latter two were reduced from $1 to 50 cents per share. This brought the total amount in dividends paid by the Bodie Company to $1,150,000, offset by assessments of only $75,000. In short, every dollar paid in assessments had returned $15.33 in dividends.

Despite stock trader uneasiness, a gold mine that makes money is compelling, and many people wanted a share in the Bodie. Even its discarded rock was of value. "A force of men are at work overhauling the old dumps of the Bodie Consolidated and sorting out the best quartz for shipment to the mill. The Indians have been making a good deal of money all summer, picking them over, and pounding up and washing out the richest pieces."[60]

THE JUPITER-OWYHEE GUNFIGHT

Given his combative personality, it is not surprising that George Daly was soon involved in another violent affair. Six months after the Mechanics Union strike, a dispute over boundary lines turned deadly.

In addition to managing the Mono Mine, Daly was superintendent and part owner of the adjacent Jupiter, a property deemed valuable because of its proximity to the Bodie Mine. When a group of men was discovered sinking a shaft on Jupiter ground, Daly ordered them off the property. The "jumpers," as Daly called them, were owners of a nearby mine called the Owyhee (a phonetic spelling of Hawaii). They had started sinking the mine shaft on high ground near the Jupiter hoisting works after striking water in their first shaft. A survey verifying Jupiter ownership was ignored by the belligerent Owyhee men. They labored nearly two more weeks while arguing and exchanging threats with the Jupiter's steadfast superintendent. On August 22, 1879, Daly approached the intruders again, this time telling them that "they could not be permitted to continue work inside the Jupiter lines."

"We'll hold this ground if we have to hold it with shotguns," the claim jumpers replied.

"If it comes to that," Daly responded, "the Jupiter Company can get shotguns also. Cartridges are cheap and men are plenty."[1]

After the Owyhee men left work that night, Daly ordered eight of his employees to arm themselves and take possession of the disputed mine shaft. They removed the windlass and filled the hole with dirt. Then they positioned a shed over the shaft and padlocked its door. Standing guard, Daly's followers were ordered to stop trespassers and have them arrested. But when the six Owyhee men saw the armed assembly on the hill, they thought their claim had been jumped, and they crept into a nearby dugout cabin to await an opportunity to take back their mine.[2]

About one o'clock the next morning, two of Daly's men happened to walk past the impromptu hideout when the Owyhee group started shooting. About "sixty or seventy shots" were fired toward the retreating men and toward their companions on the hill.

It was an old "dug out," situated about 200 feet east of the Mono shaft house, into which six of the owners of the Owyhee, armed with Winchesters, stole at 12 o'clock on the night of the 22d of August, 1879, and on the next morning done some celebrated sharp shooting at the Jupiter men; who, unaware of their concealed enemies, were standing within 63 yards.

Fired into the darkness, the volley proved inaccurate. No one was wounded or killed.

Daly's men were discussing the incident when morning light exposed their open position. A second blaze of gunfire sent bullets from the dugout, smashing through the walls of the makeshift stronghold atop the Owyhee shaft. Unable to find cover or a safe path of retreat, Daly's men hastily decided to storm the dugout and put a stop to the shooting. Firing as they advanced, the Jupiter crowd surrounded the Owyhee men, captured them, and turned them over to authorities.

A bullet fired during the assault had slammed through the dugout's door and killed the Owyhee leader, John Goff. He was a well-liked foreman and a popular member of the Miners Union.[4] Although not at the scene, Daly, who was already scorned for his anti-workingman convictions, was thought by a large portion of the community to have been responsible for Goff's death. Many felt that Daly had provoked the gunfire by ordering the armed takeover at the Owyhee shaft. "The air was filled with threats Saturday that he would be killed that night, and it was reported that a vigilance committee was forming to carry out that object."[5]

A meeting at the Miners Union hall concluded that the actions of Daly and his band of Jupiter employees were inappropriate because "the question of title should be settled by legal tribunals, and not by force." While protesting that "all

questions of this nature shall be decided legally rather than by force of arms," about 500 members of the Miners Union were joined by 500 non-members in a procession determined to take possession of the disputed ground.[6] As they surmounted the hill, the union-backed marchers fired shots into the shed at the Owyhee shaft until Daly's men fled. The crowd seized the mine then returned it to the Owyhee Company.

Later that day George Daly was arrested by the town's constabulary on charges of murder. For his own protection, he was taken to the jail in Bridgeport. Daly posted bail, then headed north to await trial in relative safety at Virginia City. A month later the county court in Bridgeport confirmed that the Owyhee shaft was on Jupiter ground, and that Daly's men had been justified in defending the company's property.

Daly's acquittal, followed by his return to Bodie, incensed the Miners Union, which abruptly adopted a resolution demanding that he and his followers leave the district. This formally reversed the leadership's earlier rule-of-law stance and incited renewed cries for vigilantism. Relentless, Daly and some 20 armed men barricaded themselves inside the Jupiter hoisting works, where they resolved to defend their rights.

Daly's written response to the union's call for his banishment was published as an open letter by local

Figure 3-5: The dugout cabin where armed Owyhee men hid on the night of August 22, 1879, then opened fire while awaiting an opportunity to take back their mine. John Goff was killed by return fire as Jupiter forces overran the hideout early the next morning. Victorious attackers are seen occupying the captured fort. (R. E. Wood stereo view. Courtesy, Society of California Pioneers, San Francisco)

newspapers. "We have been, by the laws of our country, declared innocent of any crime or wrong doing; we are American citizens, and as such are entitled to pursue our respective avocations free from molestation."[7] Daly may have been right, but the legality of his argument was lost on the wage-earning community, which overlooked the fact that the Miners Union had no authority to demand that anyone leave town.

Negotiations commenced between the Miners Union, a committee appointed on behalf of the town, and George Daly. After a ten-hour impasse an ad hoc advisory council of Bodie's leading citizens and Daly's friends intervened and persuaded Daly and his followers to surrender to injustice and withdraw from Bodie within 48 hours. To the relief of

Figure 3-6: Covered by a padlocked shed, the backfilled Owyhee shaft is guarded by Jupiter men following the battle. Despite surveys proving that the shaft was on Jupiter ground, angry Miners Union members would soon take control of the ground, then blame the Jupiter's anti-union superintendent, George Daly, for the deadly gunfight. Neither the Jupiter nor the Owyhee mine would become significant ore producers. (R. E. Wood stereo view. Courtesy, Society of California Pioneers, San Francisco)

many, an open battle and bloody reprisals were averted when the Jupiter men gathered their belongings and left for Aurora on the evening of September 23. While a crowd of silent onlookers kept watch from the sidewalk, "no attempt toward violence or insult" was made.[8]

The gunfight which killed Goff and Daly's pluck in taking up arms against the Union focused more unwelcome outside attention on the town by amplifying its violent reputation. Over the years, Bodie's newspapers followed Daly, who had inflamed so many passions.

At nearby Aurora, he and his followers found employment at the Real del Monte Mine. Then he went to Leadville, Colorado, where he was decisive in breaking a four-week strike over wages, work hours, and employee rights. The conflict had compelled the governor to declare martial law in June 1880. Daly, backed by the state militia, a 600-member committee of armed citizens, and a band of hired gunmen, reestablished mine-owner control over 6,000 striking workers.

Twenty-four months after leaving Bodie, Daly was managing a mine in New Mexico when he was killed in a tussle with Apache Indians in August 1881.[9] By then his reckless encounters in Bodie had become a source of local pride, and a newspaper commented that "the circumstances of his leaving this district were among the most exciting events in its history."[10]

The Standard and Bulwer Mines

Because most San Francisco-controlled mines had managers with reputations for stock scams, any western mining company with genuine potential strove to disassociate itself from the unsavory, depressed West Coast exchanges. A Bodie daily acknowledged: "It has become an established fact that New York is the best market in the United States for steady dividend-paying mines. New Yorkers will pay more for this class of investment than any other community."[61]

Although listed in San Francisco, the Standard Company stood above its controversial and tawdry brethren largely because of its extraordinary profits. Sixteen consecutive monthly dividends since late 1877 inspired Standard managers to seek entry into the highly regarded New York Stock Exchange. They split the company's stock in February 1879 to meet the eastern exchange's 100,000 share requirement. The Standard Gold Mining Company upgraded its name to the Standard Consolidated Mining Company and opened a Manhattan office at 26 Exchange Place.[62]

As one of the few western mining corporations listed in the East, Bodie's preeminent company was distinguished on April 10, 1879, when "Standard Con." was called for the first time in New York City. It opened at $34¾ and advanced to $35. By the end of the day, 2,000 shares had been sold. Journalists wrote enthusiastically about the Standard, ranking it as "one of the best gold mines in California" and anticipated its stock would be "very active." The Bulwer Company, having yet to mill any ore, followed suit by adopting Bulwer Consolidated Mining Company for its name and opening a New York office at 11 Pine Street.[63]

Under its fancy new name, the Bulwer Company piled ore higher and higher at the Bodie mill until water could be supplied and milling begun. On March 12, 1879 the first bar of Bulwer bullion was finally produced. Its value was $16,638, of which $15,233 was gold, the rest silver. The mill ran for three months, with a total output of $241,094. Then the mill was cleaned up so it could begin treating ore from the Bodie Mine's fabulous Fortuna lode.[64]

The discovery of the Main Standard ledge in December 1878, followed five months later by the unearthing of the Fortuna lode, excited even more interest in Bodie mining companies. Satisfying public demand, newspapers in Bodie, San Francisco, New York, Chicago, Philadelphia, and Boston now quoted Bodie stock. "The shares of all the companies have been bought right and left," noted a New York journal. "Standard has been very active, the sales amounting to 27,080 shares."[65] The Boston Daily Globe seduced investors by remarking, "Bodie district shows daily improvement, producing at the rate of $300,000 per month, the greater part of which is gold."[66]

The immense Main Standard ledge required additional milling facilities, and once again the Syndicate mill came to the rescue. After crushing Bechtel, Bodie, and the first run of Noonday ore, the Syndicate mill was put under contract by the Standard Company in May 1879. Now feeding two mills with ore hoisted through the incline shaft, the Standard Company strove to complete the main shaft. It spent the first half of 1879 finishing the hoisting works, where an air compressor that ran six pneumatic rock drills complemented the hoisting engine and boilers already in place.

Excavating commenced in June for a massive masonry foundation adjacent to the shaft's mouth that would support the heavy pumping equipment needed to extend exploration below the water at the 780-foot level. A Cornish pumping system, assembled from used parts, was shipped from Virginia City. Pumps, bobs, tanks, and other components that made up the pitwork came from the Lady Washington Mine on the Comstock. They would be installed in the shaft and powered by a big steam engine from the Comstock's Florida Mine. It was a fine engine, manufactured in the East by the best builder in the business, the Harris Corliss Engine Works. With a cylinder diameter of 20 inches and a stroke of 5 feet, it was small in comparison to other pumping engines on the Comstock, where some of the nation's largest engines were raising water more than 1,500 feet.[67] Still, it was considered adequate for the Standard. A small steam hoist dedicated to lowering the heavy iron and wooden pieces into the shaft's pumping compartment, or bringing them up for repairs, was also placed in the Standard's new works. Then two more boilers were installed to provide steam for the additional machinery.[68]

Further displaying a penchant for advanced technology, the company hired a couple of communications experts (then known as telegraphers) to install the region's first telephones. Wire for the talking devices was strung along the wooden supports that carried the aerial tramway. Voice communication between the mine and mill eliminated the arduous half-mile trek up and down the hill to deliver messages.[69]

Week after week newspapers commented on the amazing two-mill, dividend-paying Standard Mine. More people in search of work headed for Bodie, where some 60 mines were operating in mid-1879. Many employed only one or two workers, but others had payrolls ranging in size up to 100.[70] There could be no doubt: Bodie was growing, and so was its reputation as a western boomtown.

> The stage comes in daily, filled to its utmost capacity, and the departures of those who have made or lost their fortunes are as yet very small. Many idle men throng the streets. . . . Saloons and gambling hells abound. There are at least sixty saloons in the place, and not a single church. Still, the general morals are not so very bad. There has not been a man killed for a month or two. The fear, though, of such an event is always present, and when, a few evenings ago, two gentlemen, in a dispute, in a crowded saloon, merely put their hands toward their pistol pockets, the crowd made such a stampede for the street that it carried the large doors, glass and all, with it.[71]

As the denizens of Bodie's dives reached for their pistol pockets, investors across the country reached for their money pockets. The national press gave readers every reason to believe that the future was bright for anyone buying Bodie mining stocks. "It is asserted by leading New York papers that over $12,000,000 have been invested in Bodie District alone, and that the excitement there is continually on the increase."[72] While acknowledging that $12,000,000 had been poured into Bodie's mines, the publicity neglected to mention, and no one seemed to notice, that the district had only produced about $4,000,000.

One week after the citizens of Bodie celebrated Independence Day, they were rocked at about half past seven, on the evening of July 10, 1879, by a tremendous explosion on High Peak. The concussion shook the entire district, and a gigantic cloud of black smoke ascended more than a thousand feet above the hill and spread across the sky. Windows shattered downtown and people were knocked off their feet. As a hail of debris rained onto streets and clattered off rooftops, reverberations echoed into the distance, and terror-stricken townsfolk rushed to the crest of the hill where they gazed in horror at a scene of devastation. Where the Standard Company's powder magazine once stood, they saw a gaping crater 30 feet in diameter. Rubble had replaced the hoisting works at the Standard incline shaft, and a number of private dwellings nearby were destroyed, burying people in the ruins. The new hoisting works at the Standard main shaft and the works at the Bodie and Summit mines had been damaged.

Women and children cried as they searched the wreckage for loved ones. The Babcock fire brigade hitched their engine to a team of commandeered draft horses, then sped up the hill to douse the flames. Then a massive effort was organized to rescue victims. Two men were missing, two were dead, and three were dying. The Miners Union hall was turned into a makeshift hospital to care for more than 40 casualties, including a woman and her baby, both injured in the district's deadliest industrial accident.[73]

The next morning's headlines in San Francisco read: "TERRIBLE DISASTER AT BODIE. Explosion of a Powder Magazine Near the Old Standard Incline. The Shock Felt at a Distance of Twenty

Figure 3-7: A crowd of curious citizens surveys the damage after an explosion at the Standard Company's powder magazine killed seven men. The July 1879 blast also injured more than 40 people and leveled the hoisting works at the Standard incline shaft. In the foreground, scattered debris and cordwood surround the incline's hoisting machinery. At upper right, ore extraction and construction of a pumping engine foundation continue at the Standard main shaft despite broken windows. The aerial cable tramway disappears over the hill from center left, while the booming town of Bodie expands in the valley beyond. (Courtesy, California Department of Parks and Recreation)

Miles."[74] The coroner's jury reviewing the tragedy learned that about two tons of Giant, Hercules, and Vulcan high explosives stored in the magazine had inexplicably detonated. The missing men were William J. O'Brien, an employee of the Standard Company, and Charles Malloy from the Double Standard Mine. Killed were blacksmith Frank File, age 26 years, a native of Germany, and Thomas Flavin, a miner approximately 39 years of age, of Ireland. The Standard's hoisting engineer at the incline shaft, Ewen H. McMillan, 26 years old, from Canada, died that night. John McCarthy, age 36, from Ireland, died the next morning. Their funeral, conducted in the Miners Union hall, was the largest ever held in Bodie.

Flags flew at half-staff and nearly every building was draped in solemn black and white bunting as the procession of 238 miners, 302 citizens, 23 horsemen, and 12 wagons bore the caskets to the cemetery. Hugh McMillan, age 48, from Canada, clung to life for a week.[75]

The powder magazine was thought to be "as safe as any in any mining camp." It had been dug into the side of the mine's dump with its exposed sides built of stone four feet thick and banked with 10 feet of earth. The timber roof was covered by four feet of dirt, sloping to two feet. Two-inch plank doors with iron strap hinges, three-quarters of an inch thick, swung from 8 by 8-inch posts.[76]

The 4,000 pounds of dynamite in the magazine belonged to several local agents. The Hercules powder was owned by downtown merchants Gilson, Barber & Co.; the Vulcan explosives were the property of West & Bryant, also Main Street storekeepers; and the Giant powder was stored by William Irwin, superintendent of the Standard Company, who was area representative of the Giant Powder Company. As part of their duties, designated Standard Company employees distributed the dynamite to the district's mining companies and kept track of the accounts. Because no fuse or detonating caps were stored in the magazine, the cause of the calamity was at first a mystery. Slowly, eyewitness reports coalesced into the following scenario: Top carman at the Standard incline shaft, William O'Brien, was in charge of the powder magazine when Charles Malloy of the Double Standard arrived for some dynamite.

Figure 3-8

This man had also been sent for caps, and had them in his hand when he went for the powder. Both went into the magazine. The keeper was seen to come out with his box of powder, put it down, and then turn back to close the door . . . and was seen pushing heavily against it at the moment of the explosion. [Malloy was still] in the magazine when the . . . keeper attempted to close the door upon him for a joke. . . . This, the man inside, with the caps in his hand, resisted . . . and in the scuffle the caps were either set off, or were dropped, or perhaps stepped on and exploded . . . [77]

Nothing was found of either man. Oddly, miners working below on the 200-foot level felt only a slight tremble and had no idea of the ghastly mayhem above. [78]

A new gallows frame was in place over the incline shaft within a week. The machinery was repaired, and precious ore from the Bullion vein resumed its journey from the depths. Meanwhile, a new building was constructed to enclose the works. Nearby, masons at the Standard main shaft continued assembling the granite block foundation for the pumping machinery. In August the massive base was completed, the engine set in position, and the pumps, bobs, pipes, tanks, and rods placed in the shaft. [79]

In September, the west crosscut, begun in the Standard main shaft 365 feet below High Peak, reached the tunnel advancing from Bodie Canyon. The Bulwer Tunnel measured 1,860 feet from its mouth to the Standard main shaft. By eliminating

While visiting Bodie in August and September of 1979, photographer R. E. Wood set up his camera at the intersection of Main and Green streets, then captured these three downtown views. To the southwest (figure 3-8) is the Bodie House, a hotel that offered guests a bar and a reading room supplied with "all the leading papers of the day." The Miners Union hall occupies the background. The photographer then aimed his camera to the northwest (figure 3-9), where, immediately north of Boone's store on Main Street, travelers received "first-class accommodations" with "new bedding" at the Champion, Grand, and Oakland House hotels. These lodging houses also advertised dining rooms that served "the best meals at all hours," a "private waiting room for ladies," and a barber shop. An express wagon pauses in the foreground.

Figure 3-9

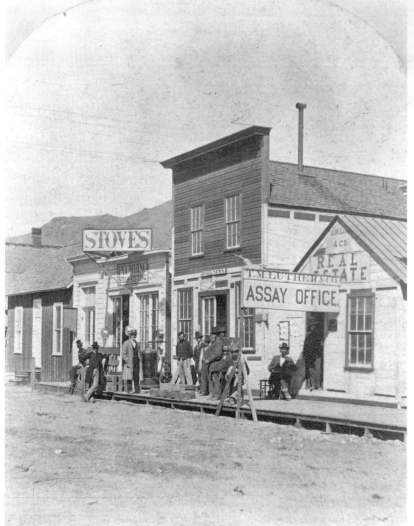

Directly across Main Street (figure 3-10) a plumbing and stove shop, the *Bodie Daily News* printing house, and an assay and real estate office are clustered immediately north of a vacant corner lot. (R. E. Wood stereo views. Courtesy, Society of California Pioneers, San Francisco)

Figure 3-10

Figure 3-11: Looking northwest on Bonanza Street in late 1879, a view captures a row of cribs where residents of Bodie's red-light district peer from doorways and windows. (R. E. Wood stereo view. Courtesy, Society of California Pioneers, San Francisco)

Figure 3-12: Midway between Green and Mill streets, a row of businesses dominate the east side of Main Street in late 1879. Depicted are the *Bodie Chronicle* newspaper office, a saddle and harness shop, West & Bryant's hardware, tin, and general merchandise store, and the Bodie Market. Bodie Bluff and High Peak appear in the distance. (R. E. Wood stereo view. Courtesy, Society of California Pioneers, San Francisco)

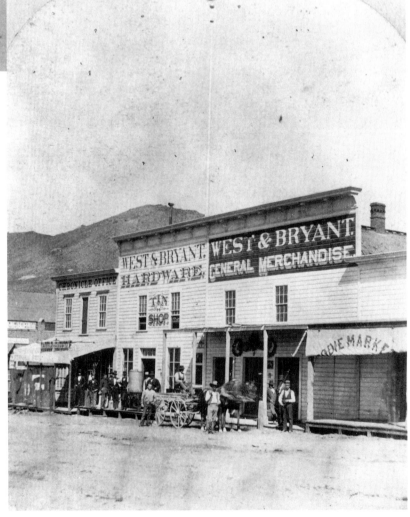

Figure 3-13: Wells, Fargo & Co.'s express office, Page, Wheaton & Co.'s general merchandise store, and Silas Smith's store are depicted near the northeast corner of Main Street and Standard Avenue in late 1879. Bodie's post office was housed in Smith's store, where "newspapers, periodicals, school books, stationary, cutlery, tobacco, and cigars" were sold until late in the year, when postal functions were relocated to a new brick building south of Green Street. The Masonic Hall occupies the building's second floor. (R. E. Wood stereo view. Courtesy, Society of California Pioneers, San Francisco)

Figure 3-14: On the northwest corner of Main and King streets, John Wagner's saloon offers imported whiskies, rum, brandy, port, sherry, champagne, California wines, and a variety of beers including Budweiser, St. Louis, Milwaukee, and Carson Lager. Wagner sold beer by the bottle, quart, gallon, or keg, either retail or wholesale. His popular establishment also featured a billiard and club room "with every convenience," and Radovich & Gillespie's Capital Chop Stand, where meals were served "day and night." (R. E. Wood stereo view. Courtesy, Gregory Bock)

Figure 3-15: A 12-mule team with two wagons pauses on Main Street in late 1879. Known as "big teams" or "jerk line teams," heavy freighting outfits like this one delivered tons of staples and machinery to the remote mining camp. The driver rode the saddled left-rear mule, and controlled the team with (mostly profane) voice commands and tugs on a single rope, or "jerk line," reaching to the left-lead mule. (R. E. Wood stereo view. Courtesy, Society of California Pioneers, San Francisco)

365 vertical feet of hoisting, it would provide an economical route for transporting ore and waste rock from the Standard Mine. The tunnel would also convey water discharged from the Standard pumps, reducing the lift by 365 feet and significantly decreasing pumping costs.

Robert Bell, who worked in the Bulwer Mine during the 1930s, described the tunnel.

The Bulwer tunnel is about seven feet wide with a single track all the way—no place for cars to pass inside. There's a gutter along the track for drainage. It was timbered for about the first 500 feet. The ground is loose there, then its all hard rock after that. It's uphill all the way from the mouth till you get to the Ralston upraise, then it's fairly flat to the Standard shaft. Loaded cars run easy coming out. Mules would take the empties back. It's pretty straight—you could see a point of light almost all the way. They drove it from both ends. The surveyors were right on line, but they were off about four or five feet on grade. They made [the tunnel] high enough to stand up in, but it's over nine feet high where they had to re-grade it. They called it the "336 level." There are two big bins at the Standard shaft and a great big station above them where they landed cars. Everything below was hoisted up to that level—anything above had to be lowered down to it.[80]

No sooner was the Bulwer Tunnel complete than the Standard and Bulwer companies began constructing a jointly-owned 30-stamp mill at its mouth. Known as the "Bulwer-Standard mill," it was strategically located at the end of the tunnel so that ore could be delivered to it directly from the Bulwer and Standard mines, and it could use wastewater pumped from the Standard shaft.[81]

The new mill was near the remains of a stone foundation that had supported one of Bodie's earliest stamp mills. In December 1865, just three months after the Empire Company completed its mill, Jack Biedeman had started the stamps on Bodie's second mill. Biedeman was one of the region's early inhabitants, and a mountain located about five miles southwest of Bodie bears his name. He was the original owner of the Homestake ledge, the predecessor of the Bulwer Mine. Satisfied by its showing, he had moved the Gregory mill from Aurora to the foot of High Peak, where it became known as the "Homestake

Figure 3-16: A plume of black smoke was drifting from the Standard mill's smokestack when visiting photographer R. E. Wood captured this late-1879 scene. The town was said to have at least 60 saloons. "Bodie is improving wonderfully," affirmed the *Bodie Morning News* in October, when the population surpassed 7,000. "Mills, hoisting works, stores and dwelling houses are going up on every hand with the greatest rapidity." Amid the building frenzy, a schoolhouse, located immediately below the mill at lower right, furnishes enlightenment to youthful scholars. (R. E. Wood stereo view. Courtesy, Society of California Pioneers, San Francisco)

Figure 3-17: From the hill above Bodie, a scene looking northward toward High Peak in late 1879 shows Bodie's principal mines at the height of the boom. At lower center, the hoisting works at the Mono Mine. Immediately beyond, the Bodie Mine's ore house nearly conceals the Bodie's hoisting works. The Standard's hoisting works, at upper right, is silhouetted on the crest of the hill. (R. E. Wood stereo view. Courtesy, Gregory Bock)

mill." Its 12 stamps, 4 pans, and 3 separators were powered by a 30-horsepower steam engine. By early 1868, like most mills in the region, it was idle, and ownership had reverted to the bank. While in office, Nevada Governor Henry Blasdel purchased the mine and mill in June of that year. Some time later, the governor moved the mill to Rockland, a small district 40 miles north of Aurora. During the early years of Bodie's mining boom, remnants of the Homestake mill's foundation were visible near the mouth of the Bulwer Tunnel, where they were a historical curiosity to passers-by.[82]

Everything appeared ready in October to start the pumps at the Standard main shaft and begin removing water that had interrupted its downward progress. Pumps and pipes were in the shaft; engine and boilers stood ready above. As Bell mentioned, there was a problem. Because of a surveyor's error, 400 feet of the Bulwer Tunnel had to be regraded so that wooden gutters, known as "boxes" (as in sluice boxes), could be buried at the correct pitch to carry water away from the main shaft. Once the grade was corrected, a track made of 4 by 4-inch wooden rails and 8 by 8-inch ties was installed to convey mine cars. The work required a full month. On November 24, 1879, the Standard pumping engine was started, and water drawn from the bowels of the earth rushed through the tunnel. By December the pumps had drained the shaft, and

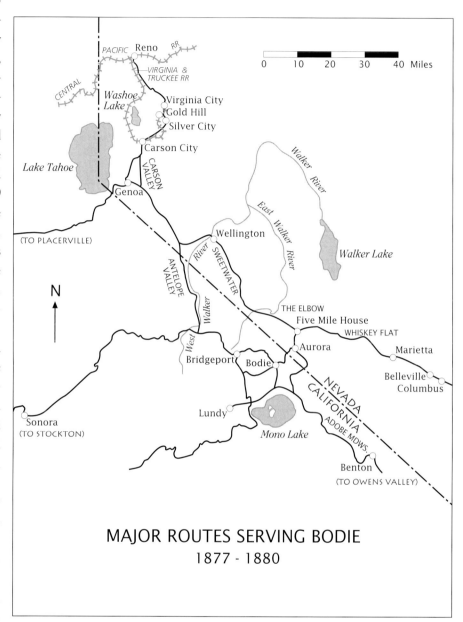

MAJOR ROUTES SERVING BODIE
1877 - 1880

Map 5: During its boom years, Bodie's main source of supplies was the railroad at Carson City, reached via Aurora, Wellington, and Sweetwater. A shorter road through Antelope Valley and Bridgeport was opened in 1879, but its usefulness was limited by winter snows. Also seasonal, the scenic road over Sonora Pass remained popular among stageline passengers seeking the most direct route to San Francisco. Freight wagons hauling fresh produce from central California's agricultural regions used this route. All roads into Bodie were toll roads, a constant annoyance to its citizens. "Within hearing of the Standard whistle there are toll houses in every direction, . . ." complained the *Daily Free Press* in May 1880. That same month, the *Daily Bodie Standard* observed that "the only public thoroughfare near Bodie is Main street, and not one dollar of road tax is being expended upon that almost impassable sea of mud."

crosscutting recommenced on the 700-foot level to pierce the great lode.[83]

During 1879, the Standard Consolidated Mining Company had produced $1,448,845 and re-established its mine's primacy as Bodie's most productive property by shipping more than half the district's total bullion. Dividends had been declared each month, though they were adjusted from $1 to 50 cents per share in February, when the number of shares were doubled during the corporate reorganization. The Standard's hoisting works over the main shaft had been equipped with an impressive Cornish pumping system, the district's second of this type, and the works at the incline shaft, destroyed by the explosion, had been replaced.[84] At the tunnel's mouth, the 30-stamp Bulwer-Standard mill was nearly complete.

Bulwer Consolidated Mining Company production remained stuck at $241,094, the output of its one run of ore at the Bodie mill during the second quarter of the year.[85] This placed the Bulwer Company third behind the Standard and Bodie in yield, a circumstance that the Bulwer-Standard mill would remedy forthwith. The company had incurred expenses while driving the Bulwer Tunnel and financing half of the new mill, but no assessments had to be levied. Buoyed by spirited reporting, anxious stockholders were dismayed that the Bulwer concluded its third year without dividends.

Bodie boasted that its mining district had paid more in dividends than it levied in assessments, a claim owing largely to the continuing stream of dividends from the Standard.[86] Despite many plaudits, usually generated by the local press, some writers urged caution and reminded overeager investors that "everything is not gold that glitters." The leading New York mining journal rebuffed Bodie in early autumn. "Our readers will do well to discriminate between the mines and the prospects, and not be induced to purchase every cheap stock offered from this district, under the belief that bonanzas are to be discovered." Further discretion was counseled a week later. "We wish to warn our readers that there are but very few mines in that district that have present value, and a very large number that have not even a prospective value."[87] Time would show the wisdom of this advice.

---

1. *Daily Bodie Standard* 30 January 1879.

2. *Daily Bodie Standard* 11 February 1879.

3. *Weekly Bodie Standard* 18 January 1879; 8 February 1879; 15 February 1879.

4. *Weekly Bodie Standard* 15 March 1879.

5. *Bodie Morning News* 20 April 1879; 27 April 1879; 25 May 1879; *Engineering and Mining Journal* 14 June 1879, 440; *Mining Record* 17 May 1879, 411.

6. *Mining Record* 17 May 1879, 411; *Bodie Morning News* 25 May 1879.

7. *Engineering and Mining Journal* 14 June 1879, 440; *Bodie Morning News* 18 June 1879; *Mining Record* 21 June 1879, 527; *Daily Bodie Standard* 3 July 1879.

8. *Engineering and Mining Journal* 28 June 1879, 478; *Mining Report* 5 July 1879, 9; *Bodie Morning News* 26 July 1879; 13 August 1879.

9. *Bodie Morning News* 26 July 1879; 3 August 1879; 30 October 1879; *Mining and Scientific Press* 27 September 1879, 197. By this time the Keystone ledge was commonly known as Ledge No. 1, the Noonday as Ledge No. 2.

10. *Bodie Morning News* 30 October 1879.

11. *Bodie Morning News* 29 October 1879.

12. *Bodie Morning News* 29 October 1879.

13. *Engineering and Mining Journal* 16 August 1879, 113; Roger D. McGrath, *Gunfighters, Highwaymen, and Vigilantes: Violence on the Frontier* (Berkeley, CA: University of California Press, 1984), 109; Michael H. Piatt, "Hauling Freight Into the 20th Century by Jerk Line," *Journal of the West* 36, no. 1 (January 1997): 82-91.

14. *Daily Bodie Standard* 4 August 1879.

15. *Mining Record* 1 November 1879, 351; *Daily Free Press* 8 November 1879; 15 November 1879; *Bodie Morning News* 9 November 1879; 23 November 1879; *Bodie Chronicle* 22 November 1879.

16. *Bodie Morning News* 18 June 1879.

17. *Daily Bodie Standard* 26 December 1879 in Loose, *Bodie Bonanza*, 114; *Daily Free Press* 26 December 1879.

18. *Gold Hill Daily News* 25 October 1877.

19. *Bodie Morning News* 1 June 1879.

20. *Mining Record* 17 January 1880, 53; *Engineering and Mining Journal* 31 January 1880, 86.

Five-stamp battery

21. *Engineering and Mining Journal* 6 September 1879, 160-162.

22. *Mining Record* 15 February 1879, 112.

23. *Daily Bodie Standard* 6 February 1879; *Weekly Bodie Standard* 8 February 1879.

24. *Daily Free Press* 13 December 1879.

25. Eliot Lord, *Comstock Mining and Miners* (1883; reprint, San Diego, CA: Howell-North Books, 1980), 404.

26. *Bodie Morning News* 4 October 1879.

27. *Bodie Morning News* 4 October 1879; 5 October 1879; 9 October 1879; 10 October 1879; 12 October 1879; *Daily Free Press* 10 November 1879.

28. Dan De Quille [William Wright], *The Big Bonanza* (1876; reprint, Las Vegas, NV: Nevada Publications, 1982), 227-230.

29. *Daily Free Press* 28 May 1881.

30. Herbert L. Smith, *The Bodie Era: The Chronicles of the Last of the Old Time Mining Camps* (TMs [photocopy] 1934), 64-65.

31. *Mono Alpine Chronicle* 8 March 1879; *Bodie Morning News* 22 March 1879; California State Mining Bureau, *Eighth Annual Report of the State Mineralogist, for the Year Ending October 1, 1888* (Sacramento, CA: Superintendent of State Printing, 1888), 390; *Engineering and Mining Journal* 26 April 1879, 306.

32. *Engineering and Mining Journal* 24 May 1879, 379; 31 May 1879, 400.

33. *Engineering and Mining Journal* 31 May 1879, 398.

34. California, *Eighth Annual Report*, 390; Mono County, *Mine Locations*, Book G, 28-29; American Institute of Mining Engineers, *Transactions of the American Institute of Mining Engineers* 38 (1908), 343-357; *Engineering and Mining Journal* 6 September 1879, 160-162; *Mining Record* 26 March 1881, 296.

35. *Bodie Morning News* 12 June 1879.

36. Robert T. Bell, interview by author, 27-30 August 1994, Nevada.

37. *Bodie Morning News* 21 June 1879.

38. *Daily Bodie Standard* 12 April 1880.

39. *Weekly Bodie Standard* 22 February 1879; 8 March 1879; *Mining Record* 15 March 1879, 208; 16 August 1879, 131.

40. *Bodie Morning News* 10 June 1879; *Daily Bodie Standard* 15 April 1880; *Engineering and Mining Journal* 19 February 1881, 131. Disruptions in ore freighting nearly made bullion production a seasonal proposition for mines without mills of their own. Nearly every mining company in Bodie successful enough to build its own mill, located it close to the mine's entrance to eliminate transportation costs. The Bodie and Standard companies were the exceptions. While the Bodie Company relied on wagons for freighting its ore, the Standard minimized transportation costs by building an aerial cable tramway between its mine and mill.

41. *Engineering and Mining Journal* 19 July 1879, 40.

42. *Mining and Scientific Press* 5 July 1879, 5.

43. *Bodie Morning News* 5 August 1879.

44. *Bodie Morning News* 22 August 1879.

45. *Bodie Morning News* 21 October 1879.

46. McGrath, *Gunfighters*, 186, 196, 199, 209, 213, 255.

47. *Bodie Morning News* 14 October 1879.

48. *Bodie Weekly Standard* 25 December 1878.

49. For a more detailed discussion of Bodie's experience with violence, see McGrath, *Gunfighters*, 102-246.

50. *Bodie Morning News* 1 June 1879. Although Bodie, Tombstone, Deadwood, and Dodge City boomed simultaneously and were known for violence, Bodie is less remembered than the others largely because it never produced fabled lawmen, outlaws, or cowboys necessary to preserve its place in western folklore. One of its few characters of notoriety was Madame Moustache, a professional card dealer from Virginia City and Deadwood who committed suicide at Bodie in 1879. For a reprint of Madame Moustache's September 8, 1879 obituary from the *Daily Bodie Standard*, see Loose, *Bodie Bonanza*, 226-227.

51. *Daily Bodie Standard* 20 January 1879; 24 June 1879;

Engineering and Mining Journal 25 January 1879, 62; 5 July 1879, 7; *Mining and Scientific Press* 22 March 1879, 181.

52. *Engineering and Mining Journal* 30 August 1879, 148; *Bodie Morning News* 9 September 1879; *Daily Bodie Standard* 1 July 1879; 8 October 1879; 18 November 1879; *Mining Record* 30 August 1879, 170; 11 October 1879, 290; *Bodie Chronicle* 22 November 1879.

53. *Daily Bodie Standard* 24 June 1879; *Engineering and Mining Journal* 20 September 1879, 203.

54. *Daily Bodie Standard* 20 February 1879; *Daily Alta California* 16 June 1879; *Bodie Morning News* 2 November 1879.

55. *Mining and Scientific Press* 20 December 1879, 389.

56. *Bodie Weekly Standard* 31 July 1878.

57. *Daily Bodie Standard* 8 September 1879.

58. *Engineering and Mining Journal* 27 September 1879, 232.

59. *Engineering and Mining Journal* 27 September 1879, 232.

60. *Bodie Morning News* 19 December 1879.

61. *Daily Bodie Standard* 7 October 1879.

62. Mono County, *Mining Deeds*, Book N, 593-597; *Daily Bodie Standard* 4 February 1879; *Weekly Bodie Standard* 22 February 1879. During the Standard Company's first 16 months of existence its shares were highly desired but rarely traded. Owned by a few individuals, the stock was reported as "closely held."

63. *Daily Bodie Standard* 15 February 1879; *Engineering and Mining Journal* 12 April 1879, 269; 10 March 1888, 192; *Mining Record* 26 April 1879, 338.

64. *Weekly Bodie Standard* 15 March 1879; 22 February 1879; 8 March 1879; *Mining Record* 5 June 1879, 9; 28 June 1879, 554.

65. *Engineering and Mining Journal* 31 May 1879, 398.

66. *Boston Daily Globe* 8 July 1879.

67. After the Sutro Tunnel was driven into the Comstock Lode in June 1879, water pumped from the mines was discharged through the tunnel, some 1,400 feet below the surface. (Lord, *Comstock Mining and Miners*, 343-346.)

68. *Bodie Morning News* 25 April 1879; *Mining and Scientific Press* 10 May 1879, 301; *Daily Bodie Standard* 30 June 1879.

69. *Daily Bodie Standard* 4 February 1879; 8 February 1879.

70. *Bodie Morning News* 8 June 1879.

71. *Daily Alta California* 16 June 1879. Men of all occupations went about armed in boomtown Bodie, but, contrary to Hollywood's popular western convention, few used holsters. An examination of newspaper articles describing shootings and shoot-outs reveals that sidearms were usually carried in coat or hip pockets. Reporters rarely distinguished a gun by model, usually referring to it simply as a "six-shooter," "re-volver," or "pistol." When identified, handguns were most often the Colt Lightning, or self-cocker; the British Bulldog, a short-barreled double-action revolver produced by several makers; and the Colt Navy. Testimony given in 1881 reveals that the firearm used by Joseph DeRoche to kill Thomas Treloar, in Bodie's most publicized murder, was a five-shot, .38 caliber, double-action revolver by Forehand & Wadsworth, a Massachusetts manufacturer that produced small revolvers for the civilian market, including British Bulldogs. "Seven shots in 5 seconds" proclaimed an 1880s Forehand & Wadsworth advertisement for its seven-shot .32 caliber British Bulldog, a popular design that was also available in six-shot .38 caliber and five-shot .44 caliber for $3.12. Shoulder arms most frequently recorded were shotguns and Henry or Winchester rifles. Also see McGrath, *Gunfighters*, 141, 185, 198-199, 213, 259.

72. *Bodie Morning News* 6 July 1879.

73. Russ and Anne Johnson, *The Ghost Town of Bodie As Reported in the Newspapers of the Day* (Bishop, CA: Chalfant Press, 1967), 63-64; Smith, *The Bodie Era*, 69.

74. *Daily Alta California* 11 July 1879.

75. Johnson, *The Ghost Town of Bodie*, 63-64; *Daily Bodie Standard* 12 July 1879; 16 July 1879.

76. *Bodie Morning News* 13 July 1879.

77. *Daily Alta California* 21 July 1879.

78. *Daily Bodie Standard* 14 July 1879; 16 July 1879; *Bodie Morning News* 17 July 1879.

79. *Mining Record* 30 August 1879, 170; *Mining and Scientific Press* 20 September 1879, 181.

80. Robert T. Bell, telephone interview by author, 2 August 1997.

81. *Engineering and Mining Journal* 6 September 1879, 167; 27 September 1879, 227.

82. *Mining and Scientific Press* 6 January 1866, 6; 7 April 1866, 214; *Esmeralda Union* 4 July 1868; Joseph Wasson, *Bodie and Esmeralda* (San Francisco, CA: Spaulding, Barto & Co., 1878), 9, 35; Mono County, *Mining Deeds*, Book V, 310-315. The precise location of the Homestake mill at Bodie remains unknown. Indications are that it was at the north end of town near the Bulwer Tunnel. It is also not known how long the governor used the mill in Bodie, nor the date it was dismantled.

83. *Mining Record* 11 October 1879, 290; *Daily Bodie Standard* 24 October 1879; *Daily Free Press* 8 November 1879; 1 December 1879; *Bodie Morning News* 13 November 1879; *Engineering and Mining Journal* 6 September 1879, 167.

84. The district's first Cornish pumping system was installed at the south end's Booker Mine in July 1879.

85. California, *Eighth Annual Report*, 396.

86. *Daily Bodie Standard* 6 August 1879.

87. *Engineering and Mining Journal* 20 September 1879, 214; 27 September 1879, 232.

Reminiscences of George Montrose

1. *Chronicle-Union* 21 December 1921; 28 December 1921; 11 January 1922

The Mechanics Union Strike

1. *Daily Bodie Standard* 12 February 1879; *Weekly Bodie Standard* 15 February 1879; McGrath, *Gunfighters*, 225-229.

2. *Daily Bodie Standard* 13 February 1879; 17 February 1879.

3. *Daily Bodie Standard* 13 February 1879; 14 February 1879.

4. *Weekly Bodie Standard* 15 February 1879.

5. *Weekly Bodie Standard* 15 February 1879.

6. *Weekly Bodie Standard* 15 February 1879.

7. *Daily Bodie Standard* 15 February 1878; *Weekly Bodie Standard* 15 February 1879.

8. For more information about George Daly and Bodie's Mechanics Union strike, see Roger D. McGrath, *Gunfighters, Highwaymen, and Vigilantes: Violence on the Frontier* (Berkeley, CA: University of California Press, 1984) and Richard E. Lingenfelter, *The Hardrock Miners: A History of the Mining Labor Movement in the American West, 1863-1893* (Berkeley, CA: University of California Press, 1974).

The Jupiter-Owyhee Gunfight

1. *Daily Bodie Standard* 29 August 1879; McGrath, *Gunfighters*, 229-234.

2. *Bodie Morning News* 24 August 1879; 9 September 1879; *Daily Bodie Standard* 20 September 1879; 10 October 1879.

3. *Weekly Standard-News* 13 April 1881.

4. *Bodie Morning News* 24 August 1879; 9 September 1879; *Daily Bodie Standard* 10 October 1879.

5. *Daily Bodie Standard* 25 August 1879.

6. *Daily Bodie Standard* 29 August 1879.

7. *Daily Bodie Standard* 22 September 1879; *Bodie Morning News* 23 September 1879.

8. *Bodie Morning News* 24 September 1879.

9. *Weekly Standard-News* 13 April 1881; 24 August 1881; *Bodie Standard-News* 31 August 1881; *Daily Free Press* 23 August 1881; 9 September 1881; 8 October 1881; Lingenfelter, *The Hardrock Miners*, 144-156.

10. *Daily Free Press* 23 August 1881. For more information on George Daly and his fiery adventures in Bodie, see Richard E. Lingenfelter, *The Hardrock Miners: A History of the Mining Labor Movement in the American West, 1863-1893* (Berkeley, CA: University of California Press, 1974), 137-140 and Roger D. McGrath, *Gunfighters, Highwaymen, and Vigilantes: Violence on the Frontier* (Berkeley, CA: University of California Press, 1984). Though McGrath includes Daly's clashes during the Mechanics Union strike and the Jupiter-Owyhee gunfight in his chapter on vigilantism (225-234), no committee of vigilance took part. In both cases, the actions perceived as mob violence were organized proceedings formalized by unions. McGrath omits a May 26, 1881, incident of mob action when about 40 white men traveled from Bodie to Mono Basin intent on driving away Chinese workers employed in building the railroad. Bloodshed was averted when the "Celestials" were spirited away aboard the steamer *Rocket* and its lumber barges to Paoha Island in Mono Lake. The unruly crowd, having brought little in the way of provisions, returned to Bodie. The Chinese resumed their work unharmed. See David F. Myrick, "The Bodie & Benton Railway," *Railroads of Nevada and Eastern California, Vol. 1* (Berkeley, CA: Howell-North Books, 1962), 307-308.

Figure 4-1: Viewed from nearly the same position as figure 3-7 (page 87), a sketch made in about 1880 shows the rebuilt hoisting works at the Standard incline shaft and the works at the Standard main shaft. From the two ore houses at lower left, one at the end of each dump, ore was loaded into iron buckets traveling along the aerial cable tramway. The tramway served both shafts on its descent to the Standard mill. ("Standard Old and New Hoisting Works." Courtesy, California Historical Society, San Francisco)

CHAPTER FOUR

"THE GREATEST GOLD MINE THE WORLD HAS EVER SEEN" 1880

The mining outlook is as cheerful as the most enthusiastic stock sharp could desire, each day adds some new and valuable contribution to the future of the camp in the way of new discoveries of large and valuable paying bodies of ore.
    —Bodie Chronicle, *March 8, 1880*

There are disappointments in every mining camp. Bodie is no exception to the general rule. Good mines have been found where they were not supposed to exist. Good prospects have proved fickle.
    —Daily Stock Report (San Francisco), *August 5, 1880*

There have been too many people there for the amount of work doing in its mines—for the number of miners employed; it has had too many saloons and gambling houses—and many of these of the lowest stamp to lead the unwary to ruin. Twenty well and respectably conducted saloons would have been all that was required to make the average Bodieite happy and content, instead of having in the neighborhood of one hundred of all kinds and descriptions.
    —Bridgeport Union *in* Bodie Chronicle, *August 21, 1880*

The Standard and Bulwer Mines

At long last, Bodie's need for more stamp mills was met. Three new mills, completed in the winter of 1879-1880, more than doubled the town's ore handling capacity. In late December 1879, the 30-stamp Noonday became the first mill built in more than a year, joining the four already in operation. It was followed in February 1880 by the 30-stamp Bulwer-Standard mill and the 10-stamp Spaulding mill in the south end.

    The Standard and Bulwer's new mill, like the Noonday, was divided into halves, allowing each company to run its 15 stamps independently of the other. The steam engine, manufactured in San Francisco by Prescott, Scott & Co., was said to move as "noiselessly as a cat." It powered 24 Washoe pans, 8 settlers, and 2 agitators fed by the stamps, which dropped on ore contained in iron mortars cast locally at the Bodie Foundry.[1] The Bulwer-Standard mill also displayed a degree of opulence befitting its predicted status as a producer of great wealth. In a district where industrial buildings were usually painted with locally-mined brown ochre, the Bulwer-Standard mill was coated with real red paint. One observer commented, "This mill is a model worth looking at, the interior is kept so clean and free from dirt of any kind, that one would not soil the finest fabric while passing through, and inspecting it."[2]

Overwhelmed by an abundance of ore from the upper levels, the two companies had been desperate for increased milling capacity. The Standard's ore bodies delivered more than the 40 stamps in the Standard and Syndicate mills could handle, and the Bulwer Company had been unable to mill any ore since June 1879, when its one contract with the Bodie

mill expired. After seven long months without a mill run, Bulwer stockholders were rewarded in the first week of February, when the company's 15 stamps began dropping on backlogged Bulwer ore. Calculating that ore shipments would lead to bullion, Bulwer investors expected handsome dividend checks.

The district's 70 new stamps meant that more mines would finally see their ore treated. Once again, however, a long winter punctuated by snow storms frequently halted the heavy ore wagons, and many mines had closed until roads were cleared. Others stockpiled their best rock, meeting payrolls by levying assessments. Attempting to soothe despondent investors, one local scrivener advised, "A good many holding stock are prone to growl at the assessments that are being levied, and feel discouraged, but the cunning ones keep cool and are full of hope as to the

Figure 4-2: Two overcrowded stagecoaches, one drawn by six horses, the other pulled by four, pause in front of the Grand Central Hotel, a few doors north of Wagner's saloon on lower Main Street. The U.S. Stage Company's office occupied ground-floor space in the hotel, where Mrs. M. E. Chesnut, shown standing on the balcony, prepared meals for guests "in a first-class manner," and kept the lodging rooms "clean and neatly furnished." (Courtesy, California History Room, California State Library, Sacramento, California)

THE BODIE FOUNDRY

A local foundry served Bodie's mines and mills. Cast-iron parts were produced by pouring molten iron into molds and machining the castings to size. The Bodie Foundry made objects of its own design as well as replacement parts that rivaled those made by distant manufacturers. Located south of town, the Bodie Foundry employed about 12 men. When it opened for business in September 1879, it was visited by a journalist. His observations were recorded by the *Bodie Morning News*.

Our reporter visited the new Bodie Foundry, yesterday, and found this latest and much needed improvement and industry nearly completed. In fact they have already commenced work in earnest, having just completed a melt and cast some very credible pieces of work, amongst which we found a sheave for the Standard mill engine. The foundry is conveniently arranged for doing all kinds of work.

The moulding shop is 40 feet square, fitted up with a fine, thirty inch cupola, having a capacity of six tons per hour, with all the latest improvements. The crane is a fine piece of work, with perfect gearing, set in a most substantial manner and capable of handling ten tons with ease. The building is well lighted, strong and substantial and could not be better arranged for a moulding shop.

The machine shop is 26 x 40 feet, the boiler and engine room 16 x 20, the blacksmith shop 16 x 25 and all connected together under one roof. The boiler is 44 inches in diameter by 16 feet in length, set in solid masonry, with

Figure 4-3: South of town, the Bodie Foundry cast products in iron and brass to meet Bodie's mining and milling needs. Buildings on Silver Hill in the background belong to the Noonday Company. (Detail, *Map of the Bodie Mining District.* Courtesy, Geography and Map Division, Library of Congress)

every protection available for fire. The engine runs like clockwork, is of 20-horse power and amply sufficient for all purposes of the foundry. The machine shop is fitted up with one of the finest iron lathes on the coast, Putnam's best make, and of 36 inch swing. This lathe is a splendid piece of machinery, and for heavy work just what is wanted in Bodie. There is also a small lathe for light work—perfect in all its parts. The drill machine is one of Putnam's latest improved, and so arranged as to drill at any angle and any size hole required. This is a heavy, massive piece of machinery, and does its work to perfection. The line and counter shafts are fitted up with patent hangers, and all the machinery

works smoothly without the slightest jar.

The pattern shop is on the second floor. It is 26 x 40 feet, and when the buzz and jig saws are set up will be as well arranged for pattern making as any foundry on the coast.[1]

Bodie's foundry produced "cams, tappets, shoes, dies, pans, settlers, and everything pertaining to milling and mining machinery."[2] The original facility was destroyed by fire in December 1881. Rebuilt the following spring, it served Bodie's industry until October 1903, when another blaze reduced it to ashes.[3]

general result."[3] At the same time, a few companies, like the Standard, Bulwer, and Noonday, with mines and mills connected by aerial tramway, tunnel, or trestle, maintained steady ore shipments.

In town, too many men and too few paychecks created chronic indebtedness during the wintry months of early 1880. "Last Night Was Unusually Quiet and the Town Turned In at 2 A.M." headlined a satirical commentary about the depressed economy.

> After dark the long stretch of Main Street does not present any great amount of life and business. The shops begin to close up at nine, and the man of family hurriedly seeks the joyful retreat of his home. . . . Lights in the saloons were put out early and dance houses closed down at eleven o'clock.[4]

The author observed that if it were not for the cheerful manner in which several all-night saloons were lit, Bodie's main thoroughfare would have resembled a dingy, big-city side street.

Winter weather might slow ore shipments and cast despondency over luckless job seekers, but it in no way impeded the stampede of new arrivals.

> There is a steady immigration of men here in search of employment. At the present time there are more men here than can find anything to do. This will be the situation until spring, as no more men will be set at work this winter than are now employed. Applications for work at the new Standard-Bulwer mill are so numerous that the superintendent is actually annoyed. Those who are here and have friends anxious to come should advise them to stay away until spring, when the field for work and prospecting will be large and fruitful.[5]

Despite the woes in town, progress in the Standard Mine continued without interruption. Pumps drained the 780-foot main shaft, and work commenced in January 1880 to drive it deeper. The opening of the Bulwer-Standard mill in February permitted ore extraction to accelerate, and the Standard's uppermost levels fed 55 stamps in the Standard, Syndicate, and Bulwer-Standard mills. These developments prompted the company to increase its monthly dividend from 50 to 75 cents per share in March. Such impressive manifestations of mineralogical affluence earned the Standard's ore formation accolades that were read from one coast to the other. "The most notable feature of the mine is the length of the main vein, which, on the 450-foot level, is exposed for a distance of nearly 1,000 feet. This is, I am told, one of the longest gold veins of which there is any record."[6]

Far below this lofty rhetoric, miners drove a crosscut eastward to explore the Standard's 700-foot level. Approximately 313 feet from the main shaft and directly beneath the expanding ore-delivering stopes, they pierced a quartz seam containing "broken vein matter."[7] Stockholders were confident that this was the Main Standard, extending from the stopes above, and that more great riches would be exposed as the main shaft descended. Believers gave the old Veta Madre theory new life. A solid core of rich ore at Bodie became the topic of discussion in smoke-filled saloons and private clubs from San Francisco to New York City. Self-styled authorities and smug investors figured that the source of Bodie's ledges lay somewhere between the 1,000- and 1,200-foot levels. After all, they reasoned, since the Big Bonanza on the Comstock was encountered 1,200 feet below the surface, the same would hold true for Bodie.[8]

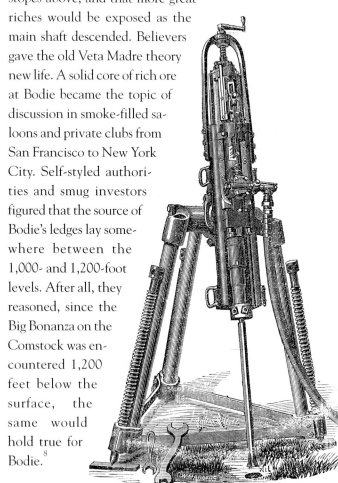

As Bodie grew, it gained refinement. Whiskey remained the most common thirst quencher, but saloons offered more in the way of liquid refreshment than distilled rotgut. The sophisticated could cultivate a taste for imported beers, California wines, choice cigars, cocktails (Tom and Jerries and hot scotches were advertised most), port, sherry, and a variety of liquors, such as brandy, rum, and scotch. Still, Bodie's preferred brand of whiskey became the brunt of many outside jokes. One Gold Hill, Nevada yarn professed that in less than 10 minutes after a woman rubbed some on her scalp to relieve a headache, her head was as bare and smooth as a billiard ball.[9] A San Francisco tale told of a visiting Bodieite who was served a mixture of alcohol, turpentine, Perry Davis patent painkiller, Jamaica ginger, and pepper sauce. After drinking the potion he exclaimed to the bartender:

> Young man, that's whiskey. I ain't tasted nothin' like it since I left Bodie two weeks ago today. That's real genuine licker, kinder a cross 'tween a circular saw and a wildcat, that takes holt quick, en hols on long. Jus' you go to Bodie and open a saloon. And with that whiskey you might charge four bits a glass for it and the boys 'ud never kick.[10]

Although Bodie's favored libations suffered abuse from distant comics, its drinking establishments were similar to those found in neighborhoods throughout the country. An important and accepted part of nineteenth-century society, the saloon provided a comfortable place for men to gather. In mining camps populated mostly by single men, saloons were also places to escape the solitude of lonely cabins and rented rooms. Men desiring refreshment and camaraderie in Bodie could choose from the Union, Comstock, Parlor, Cabinet, New Magnolia, Occidental, Oriental, Carson, Gold Brick, Dividend, Bank Exchange, Parole, Mammoth, Senate, Rosedale, and Wagner's. In addition to a congenial atmosphere for drinking and socializing, many Bodie saloons contained a food concession called a "chop stand," serving full meals (in many styles, including French) day and night. John Wagner's popular establishment, which fronted Main Street at the intersection of King, occupied a room about 30 feet wide, 100 feet long, and 15 feet high. To the left of the entrance stood an ornately carved bar extending along the wall. On the opposite wall, a long counter served as a chop stand.[11]

Bodie's saloons often offered other services as well. Most advertised "club rooms," where gentlemen could "discuss business or conduct private meetings." Some staged nightly music. One saloon catered to the erudite with a reading room, another featured a bowling alley, while a third equipped as a gymnasium accommodated evenings of sparring and wrestling. Barrooms often adjoined hotel lobbies, and two Bodie breweries had saloons where "wines, liquors, and cigars" complemented the home brew.

Gambling was next in popularity to drinking. "Nearly everybody drank, nearly everybody gambled," recalled Grant Smith.[12] Billiard tables were ubiquitous in Bodie's saloons, and games of chance, while illegal, took place openly. At many establishments, such as Wagner's saloon, "the rear of the room was literally filled with gambling-tables of one kind and another, principally faro-banks, presided over by silent, watchful dealers, with hundreds, or even thousands, of dollars in gold and silver stacked up in front of them, and a gun always within reach."[13]

Dealing faro, the West's most popular card game, was considered a respectable occupation. Smith remembered that professional gamblers in mining camps were:

> Well-dressed, quiet, gentlemanly men who conducted faro-banks, which required considerable capital. They prided themselves on dealing "a square-game," and were patronized accordingly. The profit was in the percentage. Some of these men came of good families in the East and South, more particularly "The South." Not infrequently, they were married and had children.[14]

Although Bodie was a raw, young town in 1880, it displayed attributes of established communities. Its fraternal organizations provided social diversions and engendered a sense of belonging. The Order of Knights of Pythias, Ancient Order of Free and Accepted Masons, Triennial Conclave of Knights of Templar, International Order of Odd Fellows, and the Society of Pacific Coast Pioneers offered fellowship and professed philanthropic goals. Other groups advanced more tangible charitable aims. The Ladies Relief Society and Ladies Benevolent Society provided for the poor and disabled, and the Ancient Order of United Workmen ensured disability and death benefits. There were also baseball clubs that competed on a Booker Flat diamond, a rifle club that held shooting matches at a 500-yard target range near the Red Cloud Mine, veterans of the Union and Confederacy, and the Bodie Guards, a uniformed unit of the state militia that existed primarily for camaraderie and military pageantry, and never fired a shot in battle.

Less warlike heroes could join one of the firefighting companies. When they were not battling flames, the volunteers took pleasure from donning colorful uniforms, mustering, and marching in parades. The Republican Club and the Democrats of Bodie provided forums for those interested in arguing politics. Another group, the Land League of Ireland, was established in December 1880 to give financial aid toward liberating Ireland from English occupation.[15] These organizations raised money by hosting suppers, dances, concerts, and theatrical performances, usually in the rented Miners Union hall, Odd Fellows hall, Babcock engine house, or the Masonic hall—venues where Protestant, Catholic, and Jewish worship services were also held.

There were less formal types of entertainment as well. In dance halls, often called "hurdy-gurdies," rough-hewn miners with romantic inclinations could purchase dances with engaging females. The delights of the red-light district on Bonanza Street, also known as "Maiden Lane" or "Virgin Alley," were offered in cribs and brothels conveniently located behind a concentration of lower Main Street saloons. In the Chinese district on King Street, seedy opium dens promised dim relaxation to fiends and less addicted

smokers of the drug.[16]

But these were momentary diversions. Virtually all of Bodie's citizens avidly followed developments in the mines and speculated in mining stock. None of them could glance upon the district's hills or read newspaper reports without being impressed by the improvements. "Our companies no longer scratch upon and near the surface," remarked one devotee, but "are following the seams and stratas of rich ore to such depths as will give assurance of finding heavy bodies of pay ore. Today we have 31 steam hoisting works so actively engaged in this commendable work. . . . [Investors] have full and unlimited confidence in the mining outlook and the solid merit of our mines."[17]

When spring weather came in late May, mines reopened and the economy improved. The discovery of rich ore on the 600-foot level of the Goodshaw Mine in June 1880 elicited more "expert" opinions. Pontificating nabobs felt certain that the ledges on Bodie Bluff reached to the south end. This showing in the saddle bridging High Peak and Silver Hill was seen as the "missing link," proving that Bodie's ledges sprang from one continuous lode. The connection was considered crucial to the fate of the south end, where the Noonday companies were investing a fortune, gambling that the ore there would be as rich as that in the Standard and Bodie mines.[18] The town was in its finest hour, but the enthusiasm would not last much longer.

In August, the Bulwer completed a six-month run of ore in its new mill, producing $117,498. Two mill runs since early 1878 had yielded more than $350,000 in bullion, and Bulwer stockholders figured it was time for them to receive some dividends. When none came forth, they wondered where the profits had gone. It appeared strange that there was enough money to build the Bulwer-Standard mill and drive the Bulwer Tunnel, but nothing for stockholders. Concerns were raised further when the 80-man work force was reduced to just nine miners, strongly suggesting that the ledges were worked out.

A RAMBLE AFTER MIDNIGHT

On a summer night, a reporter for the *Bodie Morning News* strolled northward on Main Street to observe and record the town's after-dark amusements. His candid report gives us a glimpse of boomtown life. He first encountered a cluster of saloons, and occasionally had to step from the sidewalk to avoid tripping over "some poor unfortunate" who had imbibed too much. A more sinister plight awaited indoors.

> The saloons have their customary quota of sleepers and men without visible means of support, many of whom, doubtless, are waiting for some poor, honest, but drunken devil to lose his head sufficiently for them to go through him and raise a stake with which to aid in the further support of a worthless existence.

The adventurous reporter resumed his tour of Bodie's seedy fringe: a dance hall, the red-light district, an opium den in the Chinese quarter on King Street, another Main Street dance hall, and a gambling room.

> At the dance-house, after midnight, the boys and girls have become warmed up to their work, and, casting aside all ideas of appearances and the future, rush madly around over the board floor to the music of the orchestra. "Come up and drink, all hands!" shouts some whisky-loaded enthusiast, perhaps a miner or teamster who has just been paid off, and the invitation needs no second but is promptly responded to by his friends.
>
> Back of Main street we find Virtue Avenue, with its dozens of lighted windows, at each of which a gaudily attired woman sits, either smoking, chatting, or in silent contemplation of the bright summer night.
>
> Along further, King street is easily recognized by its half-shut up appearance, with now and then a lantern hung outside of a dark looking shanty, either occupied as an opium den or gambling hell, by Chinese. . . . Within the walls of the dirty looking houses one can find dozens of young and old habituates, packed into the filthy places like sardines in a box.
>
> The hurdy-house is just now in full blast and the assembled multitude of men, women and others almost children, who have become excited with bad whisky and worse wine, are now reeling around in a lively dance without other purpose, apparently, than to see who can do the most kicking in the shortest space of time. Often the dance breaks up in a row, and perhaps some poor devil gets his "lights let out;" but usually everybody is good-natured and inclined to enjoy the occasion to the extent of their desires.
>
> The gentle tiger [referring to the image printed on the box from which cards for faro were dealt] purrs contentedly in various places, and the study of faces gathered around the brightly-marked table-covered cards, although old, is nevertheless interesting. From the sport, with his diamond pin and ring, clean shirt front and polished boots, one can see the dirt begrimed miner, just off shift, who is attempting to do what no man was ever known to do—beat the game.

The reporter concluded his tour with a few thoughtful lines.

> And thus, and in other ways more secret, pass the lives of thousands. The wear and tear on the constitution; the never-dying thirst for excitement; the ruined hopes and crushed ambitions and the ultimate fall and despair attending such lives are all portrayed and outlined to an inquisitive observer by a night's cruise around Bodie.[1]

The perception that the Bulwer's ore bodies, along with investors' money, had been depleted to build extravagant facilities for the Standard produced a gut-wrenching feeling among Bulwer stockholders. Exhibiting more than a twinge of hostility, the New York-based *Mining Record* presented its view of the situation.

Representations were made by the promoters of the enterprise and through various mining papers, that [the Bulwer] was one of the richest mines in all the Bodie district. . . . In May, 1879, the stock was offered as a great favor at fourteen dollars per share by the promoters, intimating that fifty thousand dollars would be paid soon in monthly dividends. The Eastern capitalists were told of the two hundred dollar [per ton] ore the mine was delivering daily to the mill. . . . Now what have been the results? . . . The ore worked has all been low grade, and hardly pays milling expenses. . . . The stock has been gradually shrinking from its highest price, fifteen dollars, until today it is selling at one dollar and a half per share."[19]

Anticipation of Bulwer dividends ended abruptly in September, when the Standard Company completed its contract with the Syndicate mill and all 30 stamps of the Bulwer-Standard mill started crushing Standard ore. Bulwer production would be postponed yet again.

The Bulwer management's symbiotic relationship with the Standard came under bitter criticism from cynics, who insinuated that the Bulwer Company existed not because it owned a great mine, but rather to enable its assets, consisting of the Bulwer Tunnel, half of the Bulwer-Standard mill, and a pool of gullible shareholders, to be exploited by the Standard. The Bodie press lashed back, defending the Bulwer by emphasizing that the company received rent from the Standard's use of its half of the mill. This rent money financed the search for more Bulwer ore without levying assessments. To be sure, the papers argued, the Standard used the tunnel, but the Bulwer used the Standard's hoist and shaft, at no cost, for transporting rock, men, tools, and timbers to and from its lower levels—areas kept dry by the Standard's pumps. Furthermore, the Bulwer benefited from Standard wastewater, used to run its half of the mill. The combative *Mining Record* responded that Bulwer stockholders had paid for most of an 1,860-foot tunnel and half of a 30-stamp mill, both of which were useless to them if their mine had no more ore.[20]

The Standard Mine, in contrast, delivered enough ore to supply 20 stamps in its own mill plus all 30 stamps in the Bulwer-Standard mill. Approximately 1,200 tons of rock were delivered to the two mills each week. Ore from the main shaft was sent through the Bulwer Tunnel to the Bulwer-Standard mill, while ore from the old incline was conveyed downhill to the Standard mill by aerial cable tramway.

While the Standard profited from the mineral wealth in its upper levels, in mid-1880 miners sunk the main shaft past the 900-foot level. The shaft's ever-increasing depth made it clear that the managers expected to find great ore bodies below, but heavier and more powerful hoisting machinery would be needed to develop them. Every day the hoist raised more than 200 tons of ore and waste rock to Bulwer Tunnel level, lowered timbers that supported the expanding underground, and delivered men and tools to the various levels.

New equipment that would more than quadruple the Standard's hoisting capacity was ordered from San Francisco in October. Press reports said the machinery was equal in power to any hoist on the Comstock, except for the one at the Union Consolidated shaft. The hoist, and a new gallows frame high enough to handle double-decker cages, required a larger building. To avoid interrupting bullion production, an imposing two-story facility would be erected over the existing machinery while hoisting and pumping continued. The building's foundation was laid in November. Far below, the Standard main shaft reached the 1,000-foot level.[21]

As early as the 1860s, when Aurora was the area's mining center, there were proposals to meet the region's industrial growth by building a railroad. Until 1864, Aurora was the primary destination. In the late 1870s, Bodie became the objective. Nothing materialized until 1880, when the Carson & Colorado Railroad Company started building a line south from the Virginia & Truckee Railroad at Mound House, six miles east of Carson City. It was widely believed that the rails would pass through Bodie, and the line was informally referred to as the "Bodie Railroad" or the "Bodie Extension." Unfortunately, the narrow gauge rails of the C&C were laid considerably east of Aurora and Bodie. Instead of a railroad, Bodie had to settle for a new wagon road to the tracks near Walker

Figure 4-4: Surveyor C. L. Anderson sketched Bodie Bluff and High Peak in 1880, showing four of the district's preeminent mines. The Standard, Bodie, and Mono occupy High Peak's southern ridge, while the Bulwer Tunnel probes the hill from the lower left. Near the tunnel's mouth stands the 30-stamp Bulwer-Standard mill. To the right is the 20-stamp Standard mill. At far left, Bodie Creek runs northward around the base of Bodie Bluff, where the Syndicate and Bodie mills are located and the Bodie Tunnel mill will be added later. The Miners mill is farther down the canyon. (Detail, *Map of the Bodie Mining District*. Courtesy, Geography and Map Division, Library of Congress)

Figure 4-5: Descending the slope of High Peak, from left, are the Standard, Bodie, and Mono mines, where large buildings house steam-powered hoisting and pumping machinery. When this view was drawn in 1880, the Bullion, Bruce/Burgess, and Fortuna lodes had already made Bodie famous. Near the lower left, a wagon hauls cordwood to the mines before the Bodie Railway and Lumber Company completed its narrow-gauge railroad in late 1881. (Detail, *Map of the Bodie Mining District*. Courtesy, Geography and Map Division, Library of Congress)

Lake, some 38 miles away. Construction of the Walker Lake & Bodie Toll Road began in September 1880.

Financed by the railroad company, the new dirt road would offer the quickest route from Bodie to the world outside. It also avoided the longer, arduous route through Aurora, bypassing that town altogether. The new road started 10 miles northeast of Bodie at the old Antelope and Del Monte mills, where the Aurora & Bodie Toll Road turned southeast. From that point it continued northward, following Bodie Creek through Del Monte Canyon. Beyond the canyon's mouth it joined the Carson-Aurora stage road at Five-Mile House (near a place later called Fletcher, named for stage-line owner and station operator H. D. Fletcher), before turning eastward onto the stage road to Columbus. After five miles, it branched toward the northeast and headed over a pass (later named Lucky Boy), then descended along a creek onto the sage-covered desert to a point where a couple of wagon roads met south of Walker Lake. After the C&C's rails arrived in April 1881, a settlement arose known as Hawthorne. It was named (with a slight variation in spelling) after W. A. Hawthorn, the contractor who built the wagon road from Bodie. From then on, most transportation to and from Bodie went through Hawthorne, which displaced Carson City (110 miles to the north) as the closest rail connection. Two years after its founding, Hawthorne replaced Aurora as the seat of Esmeralda County.[22]

During 1880, Mono County produced nearly $3,000,000 in bullion, surpassing all other California counties. The Standard contributed over half the county's yield and maintained its lead in Bodie District by increasing its yearly production to $1,858,763, nearly two-thirds of the district's year-end total. In his annual report, the director of the U.S. mint ranked the Standard first among California's mines. Others believed that it was the nation's leading gold mine. "A year ago," supporters added, "it was the wonder of the mining world. It is a greater wonder today."[23] The company had declared 12 monthly dividends during the year and paid an extra dividend in December.

By the time the timber frame for the Standard's grand hoisting works was raised, enough ore reserves had been exposed in the upper levels to ensure four more years of steady dividends. The Bulwer Mine, on the other hand, slipped to fourth place behind the Standard, Noonday, and the Bodie. Producing no dividends during its long-anticipated, but short run early in the year, the Bulwer's ore proved to be far less valuable and extensive than investors had envisioned. Instead, rental income from its half of the Bulwer-Standard mill during the final months of 1880 financed mineral exploration on the 1,000-foot level, where a crosscut from the Standard main shaft advanced toward anticipated extensions of the Ralston, Homestake, and Stonewall ledges. Predictions that something of value would be found in the Bulwer's lower levels went unfulfilled, and the mine produced no more bullion for the next five years.

The setback in the Bulwer, the closing of numerous Bodie mines, and the fact that many of the district's working mines, such as the Black Hawk, Boston Consolidated, Tioga, and Consolidated Pacific, were not producing ore, deepened problems plaguing traders at the San Francisco stock exchange. Still, Bodie's mines were producing $250,000 per month, and local newspapermen exuded confidence. "Our mines are all looking well and give promise of soon yielding a rich reward to stockholders."[24] But the demoralized Comstock, coupled with the market's seamy reputation, created universal distrust of California and Nevada mining stocks. "In San Francisco," wrote a New York correspondent, "the leading banks have refused to make advances to mining corporations. . . . Three-fifths of the brokers are, plainly speaking, 'busted'."[25] The painful news was repeated week after week. "The market continues greatly depressed, and it is stated that the whole business interest of San Francisco is more or less affected by it, and also that the general public are losing interest in mining, and that brokers and promoters are despondent."[26]

The Noonday and Red Cloud Mines

Throughout 1879 and into early 1880, the Red Cloud Company financed operations by levying one assessment after another. Plagued by the budget-busting problem of removing water and an inability to find profitable ore, the company sank its shaft only 75 feet further, where work halted at a depth of 475 feet. There was plenty of low-grade quartz in the mine, but the Red Cloud never accumulated enough ore of sufficient value to make another mill run. Occasionally the discovery of a rich seam or stringer would bring a glimmer of hope to investors, who gradually realized that the phenomenal ore body that once placed the mine among the richest in the district existed only near the surface and was already exhausted. The *Mining Record's* Bodie correspondent explained the Red Cloud's problem. "The lodes do not produce paying ore except in small quantities at intervals, which cannot be saved on account of the amount of unproductive material surrounding it."[27]

At the beginning of 1880, only two Bodie companies, the Standard and the Bodie, had paid dividends. The district's windswept hills were already dotted with abandoned and failing mines. Their owners had set forth with high expectations, but with no pay ore in sight to bolster the faltering faith of their shareholders, they could not meet operating expenses. Here, among dozens of forgotten mines, the story of the Red Cloud nearly ended. Then a twist of fate secured its survival—albeit sporadically—into the twentieth century. Nobody would have predicted it at the time, but the Red Cloud Mine was destined to play a central role in Bodie's future.

By the early months of 1880, Bodie had attained a reputation for utter disregard of law and order, an aspect of the town's notoriety that almost overshadowed mining. Emphasizing the depravity of Bodie's troublemakers, a column titled "Crime Rampant" stressed their penchant for brutality, and noted that violence usually went unpunished because of the town's listless constabulary.

Within a fortnight two men have been seriously beaten over the head with six shooters, one has been shot to death, one man and one woman have been knifed, one woman's skull crushed with a club, and she may die tonight. For these seven crimes—for those five lives jeopardized and two taken—two arrests have been made. We have constables and several deputies, whose sworn duty it is to enforce the law—and ever so many night watchmen, or private policemen, paid by property owners; and yet crime runs riot nightly in the criminal quarters of the town, and few arrests are made.[28]

Ruffians, known in the vernacular of the day as "bad men," gave Bodie a pervasive air of danger. "We do not misstate the facts when we say that Bodie has the reputation abroad of being a fearfully and wonderfully bad place, and withal decidedly unhealthy," remarked one observer, alluding to the town's troublesome element. A Comstock undertaker reportedly blamed his declining business on the departure of so many of Virginia City's toughs. They "hang around long enough to think that they are fighters," the mortician complained. Then they go to Bodie, and the "Bodie undertakers get paid for burying them."[29]

Repeated stories of mayhem distressed some Bodieites, who challenged the motives and accuracy of distant city reporting.

When the witty paragrapher of one of our metropolitan contemporaries has touched up all the live topics of the day, and still lacks a little of filling the space in his department of his paper, he dashes off a few lines about 'the bad man of Bodie' and his exploits.[30]

Indeed, the term "Bad Man From Bodie" had been coined two years earlier by a Sacramento journalist wishing to capitalize on the remote mining camp's growing reputation for violence.[31] In 1880 he broadened his impressions by citing details, with more than a hint of embellishment.

One of the peculiarities of a Bad Man from Bodie is his profanity. A Bad Man from Bodie who never used an oath is as impossible as perpetual motion or an honest election in Nevada. This trait is especially noticeable whenever he kills a man or endeavors to kill one. Whenever you hear of a man from Bodie who did not swear when he pulled his gun you may depend upon it that he is base metal, a tenderfoot, a man from Pioche, or Cheyenne, or Leadville. The oath of a Bad Man from Bodie is like the cheerful warning of the rattlesnake. . . . Meeting an eligible candidate for a place in the graveyard, he emits his stereotyped oath and blazes away. Sometimes the bad man from Bodie entertains his victim with a short oration before butchering him.

The columnist claimed to have witnessed a Bodie bad man enter a saloon and leap upon a billiard table. "Here I am again," the thug shouted, "a mile wide and all wool. I weigh a ton and when I walk the earth shakes. Give me room and I'll whip an army. . . . I was born in a powder house and raised in a gun factory. I'm bad from the bottom up and clear grit plumb through."

The journalist asserted that the bad man concluded his tirade by declaring: "I'm dry! Whose treat is it? Don't all speak at once for I'll turn loose and scatter death and destruction full bent ."[32]

Editors as far away as New York enjoyed emphasizing Bodie's wicked inclination. The prestigious *Engineering and Mining Journal* reported that "Bodie contains about 6,000 inhabitants, who support 156 drinking places, several newspapers, and many attorneys-at-law, without a single church."[33]

Amid this scandalous surge of mining camp recognition, Governor Blasdel sold his controlling interest in the Red Cloud Consolidated Mining Company.[34] Although depleted of profitable ore, the mine was purchased by the management of the adjacent Noonday, whose mine dominated production in the south end and had already delivered enough ore to surpass the capacity of the Noonday's new 30-stamp mill. The Noonday's remarkable output led Noonday and North Noonday managers to augment production by leasing the recently completed 10-stamp Spaulding mill, where they had an elevated track built to con-

Figure 4-6, facing page: The mines and mills on Silver Hill are portrayed in a sketch by C. L. Anderson, which looks north in early 1880. Shown from left: the newly-constructed Noonday 30-stamp mill; the Noonday hoisting works; the Oro Mine; and the then defunct Red Cloud, prior to the addition of powerful pumping machinery. Bodie Bluff and High Peak rise in the background, while, at the far left, the booming town of Bodie expands in the distance. "Before the first of July arrives" fretted the editor of Bodie's *Daily Free Press*, "it is no boast to say that ten thousand people will be quartered in this place." Seven months later, he bemoaned the common occurrence of "house for rent" signs as people were leaving in droves. (Detail, *Map of the Bodie Mining District*. Courtesy, Geography and Map Division, Library of Congress)

vey mine cars directly from the Noonday shaft.[35]

Below ground, the Noonday shaft and its major east-west crosscuts straddled the boundary line separating the Noonday's property from the North Noonday, and provided equal access to both claims. North of this line, a series of rich discoveries during the spring of 1880 gave the appearance that the North Noonday was the richer property. On April 16, stock in the North Noonday Mining Company reached its maximum price of $7.38 per share. This advance boosted stock in the Noonday Mining Company to its highest price of $5.50 per share.

On the 512-foot level, the east crosscut following the property line passed through the Keystone ledge 30 feet from the shaft, then continued toward the Noonday ledge. There, between the parallel-sloping Keystone and Noonday veins, miners blasted out a subterranean hoisting works. Some 60 feet long, 30 feet high, and 25 feet wide, the timber-supported cavern became the starting point of an incline shaft that would pitch downward on the property line at an angle of 57 degrees toward the east. The incline would penetrate the barren ground lying between the two veins, providing access to both ore bodies.

Like the main shaft, the jointly-owned incline shaft would contain three compartments that traced the boundary line, but instead of cages, it would use specialized mine cars that traveled on an angle. These cars, called "giraffes," carried both rock and personnel.[36] East-west crosscuts driven on various levels from the incline shaft would bring ore and waste rock

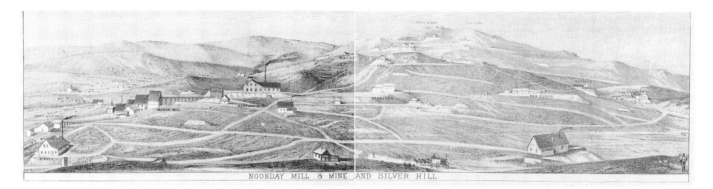

NOONDAY MILL & MINE AND SILVER HILL

from the stopes. The giraffes would then transport the rock to the 512-foot level, where it was dumped into bins. From the bins, the rock dropped into mine cars, which were pushed 50 feet westward to the main shaft, then hoisted two at a time to the surface on double-decker cages. Consisting of a gallows frame, hoist, and pumps, the underground works would be powered by compressed air piped from the main works on the surface, where three boilers were added to provide more steam.[37]

Sinking of the new incline began in May 1880, and was almost immediately retarded by ground water.[38] Despite the installation of steam pumps, incoming water halted work after the shaft had been extended only 75 feet. Downward progress had stalled, but the Noonday companies put their pumps and water-bound depths to good use. Instead of purchasing water piped from the nearby Booker Mine, where the district's first Cornish pump had been in service since July 1879, the Noonday companies pumped water from their own shaft to supply their boilers and stamp batteries.

Also during May 1880, the Noonday mill adopted a highly innovative process that promised to hasten the recovery of gold and silver from ore. Known as the "Boss Continuous Process," the method had been developed by San Francisco milling engineer Martin P. Boss. By placing the mill's machines in sequence, precious metals would be extracted incrementally from the mixture of finely-ground ore, water, and mercury as it ran from one machine to the next. Nearly automatic, the continuous system made the Noonday the most advanced mill in Bodie, where

stamp mills customarily employed the Washoe Pan Process, a method of treating ore in batches that had been developed on the Comstock during the 1860s to handle silver-rich ores.[39]

To constantly feed 30 stamps in the radically efficient Noonday mill, plus 10 stamps in the Spaulding, ore extraction in the Noonday's upper levels proceeded at a furious pace. Money invested to develop the property appeared to have been well spent. When miners driving the east crosscut on the 512-foot level tapped the Noonday ledge, local headlines on June 1, 1880 screamed: "Noondays—The Big Bonanza of Silver Hill—Gold and Silver Galore in the Lower Level." The vein had been pierced some 80 feet east of the main shaft and 30 feet beyond the incline. It was 20 feet wide—and rich. A stunned reporter described the strike: "Here the visitor, who is accustomed to the three, four, five or six-foot ledges common to Bodie District, is met with a sight which is simply astounding. He is likely to give his eyes a good sound rubbing before he can satisfy himself that what he sees is all genuine, and that he is not dreaming."[40]

Anxious to know the extent of the wealth, managers ordered a winze to probe the depths of the Noonday ledge. It would straddle the boundary line and be jointly owned. Down the miners went, prospecting the lode, until they too struck water.[41] The Noondays, like the Booker, Red Cloud, Standard, Mono, and other companies, faced the challenge and expense of removing water if their mines were to go deeper.

In June 1880 the managers of the Noonday and

North Noonday companies embraced a broad plan to drain their mine more economically than by adding more and more steam pumps. The idea was to sink one central pumping shaft with the financial aid of neighboring companies. The shaft would be deep enough for water to flow into it through passageways driven into the surrounding properties. Water collecting in the sump at the shaft's bottom would be lifted to the surface by powerful Cornish pumping machinery. Six mines controlled by the Noonday companies entered the agreement and consented to bear expenses equally: the Concordia, Maybelle, Paris, Noonday, North Noonday, and Red Cloud. These were joined by two independent companies: the Dudley and Oro.[42]

The abandoned Red Cloud offered several advantages as a site for the great pumping plant. With substantial hoisting machinery in place, the existing 475-foot shaft was already deeper than those of most of its neighboring mines. It was centrally located among the group of participating mines, and its collar was the lowest in elevation, crucial for raising water to the surface at minimum cost. A big hoisting works would also economically raise ore and waste rock, allowing the surrounding companies to reach their ground while avoiding the expense of sinking shafts individually. Furthermore, since the two Noonday ledges dipped toward the east, they were projected to intersect the Red Cloud shaft at about the 1,000-foot level.[43]

A final consideration in choosing the Red Cloud was that its shaft was on the eastern slope of Silver Hill, where water discharged from its pumps would flow away from town. Since July 1879, when the Booker started its Cornish pump, adding considerably to the discharge from numerous bailing tanks on Silver Hill, the south end companies had been under attack because water from their mines ran through town, where it flooded streets and yards. The flow, carrying residue from placer mines, backed up on Main Street, where one witness claimed that the mud created a "slough hole deep enough to drown a twenty-mule team."[44] The quagmire worsened in

early 1880, when the south end mills began adding copious amounts of tailings to the flow. Thereafter, major thoroughfares were often clogged with horses and wagons floundering in mud.[45] The thoughtless addition of domestic waste persuaded one observer to comment, "Main Street, at various points, is a sink hole and pestilence-breeding canal for sink and refuse water used in restaurants, hotels, etc. and the stench at times arising from these disease accelerators is intolerable."[46]

Public outrage led to a crusade aimed at correcting the miry problem. In the summer of 1880, the Noonday companies surrendered to civic demands by building a dam across Booker Flat where the tailings would settle. Although the dam retained the sediment, it did little to check the water, and the overflow still ran through town. The flow was especially serious when augmented by seasonal snowmelt. Flooding was most apparent on the lowland east of Main Street. One joker suggested early in 1881 that the steamer *Rocket* should be brought from Mono Lake to ply a regular course in Bodie and offer ferry service to school children crossing Mono Street. Finally, responding to heightened appeals from the unhappy citizenry, the Noonday companies would help finance a buried flume in 1881 to carry water through town.[47]

Machinery for the Red Cloud's pumping plant began arriving in July 1880. Amid an accumulation of stone and lumber for a building that would enclose it, the shaft was widened by the addition of a third compartment to contain Cornish pumping equipment.[48] A mighty compound steam engine, said to be the nation's largest (except for those on the Comstock), was bolted to a massive granite-block foundation, where it would power sequential pumps below. The engine was a marvel of power and efficiency. Its 27-inch diameter high-pressure cylinder adjoined a low-pressure cylinder measuring 48 inches in diameter. Placed horizontally end to end, the two cylinders with 8-foot strokes could pump out a mine 2,500 feet deep, raising water to the surface through two 12-inch diameter pipe columns. At a maximum

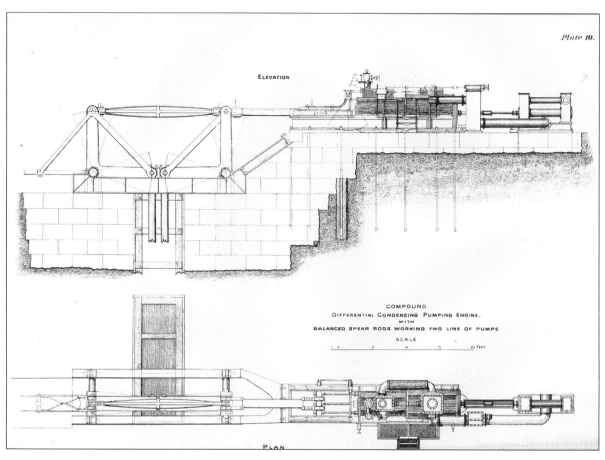

Figure 4-7: Subterranean pumps driven from the surface by a powerful engine were known as Cornish pumps. The system originated during the early 1800s in Cornwall, England, where vertical beam engines supplied the motive power. Most of Bodie's pumping engines, however, were horizontal. Drawn in San Francisco by the Risdon Iron Works, these plans depict the engine used at the Red Cloud to drive a reciprocating rod in the mine shaft. Measured from the cantilevered bob, the assembly was more than 45 feet in length. The illustration shows how a horizontal engine could simultaneously power two pump rods. (*Pumping and Hoisting Works for Gold and Silver Mines*. Courtesy, Trustees of the Boston Public Library)

speed of 15 strokes per minute, two parallel lines of pumps would throw 2,000,000 gallons of water every 24 hours. Powered by four wood-burning boilers, the Red Cloud had the largest works in Bodie, and the Noonday owners swelled with pride.[49]

In the summer of 1880, Main Street in Bodie stretched from the Bulwer-Standard mill to the Noonday mill. The center of town was crowded with businesses whose proprietors readily took advantage of anyone with money. It did not matter that most of the cash in circulation had not come from mining gold. Instead, it represented the shrinking purses of those who had not found employment, and workers'

wages financed by stockholders through speculation and assessments. That summer Bodie's population peaked. The total number of inhabitants was the subject of debate at that time—and has remained so ever since. The 1880 U.S. census counted 5,416, but the enumeration's accuracy was immediately challenged. "There are many complaints among citizens that their names are not on the census list," protested a local newspaper. "At the Standard Con. office they say no one has been around. Of the eight persons in the *Free Press* office, no one is on the list. It is safe to say that the population of Bodie is at least 7,000 instead of 5,416, as reported."[50] A competing paper agreed that the official count was flawed. "We have nine men in

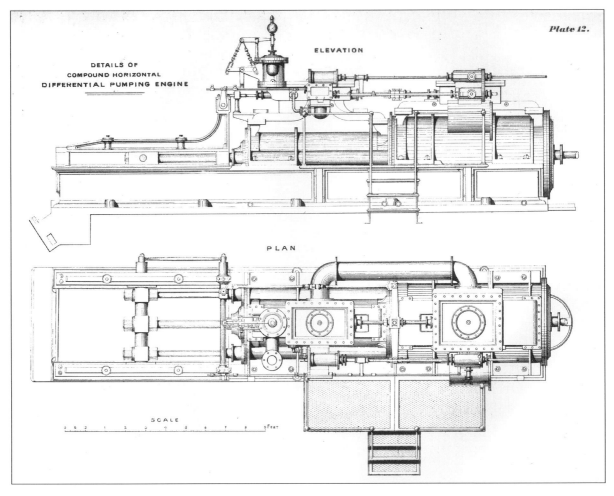

Figure 4-8: The Red Cloud's unusual pumping engine featured two cylinders and three piston rods. Two rods, driven by the large 48-inch diameter low-pressure cylinder, flank a 27-inch diameter high-pressure cylinder. Placed end-to-end, the two eight-foot cylinders made this the largest steam engine in Bodie. (*Pumping and Hoisting Works for Gold and Silver Mines*. Courtesy, Trustees of the Boston Public Library)

and about the Standard Printing House, but the census taker did not get the names of one of them that we know of. The same thing occurred at one or two other places in town. It is believed that we have nearer to 7,000 than 5,000." [51]

Since the beginning of the excitement in 1877, Bodie had witnessed a phenomenal increase in population. But for reasons that are not entirely clear, people left in droves during the fall and winter of 1880. [52] By July 1881, the population would plummet to an estimated 3,500. [53] Roughly half the town's inhabitants left during the 12 months following mid-1880—a time when more stamp mills should have stimulated mine production.

The apparent contradiction resulted from various interrelated factors. Foremost, there were more people in Bodie than its economy could support. The national Panic of 1873 had caused financial hardships across the West. These difficulties were amplified on the Comstock when the Big Bonanza pinched out beneath Virginia City in 1877. West Coast mining stocks fell to a low point, and the absorbing question in the minds of the speculating public was whether a similar bonanza might exist elsewhere. The Standard Mine's success in 1877 looked to many like the dawning of another Comstock Lode. Compelled by economic hardship in other places, more people had moved to Bodie than would have gone otherwise.

There was also a pervasive belief that the district's ore bodies were much larger than they actually were. Steady dividend payments by the Standard, and successive discoveries of the Bruce/Burgess and Fortuna bonanzas in the Bodie Mine, fueled misinformation that was disseminated by local newspapers to reinforce an illusion of immense riches.

Whether driven from other locations by adversity, or attracted to Bodie by boomtown hype, many of those arriving did not find work. By mid-1880 the unemployed apparently grasped that finding work was unlikely because few ore bodies were being discovered and the profitable mining companies already had their essential labor force in place. Those departing Bodie were described by a local newspaper as "mostly idlers and lookers-on" who left to avoid enduring another long winter without employment.[54]

A third reason for so many people to leave Bodie when expectations should have been high was an outgrowth of the mining industry's system of assessing stockholders whenever working capital was needed. Speculators initially threw money at Bodie's mines hoping to get in on the ground floor of another Comstock Lode. After the mining companies depleted this money, stockholders paid assessments a while longer expecting that rich ore would be found at greater depth. Simply put, many unproven mines were initially flush with investment capital. After this money was exhausted, they subsisted until stockholders quit paying assessments. By mid-to late 1880, time had run out for any mining company that could not demonstrate the likelihood of paying dividends. Bodie newspapers did their utmost to lure investors from the vast pool in the East, but their efforts met tepid response when circumspect eastern exchanges refused to list companies of uncertain merit.

Any mine without tangible evidence of pay ore was doomed, a hard reality that became apparent during the fall and winter of 1880. Seventeen Bodie mines with steam hoisting machinery, representing a substantial initial investment, shut down for the season. Eleven of them failed to reopen in the spring, suggesting a lack of sufficient funding to continue work. The 11 investor-backed mines that joined scores already closed were the Champion, Belvidere, Dudley, Double Standard, Defiance, Gypsy Queen, South Standard, South Bodie, McClinton, University, and the Queen Bee. Four other mines, the Goodshaw, Glynn-Dale, Spaulding, and Booker, initially planned to work through the winter, but ceased operations before spring. Ten New York companies owned mines in the district that were already idle. According to New York law, stock could not be assessed. Crippled without regular infusions of money, the Sonora Consolidated, Bodie Chief, New York & Bodie, Original Summit, King Bee, Governor Stanford Consolidated, Bolivar Consolidated, Central, Maryland, and North Standard could not pay wages, and had been among the first to stop work.

Mine closures during the autumn and winter of 1880 took the boom out of Bodie, and the glut of discharged workers disillusioned those who arrived to find no jobs.[55] While Bodie's population decreased and its hills became strewn with idle mines, the Standard, Bodie, and two Noondays, which were not dependent on skittish stockholders for funding, expanded production with a stable work force. Additional mills furnished revenue to a few marginally successful companies like the Bulwer, Syndicate, Bechtel, Bodie Tunnel, and Oro, increasing the district's overall yield.

As Bodie reached this turning point, marked by a sudden decrease in population, construction of the Red Cloud pumping plant was underway. In August 1880, a month after beginning improvements at the Red Cloud, the two Noonday companies further demonstrated their financial strength by adding another 10 stamps to their mill. Already Bodie's most progressive stamp mill, the Noonday would have a battery of 40 stamps and become the district's largest mill.[56] Enormous investments by the Noonday companies inspired confidence, and mining men were sure that the south end was on the verge of glory.

Responding to developments on Silver Hill,

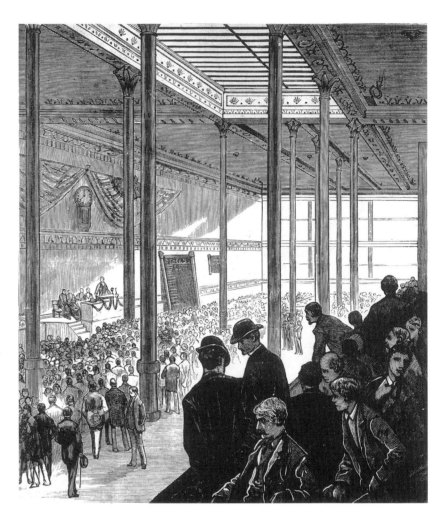

Figure 4-9: Bodie's economy was influenced by developments in its mines, as well as events in distant cities. Gold and silver mining stocks, though highly speculative, were traded daily in exchanges from San Francisco to New York City. "In this city alone," professed one New York enthusiast, "[western] mining companies are dispersing over $1,000,000 monthly in the way of dividends." Depicted here in 1880, the American Mining Stock Exchange in New York lists 32 companies, including the Standard, Bodie, and Bulwer at Bodie. (*Frank Leslie's Illustrated Newspaper* 19 June 1880. Author's collection)

Bodie's genteel population shifted southward to escape the squalor of lower Main Street. One enthusiast observed, "The filth of the town, the slum of the mills, the slums of society and the Chinese population monopolize the lower territory to the northward, while the town cries 'Excelsior!' as it builds onward and upward toward the higher ground of Booker Flat."[57]

When 1880 ended, $511,757 in bullion placed the combined Noonday and North Noonday companies ahead of the fabulous Bodie Mine for the year, and second only to the Standard. But unlike the Standard and Bodie, which had been paying dividends, the Noonday companies had yet to make a distribution. Presumably committing profits to improving facilities and developing the mine, the Noonday companies had gone to considerable expense to install Bodie's largest and most advanced pumping and milling equipment. Emboldened by the mine's incredible showing and confident in the capabilities of modern technology, the managers boasted about being prepared to fully utilize their new machines to recover riches that they were sure lay below. "The best feature of the work at the south end is that it is in the hands of men who have the financial ability to carry out the very extensive work now under way, and who are thoroughly justified in the outlay they are making by the ore almost in sight."[58]

The word "almost" would prove prophetic. Indeed, disparaging rumors were already afloat regarding the two Noonday companies. One unkind remark asserted that during the month of April the Noondays did not produce bullion of sufficient value to cover the cost of firewood consumed by the mill.[59]

The Bodie and Mono Mines

Due largely to the antics of the Bodie Company's directors, Bodie was distinguished for stock swindles.[60] The *Engineering and Mining Journal* responded to a fake dispatch received in New York, remarking:

> There has been so much rascality in connection with the operations in this stock that there is no knowing whether the mine is played out or a new bonanza discovered. . . . The Bodie rings are becoming worse than the Comstock, and although the district affords several excellent mines, unless the public is dealt with more fairly, the whole district will be shunned.

Bodie's press fired back, defending the managers of the town's second most profitable property. "This is hard talk in connection with a mine which has produced and disbursed millions in dividends."[61]

While the Bodie Company's raucous reputation was widespread, the Mono was equally known for taking from the pockets of stockholders what it lacked in pockets of pay rock. Schemes exploiting gullible stockholders were common in western mining. Three years earlier a New York-based mining journal had warned investors:

> A stranger is impressed by the vast wealth of the Golden State on seeing in every day's paper a notice of the organization of a new mining company, with a capital stock of $10,000,000; but . . . it would probably be hard to find one of these companies that could raise ten million cents.[62]

By spring, the Mono shaft was down 600 feet, and its shareholders had purchased, through a string of assessments, an impressive battery of steam pumps for the 260-, 460-, and 600-foot levels. On the surface, two additional boilers provided power, and Mono investors paid for those as well. Producing steam to pump 680,000 gallons every 24 hours, the Mono's four insatiable boilers consumed 14 cords of wood per day. Of course, Mono stockholders shouldered the cost of purchasing and transporting cordwood from distant forests by wagon. A narrow gauge railroad would not be completed for nearly two years.[63]

Water pouring from the Mono shaft gave townsfolk an opportunity to substantially improve their firefighting capabilities. Prior to this, fires had been fought with a haphazard assortment of equipment. Merchants reduced their insurance rates by purchasing hand or steam pumps, then supplying them with water by digging wells. These measures were augmented in November 1878, when the newly-organized Bodie Fire Department purchased a Babcock firefighting apparatus. Known as a chemical fire engine, the four-wheeled device carried two 60-gallon pressurized tanks containing a mixture of water, bicarbonate of soda, and sulfuric acid that delivered a stream of fire-quenching chemicals through a hose without taking time to steam up a boiler.[64] Adopting the name of the engine's manufacturer, Bodie's volunteer firefighters had formed the Babcock Engine Company No. 1, and built a fire station on Standard Avenue in early 1879 that was large enough to shelter the apparatus and accommodate meetings, banquets, and dances. Many town residents, however, questioned the wisdom of squandering $2,250—substantial funds—for a single piece of equipment. Their protests led to the April 1879 organization of the volunteer Pioneer Hook and Ladder Company No. 1, which purchased a hand-drawn hook and ladder truck, then raced to extinguish fires ahead of the Babcock unit.[65]

The Mono Mine's discharged water became the town's strongest defense against conflagration in early 1880, when a group of property owners and merchants banded together to reduce their odds of suffering ruin from fires. In the absence of a municipal government, they formed the Bodie Water Company and financed, through the sale of shares, the excavation of a 250,000 gallon reservoir to impound water from the Mono Mine.[66] A buried pipe conveyed water down the hill into the center of town, where eight hydrants were evenly spaced from one end of Main Street to the other. A pipe to the Bulwer-Standard mill and another to a hydrant near the Standard mill safeguarded the industrial buildings nearest town. To deploy the hydrants, the Water Company oversaw the establishment of two more volunteer firefighting groups: the Champion Hose Company No. 1 and the Neptune Hose Company No. 2. Each company received a hose cart with 500 feet of rubber hose. From the northernmost hydrant to the extreme southern hydrant was a distance of 2,200 feet. By adding both hoses to either end, the fire department could protect Main Street 4,200 feet along its length. The hoses also reached 1,000 feet to either side, allowing a stream of water to be played onto any downtown building within an area 4,200 by 2,000 feet, not counting the distance water was thrown.[67]

On February 4, 1880, a large group of citizens assembled on the hill to witness the water system's inaugural demonstration. Water company directors accompanied Judge Bechtel to the nearby Mono Mine, where he opened a gate that sent water flowing into the reservoir. When the reservoir was sufficiently full, the Judge made a few appropriate remarks, then turned the water into the pipe leading to the hydrants below. Downtown, the Neptune and Champion brigades attached their hoses to the hydrants, and spent the afternoon delighting cheering crowds by sending streams of water cascading over Bodie's tallest buildings and flagpoles. The aquatic display confirmed opinions that the water's pressure was sufficient to tear shingles off roofs as if they were "loose feathers."[68] The firemen then moved to the Standard mill, where they drenched buildings and sent a deluge arching over the smokestack. Exhausted from their day of training, the firefighters retired to the Pioneer Brewery to recuperate. They recovered further that evening at a champagne "blow out" hosted by the Grand Central Hotel.[69]

The Neptune and Pioneer firehouses were centrally located on the east side of Main Street, between Green and Mill streets, while the Champion's headquarters were at Main Street's extreme north end. To maintain their buildings and equipment, Bodie's firemen hosted fund-raising events, such as dances, suppers, and picnics. Should the Mono Mine ever fail as a water source, the Water Company connected its reservoir to nearby pumps at the Champion and Goodshaw mines. The group also hired wide-awake watchmen, then kept them on nightly beats with salaries collected from subscribers, who also pledged to compensate the Mono for periodically refilling the reservoir. The water company divided downtown into three districts and installed a signaling wire that allowed a watchman stationed in the belfry above the Babcock engine house to alert the engineer at the Standard mill, who directed firefighters to the scene with a coded pattern of blasts from the whistle.[70]

Because the turbid water pumped from the mines was thought to be poisoned by chemicals used in explosives, water for domestic consumption had to be obtained from other sources. But wells close to Main Street were contaminated. An 1879 news item titled "Bad Sewerage" conveyed the abominable state of downtown wells. "A vast quantity of refuse, rubbage [sic], and slop from saloons and restaurants is thrown out the rear [of the buildings, and] nearly all the wells which supply our eating houses are rendered unfit for use . . ."[71] Although not specifically mentioned, hundreds of privies must have added to the pollution.

Safe drinking water was a necessity, and those who did not possess wells dug outside the polluted center of town purchased spring water brought in barrels by wagon. These sources persisted in outlying areas even after 1882, when two competing wagon delivery companies installed separate underground pipes to convey water to their downtown customers. Construction of the first system would not begin until July, piping water from a spring at the head of Lowe Street. This source was supplemented in October 1882 by a pipe laid four miles from Potato Peak, where it tapped the headwaters of Rough Creek.[72]

Wagon deliveries, followed by pipelines, solved the drinking water problem, but rubbish disposal was not addressed. As late as mid-1882, the condition of Mono Street, which paralleled Main across a wetland, was the subject of sharp criticism. "The good people of adjacent streets have been industriously engaged in depositing rubbish and filth there until now it is one vast ocean of old cans, broken barrels, damaged boxes, worn-out boots, ruined hats, and dead cats and dogs."[73]

While the Mono Mine performed its important 1880 roles of removing water from the Bodie Mine and delivering it to the town's firefighters, the Bodie Company's management was preoccupied with getting rich. Fleecing Mono stockholders was one method, but their primary source of revenue was the Fortuna lode. On six levels below the subterranean hoisting works, crosscuts extended eastward from the incline shaft to the company's preeminent vein. The lowest level was 601 feet below the surface, and water stood 30 feet below that. Drifts, driven along the vein from each crosscut, provided access to the stopes where the ore was mined. Ore dropped into chutes, from which it was loaded into mine cars that conveyed it through the drifts and crosscuts to the incline. Skips running up and down the angled shaft delivered the ore to the hoisting station on the 433-foot level, where it was dumped into mine cars that were pushed 85 feet southward, then 140 feet westward through cave-like passageways to the Bodie main shaft. After being loaded into cages, the cars were hoisted to the surface.[74]

A problem facing the Bodie Company was the shallow angle at which the Fortuna pitched away from the main shaft. The deeper the ore, the farther the underground passageways had to extend to reach it. Expanding the workings eastward and transporting pay rock over ever-increasing distances to the shaft were expenses that could only be eliminated by a vertical shaft sunk farther east. In the fall of 1880 the Bodie Consolidated Mining Company and the Mono Gold Mining Company began a joint venture, the upshot of which was a colossal three-compartment shaft to intersect the Fortuna lode near the 1,000-foot level. Originally called the "Bodie and Mono Combination Shaft," the new shaft quickly

became known as the "Lent Shaft." It was positioned 1,000 feet east of the Bodie and Mono hoisting works and low enough on the hill to efficiently raise rock and water from both mines.[75]

Machinery, granite blocks, and timbers began arriving in August. The hoist, gallows frame, boilers, and smokestacks were removed from the Mono Mine and set up to start the Lent Shaft downward. The

relocated equipment was capable of sinking 2,000 feet, but to reach such depths the shaft would have to be kept dry. Anticipating the tremendous quantity of water to be removed, the companies purchased secondhand Cornish pumping machinery and a powerful steam engine from the Lady Washington Mine on the Comstock. Unlike the Red Cloud's compound engine, the pumping engine purchased for the Lent Shaft had only one cylinder, but it was enormous—a high-pressure cylinder 40 inches in diameter with an 8-foot stroke.[76] This surface-mounted steam engine, needed to move a huge wooden rod up and down in the shaft and deliver power to the pumps, was a duplicate of one that had been installed in 1876 at the C&C shaft in Virginia City. That engine drained the two great mines of the Big Bonanza: the Consolidated Virginia and the California. When it was built, the engine's immense size won the admiration of onlookers, and its direct-acting horizontal design, an improvement upon vertical beam engines, revolutionized pumping machinery on the West Coast.[77]

The Herculean effort required to transport the 33,000-pound casting to Bodie captivated the populace, who carefully monitored the engine's progress. "The teamsters are having a hard time," observed a local scribe as the huge cylinder drew closer.

> Its southward course is marked by a line of broken bridges. On the Springs road the wheels of the trucks on which it is loaded sank down in one place to the hubs. The freighter who took the contract has exhausted every oath . . . and the source of the creaking procession can readily be traced by the blue streak of profanity in its wake.[78]

The team pulled the big pumping engine into Bodie in December. Twelve horses were detached and the remaining 30 mules made the turn from Main to Mill Street while nearly 1,000 people assembled to witness the cornering maneuver. Then 42 horses and mules drew the huge steam cylinder up the hill to the mine.[79]

The Lent Shaft was 225 feet deep when workers began assembling the pumping machinery that would allow men to reach tremendous depths. Meanwhile, miners working through the Bodie shaft continued to exploit the Fortuna lode. As each segment was discovered, worked out, then faulted, stock in the Bodie Consolidated Mining Company fluctuated. Although press reports stressed that the famous ledge grew richer as it descended, the year's output was little more than half the 1879 yield.[80] Producing $429,818 during 1880, the Bodie Company paid a 50-cent dividend in January, reduced to 25 cents per share in February and March. Expenses incurred while sinking the Lent Shaft curtailed dividends during the remainder of the year. This brought the total in dividends paid by the Bodie Consolidated Mining Company to $1,200,000, offset by only two assessments of $75,000. Investors in the Mono Gold Mining Company were not so lucky. The Mono shaft, now abandoned and stripped of its machinery, had failed to expose any ore. Perhaps pay ore would be found deeper in the Lent, but to find out, Mono stockholders would have to keep paying assessments and wait. Another seven months would pass before the Lent Shaft reached the water level and its powerful pumps began their awesome task of draining the ground.

The Mono's proximity to the Bodie Mine's ledges fostered the belief that rich ore extended into Mono ground somewhere below. The likelihood that the biggest prize lay just ahead had seduced stockholders into paying one assessment after another. By the end of 1880, Mono investors had been assessed 10 times, for a total of $250,000, and received nothing in dividends. Meanwhile, little encouragement came from San Francisco, where the stock market failed to climb out of its doldrums. One financial columnist grumbled, "The heavy operators of the days gone by have left for the great East, taking with them their capital and energy, and leaving Pine Street, figuratively speaking, a desert waste. The brokers are doing a starvation business."[81]

While San Francisco stock traders languished in despair, yields from Bodie's mines were often upstaged by the town's reputation as a "wicked place." This aspect of Bodie's far-flung fame troubled some but delighted others.[82] Newspaper editors far and wide took great pleasure in embellishing tales of devilry and attributing it to any passing stranger who could be conveniently labeled a "Bad Man from Bodie." Such a character was said to have entered the Fern Leaf concert hall in San Francisco.

"I'm a chip from the side of Bodie Bluff," the stranger reportedly yelled as he upset a table.

Full of enthusiasm, wines, liquors, and cigars, the bad man jumped onto the stage and drove a terrified soloist into a corner.

"I'm an old stager myself," thundered the intruder, "and capture whole camps with my actin.'"

Then he pulled his gun and fired a shot. The blast extinguished footlights and sent musicians and audience members fleeing toward the door.

"This is what I call fun," proclaimed the bad man. "This old town needs shaking up a little; the boys seem to be sort o' low and need a boom."

In two minutes he was "on the sidewalk in search of a new place."[83]

Blurring the line between fact and fiction, Bad Man from Bodie stories followed a rich American tradition of exaggerating for entertainment. Tall tales that drew upon the West's ornery, unsophisticated reputation were popular across the country. Amusing East Coast readers, the *Boston Daily Globe* described a stranger who "staggered" into a tony drinking establishment. "Lurching up to the bar," the man demanded that everybody "come up and have something to drink." Giving a furious whoop and smashing a bottle on his head, the brute performed a war dance, then declared that he was a "Bad Man" and "always made it a practice to strew upon the floor the bowels of any person who declined to drink upon his invitation." Affirming his remarks, he drew an 18-inch "Arkansas toothpick from the back of his collar." Patrons scattered, many stampeding into the street.

"Who is he?" asked a bystander who had taken cover behind the bar. "From Bodie, I suppose," he thought aloud.

"Bodie, hell no!" thundered the bartender. "He's from Boston. He belongs to that Sunday-school excursion."[84]

Tales of Bodie's bad men had their whimsical side, but an escalating frequency of killings since 1879 was a serious problem. Homicides occurred with regularity, usually with impunity. Idleness among able-bodied men was a potentially dangerous problem, worsened by mine closures, job cuts, and abundant saloons. Altercations, more often than not, were between willing combatants, at least one of whom had been drinking.[85] Bodie's decent men and women were vexed by their town's reputation as a "murderer's paradise."[86] Weary of incessant crime, an ineffectual police force, and the unlikelihood that a jury would convict even a depraved killer, the local press began calling for vigilante action in February 1880. "Some-

thing should be done to relieve the town of these murderous scoundrels," argued one enraged columnist.

It is the history of every mining camp that a safety committee has had to be formed and some effective work performed in order to rid the place of hard characters. One or two examples have been sufficient to purify the place and deliver it from the hands of treacherous men. Bodie is in this condition at present and the sooner a move is made the better.[87]

By spring, rumors were heard of a mysterious organization calling itself "601," a name of unmistakable portent, since it was adopted in 1871 by Virginia City's committee of vigilance. Several Bodie wrongdoers were said to have been handed written notices expressing that "a longer stay in Bodie would be at the risk of having their oxygen supply curtailed."[88] Gossip prompted one witty editor to joke that it was better to be hanged by a lynch mob in Bodie than to live anywhere else.[89] Other opinions were more perceptive. "I am opposed to Vigilance Committees, as a general proposition," professed one prominent citizen, "but it seems to me that a little judicious hanging will stop this shooting and stabbing business."[90] Fear of mob action after two separate killings in July compelled authorities to secretly transport the accused murderers to the county jail at Bridgeport. Responding to similar threats in September, "a large force of officers and friends" redoubled security for a murder suspect detained in Bodie's jail, until the severely injured prisoner died unexpectedly.[91]

The campaign for citizen action gained strength even while the town's surplus population, and a disproportionate number of bad men, sought refuge elsewhere. Their flight failed to eliminate violence perpetrated by those left behind, at least for a while. Under the headline "More Blood," a local newspaper responded to a spate of September slayings.

Four men killed in two days is rather too much, even for Bodie, and it is high time our people should awake to the responsibility that must come of cleansing our town from men who are a terror to the community and are liable to shoot down or maim our best citizens at any moment. . . . What must be done to drive this curse from our midst? Let the good and true men of Bodie each answer this question to themselves.[92]

Another article confirmed the danger. "It is true the present condition of society in Bodie warrants, if it does not force, the carrying of firearms as a matter of self protection against the lawless element in our midst."[93] At the same time, abandoned sections of town were already falling into decay. "The north end of Main Street is growing more deserted and dreary every day," observed one reporter. "What were at one time handsome saloons are now old shells, covered with cobwebs, dust and gloom."[94] As the town's population dwindled, the cry for citizen action intensified

with a November editorial titled "Crime."

It is time that the people should seriously contemplate the situation and take into consideration what measures should be adopted to check the lawlessness which is rampant throughout the county. . . . The people tire of this and want a "change." They demand it and will have it. They simply ask that murderers be made to understand that sure and swift punishment will be meeted [sic] out to them. . . . As a general thing Courts have but little terror for murderers; a large majority escape punishment. Not so, however, with a Vigilance Committee.[95]

Two months later, on a biting cold morning in January 1881, a group of townsmen would turn this counsel into reality.

---

1. *Bodie Morning News* 22 November 1879; *Daily Bodie Standard* 27 January 1880; *Engineering and Mining Journal* 27 June 1896, 615.

2. *Mining Record* 25 June 1881, 608.

3. *Daily Free Press* 16 January 1880.

4. *Daily Free Press* 27 January 1880.

5. *Daily Free Press* 16 January 1880.

6. William M. Bunker, "Bodie—Work in the District for the Past Twelve Months," *Daily Stock Report* 5 August 1880.

7. *Daily Free Press* 29 April 1880; William Irwin, *Second Annual Report of the Standard Consolidated Mining Company for the Year Ending February 1, 1881* (San Francisco, CA: Bunker & Hiester, 1881), 38; William Irwin, *Fourth Annual Report of the Standard Consolidated Mining Company for the Year Ending February 1, 1883* (San Francisco, CA: W. T. Galloway & Co., 1883), 32.

8. *Daily Free Press* 13 June 1880; Eliot Lord, *Comstock Mining and Miners* (1883; reprint, San Diego, CA: Howell-North Books, 1980), 309, 311.

9. *Weekly Bodie Standard* 5 April 1879.

10. *Daily Bodie Standard* 27 February 1879.

11. Grant H. Smith, "Bodie, Last of the Old Time Mining Camps," *California Historical Quarterly* 4 (1925), 72.

12. Smith, "Last of the Old Time Mining Camps," 70.

13. Smith, "Last of the Old Time Mining Camps," 72.

14. Smith, "Last of the Old Time Mining Camps," 74.

15. Roger D. McGrath, *Gunfighters, Highwaymen, and Vigilantes: Violence on the Frontier* (Berkeley, CA: University of California Press, 1984), 116-117.

16. *Bodie Morning News* 14 August 1879; 27 March 1880; Herbert L. Smith, *The Bodie Era: The Chronicles of the Last of the Old Time Mining Camps* (TMs [photocopy] 1934), 106-107.

17. *Mining and Scientific Press* 22 May 1880, 326.

18. *Daily Free Press* 13 June 1880.

19. *Mining Record* 16 October 1880.

20. *Daily Free Press* 20 January 1881; 16 March 1881; *Mining Record* 5 March 1881, 218-219; 9 April 1881, 337-339.

21. *Daily Free Press* 4 September 1880; 30 December 1880; *Bodie Standard-News* 23 November 1880; *Mining and Scientific Press* 23 October 1880, 260; Irwin, *Second Annual Report of the Standard*, 35-42 and sketches.

22. *Daily Free Press* 1 September 1880; 3 September 1880; 21 November 1880; 24 November 1880; 16 April 1881; *Bodie Standard-News* 30 September 1880; *Carson Daily Index* 25 February 1881; Alan H. Patera, *Lundy* (Lake Grove, OR: Western Places, 2000), 33.

23. U.S. Bureau of the Mint, *Report of the Director of the Mint upon the Statistics of the Production of the Precious Metals in the United States [for 1880]* (Washington, DC: Government Printing Office, 1881), 38-39; Bunker, "Work in the District," *Daily Stock Report* 5 August 1880.

24. *Weekly Standard-News* 11 September 1880.

25. *Engineering and Mining Journal* 17 July 1880, 46.

26. *Engineering and Mining Journal* 2 October 1880, 226.

27. *Mining Record* 5 July 1879, 4.

28. Smith, *The Bodie Era*, 104-105.

29. Wells Drury, *An Editor on the Comstock Lode* (Palo Alto, CA: Pacific Books, 1936), 236-237.

30. *Daily Free Press* 7 January 1880. The expression "bad man" was common in the West. Recalling his notoriety in Arizona and Colorado, Doc Holliday remarked, "When any of you fellows have been hunted from one end of the country to the other, as I have been, you'll understand what a bad man's reputation is built on. I've had credit for more killings than I ever dreamed of."

31. McGrath, *Gunfighters*, 221.

32. *Sacramento Daily Bee* 12 October 1880, in *Bodie Standard-News* 16 October 1880.

33. *Engineering and Mining Journal* 31 January 1880, 86.

34. *Daily Free Press* 30 April 1880; 18 May 1880. Nevada Governor Blasdel and his son, Weaver, moved to Esmeralda County, Nevada, where they worked and invested in mines at Cambridge, Rockland, and Aurora. In Aurora they rebuilt the Antelope mill, calling it the Humboldt mill, and operated the Humboldt-West Mine. (*Daily Free Press* 28 September 1881; 5 November 1881)

35. *Daily Free Press* 9 March 1880; 21 April 1880; *Bodie Morning News* 14 April 1880.

36. Bunker, "Work in the District," *Daily Stock Report* 5 August 1880; *Mining Record* 24 July 1880, 81; *Daily Free Press* 10 August 1880. Giraffes are described in Dan De Quille [William Wright], *The Big Bonanza* (1876; reprint, Las Vegas, NV: Nevada Publications, 1982), 151-152, 225, 227-230 and Charles Howard Shinn, *The Story of the Mine: As Illustrated by the Great Comstock Lode of Nevada* (1910; reprint, Reno, NV: University of Nevada Press 1980), 225.

37. *Bodie Chronicle* 22 November 1879; *Daily Free Press* 2 May 1880; 1 June 1880; 3 August 1880.

38. *Daily Free Press* 23 May 1880; 9 January 1881.

39. *Engineering and Mining Journal* 17 February 1883, 86-87; *Daily Free Press* 9 January 1881.

40. *Daily Free Press* 1 June 1880.

41. *Daily Free Press* 9 January 1881.

42. *Daily Free Press* 23 June 1880; *Mining Record* 14 August 1880, 154.

43. *Mining and Scientific Press* 10 July 1880, 22; 21 August 1880, 114; 13 November 1880, 311.

44. *Daily Free Press* 22 November 1879.

45. *Daily Bodie Standard* 8 August 1879; 13 May 1880.

46. *Bodie Morning News* 16 October 1879.

47. *Daily Free Press* 4 February 1881; 11 March 1881; 14 September 1881; 13 November 1881; *Weekly Standard-News* 16 March 1881; 7 September 1881; 19 October 1881.

48. *Daily Free Press* 22 August 1880; *Mining and Scientific Press*, 10 July 1880, 22.

49. *Weekly Standard-News* 18 September 1880; *Mining and Scientific Press* 23 October 1880, 260; *Daily Free Press* 7 January 1881; *Weekly Stock Report* 20 January 1881.

50. *Daily Free Press* 14 July 1880.

51. *Daily Bodie Standard* 15 July 1880.

52. *Bridgeport Union* in *Bodie Chronicle* 21 August 1880.

53. *Daily Free Press* 14 June 1881. McGrath, Loose, Wedertz, Billeb, Cain, and the Johnsons failed to recognize

the significance of this sudden decrease in Bodie's population. If a boomtown is characterized by rapid growth, then Bodie's boom was over by the autumn of 1880. A population decline occurring as production in the mines was increasing raises questions as to why so many people departed in the face of apparent prosperity. Conspicuous answers are not found in the historic record. The dramatic exodus was certainly noticed by the local press, but if the underlying reasons were understood, they were left ambiguous. Most historians would assume that people drift away from a mining town because the mines have played out. At Bodie, however, people left at a time when more stamp mills were being built, the district's overall yield was increasing, and anticipation should have been high.

54. *Daily Free Press* 24 August 1880.

55. Where so many people went is not clear. Butte City, Montana Territory, and Tombstone, Arizona Territory, were the destinations mentioned most often.

56. *Mining Record* 7 August 1880, 130.

57. *Daily Free Press* 11 September 1880.

58. *Daily Free Press* 26 October 1880.

59. *Daily Bodie Standard* 8 May 1880.

60. *Engineering and Mining Journal* 7 February 1880, 104; *Mining Record* 23 October 1880, 392.

61. *Bodie Morning News* 13 February 1880.

62. *Engineering and Mining Journal* 20 January 1877, 38.

63. *Bodie Morning News* 12 March 1880; *Engineering and Mining Journal* 29 May 1880, 373; *Mining and Scientific Press* 29 May 1880, 340.

64. The firefighting apparatus placed in service in 1878 was a No. 3 Babcock chemical fire engine produced by the Babcock Manufacturing Company of Chicago, Illinois. It was equipped with two 60-gallon pressurized tanks filled with a mixture of water and dissolved bicarbonate of soda (baking soda). When the unit (essentially two large soda-acid fire extinguishers on wheels) reached the scene, a canister of sulfuric acid was upset inside one of the sealed tanks, and the resultant chemical reaction created enough carbon dioxide gas to force the solution through a hose at high pressure. When the tank was spent, the second tank was activated, and fire fighting continued while the first tank was recharged. By alternating tanks, the stream of solution continued uninterrupted. The device was furnished with 200 feet of hose wound on a mounted reel, and, typical of firefighting apparatuses of this era, it had attachments that allowed it to be hand pulled or horse drawn. Because chemical fire engines had no boilers to steam up, their response time was faster than that of steam-powered pumpers. They were also more reliable, and the chemical solution was believed to extinguish flames more effectively than plain water. Based on their advantages, chemical fire engines served as the first line of defense against fire in many towns and cities across the country. For more information on chemical fire engines, see W. Fred Conway, *Chemical Fire Engines* (New Albany, NY: Fire Buff House, 1987), 9-15, 75-82.

65. *Bodie Weekly Standard* 6 November 1878; *Mining and Scientific Press* 9 November 1878, 300; *Mono Alpine Chronicle* 15 February 1879; *Daily Bodie Standard* 31 December 1878; 18 May 1880.

66. An adjacent reservoir built by the Standard Company supplied water to the Standard mill.

67. *Daily Bodie Standard* 3 March 1880.

68. *Daily Free Press* 20 January 1883.

69. *Daily Bodie Standard* 27 December 1879; *Bodie Chronicle* 10 January 1880; 7 February 1880.

70. *Bodie Standard-News* 26 July 1880; 31 July 1880.

71. *Weekly Bodie Standard* 8 March 1879.

72. *Daily Bodie Standard* 8 February 1879; 5 August 1879; *Daily Free Press* 6 May 1882; 14 July 1882; 3 October 1882; 26 November 1882.

73. *Daily Free Press* 23 June 1882.

74. *Daily Free Press* 31 December 1880; *Engineering and Mining Journal* 15 January 1881, 42.

75. *Bodie Standard-News* 21 August 1880; *Daily Free Press* 3 August 1880.

76. William R. Balch, *Mines, Miners, and Mining Interests of the United States in 1882* (Philadelphia, PA: The Mining Industrial Publishing Bureau, 1882), 1121.

77. *Gold Hill Daily News* 6 August 1875; *Mining Record* 14 August 1880, 154; *Bodie Standard-News* 6 December 1880; Joseph Moore and George W. Dickie, *Pumping and Hoisting Works for Gold and Silver Mines* (San Francisco, CA: A. L. Bancroft & Company, 1877), 5-53 and plates.

78. *Daily Free Press* 23 November 1880.

79. *Daily Free Press* 15 December 1880.

80. *Mining and Scientific Press* 5 February 1881, 85.

81. *Bodie Standard-News* 6 October 1880.

82. *Daily Free Press* 9 February 1881.

83. *Daily Free Press* 6 January 1881.

84. *Boston Daily Globe* 7 July 1879.

85. McGrath, *Gunfighters*, 184, 198, 199, 255.

86. *Weekly Standard-News* 11 September 1880; *Daily Free Press* 7 January 1880.

87. *Daily Free Press* 19 February 1880.

88. *Daily Bodie Standard* 7 April 1880.

89. *Bodie Chronicle* 2 April 1880.

90. *Daily Bodie Standard* 8 July 1880.

91. McGrath, *Gunfighters*, 127-129, 136, 220.

92. *Weekly Standard-News*, 11 September 1880.

93. *Weekly Standard-News*, 11 September 1880.

94. Russ and Anne Johnson, *The Ghost Town of Bodie As Reported in the Newspapers of the Day* (Bishop, CA: Chalfant Press, 1967), 32-33.

95. *Bodie Chronicle* 13 November 1880.

The Bodie Foundry

1. *Bodie Morning News* 21 September 1879.

2. *Weekly Standard-News* 1 March 1882.

3. *Daily Free Press* 30 December 1881; 11 February 1882; 25 February 1882; *Weekly Standard-News* 04 January 1882; 25 January 1882; 15 February 1882; 1 March 1882; *Bridgeport Chronicle-Union* 25 October 1902; 24 October 1903.

A Ramble After Midnight

1. *Bodie Morning News* 14 August 1879.

Figure 5-1: The 16-stamp Empire mill, built in 1865, stood idle for nearly a decade before it was purchased in 1875 by the Syndicate Company. The rich ore it crushed from the Standard Mine in 1877 catapulted Bodie into national fame. After the mill was enlarged to 20 stamps in early 1878, it astounded the world again, when its batteries clogged with pure gold from the Bodie Mine. Adjoining the mill, the Syndicate Tunnel was one of Bodie's three major tunnels. Although an inconsistent producer, the Syndicate paid eight dividends between 1884 and 1885. Shortly before 1900, Warren Loose, brother of the Bodie Mine's original owner, purchased the Syndicate property, where he poses with his wife in about 1903. (Courtesy, Robert T. Bell)

CHAPTER FIVE

BOOM AND BUST ON SILVER HILL
1881-1882

The Standard Con. at the present time has a larger ore development than the Comstock has shown for two years, and the same may be said of the Noondays; and still our mines have scarcely been prospected.
 —Daily Free Press (Bodie), January 29, 1881

The population of Bodie, which at one time was estimated at 7,000, is now not more than 3,500, but those who are standing by the camp are pretty sure of their final reward.
 —Daily Free Press (Bodie), June 14, 1881

To be sure stocks are down, but that is nothing new; business is dull, but that is a familiar state of affairs.
 —Daily Free Press (Bodie), June 3, 1882

The Noonday and Red Cloud Mines: 1881

Most crimes, including murders, went unpunished in boomtown Bodie. Even when culprits were prosecuted, convictions were unlikely. This indifference toward justice, however, was about to become less assured. Demonstrating Bodie's transformation from a chaotic Wild West mining camp into an orderly community, an incident during the early days of 1881 struck terror in the hearts of desperate characters.

On the bitter cold morning of January 14, a bullet was fired into the head of Thomas Treloar as he and Joseph DeRoche left a dance at the Miners Union hall. Eyewitnesses identified the assassin as DeRoche, who had been romantically involved with Treloar's wife. The killer was quickly taken into custody. After DeRoche escaped that night, his flight was rumored to have been permitted by a drunken police officer. The cold-blooded murder, followed by the perpetrator's escape, spurred determined citizens to action.

Squads of men searched for the fugitive. He was recaptured two days later at a wood ranch about eight miles from town and returned to the Bodie jail. That afternoon authorities escorted the prisoner through a growing crowd of agitated citizens to an upstairs courtroom. After witness testimony confirmed that Treloar's killer was DeRoche, the accused was returned to his cell to await trial. In the dark of night, 200 members of a secret order gathered in the snowy street for a long, deliberate meeting. At about 1:30 in the morning of January 17, the throng, whose strength had increased to 500, removed DeRoche from the cell and hanged him from a blacksmith's wagon-hoisting frame that had been placed over the still-bloody murder site. While the body hung from the makeshift gallows, someone pinned a note on its chest, reading: "All others take warning. Let no man cut him down. Bodie 601." Meanwhile, the police officer whose incompetence had allowed the prisoner's escape fled to Carson City.[1]

Bodie's bad men had clearly worn out their welcome. The town's committee of vigilance proved that emboldened citizens were ready to confront crime. Taking advantage of an improving social climate, enterprising and orderly people had done what an ineffective legal establishment could not do. Few newspapers spoke more truthfully about Bodie's move to amend its wicked reputation than Virginia City's *Territorial Enterprise*.

[The lynching] by the Vigilantes of that reckless camp will probably have the effect of checking, if not of crushing out the spirit of lawlessness which has so long terrified its people. . . . Bodie, like all other towns that have sprung up in a night and become the centre of a large population drawn from all points of the compass, has suffered severely from the rein [sic] of ruffianism. . . . Once [the peaceable citizens have been] aroused to action, the beginning of the end of lawlessness is at hand.[2]

The paper's prediction proved accurate. The execution of Joseph DeRoche would be the only vigilante lynching in Bodie's history.

On February 23, 1881, little more than a month after DeRoche was hanged, Silver Hill's ponderous pumping engine at the Red Cloud was set in motion to begin draining the south end mines. The Red Cloud's new role inspired awe. By April, the shaft was clear of water, and miners pushed downward toward "hidden riches."[3] Eight participating compa-

nies—some with proven ore bodies, and others hoping to find them—drove crosscuts from the Red Cloud toward their ground. As the water receded below Silver Hill, glowing reports of weekly progress at depths previously inaccessible were telegraphed to journalists across the country. On the hill's far side, Bodie's eighth mill, the 10-stamp Silver Hill mill, awaited developments. Completed in late January with parts from the Dunderberg mill near Bridgeport and the Comstock's Succor mill, Bodie's newest stamp mill was well suited to treat the south end's silver-rich ores. It had been built on speculation by the Silver Hill Quartz Mill Company, who expected an influx of ore.[4]

Noonday managers also anticipated increased quantities of ore. With 10 additional stamps and a new 350-horsepower engine, the Noonday mill was a 40-stamp rock-pounding extravagance, and Bodie's largest. Its April start-up brought the total number of stamps in the district to 144.[5] Seemingly built without regard to cost, the Noondays' hoisting, pumping, and milling facilities were surpassed only by those of the Standard Consolidated Mining Company.

As these monumental events took place on Silver Hill, Judge Briggs stood in front of the Occidental Hotel overseeing the auction of 200 town lots, the owners of which were delinquent in their mortgage payments. Most debtors had simply skedaddled, leaving property and financial obligations behind. On Monday, May 2, 1881, 55 parcels were sold in moderate bidding on the first day.[6]

Spring runoff and discharged water from south end mills intensified complaints from annoyed citizens, who already suffered flooded residences and impassible streets. Another six months would pass before a buried flume carried the interminable surge through town, where it would join a torrent from mines and mills on High Peak and Bodie Bluff. Reflecting upon soggy neighborhoods that had been vacated by hordes leaving town, a reporter jotted down a few disparaging words about lower Main Street.

There are pools of green, foul, stagnant water that cannot run off, deserted cabins are surmounted with slime and odoriferous mud, and it is only lately that the stages could pass along. Coming south, heaps of manure are encountered; here and there a coal oil can looms up out of the mire, and such common articles as old boots and cast off pantaloons are quite prominent. With all this, a dozen different kinds of odors go up at all hours to remind the passer-by that filth is ever with us. Heaps of oyster shells adorn the front of elegant business houses, and it would take a six-mule team to haul off all the cigar stumps, discarded cards, and decayed fruit and vegetables that choke up the gutters.[7]

Containing not more than 3,500 inhabitants by mid-1881,[8] Bodie was decidedly losing its rip-roaring manner. With the increasing industrialization of the mines, Bodie's population had become more stable, both in the sense of reduced numbers and middle-class values. A Victorian melodrama performed upon the Miners Union hall stage thrilled audiences and exposed them to the fine arts. "The production of *Ingomar* last evening by a company of Bodie ladies and gentlemen was a credit to those who took part in the performance," declared a local reviewer. "*Ingomar* is one of the grandest plays Bulwer ever wrote. It is replete with romance, poetry, and deep thought."[9] Cultural refinement notwithstanding, some mining camp traditions proved difficult to amend. When a touring temperance lecturer's dissertation condemning drunkenness was enthusiastically received, one saloon owner proposed a toast to the fine oration, then retorted, "If they think they can deliver more temperance lectures than I can sell whisky, why, let 'em keep it up."[10]

In June 1881, four months after the Red Cloud pumps were started, water began subsiding 1,200 feet away in the Noonday Mine. As it receded below the 512-foot level, where downward progress had stopped a year earlier, miners resumed sinking an exploratory winze into the Noonday ledge.[11] Investors waited with confidence, expecting at any moment to learn that great riches had been found.

As 1881 came to a close, the Red Cloud's great shaft reached the 700-foot level. Its powerful pumps drained the ground, allowing an army of miners below. Subterranean workings expanded at a tremendous rate, and mines all around were pushed deeper. Taken from levels above, the Noonday and North Noonday companies' $244,000 contribution to the district's 1881 product received praise. In fact, it represented an output only about one-tenth that of the Standard Mine, dropping the two south end companies to third place behind the Standard and Bodie. Still waiting for a dividend, weary Noonday investors wondered why their splendid mill, running at full capacity, had produced less bullion with 40 stamps than it did with 30. The situation became more distressing when annual reports disclosed that the 1881 yield was less than half that of the previous year. Underscoring stockholders' fear was the observation that every dividend-paying mine at Bodie was in the district's north end.[12]

The Bodie and Mono Mines: 1881

The Bodie Consolidated Mining Company continued exploiting the Fortuna lode through the old Bodie shaft, while work progressed at the Lent to the east. The Lent Shaft reached the 500-foot level in March as its majestic hoisting and pumping works climbed skyward from the surface.

The premises are swarming with machinists, stone cutters, masons and laborers, all busily engaged in preparing the foundations and putting the machinery in place. Forty-three of the three-inch foundation bolts have been set, the foundations for the engine and pump bob are being laid of huge blocks of granite of the finest quality, and everything about the new works bears evidence of the best workmanship and most massive and substantial material.[13]

The hoisting works was an engineering triumph of immense size. Its Cornish pumping machinery would be capable of lifting water 2,000 feet. In June, pumps were positioned in the shaft and connected to a massive timber rod that reached from the surface, where the huge engine waited to set the assem-

PROFITS FROM WASTE PRODUCTS: BODIE'S TAILINGS MILLS

Stamp mills, which turned ore into bars of bullion, also produced vast amounts of waste known as "tailings." This material consisted of water and finely ground ore from which most of the valuable metals had been removed. Although technically a waste product, tailings were in fact a potential source of revenue because they contained traces of gold and silver that had escaped capture by the treatment process. Tailings also contained mercury, an essential but costly element in milling that was reused whenever possible.

During the Comstock's early years, sluices of extraordinary length were built in the canyons below Virginia City and Gold Hill so that tailings leaving the mills passed over several miles of blankets and riffles.[1] Later, Comstock mill owners replaced the sluices with combinations of mechanical concentrators, grinders, amalgamators, dryers, and chemical additives to coax more value out of the waste material before it was discarded. Other entrepreneurs subjected tailings to treatment in facilities known as "tailings mills." Working and reworking tailings became an industry that employed a large number of men.[2]

At Bodie, recovering profits from tailings was much less elaborate. Most of the tailings were impounded in ponds adjacent to the stamp mills. The Standard and Bodie companies periodically ran their tailings through their mills. Other companies made no such effort, and tons of the valuable material remained in reservoirs and deposits along the banks of Bodie Creek. Depending on the mill's efficiency and the characteristics of the ore it had been processing, a mill at Bodie usually wasted between 10% and 20% of the ore's gold and silver. District-wide, these losses averaged about 12% of the ore's assay value, resulting in tailings containing between $2 and $183 per ton—an asset of considerable importance, especially if the mill had been crushing rich ore.

Two small tailings mills below Bodie treated tailings washed down Bodie Canyon. These crude affairs employed machinery similar to an ordinary stamp mill, plus sluice boxes and riffles to concentrate anything of value that escaped the machines. With some tinkering, these small-scale operations could be quite profitable despite the expense of purchasing, hand shoveling, and trans-

bly in motion.

In July 1881, water was struck at the bottom of the Lent Shaft, 635 feet from the surface. Slowly, the powerful engine began working the heavy rod up and down and pumps below forced a torrent to the surface. The Lent Shaft engine joined two others at the district's deepest shafts, taking over for an army of small pumps now idle in abandoned mines. The Standard, located about ¼ mile northwest of the Lent, was already 1,000 feet deep and being pushed deeper. The Red Cloud, less than a mile to the southwest, had reached a depth of 550 feet.[14] Bodie's fate, the *Mining and Scientific Press* reminded readers, would be decided by developments in these formidable shafts. "The three companies that control these properties are the ones who will determine whether or not the rich veins found near the surface extend to great depth—1200, 1500 or 2000 ft. beneath the surface."[15]

Ever since the Mono hoisting works was dismantled in August 1880 to furnish machinery for the Lent Shaft, the Bodie Water Company had been without its principal means of replenishing the reservoir that supplied water to the town's fire hydrants. Every time firemen doused a blaze, a hat was passed along Main Street to raise funds for the idle Champion Mine to steam up and refill the reservoir. Collections were porting the tailings. Since frozen ponds were impossible to excavate, treatment of tailings at Bodie was a seasonal proposition.

The first tailings mill at Bodie was built in the autumn of 1879. It was located a mile below the Bodie mill and included a dam that held tailings in a pond known as the "Johnson Reservoir." A steam engine powered four stamps (unusual for a tailings mill since the material had already been pulverized) and six amalgamating pans that captured gold, silver, and mercury. Sluices were added for good measure. The mill ran throughout the following season. In the fall of 1881, the property and machinery were purchased by Bodie businessmen John Wagner and Adam Gillespie. Thereafter it was commonly known as John

Wagner's tailings mill. During each of the six seasons it ran, the mill yielded between $8,000 and $25,000, adding to the district's total production.[3]

A second tailings mill was built three miles farther downstream in the autumn of 1881, about the same time John Wagner was taking over the older operation. It was situated midway between Bodie and Aurora on the California-Nevada state line at Sunshine, where natural springs had figured prominently in Bodie's early history. In 1864, Sunshine had been under consideration as a site for the Empire Company's steam-powered mill. Instead, the mill was built at the foot of Bodie Bluff, nearly six miles closer to the mine. Sometime around 1870, area pioneer Judge F. K. Bechtel erected Bodie's third

stamp mill at Sunshine—a tiny water-powered contrivance with but two stamps. It is unknown when this unlikely facility ceased operating, but it seems to have survived, at least in ruins, until 1877.

Located off the main road to Hawthorne, Sunshine was the home of a number of commercial enterprises, including a toll house, stage station, hotel, and a scattering of unremarkable mines. Sunshine residents George Storrs, William Davidson, and Jonathan Lockwood built a tailings mill in 1881, taking advantage of the location's reliable water supply. A 16-foot diameter waterwheel ran an amalgamating pan, while thick woolen blankets in sluices caught any gold, silver, and mercury in the residue.[4]

made about twice a month. Subscribers, generally property owners and businessmen who stood to lose the most from fire, had readily paid installments during prosperous years. But as real estate values declined, they saw less need for protection. Collecting their obligations became increasingly more difficult, and urgent appeals from firemen and newspaper editors were necessary.

Eventually, in May 1881, the citizens approved a special property tax to finance the pumping. When water began pouring from the mouth of the Lent Shaft two months later, an elaborate scheme was engineered to ensure that the reservoir was kept full. Water from the depths of the Lent Shaft was dis-

charged into buried wooden pipes that delivered it to either the reservoir supplying the fire hydrants, or around Bodie Bluff to supplant the tentative water sources at the distant Bodie mill.[16]

The Lent Shaft reached the 700-foot level in August 1881. From there, miners drilled and blasted a westward crosscut to the Fortuna lode. When they reached it, rich ore was sent out of the Bodie Mine through two shafts. Ore from the upper levels was hoisted through the Bodie shaft, while ore from below came out through the Lent. The shaft reached the 800-foot level in November, where another crosscut was driven to pierce the Fortuna lode. The company averaged 150 men on the payroll, working both mine and mill.[17] Everything about the mine was looking well, except that stockholders had not received a dividend in more than a year. In December, instead of a dividend, the Bodie Consolidated Mining Company levied its third assessment.

Considering the outlay of funds for the Lent Shaft, no one should have been surprised, yet concerns were raised because the company was ostensibly mining the richest lode in the district. One local editor rationalized:

> But life is made up of unexpected events, and the true philosopher bears up under each one, and draws a lesson therefrom. The Bodie Con. Mining Company has of late been forced to expend a great deal of money [but] is doing some good prospecting and is paving the way for deep mining in this district.[18]

Of particular interest at the end of 1881 was that Bodie District recorded its biggest year in gold and silver production, the result of an extraordinary yield from the Standard and uncharacteristic bursts of productivity by the Syndicate, Bechtel, and Oro mines. The output for the Bodie Consolidated Mining Company, however, was down from the previous year. A yield of $372,801 placed the bonanza mine second in the district, but its output was less than one-sixth that of the Standard. Investors in the Mono Gold Mining Company were far worse off. Mono miners working through the Lent Shaft had not found any ore. Then, in December, the company levied its 13th assessment.

The Standard and Bulwer Mines: 1881-1882

The new hoisting machinery at the Standard main shaft was ready for steam in May 1881. Towering above a three-story building that dominated the horizon, its smokestacks seemed to leap into the sky above High Peak. The facility included new blacksmith, carpenter, and machine shops. After the old hoist and gallows frame were removed, new steel cables were wound onto two sturdy 12-foot diameter reels. Then sinking resumed, sending the vertical shaft beyond the 1,000-foot level.[19]

That same month, the San Francisco businessmen who had organized the Bodie Wood and Lumber Company in 1878, then formed the Bodie Railway and Lumber Company in February 1881, now began construction of a narrow gauge railroad to bring low-cost mine timbers and cordwood from the pine forest south of Mono Lake. The directors, many of whom were large stockholders in Bodie's preeminent mines, included three principal owners of the Standard: Seth and Daniel Cook, and Robert N. Graves, a Comstock millionaire who had also invested heavily in the Syndicate Mine.

These three men were joined by another owner of the Syndicate Mine, Henry M. Yerington, president of the Carson & Colorado Railroad and superintendent of the Virginia & Truckee Railroad. Through these positions, Yerington had formed working relationships with powerful bankers and railroad financiers. Most prominent among his contacts was Darius Ogden Mills, another Comstock millionaire and onetime president of the Bank of California. Though living in New York City in 1881, Mills was president of the V&T. Another Yerington affiliate was Comstock millionaire and former U.S. Senator William Sharon. Both Mills and Sharon had backed construction of the C&C in 1881, while dominating Comstock shipping through their stranglehold on the V&T.[20]

Bodie ran on wood, yet the wisdom of building the railroad was immediately questioned because so many mines were idle, and none of the deep shafts had been sufficiently explored to assure the district's longevity. Graves took a contrary view that developments would make the district profitable well into the future. He recognized that "Virginia City had been in worse condition than Bodie . . . when the Virginia & Truckee Railroad was built." He reminded listeners that "the people who had faith and stuck to the camp when it was down were the ones who came out right in the long run."[21]

While grading the Bodie railroad, the company

Figure 5-2: A view looking southeast toward Taylor Gulch and Nevada Hill shows the two-story hoisting works at the Standard main shaft that replaced the works seen in figures 3-7 and 4-1. Construction began in November 1880, when the shaft was 1,000 feet deep. A year after the works was completed in May 1881, the shaft reached its final depth of 1,200 feet. The Bulwer Tunnel lies 365 feet below. This building, shown only months before it was destroyed by fire in August 1894, housed the Standard Mine's magnificent steam-powered hoisting and pumping machinery. (*Engineering and Mining Journal* 13 May 1893. Courtesy, Engineering and Mining Journal)

built an enormous steam-powered sawmill south of Mono Lake in the timber-rich foothills. It was touted as larger than any Sierra sawmill that had supplied wood for the great mines of the Comstock Lode. Its size was strong evidence that the owners had immeasurable confidence in Bodie's mines—or that they intended to sell lumber to outside markets. The mill was officially called the "Mono Saw Mill," but together with the railroad yard, blacksmith shop, machine shop, commissary, saloon, two stores, company buildings that quartered workers, and about 30 small houses, the settlement at the south end of the tracks became known as Mono Mills.[22]

The railroad's route from the sawmill to Bodie was 31.74 miles. Emerging from the timberland, it descended onto the flat of Mono Basin, headed northward along the eastern shore of Mono Lake, then climbed the hills toward Bodie. The final 12 miles wound around sharp curves, without using tunnels, on grades that reached 3.8% (200 feet per mile), requiring two switchbacks and three trestles. Finally, rounding Nevada Hill, the tracks crossed the head of

Taylor Gulch and entered the mining district just below the Red Cloud. The rails terminated at a switch yard in the saddle between High Peak and Silver Hill. From there, wagons distributed timbers to mines and cordwood to mines and mills. At the two terminals (Mono Mills and Bodie) water tanks replenished locomotives and turntables spun them around for return trips.[23]

As track laying advanced through distant hills, the Standard Mine shipped ore from its 300-, 385-, 500-, and 550-foot levels. Its vertical shaft was 1,034 feet deep when William Irwin, superintendent of the company, prepared to serve as Grand Marshal of Bodie's 1881 Fourth of July parade. Then, two days before Independence Day, the holiday festivities were almost canceled. In far-off Washington, D.C. an assassin had seriously wounded recently-inaugurated U.S. President James Garfield. A last-minute telegram assured Bodie's Committee of Arrangements that the lingering President was improving, and the patriotic observance took place as planned.

The next morning the banners were struck and

Figure 5-3: After it was completed in November 1881, Bodie's railroad hauled cordwood to fuel steam-powered mining machinery and timbers to support underground workings. Trains also delivered wood for domestic fuel. Photographed in 1889, Locomotive No. 1, the wood-burning *Tybo*, was purchased secondhand by the Bodie Railway and Lumber Company in June 1881. The narrow gauge 2-6-0, manufactured in 1874 by the Baldwin Locomotive Works at Philadelphia, assisted in construction of Bodie's 32-mile railroad, where it served until it was sold to the Inyo Development Company in 1899. (Hawes Studio, Carson City, Nevada. Courtesy, Mallory Hope Ferrell)

everybody went back to work and awaited news of the President's fate. His life hung in the balance for another 2½ months, until the gunshot proved fatal on September 19. The dead president was mourned in Bodie by another procession, amid buildings draped in solemn black bunting.

The spirited whistle of a locomotive was heard for the first time on the hill above town on Tuesday, November 8, where it mingled with scattered steam whistles from mills and hoisting works. Six days later the last spike was driven, and the Bodie Railway and Lumber Company delivered two carloads of timber for the Standard Mine. In addition to its locomotives, the three-foot gauge railroad owned 40 cars, most of which, if not all, were flatcars built at the

V&T's Carson City shops for hauling lumber products.[24]

Locomotive No. 1 (*Tybo*), an elegant 2-6-0 Mogul manufactured in 1874 by the Baldwin Locomotive Works of Philadelphia, had been purchased secondhand from the Eureka & Palisade Railroad in northeastern Nevada. Locomotive No. 2 (*Inyo*) was an 0-6-0 built in San Francisco for the Bodie railroad by Prescott, Scott & Company. Arriving within the month, Engine No. 3 (*Mono*), was nearly identical to the *Inyo*. Each of these locomotives was hauled to Mono County in pieces by wagon, then assembled on newly laid BR&LCo tracks. At some point, the *Inyo* and *Mono* were converted to 2-6-0s by the addition of pilot trucks, which prevented derailments on

Figures 5-4 and 5-5: In November 1881, the BR&LCo purchased Locomotive No. 2, the *Inyo*, and No. 3, the *Mono*. Nearly identical wood-burning 0-6-0s, they were manufactured in San Francisco by Prescott, Scott & Co. The *Inyo*, viewed from the front, and the *Mono* are shown after pilot trucks were added to prevent derailments. (Emil Billeb collection. Courtesy, Vickie Daniels)

Figure 5-6: Locomotive No. 4, the *Bodie*, was a little Porter 0-4-2T saddle-tanker that arrived in June 1882 to work at the logging end of the tracks. The locomotive is seen near Mono Mills after 1900. The *Inyo*, *Mono*, and *Bodie* remained in use until scrapped shortly after the railroad was dismantled in 1917-18. (Emil Billeb collection. Courtesy, Vickie Daniels)

sharp curves by guiding the engines around bends and keeping their big drive wheels from climbing the rails.[25]

The closing days of 1881 brought further gratification to those interested in Bodie's future. Early in December the Bulwer Consolidated Mining Company surprised yearning shareholders by declaring its first dividend. No ore from the mine had been milled since early in 1880, but rent received from the Standard Company for using the Bulwer's half of the Bulwer-Standard mill gave Bulwer investors a long-hoped for dividend. The troublesome fact that these profits were not the result of mining gold was conveniently overlooked, and the news was proclaimed from San Francisco to New York City that Bodie had three dividend-paying mines. On Christmas Eve, the Bulwer Company amazed everyone again by declaring a second dividend. Townspeople beamed with pride and Bulwer stock edged up to $3 a share, even

though each dividend amounted to a mere 10 cents per share.[26]

Bodieites had another reason to be proud. Anticipating that their mines would produce even more riches, they celebrated the completion of the district's ninth quartz mill. This one was not a stamp mill in the usual sense. Instead of employing stamps to crush the ore, the Bodie Tunnel and Mining Company equipped its mill with a newfangled rotating contraption called a Howland pulverizer. It was the invention of W. H. Howland, who advertised it as equivalent to 20 stamps and more economical. Beset by breakdowns because the ore was too hard, the high-speed machine was a dismal failure. In January 1882, one month after it started up, the Howland pulverizer was thrown out to rust on the dump, and the Bodie Tunnel Company refitted its mill with 15 conventional stamps.[27] This brought the total number of stamps at Bodie to 159, a figure that does not in-

"THE DAY WAS SIMPLY LOVELY": INDEPENDENCE DAY 1881

The Fourth of July was the year's most festive holiday in nineteenth-century America. At Bodie, buildings throughout town were adorned in patriotic colors by 10 o'clock in the morning. People crowded streets and sidewalks, and every available balcony was occupied by parade viewers. The 1881 Independence Day celebration was recorded in rich texture by a local scribe. He prefaced his column with "The day was simply lovely."

THE FOURTH
HOW THE DAY WAS OBSERVED
IN BODIE

Anxiety About the Presi-
dent the Only Draw-
back—The Parade—
The Literary
Exercises—
Etc., Etc.

. . . At daybreak the Standard Artillery was brought out, and a salute was fired by Jules Renault, the veteran French soldier. Upon this occasion the new cannon recently made at the Standard mill was brought into use. Five pounds of powder were used in every charge, and the echo along the canyon was remarkably distinct.

THE DECORATIONS.

At an early hour the town was all life and activity. The small [boys were] out with cracker and bomb, making all the noise possible; frightening horses, timid ladies and prowling dogs. Nearly all of the business houses on Main street were decorated. Some were elaborately decked with flags, bunting and green boughs; others only displayed moderate taste, and again a few gave out no evidence that the anniversary of our national independence was upon us in all its magnificence. The decorations this year were not so elaborate as last year, yet the main thoroughfare looked inviting. On the outer edge of the sidewalks was an almost continuous row of cottonwood and pine boughs. These added freshness to the scene and made one almost feel that he was in a land of luxuriant vegetation. The saloons for the most part were particularly elegant, and if patriotism is to be measured by Fourth of July decorations, then they who preside over the destinies of the bar are entitled to a large share of the cake—if such an expression is not inconsistent with the dignity of the Fourth. The hoisting works on the hill—many of them—had the Stars and Stripes unfurled, and the mills were not without national trappings. Many private residences were also decked in holiday attire. . . . The three divisions of the procession formed on South Main, East and West Green streets. At 10:30 o'clock everything was ready and

THE PROCESSION.

Started on its way. First came a platoon of police, . . . Next came Grand Marshal William Irwin and five aides abreast and all mounted on handsome horses. Immediately following was the band discoursing patriotic airs. The musicians were backed up by the War Veter-ans, twelve in number, under Captain George Temb. Owing to the illness of an old comrade—President Garfield—many of the veterans declined to parade, feeling as though it was out of place under the circumstances. Next came the Standard Flying Artillery. Thirty-five mounted horsemen led the two field pieces. They presented a handsome appearance. The animals were all good and they were admirably managed. The Booker Artillery followed. The miniature cannon was drawn by twelve equally small boys dressed in pretty caps, red shirts and dark pantaloons. The Car of State was constructed to represent a sailing vessel, and it was called "Independence." Each State and Territory was represented by a little girl. The Goddess of Liberty was in the center, and the good ship was officered by boys dressed in sailor suits. The costumes of the children were exceedingly pretty and some of them were even elegantly dressed. . . . However, the Car of State was one of the best features of the procession. Ninety-two members of the Miners' Union came next, headed by their beautiful silk banner. The Union had an excellent representative of its members. The Officers of the Day, in carriages, . . . completed the First Division.

THE SECOND DIVISION.

Started off with thirty-one members of the Knights of Pythias, under command of T. A. Stephens. They were mounted on horses and dressed in the full uniform of the order. Their appearance was inspiring. Nothing in the whole procession attracted more attention. They received the admiration of the fair sex and the envy of less fortunate gentlemen—those who were not Knights and were on the ground, for instance. A large delegation of school children in a decorated car was the next feature. Then came Fire Commissioners . . . in a carriage. Chief Engineer Sam Williamson and First Assistant Charles Cummings headed the firemen's portion of the procession. The Babcock engine was drawn by ten members and two horses, with Mr. C. Blanchard holding the ribbons. The engine was elegantly and elaborately decorated. Under a beautiful canopy sat Miss Midgley, the fire queen. She was dressed to perfection and carried in her hands a bouquet of rare flowers. The Hook and Ladder Company followed. Thirty-eight men had hold of the rope. The truck was also neatly decorated. The Champion Hose Company followed, with thirty-four in line, arrayed in their usual bright uniforms. Miss Luella Richey was the fire queen. She sat in her seat surrounded by fairylike decorations. The cart was trimmed to perfection with flags, flowers and evergreens. Following the Champions came the Neptune boys. There were thirty-two of them. They were led by a delegation of "pioneers" wearing large white capes and bearing axes. The Neptunes never appeared to better advantage. The hose cart was properly decorated with flowers, etc., and the house of the fire queen was a masterpiece of neatness. Rich curtains hung on each side, and suspended from the roof were bird cages. Miss Mabel Richey, a sister of the Champion queen, acted in a similar capacity for the Neptunes.

THE THIRD DIVISION.

The Mexican portion of the community was represented in this Division by twenty-two pedestrians, wearing red, white and green silk sashes. The leader bore a magnificent silk banner which bore the Mexican coat of arms. Next came several wagons of business men, among whom was Fred Webber. He had a full rigged blacksmith and horseshoing establishment on board. The trades were not so generally represented this year as upon former occasions, hence the procession was somewhat curtailed. Next came a long line of citizens in carriages and citizens on horseback, who were followed by something like one hundred and thirty Piute bucks, all well mounted and painted in the highest style of the Indian art. They were commanded by Captain John who took his orders from Colonel Ferguson. The Piutes enjoyed the business hugely. Delegations from every quarter of Mono county were in line and Esmeralda county also furnished a respectable company. The patriotism of the average Indian marks the spirit of the age and his conduct upon the national holiday should inspire some of the communistic white people with loftier sentiments than they seem to possess. This competed the procession. Owing to a scarcity of musicians in town but only one band could be obtained; hence the rear end of the column was obliged to keep step to the music of patriotism and not of a brass band.[1]

The serpentine line of march wound through town. It began on Main Street and progressed northward to the Bulwer-Standard mill, then back to Green Street. After strutting a short distance west on Green, the paraders turned southward onto Fuller Street, following it as far as the Bodie Foundry. Then Main was traced northward to Green Street. The procession turned east on Green, then north on Wood Street. At the Standard mill the marchers turned west onto Mill Street, disbanding at the grandstand on Main Street.

The day's events included a prayer for wounded President Garfield, a reading of the Declaration of Independence, music, the recital of a poem titled "Independence Bells," and another poem about the battles of Lexington and Concord. Orations followed by Judges Ryan and Briggs. After the literary exercises a mad dash to Booker Flat ensued, where Bodie's newly organized Jockey Club delighted betting crowds by racing horses around a 600-yard oval track.

At day's end, a moment of uneasy excitement seized onlookers, when artillerymen fired the sunset salute from the hill behind the Standard mill. On the 38th shot (one for each state), the cannon burst after being loaded with a heavy charge. Machined at the Standard's machine shop from a discarded piece of iron shafting, the barrel split from "butt to muzzle." Half of it went sailing high in the air; the other fragment smashed through the gun carriage. Since no one was injured, the explosion provided a grand finale for a splendid day. A ball commenced at the Miners Union, keeping the celebration going well into the early morning hours.

Figure 5-7: The Bodie Tunnel mill in about 1884. Completed in December 1881, the Bodie Tunnel mill was the last mill built during Bodie's heyday. Located at the mouth of the Bodie Tunnel Mine, the mill was originally equipped with a Howland Pulverizer. The pulverizer fizzled, and was soon replaced with 15 conventional stamps. (Emil Billeb collection. Courtesy, Vickie Daniels)

clude four stamps in John Wagner's tailings mill and ignores the nagging fact that 24 stamps in the Spaulding, Silver Hill, and Miners mills were idle almost all of the time.

When the results of 1881 were summed up for the district, the Standard shaft had reached a depth of 1,139 feet, the Lent Shaft 825 feet, and the great Red Cloud shaft was 700 feet deep. Their three pumping plants kept mines dry throughout the district, and trains now delivered cordwood and timbers. Anyone watching locomotives, hoisting works, pumping engines, and stamp mills belching smoke and steam from the hills above Bodie had no doubt that the town was in the business of mining gold. Although the population had dipped to around 3,000 as excess humanity spilled out of town, Bodie's inhabitants showed mining town pluck when a new state law forbidding saloons to open on the Sabbath was flagrantly ignored.[28] Prudent county officials rationalized that it was "almost impossible" to find a jury that would convict "Sunday law violators" in Bodie. "When it comes to gambling," they reasoned, "it will be still harder to prosecute."[29]

The Standard Company had 150 men on its payroll, half of whom were underground miners. Twelve more monthly dividends of 75 cents each had been paid during the year, and another extra dividend was declared in December. Standard stock sold for $19.25 per share. The year's bullion yield, having increased to $2,168,576, was the largest in the mine's history and two-thirds of the district's 1881 total. The Standard Mine was also acclaimed as the most pro-

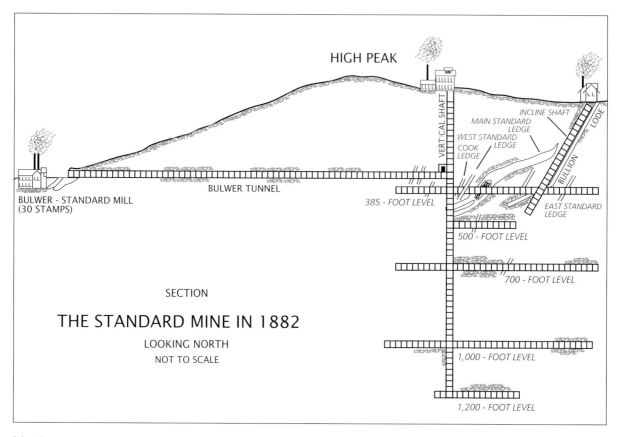

HIGH PEAK

VERTICAL SHAFT

INCLINE SHAFT

MAIN STANDARD LEDGE

WEST STANDARD LEDGE

COOK LEDGE

BULLION LODE

BULWER TUNNEL

BULWER - STANDARD MILL (30 STAMPS)

385 - FOOT LEVEL

500 - FOOT LEVEL

EAST STANDARD LEDGE

700 - FOOT LEVEL

SECTION

THE STANDARD MINE IN 1882

LOOKING NORTH

NOT TO SCALE

1,000 - FOOT LEVEL

1,200 - FOOT LEVEL

Map 6.

ductive mine in California and Nevada.[30] Its growth, augmented by unusually large outputs from the Syndicate, Bechtel, and Oro mines, was enough to overcome diminishing returns elsewhere in the district. Bodie shipped $3,160,067 in bullion during 1881, a year that would prove to be its best.

The record production, however, went almost unnoticed. Shunned by investors, the district could not overcome contempt brought about by its association with the shadowy world of mining stock traders and the corrupt, depressed San Francisco Stock and Exchange Board. Instead of mining stocks, wary speculators were turning to safer investments in railroad and utility companies.[31]

At the beginning of 1882, Bodie's railroad reorganized and was renamed the Bodie and Benton Railway and Commercial Company. In May, the new company started grading a branch line to connect its rails to the C&C, which was advancing southward

from Hawthorne to Benton, California. The Bodie extension's planned route was to leave the main line at Warm Springs near Mono Lake, heading southeasterly across Adobe Meadows to the proposed point of intersection at Benton Station. The tracks of the C&C were still 20 miles from Benton, but when the two railroads met, the Bodie railroad would be able to profit from selling lumber products to distant markets. Bodie, it appeared, would have its long-awaited rail connection to the outside world.

It was not to be. Grading of the branch line progressed only nine miles from Warm Springs before work abruptly ceased in July 1882. With 15 miles to go, 100 Chinese and 25 white workers were discharged before a single rail was spiked down. No clear explanation was given for this crucial decision, but the Bodie press believed that "the C. and C. people, who are in the lumber business, like the Bodie and Benton Company, intend putting on such a tariff on the business of the latter company as to exclude them from any profit in that business to outside points."[32]

Simply stated, the V&T monopolized one segment of a vast logging industry that had been supplying wood to the Comstock mines for years. This lumbering complex included sawmills, railroads, and flumes that brought lumber from the Sierra Nevada to yards immediately south of Carson City. From there, the V&T provided the final transportation link to deliver this vital commodity to Washoe's mines. When a decline in silver mining created a need for new markets, the V&T's management secured the Owens River Valley by building the C&C southward from their tracks at Mound House east of Carson City. The Bodie railroad's attempt to break into this supply line at Benton died because the plan conflicted with more powerful interests.[33]

Still, it was widely believed that, eventually, Bodie would be connected to an outside railroad. During 1881-82 no fewer than seven railroads announced plans to pass through town or to intersect its railroad somewhere on Mono Basin. Some railroads proposed east-west lines to unite Great Basin states with San Francisco Bay and the agricultural regions of central California. Others planned north-south routes to join Oregon to southern California. Several enterprises actually surveyed their intended routes, and a few even broke ground. In the end, however, only the C&C entered Mono County, and Bodie remained forever isolated.[34]

Although Bodie's railroad dream did not materialize, its own line made two additions in 1882. In June, Locomotive No. 4 (*Bodie*) arrived, a little Porter 0-4-2T saddle tanker purchased new for logging operations at Mono Mills.[35] At the Bodie yard, the company extended its tracks to the Standard main shaft, where the steam-powered hoisting works consumed huge amounts of cordwood and lowered timbers into the mine to support the underground.[36] Nearly all of the ground from which ore was taken required shoring. Because the Standard's ore bodies were large, the amount of timbering was tremendous. The wooden supports also demanded frequent re-

placement. Ground swelling due to included clay caused 12 by 12-inch timbers to be "broken and crushed into pulp, as though they were corn stalks." Timbering and retimbering the Standard Mine consumed 5,500 board feet of lumber each month.[37] The railroad's spur track reached the shaft by climbing the southeastern flank of High Peak, where three switchbacks overcame the 200-foot difference in elevation between the switch yard and hoisting works.

In April 1882, the Standard main shaft, Bodie's deepest, reached the 1,200-foot level.[38] While some miners explored the 700-, 1,000-, and 1,200-foot levels, others extracted ore from the upper levels. Meanwhile, the Bulwer's six miners prospecting the 500-, 700-, and 1,000-foot levels through the Standard shaft had not found any ore worth milling. The Bulwer, however, paid dividends, the result of criticism generated in New York about misused Bulwer funds and annoyed investors. Recognizing that 98.8% of its stock was held in New York, the Standard indulged Bulwer shareholders with monthly dividends through 1882. These payments, ostensibly financed by renting the Bulwer half of the mill to the Standard, continued to be only 10 cents per share.[39]

Bodie's citizens remained confident for the moment. Their town had matured and its economy appeared relatively immune to the effects of a national depression that plagued mining stocks. Feelings were different among distant stock traders. One San Franciscan was sure that the mining stock market was about to rise out of its doldrums, though his logic was somewhat antagonistic. "This opinion is based on the fact that nearly all the stock now being sold is purchased by the 'insiders,' and when the 'outsiders' are cleaned out, an advance will be the result."[40] Even insiders could not conjure up a bull market, and those who were willing to gamble on Bodie's mines were getting harder and harder to find. In the month following the suspension of work on the railroad extension, the town was disappointed by news that the Standard Company planned to reduce its monthly dividends from 75 cents to 25 cents per share in September. The *Engineering and Mining Journal* expressed concern that the Standard Mine had "reached the end of its bonanza." Reporting that only large quantities of "low-grade ore" remained in the mine provided little encouragement.[41]

The discovery of another bonanza might interest investors so that more Bodie mines could reopen, but bad news seemed overwhelming in late 1882. Crosscuts on the 700- and 1,000-foot levels of the Standard Mine failed to uncover anything of value.[42] Furthermore, water regularly impeded work on the 1,200-foot level, where increasing inflow from the mine's expanding depth and breadth challenged the company's undersized pumping engine, which now struggled to keep the deepest work areas dry.

The Standard declared 12 monthly dividends in 1882, but its stock had slumped to $7 per share after dividends were decreased in September. Even though the mine shipped between 1,100 and 1,500 tons of ore from its upper levels every week, 50 stamps in the Standard and Bulwer-Standard mills had recovered only $1,258,057, little more than half the previous year's yield and proof that the quality of the ore was decreasing. Meanwhile, prospecting progressed eastward in the lower levels. On the 700-foot level, the east crosscut had been advanced 1,020 feet, cutting several seams of quartz, but finding nothing profitable. Below it, the crosscut on the 1,000-foot level was in 1,129 feet. Although extending to the far reaches of the property, it exposed quartz formations that carried no exploitable ore. Deeper yet, water repeatedly disrupted progress on the 1,200-foot level, where the crosscut was only 300 feet in length and had yet to reach the veins.[43]

The Bodie and Mono Mines: 1882

Stark contrasts confronted the folks in Bodie as spring arrived in 1882. The district's yield had increased steadily since 1877, yet the town was laden with scores of vacant houses and commercial buildings. The Standard, Bodie, Bodie Tunnel, Syndicate, and two Noonday mines supplied as much ore as their mills could handle, but the hills were studded with abandoned hoisting works. The Standard and Bodie companies had paid thousands of dollars in dividends, but other companies could no longer collect assessments from disappointed stockholders. Big Cornish pumps at the Red Cloud, Standard, and Lent shafts had successfully lowered the water table, yet only the Goodshaw, Belvidere, and South Bodie sprang back to life and took advantage of the dry ground by exploring their lower levels. Although the Bechtel, Oro, Black Hawk, Boston Consolidated, Union Consolidated, Tioga, and Consolidated Pacific were worked right along, only the Oro and Boston Consolidated still showed signs of ore worth milling. The Boston Consolidated's rock was processed early in the year by the little Miners mill, which then closed down in company with the already silent Spaulding and Silver Hill mills in the south end.

In town, unoccupied buildings had become a fire hazard. An article titled "Wasting Property" called attention to these derelicts and complained about "small youth and poker playing Indians" who roamed at liberty through the deserted structures.

> As a result petty larceny thieves find a field for their labors in stripping these uncared for places of anything and everything of value, . . . racking and bringing to ruin everything on the premises. Persons having property in charge—either their own or that of some one else—should look to it that it is not packed off piece by piece.[44]

On a similar theme, the newspapers noted that stagecoaches departing at 2:00 A.M. provided easy escape for debtors slipping out of town.

> Several of the "boys" have of late taken their departure, leaving utterly confiding creditors behind in ignorance of anything wrong until it is supremely too late. When a man gets to Sunshine [at the Nevada state line] he cannot be taken back for debt. . . . The fact is, this habit of 'jumping' is getting too too common.

Still, the town displayed vitality every month on payday. "During the early part of the evening Main Street contained a great many people. It looked like old times to see the crowds out. A great deal of money was paid out during the day by some of the leading companies."[45]

During the mining boom, Bodie had supported two banks: the Mono County Bank and the Bodie Bank. In April 1882, the latter institution closed its doors. By an amicable arrangement, the accounts were transferred to the Mono County Bank, leaving the brokerage and banking business to be carried on by only one firm.[46] A month later, the building that had housed the Bodie Bank reopened as the Pioneer Boot & Shoe Store.

In March, the upper levels in the Bodie Mine, having been stripped of their best ore, were abandoned except for a few miners prospecting for new ore bodies. The Bodie's directors, like those of the Mono Gold Mining Company, now focused on opening the 700- and 800-foot levels through the Lent Shaft and sinking the shaft deeper. To accomplish these tasks, a more powerful hoist and air compressor were purchased from the Comstock's Rock Island Mine.

In June 1882, the Lent Shaft extended 971 feet into the earth, passing the bottom of Bodie's deepest mine—the 1,200-foot Standard shaft. A month later, the Lent reached its 1,000-foot level, from which another crosscut was started toward the Fortuna. At the same time, the pumps delivered between 346,000 and 361,000 gallons of water to the surface every 24 hours.[47]

For the year 1882, the Bodie Consolidated Mining Company recorded production of $484,890, up slightly from the year before and enough to maintain second position behind the Standard. From the Lent Shaft, 100 to 150 tons of ore per week were hauled down the hill to the mill. Happy Bodie Company stockholders received a 25-cent dividend in August, their first dividend in more than two years. Dividends of 25 cents each followed in September and October, then one of 20 cents in November.[48] The activ-

DIVIDENDS.

SAN FRANCISCO, Aug. 28, 1882.

THE BODIE CONSOLIDATED MINING COMPANY has declared Dividend No. 10, of Twenty-five cents per share, payable on the 15th of September. Eastern stockholders of record will be paid at the office of Laidlaw & Co., 14 Wall Street, N. Y. Transfer-books close September 2d.

WILLIAM H. LENT, Secretary.

Figure 5-8: Speculators could choose from hundreds of western mining companies, but few investments brought capital returns. Dividends, however, kept Bodie on the financial pages in New York and San Francisco for nearly four decades. Published in a New York mining journal, this notice advises stockholders that the Bodie Consolidated Mining Company has declared a dividend. (*Engineering and Mining Journal* 9 September 1882. Courtesy, Engineering and Mining Journal)

ity at the Lent Shaft inspired confidence. A locally-based New York correspondent described Bodie with words of approval. "I must state that I find this place has a very prosperous future; notwithstanding many hoisting works are at present idle; but I am assured that they will be started up very soon and that this place will once more resume its former businesslike activity."[49]

Meanwhile, unlucky investors who owned Mono stock paid four more assessments. So far they had been assessed 17 times for a total of $422,500. An 1882 overview summarized the Mono Mine's unfortunate state.

Several quartz veins were explored by the workings from the old shaft, nearly all carrying pay ore in small quantities, but not in any exploitable body. The most promising deposit was found at the 575-foot level, from which we were driven by the water; none of the old workings extended far enough east to reach the Fortuna.

The report offered one ray of hope by reinforcing the concept that the Lent Shaft's aim was to reach and explore "that portion of the Fortuna vein that extends into the Mono ground."[50]

The Noonday and Red Cloud Mines: 1882

In the south end of the district, the Red Cloud Mine's magnificent pumping machinery worked tirelessly. The year 1882 opened with guarded expectations as water receded beneath Silver Hill. Abundant ore from the Noondays' upper levels kept the 40-stamp mill running at full capacity, when titillating rumors of a rich strike began circulating early in March. Unleashing exuberant optimism, the local press predicted success. Stock in the Noonday and North Noonday mining companies increased in value, creating a sensation in San Francisco when prices doubled. Within two weeks they had climbed from the usual two bits per share to $1.75. On March 25, 1882, the *Daily Free Press* confirmed the rumors. "A Young Bonanza," the paper proclaimed. "An Important Development in the Noonday Mines." Miners following the Noonday ledge in the exploratory winze had discovered a pocket of rich ore below the 512-foot level.[51]

Bodie's leading citizens and eminent mine superintendents were guided on a tour of the mine. A reporter accompanying the group described the ore as resembling that of the great Comstock Lode. One assay exceeded $1,800 per ton! A sample of the rock, gleaming with streaks of precious metal, was displayed at Noonday headquarters in San Francisco to thrill investors, who gazed at it in wonder.[52] Mining men were sure that the district's south end would at last produce a dividend-paying mine. William Stewart arrived from San Francisco to examine the vein, then declared, "I have never seen the Noondays looking so well."[53] The stock fell back slightly, then quivered around $1 per share as everyone waited in breathless anticipation for the incline shaft to attain a depth from which the rich ore could be extracted in earnest. From a point 275 feet below the 512-foot level, miners drove a crosscut eastward, intersecting the ledge in late May.[54]

A miner's guidebook once cautioned that a prideful prospector might select the best looking pieces of ore for assaying, "but that will not give him much information. . . . Assays of picked specimen-rock are very likely to be deceptive."[55] Such advice was not heeded by the Noonday companies. Despite glowing reports from Bodie's press (and emphatic denials that they were paid to write them) there was no bonanza. Except for a rich seam, the ore was low grade. As it became clear to even the most optimistic speculator that no dividends were forthcoming, the Noondays' stock began a gradual decline. It was back to 35 cents per share at the end of September, when the company levied its sixth assessment.

A close look at the district during the fall of 1882 revealed that only seven mines were taking out ore: the Standard, Bodie (worked through the Lent Shaft), Bodie Tunnel, Noonday, North Noonday, Syndicate, and Oro. Five others were working without success: the Bulwer, Bechtel, Tioga, Goodshaw, and Mono (also accessed through the Lent Shaft). The Belvidere, South Bodie, Boston Consolidated, Summit, Dudley, Addenda, White Cloud, Jupiter, Black Hawk, Union Consolidated, Consolidated Pacific, and Richter had suspended work altogether. So little profitable rock had been found that only six of the nine mills were still running at capacity. Shipments to the Miners, Spaulding, and Silver Hill mills became so infrequent that the stamps sat idle most of the year.

Still, Bodie was a mining camp with spirit, especially on Saturday nights. "There were a great many people on the streets last evening and considerable life and money were thrown into the town generally. Occasionally an inebriated citizen would howl, get knocked down or fall off the sidewalk. Many of the businessmen did a good business."[56]

Religious services had been held all along in various meeting halls, but it was not until September 1882 that Bodie's first house of worship was completed. It was a Roman Catholic church, named Saint John the Baptist.[57] A month later the Silver Hill mill, denied by the infrequency and, finally, the absence of ore shipments, succumbed to the uncertainties of its industry and was torn down. It was rebuilt near Aurora as the Gregory Flat mill.[58]

Figure 5-9: South of Mono Lake, the sawmill at Mono Mills supplied finished lumber and fuel for Bodie's mines 32 miles away. The mill is seen in this early twentieth-century view as the *Mono* prepares to depart. Trains leaving Mono Mills usually consisted of 10 to 12 flatcars. Because of switchbacks and steep grades beyond Mono Basin, the engine delivered three or four cars at a time to Bodie while the remaining cars waited at Lime Kiln station. The railroad owned no passenger coaches and published no timetables. Anybody wanting a ride did so at their own risk while seated on an empty flatcar, or perched upon a load of wood. (A. A Forbes photograph. Courtesy, Gregory Bock)

The gallant Red Cloud pumps kept pace as the great shaft was pushed downward. Water receded further at the Noonday, where the incline descended into the darkness beneath Silver Hill. Working three eight-hour shifts, miners drilled into the rock, then blasted it away, hoping that more high-grade would be found deeper. Their pace was feverish, pausing only long enough to allow workers at the nearby Red Cloud shaft to achieve sufficient depth to remove water ahead of the Noonday incline.

The pumps worked magnificently, allowing the Red Cloud shaft to reach the 870-foot level in late November. From the Noonday's incline, miners cross-cut toward the Noonday ledge 325 feet below the 512-foot level.[59] Below them, the incline reached 387 feet below the 512-foot level. Then disaster struck. On December 2, 1882, the town was stunned by news that the Noonday, North Noonday, and Red Cloud companies had been served with foreclosure notices, and the mines were shut down. Dazed citizens gathered to read the local newspapers. A New York mining journal summed up the events.

On December 2d [1882] attachments, amounting to $460,000, were placed on the Noonday, North Noonday, and Red Cloud mines by Wells, Fargo & Co.'s bank. This large sum, it is understood, has been advanced . . . to these corporations . . . over and above the amount derived from milling ores and from assessments during the past three years. The mines and mill are now in the hands of the sheriff, and have been closed down. The work of raising [removing] the pump columns in the Red Cloud shaft is now in progress. The stoppage of the Red Cloud pump is a very serious matter, as that has thus far drained the entire south end.[60]

Figure 5-10: Logs were dragged from the forest with high-wheeled vehicles known as "Michigan wheels." As the team pulls, a lever and reel mechanism on the axle lifts the front end of the logs to ease the work of dragging them. (Emil Billeb collection. Courtesy, Vickie Daniels)

Figure 5-11: The *Mono* delivers a trainload of logs to the sawmill at Mono Mills. (Emil Billeb collection. Courtesy, Vickie Daniels)

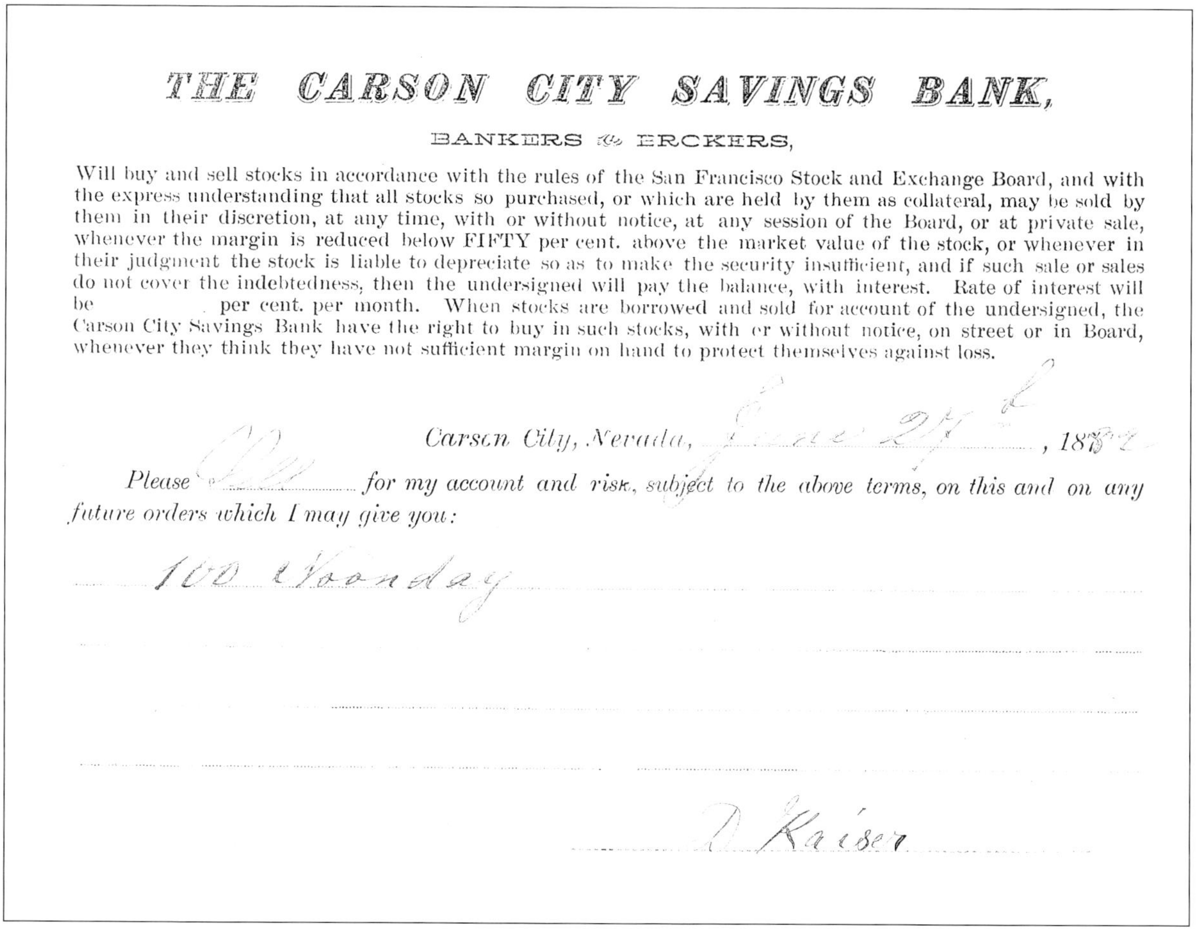

THE CARSON CITY SAVINGS BANK,

BANKERS & BROKERS,

Will buy and sell stocks in accordance with the rules of the San Francisco Stock and Exchange Board, and with the express understanding that all stocks so purchased, or which are held by them as collateral, may be sold by them in their discretion, at any time, with or without notice, at any session of the Board, or at private sale, whenever the margin is reduced below FIFTY per cent. above the market value of the stock, or whenever in their judgment the stock is liable to depreciate so as to make the security insufficient, and if such sale or sales do not cover the indebtedness, then the undersigned will pay the balance, with interest. Rate of interest will be ____ per cent. per month. When stocks are borrowed and sold for account of the undersigned, the Carson City Savings Bank have the right to buy in such stocks, with or without notice, on street or in Board, whenever they think they have not sufficient margin on hand to protect themselves against loss.

Carson City, Nevada, *June 27* , 188_

Please *buy* ____ for my account and risk, subject to the above terms, on this and on any future orders which I may give you:

100 Noonday

D. Kaiser

Figure 5-12: An example of documentation common in mining stock transactions. A shareholder, perhaps with inside information, sells 100 shares of Noonday stock in June 1882. The transaction occurred shortly after a discovery of rich ore invited exaggerated reporting that boosted stock prices to $1.75 per share. "The development," professed a telegram published in the *Engineering and Mining Journal*, ". . . will probably produce a general revival of work in the mines along the mineral belt which have been closed down for months." Instead, Noonday stock prices slid during the ensuing six months, until the mine closed in December. (Author's collection)

It was disclosed later that the Noonday companies, celebrated as two of Bodie's biggest producers, had been running on credit for years. Most of the cash infusions had been provided by two principal stockholders, James B. Haggin and Lloyd Tevis.[61] These men, famous as industrial entrepreneurs, owned financial empires stretching from San Francisco to the Black Hills. Their holdings included the Southern Pacific Railroad, the Anaconda Mine in Montana, and the Homestake Mine in Dakota. Tevis was also the president of Wells, Fargo & Company. The Noondays had incurred an enormous debt to these men and others in a daring gamble to reach below the water line. They had also run up costs by building a huge mill and introducing a novel ore treatment process. Heralded at the time as proof of the mine's great wealth, these improvements were little more than futile attempts to turn a profit by processing large quantities of low-grade ore. The managers were mistaken on all accounts. Simply put, the ore in the mine, although extensive in volume, could not be made to pay no matter how much was processed. The Noonday, North Noonday, and Red Cloud companies were ruined.[62]

Stopping the Red Cloud's pumps effectively ended mining in the south end. One by one, the few companies still working on Silver Hill ceased operations as rising water flooded their workings. Placer mining in Taylor Gulch came to a halt when watercourses went dry. Liens were filed against the Red Cloud Consolidated Mining Company by 26 employees seeking unpaid wages. Workers placed 37 liens on the Noonday and North Noonday companies.[63] Before the year ended, the three companies had been stricken from the San Francisco Stock and Exchange Board.

One oft-told tale that resulted from halting the Red Cloud's pumps involved a miner employed at the nearby Oro Mine. When the Oro closed down, its employees received checks for back wages amounting to one-third of what they were due, the balance to be paid in 60 days. With one exception, the men accepted the terms, albeit reluctantly. The holdout was Mike McCallum, who wanted his check written in full. He visited the mine office to discuss the matter with Superintendent Thomas Steel. William Barker, who was present when the distressed miner arrived to take his pay, described the confrontation.

"How are you going to get it?" asked Steel.

"I am going to make you give it to me," McCallum threatened.

"I am not heeled. Are you?" the superintendent inquired, indicating he was unarmed.

"Yes, I am," affirmed McCallum as he drew from his pocket a six-shooter "about a foot long."

"Is it loaded?" inquired Steel, thoroughly interested.

"Yes," said McCallum as he pointed the pistol out the door and fired a shot. "Now, the d——d company owes me this money, and I want it right off."

Steel knew he was in a fix. He had no authority to issue the check, but the enraged miner appeared intent on killing him if he refused to do so.

"Mr. Barker," Superintendent Steel cried. "What would you do if you were in my place?"

"Do?" the terrified Barker exclaimed. "I would make out the check d——d quick."

McCallum kept his gun in his hand while the superintendent completed the draft, then went directly to the bank and cashed it.[64]

McCallum was not seen until he was arrested the following day and charged with robbery. In Bridgeport the judge ruled that there was insufficient evidence to hold the prisoner and released him. The decision received "demonstrations of approval by the spectators in the court room."[65]

The Noonday and North Noonday had produced more bullion than any other property in the south end. During their years of operation, 1878 through 1882, their annual production consistently ranked the pair among the district's best mines. The California state mineralogist placed their total yield at $1,023,290, most of which had come at high cost from low-grade ore. Earnings were so meager that neither the Noonday Mining Company nor the North Noonday Mining Company ever paid a single dividend. They each levied seven assessments, costing their stockholders $243,000 and $252,000 respectively. The Red Cloud Consolidated Mining Company, which also paid no dividends, levied 11 assessments totaling $255,000. Although by then the district had produced some $18,000,000 in gold and silver, only the Standard, Bodie, and Bulwer had declared dividends. The sudden collapse of the Red Cloud and the two Noonday companies, followed by closures of the south end's Oro and Goodshaw and the Tioga on Bodie Bluff, left only the Standard, Bodie, Syndicate, Bodie Tunnel, Bulwer, Mono, and the Bechtel (all in the north) still working, and only the first four mentioned were extracting ore.

Downtown, people lined up to buy one-way tickets out of Bodie.

There is considerable bustle and confusion in and around the stage office these mornings. A great many people are going away. Some are taking a permanent

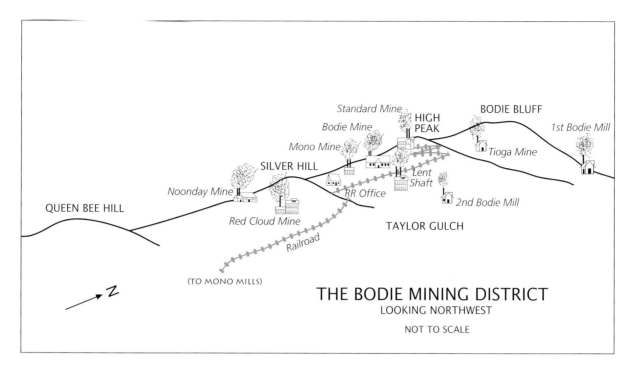

THE BODIE MINING DISTRICT
LOOKING NORTHWEST
NOT TO SCALE

Map 7: Scores of mine shafts were sunk during Bodie's heyday, but most of them had been abandoned by late 1881. Thereafter, the eastern slope was dominated by pumping and hoisting works at the Red Cloud, Standard, and Lent shafts. A narrow gauge railroad, approaching from the south, climbs to a switch yard, from which a spur track ascends High Peak to the Standard shaft.

leave of Bodie. . . . It is quite noticeable that the trunks to be shipped are of unusual size. In the early excitement of this camp a majority of the people coming here had no trunks at all. They were not troubled with a wealth of clothing or an abundance of coin. If it is an indication of wealth to own a big trunk, there then are a great many wealthy people in Bodie.[66]

If Bodie's mines were showing signs of weakness, its devout were not. A Methodist-Episcopal church had been built to welcome those of the Protestant faith. Unlike the Catholic church, the new church had a belfry. When its bell rang on Christmas Day 1882, it was the first church bell to be heard in Mono County.

In January 1883, the Red Cloud, Noonday, and North Noonday companies petitioned the Superior Court for insolvency. Nearly a year later, on November 19,

the properties were sold at public auction to satisfy judgments exceeding $550,000.[67] Creditors would keep the properties entangled in litigation for years. As the south end grew silent, the abandoned Noonday hoisting works stood quietly on the crest of Silver Hill as a painful reminder of the vicissitudes of Bodie's industry. Below it, overlooking the road to Mono Lake, the extravagant Noonday mill lay in ghostly silence. Behind Silver Hill, a mighty pumping engine that had run fewer than two years watched over the flooded Red Cloud shaft. The engine was so powerful that it conquered the water while never running faster than half speed. As time passed, only these decaying monuments to unwarranted risk-taking recalled the drama that had unfolded in the south end.

Six years after the south end's preeminent mines were closed, the Noonday and Red Cloud's surface facilities were dismantled. During July and August 1888, citizens of Bodie watched a stream of freight wagons rumble through town, the big teams straining to pull their loads of rusting machinery. In Hawthorne the equipment was transferred to the C&C and shipped to the Anaconda Silver Mining Company in Butte City, Montana.[68] For another three years there remained one last survivor of the south end's heady days, when impassioned mining companies had built more mills than the mines could supply. Then, in 1891, the lonely Spaulding mill was taken apart and shipped to the nearby Homer mining district at Lundy Lake.[69]

1. *Daily Free Press* 16 January 1881; 18 January 1881; 23 January 1881; 9 February 1881. Grant Smith remembered an earlier lynching not found in existing documents. Describing the September 1880 incident, he wrote: "An opium-fiend who had been thrown out of a saloon by a bartender, and returned with a shotgun, stood in the doorway, and filled the bartender full of buckshot." (Smith, "Last of the Old Time Mining Camps," 71) Smith recalled that the murderer was taken out of jail and hanged by a mob. A later researcher found that the accused died in jail amidst rumors of the "601." (McGrath, *Gunfighters*, 127-129) For more information on the murder of Thomas Treloar and the vigilante hanging of Joseph DeRoche, see Roger D. McGrath, *Gunfighters, Highwaymen, and Vigilantes: Violence on the Frontier* (Berkeley, CA: University of California Press, 1984), 234-244. A contemporary newspaper account is reprinted in Warren Loose, *Bodie Bonanza: The True Story of a Flamboyant Past* (Las Vegas, NV: Nevada Publications, 1979), 169-171.

2. *Territorial Enterprise* in *Daily Free Press* 23 January 1881. That Bodie was changing was undeniable. A year earlier the town supported five daily and three weekly newspapers. By the time of the lynching, only two dailies and one weekly remained to report it.

3. *Daily Free Press* 24 February 1881.

4. *Daily Free Press* 19 May 1880; 8 October 1880; 2 November 1880; 13 January 1881; *Bodie Standard-News* 9 November 1880.

5. *Weekly Standard-News* 30 March 1881; *Engineering and Mining Journal* 9 April 1881, 252; *Mining and Scientific Press* 23 April 1881, 261.

6. *Daily Free Press* 4 May 1881.

7. *Daily Free Press* 18 May 1881.

8. *Daily Free Press* 14 June 1881.

9. *Weekly Standard-News* 15 June 1881. Bodie's gushing reviewer incorrectly attributed the drama to British author Edward Bulwer-Lytton (1803-1873), who wrote several successful plays, but not *Ingomar*.

10. *Weekly Standard-News* 26 October 1881.

11. *Daily Free Press* 1 June 1881.

12. California State Mining Bureau, *Eighth Annual Report of the State Mineralogist, for the Year Ending October 1, 1888* (Sacramento, CA: Superintendent of State Printing, 1888), 396.

13. *Mining Record* 5 March 1881, 226.

14. *Engineering and Mining Journal* 19 February 1881, 131; 28 May 1881, 371; *Mining and Scientific Press* 12 February 1881, 101; *Weekly Standard-News* 29 June 1881; 2 November 1881; 16 November 1881; *Mining Record* 18 March 1882, 251. Because of its enormous low-pressure cylinder, the two-cylinder pumping engine at the Red Cloud was by far the largest and most efficient steam engine in Bodie. It is impossible, however, to determine if it was the district's most powerful. Rudimentary calculations based on available data indicate that the huge single-cylinder engine at the Lent Shaft was very close in horsepower to that at the Red Cloud.

15. *Mining and Scientific Press* 19 November 1881, 333.

16. *Daily Bodie Standard* 11 May 1880; *Bodie Standard-News* 26 July 1880; 18 November 1880; *Daily Free Press* 19 May 1881; 27 May 1881; 5 August 1881.

17. U.S. Bureau of the Mint, *Report of the Director of the Mint upon the Statistics of the Production of the Precious Metals in the United States [for 1882]* (Washington, DC: Government Printing Office, 1883), 68; *Mining and Scientific Press* 20 August 1881, 117.

18. *Daily Free Press* 8 December 1881.

19. *Daily Free Press* 14 April 1881; *Weekly Standard-News* 20 April 1881; 4 May 1881; *Engineering and Mining Journal* 7 May 1881, 319.

20. *Weekly Standard-News* 4 May 1881; Karen Colbourne McAbeer, "The Bodie Railroad" (Master of Arts Thesis, California State College, Sonoma, CA, 1973), 18-19, 43, 70-71.

21. *Carson Daily Index* 21 May 1881.

22. *Daily Free Press* 7 August 1881; *Weekly Standard-News* 12 October 1881.

23. *Daily Free Press* 15 November 1881; 27 October 1882. For more information on Bodie's railroad and its logging operation, see David F. Myrick, "The Bodie & Benton Railway," chap. in *Railroads of Nevada and Eastern California, Vol. 1* (Berkeley, CA: Howell-North Books, 1962), 298-313, and George Turner, "Bodie & Benton Railway," chap. in *Narrow Gauge Nostalgia: A Compendium of California Short Lines* (Carona del Mar, CA: Trans-Anglo Books, 1971), 9-25. Firsthand ac-

counts with photographs are found in: Emil W. Billeb, *Mining Camp Days* (Berkeley, CA: Howell-North Books, 1968), 35-75; Emil W. Billeb, "Bodie's Railroad That Was," *The Pony Express* 24 (June 1957): 1-12; Jay Ellis Ransom, "Old Timer Relives Days When Railroad Was Built In the Sky," *The California Highway Patrolman* 13 (September 1949): 16-17, 121, 124, 128-130. Rationale for extending the railroad to outside markets is presented in: Karen Colbourne McAbeer, "The Bodie Railroad" (Master of Arts Thesis, California State College, Sonoma, 1973).

24. *Daily Free Press* 4 October 1881; 10 November 1881; 15 November 1881; 24 November 1881; Billeb, "Bodie's Railroad That Was," 10.

25. Rod MacDuff, "Prescott & Scott—A Short History of the Builders of BR&LCo Locomotives #2 and #3," *Link & Pin: Friends of Bodie Railway & Lumber Co. Inc. Newsletter* Spring 1998, 2-3; Mallory Hope Ferrell, *Locomotives of the Bodie Railway & Lumber Co.* Letter and photographs to the author 25 May 1999; *Daily Free Press* 24 November 1881. The railroad had little effect on the town's growth. At the time the line was completed in November 1881, Bodie had an abundance of vacant structures. The railroad was never intended to carry passengers, and its rails never reached downtown. Throughout its 36-year life the line's primary purpose was to convey timber and cordwood for Bodie's mines.

26. *Mining Record* 17 December 1881, 584; *Engineering and Mining Journal* 31 December 1881, 437.

27. *Daily Free Press* 5 November 1881; 9 December 1881; 18 December 1881; *Weekly Standard-News* 14 December 1881; *Engineering and Mining Journal* 5 March 1881, 161; U.S. Bureau of the Mint, *Report of the Director of the Mint upon the Statistics of the Production of the Precious Metals in the United States [for 1881]* (Washington, DC: Government Printing Office, 1882), 54-55. The Howland Pulverizer installed at the Bodie Tunnel mill was described in 1882: "In appearance it considerably resembles an ordinary pan, except that it is about half the depth, and the sides, instead of being perpendicular, are concave or dome-shaped. Its diameter is but 5½ feet. A muller in the center revolves at the rate of 175 times per minute. This carries with it 12 loose shoes, each of which weighs 60 pounds. These shoes resemble hubs, being round and hollow, and flat on their ends, on which they stand. The shoes do not pass around with the same rapidity as the muller, on which they ride, as they come in contact with a stationary rim near the outer edge of the pulverizer. The centrifugal force given them by the muller keeps them pressed against this rim, and the friction thereby induced causes the shoes to revolve and grind on the muller." (U.S. Mint 1882, 54-55)

28. *Daily Free Press* 4 November 1881.

29. *Daily Free Press* 27 November 1881; 15 January 1882.

30. U.S. Mint, *Report of the Director [for 1881]*, 52.

31. It is useful to compare Bodie's most prolific mine at the height of its production with the richest mines on the Comstock. The famous ore body below Virginia City, known as the "Big Bonanza," was discovered in 1873 in adjoining mines: the Consolidated Virginia and the California. The ore extended from the 1,200-foot level to the 1,650-foot level and kept two mills, with 60 and 80 stamps, running 24 hours a day. In 1876, at the height of production, the Consolidated Virginia yielded $16,657,649 and the California $13,400,841. The highest price per share of their stock hovered at $710 and $790 respectively. At that time each company paid between $3 and $10 per share in monthly dividends.

32. *Daily Free Press* 12 July 1882.

33. *Daily Free Press* 27 January 1882; McAbeer, *The Bodie Railroad*, 84-85. After halting construction of the connecting

line, Yerington, Graves, and the Cooks used the railroad to supply lumber to Bodie for about another year and a half. Although they retained ownership of the railroad, sawmill, and timberland, the business of running the operation was turned over to a lessee in January 1884. Construction superintendent Thomas Holt was first of several lessees to try his hand at making a living from the railroad.

34. Three railroads planned to pass through Bodie: The Nevada & Oregon; the California & Nevada; and the Modesto, Tuolumne, & Mono. Four others intended to cross Mono Basin: The Salt Lake & Western; the Southern Pacific; the California & Yosemite Short Line, a branch of the California Central; and a branch of the Carson & Colorado.

35. *Daily Free Press* 23 June 1882; Ferrell, *Locomotives*; Emil W. Billeb, *Mining Camp Days* (Berkeley, CA: Howell-North Books, 1968), 67, 70.

36. *Daily Free Press* 14 December 1881; 28 June 1882.

37. *Daily Free Press* 30 December 1880.

38. *Mining Record* 18 March 1882, 251; 22 April 1882, 371. At this time, Bodie's second deepest shaft was the Tioga, located high on Bodie Bluff. The Tioga shaft reached a depth of 1,100 feet early in November 1882, without pumps. Water was brought to the surface in bailing tanks. The mine closed one month later. (*Daily Free Press* 14 June 1881; 7 November 1882; 6 December 1882) The Tioga's position as Bodie's second deepest shaft was not challenged until December 1887, when the Lent Shaft passed the 1,100-foot level as it was excavated to a final depth of 1,200 feet.

39. *Mining Record* 18 February 1882, 151; William R. Balch, *Mines, Miners, and Mining Interests of the United States in 1882* (Philadelphia, PA: The Mining Industrial Publishing

Bureau, 1882), 1139.

40. *Daily Free Press* 30 July 1882.

41. *Engineering and Mining Journal* 26 August 1882, 105; *Daily Free Press* 4 October 1882.

42. *Engineering and Mining Journal* 16 September 1882, 151.

43. William Irwin, *Fourth Annual Report of the Standard Consolidated Mining Company for the Year Ending February 1, 1883* (San Francisco, CA: W. T. Galloway & Co., 1883), 31-33; Balch, *Mines, Miners, and Mining*, 1177.

44. *Daily Free Press* 10 February 1882.

45. *Daily Free Press* 15 January 1882; *Daily Free Press* 8 February 1882.

46. *Daily Free Press* 2 April 1882.

47. *Engineering and Mining Journal* 4 March 1882, 123; 18 March 1882, 147; *Daily Free Press* 25 May 1882; Eliot Lord, *Comstock Mining and Miners* (1883; reprint, San Diego, CA: Howell-North Books, 1980), 314a; *Mining Record* 3 June 1882, 516; 22 July 1882, 83; 29 July 1882, 107.

48. Balch, *Mines, Miners, and Mining*, 1121.

49. *Mining Record* 11 March 1882, 223.

50. Balch, *Mines, Miners, and Mining*, 1119.

51. Balch, *Mines, Miners, and Mining*, 1160; *Daily Free Press* 12 March 1882; 25 March 1882; 28 March 1882; *Weekly Standard-News* 15 March 1882.

52. *Daily Free Press* 30 March 1882.

53. *Daily Free Press* 18 April 1882.

54. *Daily Free Press* 30 May 1882; 31 May 1882.

55. *Mining Industry and Tradesman* 25 February 1892, 92.

56. *Daily Free Press* 6 August 1882.

57. *Daily Free Press* 12 September 1882.

58. *Bodie Evening Miner* 14 October 1882; *Daily Free Press* 3 November 1882; 31 December 1882.

59. Balch, *Mines, Miners, and Mining*, 1162; *Daily Free Press* 22 March 1882; 28 November 1882; *Mining Record* 28 October 1882; *Bodie Evening Miner* 28 November 1882.

60. *Engineering and Mining Journal* 16 December 1882, 324.

61. James B. Haggin (1827-1914) and Lloyd Tevis (1824-1899).

62. *Daily Free Press* 3 December 1882; 5 December 1882; 6 December 1882; 27 December 1882; 4 January 1883; 10 January 1883; 16 January 1883; 20 January 1883; 23 January 1883; 28 January 1883; 30 January 1883; 18 April 1883; *Mining Record* 18 September 1880, 273; U.S. Mint, *Report of the Director [for 1882]*, 69.

63. Mono County, *Liens*, Book A, 417-529.

64. *Daily Free Press* 27 December 1882.

65. *Daily Free Press* 31 December 1882.

66. *Daily Free Press* 14 December 1882.

67. *Chronicle-Union* 27 January 1883; *Mining Record* 17 February 1883, 129; *Engineering and Mining Journal* 1 December 1883, 345; 29 December 1883, 400.

68. *Walker Lake Bulletin* 18 July 1888; 15 August 1888. No photographs have been found depicting the south end mills, which includes the huge 40-stamp Noonday mill. Similarly, not a single image is known that shows the great Red Cloud pumping plant.

69. *Walker Lake Bulletin* 1 July 1891; 15 July 1891.

Profits From Waste Products: Bodie's Tailings Mills

1. Rossiter W. Raymond, *Statistics of Mines and Mining in the States and Territories West of the Rocky Mountains* (Wash-

ington, DC: Government Printing Office, 1870), 697-698; Dan De Quille [William Wright], *The Big Bonanza* (1876; reprint, Las Vegas, NV: Nevada Publications, 1982), 163.

2. "A Fine Tailings Mill," *Mining and Scientific Press* 7 June 1873, 362; "Tailings," *Gold Hill Daily News* 12 November 1877.

3. *Engineering and Mining Journal* 9 August 1879, 94; Mono County, *Deeds, Book J*, 287-295; Mono County, *Deeds, Book H*, 576; *Daily Free Press* 28 September 1881.

4. Benjamin Silliman Jr. and William P. Blake, *Prospec-*

tus of the Empire Gold & Silver Mining Co. of New York (New York, NY: William H. Arthur, 1864), 32-33; Joseph Wasson, *Bodie and Esmeralda* (San Francisco, CA: Spaulding, Barto & Co., 1878), 9; *Mining Record* 17 September 1881, 272; *Daily Free Press* 14 March 1882.

"The Day Was Simply Lovely": Independence Day 1881

1. *Daily Free Press* 6 July 1881.

Figure 6-1: An 1895 scene, looking eastward, shows the Lent Shaft's hoisting works. Five smokestacks are evidence of the massive steam-powered machinery that pumped a flood of water and hoisted tons of rock. Begun in 1880 by the Bodie Consolidated Mining Company and the Mono Gold Mining Company to intersect the Fortuna Lode, the Lent Shaft attained a depth of 1,000 feet in 1882. It was extended in 1887, reaching the 1,200-foot level in 1888. The lower levels were abandoned a year and a half later, having produced little of value. (Francis H. Frederick collection. Courtesy, California Division of Mines and Geology)

CHAPTER SIX

"A QUIET TOWN IS BODIE TODAY"
1883-1889

There was considerable decrease in value of ore stoped during [the] past week. It is gradually getting lower grade and now leaves very little margin for profit.
　　—Mining Record, November 29, 1884

What is needed now is explorations on the lower levels. To do that successfully the Lent Shaft must be kept free from water; that will drain the Standard to the 1,200 level. Then that mine, as well as the Bodie and Mono, can be thoroughly prospected.
　　—Financial and Mining Record, May 15, 1886

When we take into consideration the idleness on the part of so many of our mines and mills, and the limited number of men who have been employed in the mines of the district during the year, the showing is not a very bad one for a camp that has had the bottom so completely knocked out of it by the pessimists as has Bodie.
　　—Mining and Scientific Press, January 29, 1887

There will surely be a mining boom at Bodie ere long. It is impossible for a camp surrounded with mines, such as those which environ that place, to escape a good old-fashioned mining boom.
　　—Mining and Scientific Press, September 17, 1887

The Bodie and Mono Mines

The closure of the Noonday and Red Cloud Mines brought with it a sudden and dramatic decrease in Bodie's population. Within a month, 250 former employees of the south end mines, and their families, had left town.[1] "The exodus steadily continues," affirmed a nearby newspaper. "All classes of people are leaving, business houses are closing and property and rents are about down to zero."[2]

As residents of Bodie well knew, 15 district companies had been removed from the San Francisco stock exchange during the previous year for failure to pay the annual $100 membership fee.[3] Disregarding the obvious scarcity of profitable ore, the local press blamed the Miners Union for the district's misfortunes, claiming that the union's arbitrary canon of $4 per day pay for miners depleted capital and discouraged investors. Graphically displaying this viewpoint, an editor penned Bodie's epitaph.

HERE LIES
The Remains Of Bodie
A Once Flourishing and Prosperous Camp,
Which departed this life in the flower of its youth,
And in the noontide of a brilliant future.
KILLED
By the Four-Dollar-a-Day Rule of the Miners'
Union.[4]

In 1883, Bodie was one of only a few western mining districts where $4 per day was still paid to miners. Industry-wide, wages had dropped steadily since the 1860s, when Comstock quartz miners received $6 to $8 per day for underground work, earning western boomtowns a reputation for the nation's highest pay rates. Mine owners paid lavishly during flush times, but in a business that was based upon depleting its source of revenue, few companies could sustain such extravagance for long, and wages invariably dropped. By the 1870s, $4 per day had become the Comstock standard for underground miners, and the benchmark from which pay scales were measured throughout the West. Actual wages, however, varied from town to town, depending on local conditions.

Mine owners, facing nationwide economic problems during the 1880s, sought to reduce wages further, asserting that high operating expenses would shorten the working lives of the mines.[5] However extravagant, wages should be high, countered the unions. Underground work was dangerous, and living expenses were exorbitant in remote mining towns. Despite union opposition, wages fell in many districts, but the scale for Bodie's underground miners remained fixed at $4 per day. This was a source of local pride among the laboring class, but a luxury that faced sharpening criticism each time a mine closed.

As an industry standard, $4 per day applied mostly to miners and other underground workers. Some mineworkers earned more, some less. The payroll for one mine at Bodie reveals that during the mid-1880s, laborers and surface hands earned $3.50 per day. While miners received $4 per day, so did carmen, station tenders, and timbermen. Shift bosses and skilled tradesmen, such as engineers, blacksmiths, and carpenters, earned $5 a day.

In June 1883, the Bodie Company purchased the neighboring Jupiter Mine, whose principal ore bodies had been auspiciously named the Lent and Boyd ledges.[6] Their proximity to the Bodie Mine turned out to be the Jupiter's primary asset. Four years earlier, the mine's superior position had given rise to Bodie's most celebrated shoot-out, when Jupiter employees fought intruders from a neighboring mine in a deadly battle over ownership. Later, the Jupiter's lower levels were easily explored through the Lent Shaft, but the mine never developed into a big producer, and its excellent location was of no benefit to stockholders.

Through most of 1883, miners in the Lent Shaft worked the Fortuna lode from the 700-, 800-, and 1,000-foot levels, while massive pumping machinery kept the mine well drained. There was even talk of sinking the shaft deeper. Then, in October, townspeople learned that pumping in the Lent's lower levels had ceased, and the Bodie and Mono's deepest regions would flood. The big engine slowed, then sustained a pace to just meet the water needs of the distant Bodie mill.[7] Faithfully casting events in a positive light, a local newspaper rationalized that stopping work on the 1,000-foot level would not affect profits, because the Bodie Company's best rock came from above the 800-foot level. The report carefully emphasized that ore taken from the higher levels "has been of better quality than heretofore, and the bullion shipments have been larger." The "appearance" of the mine, it affirmed, "is better than it has been for some time."[8]

Such unfounded assurances did little to buoy spirits, especially when workers were laid off as water filled the Lent Shaft's 1,000-foot level, then gradually rose above the 700-foot level. The town's tattered economy was further imperiled when the Lent's near-idle pumps allowed water to rise in the Standard Mine, 1,000 feet away. Defying the Standard's capacity to remove it, the silent tide filled the deepest part of the district's most productive mine, forcing workmen out and dashing all hopes of finding ore bodies in the lower levels.[9]

The quick response of workmen momentarily restored some dignity to the Lent Shaft later that autumn, when fire broke out downtown in Brown's Hotel on November 3. Alarms sounded, and the Lent's pumps and bailing tanks immediately replenished the neglected reservoir. After the hose companies reached the hydrants and found abundant water, a local newspaperman declared with obvious relief that Bodie had been saved from "total destruction."[10]

Late in 1883, miners reopened the old Bodie shaft, initiating a search for pay ore in the upper levels. It was the Lent Shaft, however, that had yielded most of the year's take before pumping costs proved prohibitive and its lower levels vanished under the murk. The Bodie Consolidated Mining Company realized $246,820—barely half that of the previous year. Although ranked second in the district, its yearly production was little more than one-fifth that of the Standard.

The Bodie had also levied three assessments and paid no dividends. Mono shareholders, convinced that the Lent's flooded 700-, 800-, 900-, and 1,000-foot levels had been their best hope for dividends, found little comfort when the heretofore unproductive Mono shaft was reopened. Hoisting machinery taken from the Mono for sinking the Lent Shaft was returned, and exploring resumed in the Mono's upper levels.[11]

By the end of 1883, fewer mines were worked, and fewer were producing bullion than at any time since 1877. Of the nine original mills, only three were running steadily: the Standard and Bulwer-Standard, which were crushing ore for the Standard Company, and the Bodie mill. The town's population had declined to about 2,500.[12]

As disappointments mounted during the opening days of 1884, San Francisco traders watched in disbelief as Bodie Con. stock began to rise. Inexplicably, prices doubled, then tripled, climbing from $1.50 to $12.50 per share in just three weeks. Purchase orders poured into the city. One newspaper, well-seasoned by lavishly staged stock swindles, suggested that the mine's directors had trotted out a stash of high-grade ore to drive stock prices up. William Lent's ring of insiders, unaware of any developments in the mine, issued a blunt statement insisting that there was nothing to warrant a stock advance. This prompted accusations that management was trying to hold prices down until dramatic news from Bodie could be exploited to greatest effect. With such opinions flying around San Francisco, the younger Lent was dispatched to Bodie to find out just what was happening.[13]

The public learned the facts on February 2, after a couple of talkative miners from the Bodie Mine spoke to the *Homer Mining Index*. There had been not one, but two discoveries, both in the old workings of the Bodie Mine. On the 306-foot level, workmen found that an abandoned drift had caved, exposing a previously unknown segment of the famous Fortuna lode. The other discovery, on the 206-foot level, was a vein extending from the Mono Mine known as the "Vulcan ledge." It was thought to be barren until this ore-bearing section was found on the Bodie side of the boundary. When the surprised miners realized the extent of their discoveries, they concealed them from the superintendent and raced into town to buy Bodie Con. stock. This drove prices to a high of $13.25, but their zeal to purchase as much stock as possible had tipped their hand by drawing attention to the plot.[14]

Superintendent Henry A. Whiting had unwittingly allowed miners to get the jump on management—something rarely seen in western mining. Whiting was fired as soon as the situation became clear. "Never on the Pacific Coast," wrote a local editor, "have the insiders been left so completely out in the cold as when the recent bonanza was struck in the Bodie Consolidated."[15] The oversight also triggered blistering accusations of incompetence and mismanagement from investors. At a scheduled meeting of stockholders a week later, Lent and his crowd were voted out of office. The overthrow was "very quietly effected," reported the San Francisco Post. "We are informed that this change practically retires the Lent party, and that the control now rests in the hands of . . . operators who hold a very large amount of the stock."[16]

Two and a half months later, on April 23, 1884, the younger Lent was found dead on a San Francisco park bench. Although the bullet in his chest appeared suspicious, it was concluded that William H. Lent committed suicide because of ill health.[17]

The two recently-discovered veins were not as rich as the Bruce/Burgess nor the Fortuna bonanzas, but their combined size ensured profits. The new management quickly declared a dividend, then leased the 15-stamp Bodie Tunnel mill in March. With two mills crushing ore, weekly shipments increased from approximately 150 to 500 tons. Once again the Bodie Mine was alive with activity. Miners on the 200- and 300-foot levels stoped the Vulcan, and on the 300-, 400-, and 500-foot levels, the Fortuna. Aware that the contract with the Bodie Tunnel mill was about to expire, the Bodie Company secured the Bulwer's 15 stamps for a six-week run. Utilizing the Bodie mill, Bodie Tunnel mill, and half of the Bulwer-Standard mill, the Bodie Company impressed its investors by reporting that there were 40 stamps dropping on its ore in June 1884.

In July, while the Bulwer-Standard mill was still crushing ore from the Bodie Mine, the Bodie Company diverted its own mill to treating tailings. Assaying at about $6 per ton, tailings represented a source of gold, silver, and reusable mercury readily available in ponds near the mill.[18] All told, 1884 proved to be the Bodie Company's best year since the bonanzas of 1878 and 1879. By increasing production, the Bodie's $618,024 yield nearly tripled its previous year's output. The company also paid two 50-cent dividends, its first disbursements in 16

months, and levied no assessments. Speculators, however, were well aware that the newfound ore was of poor grade. Because the day-by-grubby-day mining of subsistence-grade ore did not possess the glamour of previous bonanzas, apathy toward the company's stock blurred its accomplishment.

Investor disinterest proved to be justified when, in late 1884, a setback befell the Bodie Company. Their mine ran out of profitable ore. Ore shipments to the Bulwer-Standard mill ceased in August, followed in late December by an end to deliveries of tailings to the Bodie mill. Shutting down the Bodie mill sent an unmistakable message to investors that the mine had fallen on hard times, and stock prices softened to $2 per share.

Giving events their usual positive interpretation, local reporters cited one excuse after another with unshakable loyalty: muddy water had ruined the mill's boilers; its water supply was frozen; the mine was being prospected for more ore.[19] In reality, the ore was of such low grade that it no longer paid to transport it to the mill. Extraction came to a standstill until higher-grade rock could be found. Stating the cold facts at the end of 1884, the director of the U.S. Mint explained that "indications are that the [Bodie Mine's] best ore has been worked out."

The director's report did little to reverse the district's shriveling appeal.

The following mines which a few years ago were in active operation, are now closed down: Noonday, North Noonday, Bodie Tunnel, Spaulding, Red Cloud, Concordia, Addenda, Oro, May Belle, Goodshaw, Dudley, Defiance, University, Maryland, Queen Bee, King Bee, Boston, East Noonday, Glendale, Champion, South Bodie, Gipsy Queen, Consolidated Pacific, South Standard, South Bulwer, Tioga, Blackhawk, Summit, Double Standard, Bodie Bluff, and Union.[20]

The chilling conclusion was daunting. "The impression seems to be that Bodie, as a great mining camp, will soon be among the things of the past."[21]

Others, especially Bodie's eternal optimists, felt that 1884 ended on a positive note. The Syndicate

Mining Company, whose mill had been built 20 years earlier by the Empire Gold and Silver Mining Company and had crushed the celebrated first runs of bonanza ore from the Standard and Bodie mines, had unexpectedly paid a string of dividends. The company had survived during the late 1870s on a diet of marginal ore, or no ore at all. When its ore was not worth milling, the Syndicate leased its mill to finance the search for high-grade ore. Bullion shipments increased during the early 1880s, then, to the surprise of all, between January 1884 and September 1885 the Syndicate Mine produced enough exceptional ore to pay stockholders eight dividends. Bodie thus had four dividend-paying mines. The situation revitalized the confidence of some investors, and the Goodshaw, Consolidated Pacific, and Champion mines were reopened.

The Bodie mill, on the other hand, did not start up again until March 1885. It ran only one month on ore from the Bodie Mine, from which $48,633 was produced and another dividend paid. The mill then shut down in April. Once again, the ore had become so poor that its bullion did not cover operating expenses.[22]

While the Syndicate Company delighted its investors, and the Bodie Company struggled to find profitable ore, the Mono Mine had been reporting since late 1884 that it had rich ore on its 550-foot level. After years of deceptions, such reports were not out of character for the Mono Mine, and few readers took notice. With only 11 surface and underground workers, the Mono appeared more on the brink of failure than of riches. Truly rich ore in the Mono was unlikely, and its stock generated no interest. Only one trade took place during the first nine months of 1885.

Contrary to the accepted presumption that favorable indications in the Mono Mine were fake, the Bodie mill started running in September 1885 on Mono ore![23] Any lingering doubts were erased when superintendent John Kelly escorted two cage-loads of Bodieites down the Lent Shaft and showed them the development. Landing at the 550-foot level, the party worked their way through the south drift into Mono ground. From there they descended ladders another 100 feet and tramped, wide-eyed, 75 feet through a drift showing "stringers of rich ore." Peering down a six-foot winze, the awestruck spectators beheld rock "bright with native wire silver, and show[ing] flecks of gold." Using the point of a miner's iron candlestick, the group broke loose specimens that closely resembled the rich ore once mined on the Comstock.

An excited correspondent emerged from the Mono Mine and raced into town, where he frantically telegraphed his New York editor. "Strike, at its comparatively great depth, in unexplored ground, remarkable richness, and all, is the most important event Bodie has experienced in some years."[24] Mono stock shot from $2 per share to a high of $8.62 on November 5, as the Mono Gold Mining Company rushed headlong into production. Wagons hauled Mono ore down the road to the Bodie mill during the final four months of 1885, while stockholders awaited reports of bullion shipments and contemplated big profits.

The 1885 yield of the Bodie Consolidated Mining Company was less exciting. Its brief run had delivered less than one-tenth of the previous year's production. The Lent Shaft's pumping machinery was running, but only enough to supply the mill with water and expose the 700-foot level, where the company had been forced to return, hoping to reverse its fortunes.[25] Success would be slow to come. The single dividend of 50 cents per share funded by the mill run in March and April was the last one the Bodie Company would pay for nearly a decade.

The seemingly impossible happened in March 1886. The Mono Gold Mining Company declared a dividend! This surprise came after eight years with nothing to its credit but ridicule and a long procession of assessments. The dividend was only 25 cents per share, but it was the first the company ever paid. It would also be the last. Over the years, the Mono had levied 22 assessments totaling $560,000 and this one dividend returned a paltry $12,500 to investors.[26] Nevertheless, the Mono Gold Mining Company was added to the district's modest inventory of dividend-paying mines, where it joined the Standard, Bodie, Bulwer, and Syndicate. The Mono would be the final addition to the list.

The Mono's long-awaited triumph collapsed after only eight months. Ore shipments were suspended in April 1886, the month after the dividend was declared. The problem facing the Mono was twofold: Its only known ore body descended below the water line, and the ore remaining above water did not justify the expense of transporting it to the Bodie mill. Cutting significantly into dwindling returns, the costly long haul to the mill had finally become a critical concern.

Transportation costs were addressed first. The Bodie mill was disassembled in July 1886 and moved from the confluence of Taylor Gulch and Bodie Canyon to a site next to the Lent Shaft's hoisting works. Convenient to the mine's main entrance and directly above its supply of water, the relocated Bodie mill was the only stamp mill on the district's eastern slope.[27]

The problem of underground water was less complex. The Mono's submerged ore supply lay in areas that had been under water since 1883, when pumping was discontinued in the Lent Shaft's deepest levels. Anticipating the huge cost of lowering the water level, Mono managers, working in cooperation with their Bodie Mine counterparts, entered into a deal with the Standard Consolidated Mining Company to share expenses. The pumps in the Lent Shaft, still checking encroaching water at the 700-foot level, increased their speed and cleared the 800-foot level just as the relocated Bodie mill became operational in September, ready to resume crushing Mono ore.[28]

The Mono Company was rewarded by the discovery of part of the long-sought Fortuna lode. "These pieces of quartz are quite large and are exceedingly rich in gold," reported one impressed observer. "In fact, there is about as much gold as quartz in them." One piece was "thickly covered in many places with

silver."[29] The Mono Company's books showed a total production of $116,392 for 1886, the richest year in the mine's history.[30] Unfortunately, except for the 1886 dividend and a 20-month period absent of assessments, investors had realized little from the company's good fortune. Instead of more dividends, profits had been consumed by pumping.

Summarizing the ambiguities of 1886, the *Bodie Evening Miner* reflected: "When we take into consideration the idleness on the part of so many of our mines and mills, and the limited number of men who have been employed in the mines of the district during the year, the showing is not a very bad one. . . . This district is not dead yet."[31] Aiming to lift the region out of its doldrums, economic and otherwise, a Hawthorne journalist at the *Esmeralda News* pontificated, "It takes a long time to thoroughly develop a good mine, but when done it can never be worked out, and such is the character of the mines at [Bodie]."[32]

Fortified by such rhetoric, people in Bodie looked forward to the lower levels restoring prosperity to their community. The remarkable pumping endeavor, championed by speculators in San Francisco and New York, renewed interest in mining shares, and the few Bodie companies still listed on the exchanges enjoyed a marked increase in daily stock transactions.[33]

By April 1887, the pumps had drained the 900-foot level. By May, the 1,000-foot level was dry. The Lent's pumps battled around the clock against a torrent, while the boilers that powered them devoured fuel—and funds—at an alarming rate. As the companies struggled to maintain a positive cash flow, men cleaned out and repaired work areas that had been under water for three years. Miners once again explored the deepest parts of the Bodie and Mono mines.[34]

Desperate for good news from the Lent Shaft, Bodie's citizens watched events unfold, pinning their futures on the discovery of more rich ore. Instead, the news from the lower levels was devastating. The

Figure 6-2: Pulling two wagons, a 12-mule team pauses at the intersection of Main and Green Streets. The wagons strain under an enormous load of flanged iron pipe, similar to the pipe used in the Lent Shaft for the vertical column through which water was pumped 1,200 feet to the surface. Because Bodie's railroad supplied only lumber products, mining machinery and other commodities were hauled into town by commercial wagon freighting outfits. It was not until the 1920s that motor trucks replaced these big teams. (Courtesy, Russ and Anne Johnson)

Mono's ore body pinched out immediately above the 800-foot level, and nothing of value was found below that. With nowhere else left to look, the managers of the Bodie and Mono mines pondered their next course of action, then decided to sink the Lent Shaft 200 feet deeper. This engineering challenge would determine once and for all whether pay ore existed in the lower levels. After all, local oracles reasoned, Bodie occupied the same relative position along the Sierra Nevada as did the Comstock Lode. Another 200 feet deeper, and Bodie's underground would reach a depth comparable to that of the Comstock's Big Bonanza.[35]

In October 1887, equipment and supplies for the massive undertaking began to arrive. A second 12-inch diameter pipe column was installed in the Lent Shaft along with another line of pumps. At the Carson & Colorado railroad yard in Hawthorne, freight bound for Bodie invited inquiry. "Bodie is not dead yet," was tendered as the explanation. "Earl & Co. have been loading machinery for the Lent shaft for three or four days, four carloads have arrived and two more are expected. Another 16-animal team has been put on the road, as there is an increase in all kinds of freight."[36] The project captivated the mining world, attracting enough attention that two less noteworthy district mines, the Oro and Booker, were reopened.

Stock in the Bodie Consolidated Mining Company advanced from $1.25 to $3.25 in anticipation of great discoveries, though the company recorded a pitiful 1887 production of $19,186 with ore from

Figure 6-3: The Lent Shaft has been credited with being Bodie's deepest. Its hoisting works, where boilers consumed 24 cords of wood per day removing water from the 1,200-foot level, is pictured looking northeast in 1895. To deliver the fuel, the narrow gauge railroad refilled its locomotives from the water tank seen immediately below the Jupiter Mine, to the left, where a spur track with three swithchbacks began climbing High Peak to the Standard shaft. Above, the Summit Mine is silhouetted on the horizon, while to the far right, the gable of a building, probably the second Bodie mill, appears beyond the dump. (Francis H. Frederick collection. Courtesy, California Division of Mines and Geology)

above the 700-foot level, and paid no dividends, while levying two more 50-cent assessments. The Mono Company produced nothing during 1887, and also levied two 50-cent assessments. Nonetheless, the monumental task of sinking the Lent Shaft to the 1,200-foot level was underway.

Every dollar available to the Bodie Consolidated Mining Company and the Mono Gold Mining Company was exhausted in driving the Lent Shaft deeper. The 1,200-foot level was reached in January 1888.[37] Water poured from the mine as pumps discharged 800,000 gallons of water every 24 hours. "The water

is taxing all our power at present," exclaimed Superintendent Kelly, "but I hope to have it decreased soon. We are burning from 23 to 24 cords of wood per day."[38] Even so, incoming water overwhelmed the pumps, and the hoist had to be brought into play with bailing tanks. As water spilled over the hillside, industrious individuals on the surface commenced placer mining. "Two or three white men and as many Chinamen are at present engaged in mining the auriferous surface deposits eastward of the Lent Shaft."[39]

The Lent's pumps persevered, but lack of ore left the Bodie mill idle. Two 50-cent per share assessments in 1888 by the Bodie Company and one by the Mono drove stock prices downward. The two companies spent their feeble resources to stay ahead of the incessant flow, while underground miners kept up a desperate search for rich ore bodies 1,200 feet below the surface. When a new hoisting cable arrived for the Lent Shaft in February 1889, the *Homer Mining Index* predicted that the wire rope's 1,500-foot length was proof that the shaft would be driven deeper.[40] Instead, investors were called upon to reach deeper into their pockets. A Bodie Company assessment of 50 cents per share in March 1889 was followed by another of 25 cents in November. The Mono followed suit, financing the Lent Shaft's costly pumping with 25-cent assessments in March, July, and November. A cynical San Francisco correspondent scoffed, "The Bodie officials appear happy, as the stock has been assessed, which insures the regular payment of their salary, provided the public pays it."[41] Meanwhile, the Bodie mill stood idle, awaiting a shipment of ore from the district's deepest mine.

As the decade came to a close, it looked to many as if the Bodie and Mono companies provided the town's best opportunity for revival, and the Lent Shaft was where they placed the district's last hope. While eyes strained toward the Lent for signs of good news, few in Bodie realized that the fate of their community actually rested upon the Standard and Bulwer mines.

The Standard and Bulwer Mines

The unexpected collapse of the Noonday and Red Cloud companies in late 1882 triggered vast changes in Bodie that were appreciated by at least one early 1883 resident.

> For the first time in her history Bodie is without a dance hall; the opium joints are closed—or at least are doing no business . . . The bullies and toughs have pretty nearly all left and the moral aspect of Bodie wears a placid and contented appearance. When a camp of Bodie's size gets rid of the class which comes in on the first flood tide of excitement, it is a sure sign that it is

setaling [sic] down on a firm basis—a basis that will be lasting. A quiet town is Bodie today; yet its moral atmosphere is healthier and its business upon a firmer basis than was the Bodie of 79-80.[42]

A day later, an item noting decay overtaking abandoned neighborhoods eerily foreshadowed Bodie's fate.

> The lower end of Bodie presents a lonesome aspect at present. Many of the buildings are going to ruin; the sidewalks are cranky; unlatched doors swing on rusty hinges; demolished stovepipes sway to and fro and here and there the legends "for rent" and "for sale" stand out with great prominence. Nothing is quite so depressing as a row of deserted houses.[43]

While north end buildings were being torn down and loaded onto wagons headed for Hawthorne, the Standard Mine maintained weekly production at $13,000 to $33,000 from ore taken on the 385- and 500-foot levels. Explorations on the 700-, 1,000-, and 1,200-foot levels, however, continued to reveal what the superintendent described as ore "of no particular value," consisting of "small veins of low grade quartz" that contained "nothing of any importance."[44]

Then, one fateful day in May 1883, the unmistakable sound of crashing metal and the roar of escaping steam echoed from the Standard mill. Debris flew across the mill's engine room as machinery thrashed itself into ruin. Parts linking the engine's piston to the connecting rod had fractured, allowing the piston to slam against the cast-iron cylinder head. The head broke into a dozen pieces, the largest of which was hurled six feet. As men ran for cover, the 19,900-pound flywheel spun until its flailing connecting rod jammed against the frame and lifted the huge wheel off its bearings, breaking a spoke and twisting the crankshaft before it came to a lurching halt.[45]

A set of old hoisting engines from the Standard Mine was brought down to run the mill until a replacement engine could be ordered and freighted from San Francisco. It was all accomplished quickly. After only a week, the shriek of the Standard whistle was heard again "as though nothing had happened." The welcome tone sent the local press into ecstatics, and "caused a pleasurable thrill to tingle along the spinal marrow of all who heard it." [46]

In January 1883, the Bulwer Company reduced its monthly dividend to five cents per share. Then it failed to pay dividends in April, May, and June. In July, it declared its eighteenth dividend — a substantial 15 cents per share. Optimism was tempered, however, when stockholders learned that it was a *quarterly* dividend. [47] Despite the insinuation that quarterly dividends would be regular, none were paid until early the following year. Missed dividends did little to lift spirits, especially at the exchanges, where weekly financial columns remained lackluster. "Bodie stocks were very quiet," read the familiar litany. "Bodie Consolidated was weak at 39 to 35¢. Standard was steady, under small transactions, selling from $5.00 to $6.00. Bulwer records one transaction at 70¢." [48]

The Standard mill was back in operation, but the Standard Mine confronted mounting problems. Braving an onslaught of water, its pumping engine fought progressively harder to keep the mine dry. Recognized as underpowered from the outset, it faced increasing inflow as greater depths were achieved and neighboring mines closed and stopped their pumps. When pumping at the Lent Shaft was halted in October, the Standard's engine stood alone against the flood. It battled in vain. By the end of 1883, the 1,200-foot level was under water, and the engine was straining to keep the 1,000-foot level dry. [49]

On that level, the east crosscut had been advanced 1,422 feet, but the search for pay ore brought little comfort to investors. Superintendent Irwin could only report that "prospects for the coming year are fair. We have large, low grade ore reserves on all the upper levels, and the recent improvement on the 700-foot level is very encouraging." [50] The company had disbursed its usual 12 dividends of 25 cents, plus one extra. Nonetheless, the ore was diminishing in value. Four years earlier, rock from the mine had av-

eraged $60 per ton. At the end of 1883, it was worth only $16.50 per ton—barely worth mining. The depleted supply of rich ore curtailed a common strategy used to maximize profits from poor ore. As a matter of course, high-grade had been mixed with low-grade rock to make use of ore that would otherwise be left behind. [51] With the rich reserves now gone, the yield for 1883 dropped to $1,155,182.

Slipping into financial difficulty for the first time in its history, the Standard paid dividends of 25 cents per share during each of the first three months of 1884, then skipped the anticipated April dividend— the first month without a distribution since the Standard began paying dividends in September 1877. "Our mine is not looking well," disclosed a March 13 telegram from the superintendent to the company's vice president in New York. "The ore has very materially diminished in quality. The last thirty days we have been doing the best we can, but the results are not entirely satisfactory." Another dispatch wired by the secretary in San Francisco revealed that "final receipts of bullion, [were] less than usual, owing to diminished value and quantity of ore." [52]

When a large number of Standard miners were discharged the following week, ore production slumped by two-thirds. The editor of the *Mining Record* groused, "The last dividend of $25,000 was declared in the face of the knowledge . . . that its payment would certainly leave the company in debt." [53] Reporting to absentee directors, the superintendent acknowledged the mine's dire condition.

> There is exposed throughout the 500 and 385-foot levels of the Standard mine an immense quantity of ore . . . but the greater part of it is very low grade, and will not pay to take out of the mine. . . . The paychutes in the main Standard vein have been getting scarcer and poorer, as shown by the gradual decrease in the amount of bullion produced. . . . On the 1,000-foot level, no ore has been found of any value, except in stringers too small to pay for working. [54]

A sudden surge of ground water in mid-1884 inundated the 1,000-foot level, ending the Standard's "search for another bonanza." Managers abandoned pumping in order to save money, and water slowly rose another 100 feet in the shaft, where a bailing tank hoisted it to tunnel level to supply the Bulwer-Standard mill. Bailing water to sustain milling, however, tied up the hoist and one compartment of the shaft, interrupting mining whenever the mill was running.[55]

On May 1, 1884, the unthinkable finally happened. After the noon whistle sounded at the famous Standard mill, the clatter of its stamps ceased. Boiler fires died and cogwheels on the aerial tramway creaked to a stop. Then silence settled over "Old Reliable." One stunned observer remarked that "many persons would not have been more surprised to see the sun stop."[56] Small groups of uneasy men stood on streets theorizing and discussing possible explanations. The facts were soon learned. The Bullion lode's best ore had been exhausted. Abandoning the old incline, whose ore had been treated at the Standard mill, eliminated the cost of hoisting rock to the crest of High Peak, then transporting it by aerial tramway for treatment. Overcoming this inefficiency, all ore would be conveyed through the Bulwer Tunnel and treated at the Bulwer-Standard mill.

Another missed dividend in May sent Standard stock prices plummeting from $6.50 to 90 cents per share. The company mined low-grade ore and struggled to reduce its debt with tailings worked by renting the Bulwer's half of the mill. Assaying at $10.94 per ton in gold and silver, tailings from ponds below the Standard mill were nearly as valuable as ore in the mine. The ponds contained 7,000 tons of revenue-producing sand ready for the taking, at least until they froze in winter.[57]

If closing the Standard mill was unthinkable, the truly inconceivable took place in October 1884, when the formidable Standard Consolidated Mining Company levied its first assessment.[58] The assessment provoked a series of scathing news items a continent away in New York. "The reports from the famous Standard mine show that the last traces of

the company's bonanzas are disappearing, and instead of the regular dividend, assessments will no doubt soon be the order."[59] The Standard was facing its darkest hour. Stocks tumbled to as low as 30 cents per share, and were expected to go lower.[60]

The Standard's mine and tailings ponds yielded only $304,295 during 1884, less than a third of, and almost $1,000,000 short of the previous year's production. Income from the 25-cent per share assessment lowered the debt, but the mine produced no more than half the revenue of the neighboring Bodie, where two discoveries in the upper levels had generated optimism and enough bullion to outproduce the Standard for the first time since 1878. The Bodie Company, though financially shaky, now appeared to be the district's best hope.

Contradictions were evident elsewhere. While the embattled Standard slipped closer toward ruin, the Syndicate, the oldest mining company working in the district, paid the first in a succession of eight dividends. These dim assurances did little to inspire the director of the U.S. Mint, whose 1884 report concluded, "The Standard Consolidated, which has produced so largely in years past and regarded as one of the leading mines of the State, has been virtually closed down, only 15 men being employed in the mine."[61]

Difficulties spilled over to the Bulwer, where intermittent rental of its 15 stamps was the only source of income. One Bulwer dividend of 10 cents per share was paid in January 1884. Twelve months later, stockholders faced an assessment of 20 cents per share. Those selling Bulwer stock considered themselves lucky to get four cents per share. No Bulwer ore had been mined since 1880, but the assessment would ostensibly sustain the search for more ore. The only good news came when the company leased its half of the mill to the Standard, and the Bulwer's bank account saw a few deposits from rent money. Suffering from pervasive gloom, investors in both companies were comforted whenever both halves of the Bulwer-Standard mill were running.[62]

As the Standard Company reduced its indebtedness, its stock advanced to $1.50 per share. "There is plenty of virgin ground to be explored," stressed president Augustus Pettibone, emphasizing the positive (while ignoring the troublesome fact that the 1,000 and 1,200 foot levels remained flooded). "The various theories advanced respecting the existence of ore bodies equal to those worked in the past appear to be well founded."[63]

Indeed, a nice little ore pocket found in May 1885, extending from the 500- to the 700-foot level, averaged $130 per ton. But there was only enough to keep the mill's 30 stamps running for two months.[64] After ore shipments dropped to 300 tons per week in July, half of the stamps were left idle. At the Standard's 400-foot level, values held steady at $12 to $20 per ton, hardly enough to show a profit. The Bulwer Company, barely sustained by sporadic rental payments, ordered another assessment of 20 cents in October. Then, once again, it rented its 15 stamps to the Standard, which finished 1885 crushing ore from the 280-, 400-, 500-, and 700-foot levels.

When the Standard's yield was entered into the books, its 1885 production had slipped to $214,561, down by almost a third from the previous year. It was the first year in company history during which the Standard failed to pay a dividend. Although no assessments were levied, by December stock in the Standard Company rarely traded. When sold, it brought only about 80 cents per share.

Little changed during the long winter season. Then, in May 1886, miners on the Bulwer's 400-foot level scrutinized the rock that they had just blasted and began to feel some excitement. It was a small streak showing 14 inches of high-grade quartz. After years of fruitless searching, here was pay rock 302 feet south of the tunnel. On June 14, the Bulwer started shipping ore for the first time in years. Getting it out of the mine required some effort. It had to be transported in mine cars on tracks laid north through a drift, then east through a crosscut to the Standard shaft, where it was hoisted to a station 40 feet above the Bulwer Tunnel level. The cars were dumped into two large

underground storage bins, from which the ore was transported 1,860 feet through the tunnel to the Bulwer-Standard mill.[65]

Initially, the Bulwer's newfound ledge appeared to increase in width as it ascended toward the surface. Prompted by the showing, miners drove toward it on the 200-foot level, where they discovered the vein was "small," but worth between $19 and $30 per ton. Then, in September, to the surprise of miners crosscutting on the 100-foot level, an abandoned drift was found that revealed another vein 2½ feet wide, assaying at $80 per ton. Chutes were quickly built allowing ore to be dropped to tunnel level without need for the Standard's steam hoist.[66]

As the Bulwer's prospects improved, Bodie District enjoyed a modest resurgence in popularity. Alluring reports, enhanced by news of the Mono's dividend, reached former Bodieites, many of whom began drifting back from the "land of cactus and rattlesnakes" where they had relocated years earlier. Exhibiting contempt for unproven camps in Arizona, Montana, Idaho, and Utah, the *Territorial Enterprise* in Virginia City explained, "Old miners from the Nevada and California mountains do not take kindly to tenderfoot camps." The incoming population gave rise to the belief that Bodie was experiencing a population boom, and the distant editor surmised with unwarranted exhilaration that "Bodie has a brighter outlook today than for a long time past."[67]

Indications in the Bulwer Mine, recent dividends by the Syndicate and Mono companies, and a massive pumping effort at the Lent Shaft afforded the town an affectation of certainty. Stock sales responded accordingly. "The Bodies were out in full glory!" wrote an approving New York columnist. "Bulwer gained one dollar; the highest point reached was $2.15; today, $2.05. Standard, which has been sorely neglected of late, came forward on Tuesday at $1.25; today it was quoted at $2."[68]

The Bulwer Company milled ore from its 100-, 200-, 300-, and 400-foot levels for 3½ months during 1886, producing the company's first bullion in six years. Disappointing stockholders, the feeble

$20,144 yield was not enough for a dividend. The Standard Mine's 280-, 400-, 500-, and 700-foot levels yielded slightly more than the previous year by producing $228,085, but meager profit margins resulted in a second year without dividends.

Bodie District was noted in 1887 not for developments in the Standard Mine, but for the monumental pumping effort carried on by the Bodie and Mono companies to clear the 1,000-foot Lent Shaft and sink it 200 feet deeper. Taking advantage of the low water to probe the Bulwer's unexplored depths, miners on the 1,000-foot level drove a crosscut from the westernmost reaches of the Bodie Mine. A 20-cent per share assessment in July 1887 subsidized the Bulwer's search, while it accumulated enough ore from the upper levels to begin another mill run.

Not until September did Bulwer miners pierce company ground on the 1,000 foot level from the Lent Shaft, permitting them to reach some 200 feet deeper than earlier explorations conducted from the Standard shaft.[69] The effort was yet to produce anything of value, but in October the Bulwer half of the mill began running for three months on ore from higher levels. Like the previous year's production, the outcome was modest and did not result in a dividend. At the end of 1887, the Bulwer Company reported a yield of only $16,102, and its stock slumped to $1 per share.

As mining men awaited developments from the Bulwer, the Standard Mine maintained steady ore shipments. The Standard Company's 15 stamps in the Bulwer-Standard mill remained active throughout the year, producing $287,555, with dividends in November and December of five and ten cents, respectively. Stock rallied to $2.35 per share. "The people of Bodie have every reason to be hopeful of

their camp," concurred the *Esmeralda News* in Hawthorne, "for there is no doubt about their being surrounded by mines which have already become noted by their immense yield and which contain millions to be extracted."[70] Despite the appraisals, empty buildings that had comprised the Standard hoisting works at its abandoned incline shaft were sold in December. They were moved to Bridgeport along with three other Bodie buildings and converted into barns.[71] The removal of these structures from High Peak brought to an end the story of the famous gold-laden Bullion Lode, the ore body that had been partially developed in 1875 by Peter Eshington and Louis Lockberg, and had then fueled the district's boom in 1877.

In January 1888, Bulwer miners were following the vein on the 200-foot level when they unexpectedly broke into one of the Standard's abandoned stopes. A survey by the Bulwer determined that the backfilled excavation was in Bulwer ground, and that the Standard Company had taken Bulwer ore. Public accusals and recriminations began. To no one's surprise, a survey ordered by the Standard indicated that no encroachments had been made.[72]

Boundary disputes, common in Nevada's Pioche,

Eureka, Aurora, and Washoe districts, had been remarkably rare in Bodie. Most Bodie companies had learned from examples on the Comstock that protracted litigation wasted tremendous resources and rarely brought financial gain. Misspent funds on the Comstock, where mine owners squandered an estimated $9,000,000 to $10,000,000 on litigation between 1860 and 1865, represented a fifth of production, considerably more than was paid in dividends during the same period. Nevertheless, in March 1888, the Bulwer Company initiated a lawsuit to recover revenue lost from ground allegedly worked by the Standard.[73] At issue was the location of ore that had been removed and ore recently discovered that the Bulwer wanted to remove.

The squabble created enough dissension between corporate directors that the Bulwer and Standard companies separated. Those managing the Bulwer, including John F. Boyd, formed new alliances with the Bodie and Mono companies. Thereafter, Boyd occupied prominent board positions with all three corporations until he retired in 1889. Captain John Kelly, a Comstock-trained superintendent, managed the three mines until his death in 1891. His cousin, John W. Kelly, then succeeded him.

Bickering over the boundary line that separated Bulwer property from the Standard's continued for the next 2½ years. Legalities were argued in corporate boardrooms as well as in the press. "We had some trouble with Standard Con. in stopping them from taking out ore from the ground in dispute," complained a Bulwer memo released for public consumption. "We have again agreed to leave ore undisturbed until courts shall decide or directors of Standard and Bulwer shall agree to whom it belongs."[74]

The rift jeopardized the district's standing on the stock exchanges. Jittery investors quickly realized that the rivals shared two essential assets: the Bulwer Tunnel and Bulwer-Standard mill. If disharmony entangled these facilities, mining would be impeded. The potential for the conflict to disrupt production sent stock prices tumbling until they "almost dropped out of sight."[75] Further weakening

Bodie's precarious economy was a May assessment of 20 cents levied by the Bulwer Company. The assessment drew attention away from explorations underway in the Bulwer mine, and clouded a Standard Company run of six more five- and ten-cent dividends between January and June 1888.

Apprehensiveness was expressed at year's end in a New York market summary. "No interest is manifest in Bodie stocks. Bodie Consolidated shows one sale at $1.80. Some 600 shares of Bulwer changed hands at 50¢. A few shares of Mono sold at 90¢, and Standard at $1."[76] When the figures were tabulated for 1888, only 15 of the district's stamps had been operating. They were on the Standard's half of the Bulwer-Standard mill, and had run only until July, putting an end to dividends for the final six months of 1888. The Standard Mine produced only $118,371 in bullion, the smallest annual yield in its history, putting the company in peril.

The situation was recounted in late 1888 by the California State Mineralogist.

In the once populous town of Bodie there are not more than five hundred inhabitants. And whereas, in 1879-81 there were between forty and fifty mines in active operation, there are now but three [Standard, Bulwer, and the Lent Shaft], and of these only one is extracting and milling ore, the Standard namely. . . . Present interest in Bodie District, and hope in its future are centered in the work now doing through the Lent shaft at its deepest levels.[77]

Attempting to bolster local confidence, the *Bodie Evening Miner* opined that the "outlook for the Spring of 1889 is not bad." It published a column titled "Bodie's Prospects" that, not surprisingly, accentuated the positive. "The staid, sturdy, solid old reliable Standard Con. mine still gives steadily regular employment to some sixty men." The columnist also applauded discoveries in the Lent Shaft, where a high-stakes probe had reached 1,200 feet below the surface. "Are not those rich little streaks liable to lead into a young bonanza any day?"[78]

During 1889, the Standard Company searched for any ore that was fit to mill, stockpiling whatever was found until the accumulation warranted a mill run. Miners found only enough to run 15 stamps about two weeks out of each month. To generate additional income, the Standard began allowing outsiders to lease parts of the mine and remove ore at their own expense. The Standard's underground consisted of numerous mines that had been acquired over the years. Their interlaced, layered workings exceeded 25 miles in length, most of which were long abandoned and obstructed by caving. Anyone willing to invest in hoisting machinery and retimbering could reach just about any location inside High Peak. The Standard's 1889 percentage of lessee yields turned out to be a significant $8,881, adding substantially to the company's meager accomplishments elsewhere.[79]

A countersuit filed in April 1889 by the Standard Company accused the Bulwer of extracting ore from the disputed ground and sought to recover damages. An injunction was obtained to restrain the Bulwer Company. On June 25, the Bulwer's initial suit against the Standard came to trial in Bridgeport. Testimony was expected from a San Francisco mining expert, but no evidence was taken and the judge dismissed the case. Certain that legal expenses would impair both companies, shareholders were momentarily gratified, until the Standard's countersuit went to trial a week later. The verdict established Standard ownership of the ledges, and awarded the company $3,000 in damages and costs.[80] The Bulwer Company appealed the decision.

At the end of 1889 the Bulwer's 1,000-foot level was abandoned, having disclosed nothing of interest. A share of Bulwer stock brought only two bits, and stockholders had been assessed two more times at 25 cents per share. One New York columnist remarked, "The 25 cent assessment and the seemingly interminable lawsuits in which the Bulwer Company is involved seem to keep purchasers away from this stock."[81]

The Standard Company, at the same time, had amassed $26,000 in legal expenses—more than it could afford—and paid no dividends during the year. President Pettibone offered little to lift community spirits. The mine, he said, "has not yielded a quality of ore, during the year, to quite pay current expenses."[82] In short, the region's most important employer, the Standard Consolidated Mining Company, had produced only $127,341 during 1889—barely enough to cover operating costs—and was in debt again.[83]

Put off by the Standard and Bulwer companies, citizens and distant investors alike scrutinized developments in the Lent Shaft, from which they longed for one shred of good news to emerge. The pumps persevered as the Bodie and Mono companies levied more assessments.

---

1. *Daily Free Press* 4 January 1883.

2. *Chronicle-Union* 27 January 1883.

3. These were the Noonday, North Noonday, Red Cloud, Maybelle, Concordia, Belvidere, Black Hawk, Booker, Queen Bee, Consolidated Pacific, Dudley, Boston Consolidated, Oro, Paris, and Addenda.

4. *Daily Free Press* 10 March 1883.

5. Richard E. Lingenfelter, *The Hardrock Miners: A History of the Mining Labor Movement in the American West, 1863-1893* (Berkeley, CA: University of California Press, 1974), 157-181; Mark Wyman, *Hard Rock Epic: Western Miners and the Industrial Revolution, 1860-1910* (Berkeley, CA: University of California Press, 1979), 35-37, 151-165; *Mining and Scientific Press* 25 July 1885, 72.

6. *Bodie Morning News* 9 September 1879.

7. *Bodie Evening Miner* 9 October 1883.

8. *Engineering and Mining Journal* 20 October 1883, 250.

9. *Engineering and Mining Journal* 27 October 1883, 266.

10. *Bodie Evening Miner* 3 November 1883.

11. *Bodie Evening Miner* 11 March 1884; *Engineering and Mining Journal* 22 March 1884, 221.

12. *Engineering and Mining Journal* 2 February 1884, 89; *Bodie Evening Miner* 22 March 1883; Grant H. Smith, "Bodie, Last of the Old Time Mining Camps," *California Historical Society Quarterly* 4 (1925), 76.

13. *Bodie Evening Miner* 4 January 1884; *Engineering and Mining Journal* 5 January 1884, 11; *Mining and Scientific Press* 12 January 1884, 20; 19 January 1884, 36; *Mining Record* 26 January 1884, 61.

14. *Mining Record* 2 February 1884, 70, 71, 77; *Mining and Scientific Press* 23 February 1884, 142.

15. *Bodie Evening Miner* 16 February 1884.

16. *Mining Record* 23 February 1884, 120.

17. *Engineering and Mining Journal* 26 April 1884, 316; *Bodie Evening Miner* 24 April 1884.

18. *Mining and Scientific Press* 8 March 1884, 179; 14 June 1884, 404; *Bodie Evening Miner* 10 June 1884.

19. *Mining and Scientific Press* 20 December 1884, 392.

20. U.S. Bureau of the Mint, *Report of the Director of the Mint upon the Production of the Precious Metals in the United States During the Calendar Year 1884* (Washington, DC: Government Printing Office, 1885), 112. To this list should be added: the White Cloud, Jupiter, Richter, Belvidere, McClinton, Glynn-Dale, Booker, Butler, Bodie Chief, Original Summit, New York & Bodie, Sonora Consolidated, King Bee, Governor Stanford Consolidated, Bolivar Consolidated, Central, Maryland, and North Standard.

21. U.S. Mint, *Report of the Director [for 1884]*, 113.

22. *Engineering and Mining Journal* 14 March 1885, 179; 21 March 1885, 196; *Mining and Scientific Press* 18 April 1885, 256.

23. *Mining and Scientific Press* 13 December 1884, 376; *Mining Record* 3 January 1885, 423; *Engineering and Mining Journal* 13 December 1884, 399; 19 September 1885, 205.

24. *Financial and Mining Record* 14 November 1885, 311.

25. *Engineering and Mining Journal* 6 June 1885, 392; *Mining and Scientific Press* 15 August 1885, 120.

26. *Engineering and Mining Journal* 6 March 1886, 181-182.

27. *Engineering and Mining Journal* 17 April 1886, 289; *Mining and Scientific Press* 21 August 1886, 124. No photographs have been discovered of either Bodie mill.

28. *Financial and Mining Record* 15 May 1886, 311; 24 July 1886, 54; 28 August 1886, 133-134; 4 September 1886, 149; *Engineering and Mining Journal* 22 May 1886, 378; 25 September 1886, 226.

29. *Financial and Mining Record* 12 June 1886, 385.

30. The Mono's short-lived production between September 1885 and December 1886 produced $122,368, the mine's only recorded bullion.

31. *Mining and Scientific Press* 29 January 1887, 74.

32. *Mining and Scientific Press* 17 September 1887, 181.

33. *Financial and Mining Record* 20 November 1886, 321.

34. The Bodie Company employed only five miners, but shared with the Mono three engineers and three firemen who ran the steam engines, two carmen, one carpenter, four miners, one pumpman, two shaftmen, one watchman, a blacksmith with his helper, and one foreman. *Mining and Scientific Press* 14 May 1887, 320.

35. *Mining and Scientific Press* 17 September 1887, 181; *Engineering and Mining Journal* 24 September 1887, 227; *Financial and Mining Record* 24 July 1886, 54; Eliot Lord, *Comstock Mining and Miners* (1883; reprint, San Diego, CA: Howell-North Books, 1980), 309, 311. Everyone ignored that nearby Aurora's ore bodies were shallow.

36. *Mining and Scientific Press* 26 November 1887, 328.

37. *Financial and Mining Record* 4 February 1888, 71; *Engineering and Mining Journal* 11 May 1889, 440; *Mining and Scientific Press* 17 August 1912, 209. The Standard Company's shaft was also 1,200 feet deep, but because the collar of the Lent was 229 feet lower in elevation than that of the Standard shaft, the Lent Shaft has received credit for being Bodie's deepest. (Anderson Survey 1880) The Lent and the Standard were Bodie's deepest shafts, yet they were by no means notable among the world's deepest mines. The *Mining and Scientific Press* provided some perspective by publishing the vertical depths of deep mines in 1897. The world's deepest shaft, measuring 4,900 feet, was the Red Jacket in the iron region near Lake Superior. The deepest mine on the Comstock was the Yellow Jacket measuring 3,123 feet. In California, the deepest was the Kennedy Mine at 2,200 feet. Neither the Lent nor the Standard appeared on the list of 62 deep mines worldwide. (*Mining and Scientific Press* 13 February 1897, 133)

38. *Financial and Mining Record* 29 June 1889, 407.

39. California State Mining Bureau, *Eighth Annual Report of the State Mineralogist, for the Year Ending October 1, 1888* (Sacramento, CA: Superintendent of State Printing, 1888), 393.

40. *Mining and Scientific Press* 9 February 1889, 94.

41. *Mining and Scientific Press* 16 November 1889, 386.

42. *Bodie Evening Miner* 27 February 1883.

43. *Daily Free Press* 28 February 1883.

44. William Irwin, *Fifth Annual Report of the Standard Consolidated Mining Company for the Year Ending February 1, 1884* (San Francisco, CA: W. T. Galloway & Co., 1884), 33.

45. *Mining and Scientific Press* 2 June 1883, 372.

46. *Bodie Evening Miner* 26 May 1883.

47. *Engineering and Mining Journal* 23 June 1883, 371.

48. *Engineering and Mining Journal* 18 August 1883, 105.

49. *Engineering and Mining Journal* 27 October 1883, 266.

50. Irwin, *Fifth Annual Report of the Standard*, 34.

51. *Engineering and Mining Journal* 1 November 1884, 293.

52. *Engineering and Mining Journal* 15 March 1884, 204, 207.

53. *Mining Record* 22 March 1884, 178.

54. *Engineering and Mining Journal* 2 April 1884, 271.

55. *Engineering and Mining Journal* 1 November 1884, 293; *Financial and Mining Record* 24 July 1886, 55. The 1,000- and 1,200-foot levels would remain under water until pumping resumed in the Lent Shaft 2½ years later.

56. *Mining and Scientific Press* 10 May 1884, 324; *Mining Record* 17 May 1884, 311.

57. *Bodie Evening Miner* 22 July 1884; *Engineering and Mining Journal* 15 November 1884, 335.

58. *Engineering and Mining Journal* 1 November 1884, 305.

59. *Engineering and Mining Journal* 20 December 1884, 416.

60. *Engineering and Mining Journal* 29 November 1884, 369.

61. U.S. Mint, *Report of the Director [for 1884]*, 111.

62. *Engineering and Mining Journal* 31 January 1885, 77.

63. *Mining and Scientific Press* 11 April 1885, 240.

64. *Engineering and Mining Journal* 23 May 1885, 362.

65. *Financial and Mining Record* 15 May 1886, 311; 24 July 1886, 55; *Engineering and Mining Journal* 26 June 1886, 468.

66. *Engineering and Mining Journal* 26 June 1886, 468; 25 September 1886, 226; 2 October 1886, 244; 23 October 1886, 298.

67. *Mining and Scientific Press* 21 August 1886, 124.

68. *Engineering and Mining Journal* 4 December 1886, 411.

69. *Financial and Mining Record* 17 September 1887, 181; 1 October 1887, 215.

70. *Mining and Scientific Press* 17 September 1887, 181.

71. *Walker Lake Bulletin* 7 December 1887.

72. *Financial and Mining Record* 7 January 1888, 8; *Engineering and Mining Journal* 7 January 1888, 23; 14 January 1888, 42; 28 January 1888, 76.

73. Lord, *Comstock Mining and Miners*, 172-173; *Engineering and Mining Journal* 31 March 1888, 239.

74. *Financial and Mining Record* 26 May 1888, 327.

75. *Engineering and Mining Journal* 19 May 1888, 376.

76. *Engineering and Mining Journal* 22 December 1888, 535.

77. California, *Eighth Annual Report*, 383, 392.

78. *Walker Lake Bulletin* 15 May 1889.

79. *Engineering and Mining Journal* 23 March 1889, 284; *Bodie Miner* 31 July 1909.

80. *Engineering and Mining Journal* 6 July 1889, 15; 3 August 1889, 100.

81. *Engineering and Mining Journal* 17 August 1889, 147.

82. *Engineering and Mining Journal* 17 August 1889, 147; *Financial and Mining Record* 18 January 1890, 35.

83. Charles W. Chesterman, Rodger H. Chapman, and Cliffton H. Gray, Jr, *Geology and Ore Deposits of the Bodie Mining District, Mono County, California (Bulletin 206)* (Sacramento, CA: Division of Mines and Geology, 1986), 32, 33.

Figure 7-1: After standing idle for five years, the Standard mill emerged from an 1890 renovation sporting amalgamating plates, Frue concentrators, and the Boss continuous process. Because the precisely-tuned concentrators required a power source independent of the heavy milling machinery, another smokestack was added. Soon after this photograph was taken, the mill was updated again, this time with electric power. (*Engineering and Mining Journal* 13 May 1893. Courtesy, Engineering and Mining Journal)

CHAPTER SEVEN

"THERE IS MUCH ENCOURAGEMENT TO LOOK FORWARD TO"
1890-1899

New York and the eastern cities have been so frequently victimized by mining swindles that . . . it has been almost impossible to effect the sale of a mine or do any business in mines during the past few years in the East. There is a great deal of capital lying idle awaiting investment in the East that could be profitably employed in mining, and many people owning it would be willing to invest a portion in mines; but prejudice and want of confidence prevents them from doing so.
 —Mining and Scientific Press, *August 27, 1892*

The money derived from assessments seems to go mainly to maintain a horde of useless officials who do nothing particularly toward mining development. For development, actual miners are needed, yet comparatively few are employed. Of course there must be some, but they are getting fewer and fewer. But the useless officials do not seem to let go. They still hold their positions and draw their salaries.
 —Mining and Scientific Press, *May 27, 1893*

The Bodie and Mono Mines

Predictions that the Lent Shaft would be sunk below the 1,200-foot level proved wrong when San Francisco received news, on January 1, 1890, that the pumps in the lower levels had been stopped. The massive effort to find profitable ore at depth had lasted slightly more than two years and placed men 1,200 feet below the surface. There they had blasted away 2,100 linear feet of underground passageways searching for riches that they could not find. Even the dependable Fortuna lode was nearly barren in its deepest extremities. "In these lower workings," revealed Superintendent Kelly, "the Fortuna is found to carry quartz only in small, isolated bunches and veinlets, which are occasionally rich in precious metals, but are insignificant in extent."[1] The 1,200-, 1,000-, 900-, and, eventually, the 800-foot levels of the Bodie and Mono mines were surrendered to the water. Disappointment among stock speculators, who once believed that riches lay below, turned to indifference. A week after the pumps were stopped, stock in the Bodie Company plummeted from 75 to 35 cents per share. The gamble had failed because of high fuel costs and paltry indications at deep levels.[2]

An alternative proposal to drain the mines was considered: Drive a three-mile tunnel from Mono Basin, similar to Adolph Sutro's famous 3.9-mile tunnel on the Comstock, to intersect Bodie's underground at the 1,000-foot level. The workings would become self-draining above that point, and deeper mines would only have to raise water to tunnel level. Water discharged in Mono Basin could power scores of stamps, at no additional cost, and then be sold for irrigation. By eliminating the appalling cost of pumping water 1,000 feet or more to the surface, deep-level mining of even low-grade ore would become profitable. It was an enticing scheme, but never came to be.[3]

Late in 1890, the hoisting works at the old Bodie shaft was reopened, and miners returned to the upper levels, famous for the Bruce/Burgess and Fortuna bonanzas, where they now stoped progressively poorer ore.[4] The Bodie mill ran only part time, lying idle or working tailings until enough ore accumulated in its bins to make a run worthwhile. Transportation costs reappeared on the debit side of the account books as the company faced its former problem of hauling ore to the mill by wagon and team. This time, ore had to be conveyed from the Bodie shaft to the mill near the Lent.

At the Lent Shaft, the Bodie and Mono companies explored the 700-foot level, kept dry by pumps running at minimum speed. Occasionally a rich seam was found, spawning carefully crafted press releases that suggested another bonanza was within reach. Expectations, however, always exceeded the outcome, and exaggerated reporting could not overcome investor apathy. One analyst complained: "This market is like a graveyard, quiet and sad. Those persons who are out don't want to go in, and those who are in can't get out."[5]

A decade-long market slump in trans-Sierra mining shares was conspicuous in 1890, when Henry DeGroot described Mono County for the State Mineralogist.

With mining so depressed all other interests and branches of business have suffered in like degree. The town of Bodie and its surroundings show everywhere signs of decay. The former population of the place amounting once to several thousand, has shrunk to a few hundred, more than half its stores and dwellings being empty. The big mills are all idle. A number of mills and hoisting works, once standing in the vicinity have been torn down and removed elsewhere, some of those left being partially dismantled or dilapidated beyond repair. . . . The sawmills in the Sierra have shut down and the woodchopper's occupation is gone, while the stock raisers and farmers, left without an available market for their products, are generally poor.[6]

Weekly statements issued by Bodie and Mono managers outlined advances made underground and hyped the smallest discoveries. Their fervent resonance did little to buoy credibility, and even the most naive investors realized that the rich ore was gone. It was only by sheer luck, confessed the company president, that a collapse of timbering had exposed enough ore to pay the Bodie Company's last dividend, five years earlier. Perceiving that improved extraction at the mill could elicit profits from a shrinking ore supply, management undertook repairs designed to recover more value from the remaining ore. In June 1892, additional amalgamating pans and settlers, taken from the Bulwer's side of the Bulwer-Standard mill, were installed at the Bodie mill to increase capacity and efficiency.[7]

The specter of fire was an ever-present concern in a town consisting mostly of wooden buildings. On July 26, 1892, a kitchen fire started on the west side of Main Street. As soon as the alarm sounded, firemen hauled out the hose carts and attached hoses to hydrants. Residents were shocked to discover that, although the Lent's pumps had kept the emergency reservoir full, there was no water! A valve allowing water into the system had been inadvertently closed. When the problem was discovered and the valve opened, the sound of rushing water brought hope to those whose property had thus far escaped the flames. It was too late, however, to save 64 buildings in the business district north of the bank. When the fire was finally extinguished, the number of buildings in town had been reduced to a figure more proportionate to Bodie's population of about 600.[8]

By the end of 1892, the Bodie Mine had yielded only $1,914. The Mono did somewhat better. Ore from a winze beneath the Lent Shaft's 700-foot level produced $34,190 during a six-month run in the Bodie mill. All of the earnings, however, were consumed by fueling the pumps, whose increased speed allowed miners to reach the ore, and there was nothing left from which to declare a dividend.

Addressing the town's economic difficulties, the State Mineralogist blamed earlier insider excesses that had victimized Bodie's working-class investors.

The principal owners, after realizing large revenues from the mines, scenting reverses ahead, managed to dispose of their shares while they were yet at a premium, and pocketing the proceeds, left the country to its fate. As a rule, the shares so disposed of fell into the hands of the working miners, and other persons of small means, who, being residents of Bodie and naturally confiding in the future of the mines, invested freely in these worthless "securities," to their general undoing.[9]

In February 1893, the Mono Gold Mining Company levied a 25-cent assessment. When stockholders ignored the call, the company closed its half of the mine. The Bodie Company continued working its upper levels with five miners underground and two men at the hoist. A carpenter and a blacksmith worked part time. During the winter of 1893-1894, a correspondent of the Mason Valley *Tidings* wrote disparagingly of Bodie.

It is a strange camp. The horses wear snowshoes in the winter and the women wear long-legged gum boots. The snow falls deep and drifts deeper. The miners going and coming from work often get lost within a hundred yards of town. It is called a gold camp but there is too much silver in the bullion to make the name good and too little to make the thing pay.

Referring to Bodie's relatively high wage scale

of $4 per day for underground miners, the reporter concluded: "It is a four dollar camp, but the men don't work days enough in a week to average two. Bodie is a good place to keep away from, for the climate is tough and the people are tougher."[10]

Operations in the Bodie Mine were confined to the 300-foot level, where some high-grade ore was unearthed in early 1894. When the mill's stamps began a six-month run, stock advanced from 10 cents per share to $4.15 in May. Insiders and the company itself seized the opportunity by disposing of their holdings. A week later the stock had fallen to $1.25 and was declining steadily. By the end of the year, a share of Bodie Con. did not fetch six bits. The company used the $122,469 produced from the ore and proceeds from stock sales to reduce its debt and pay two more dividends, but these would be its last.

Years of low yields, diminishing ore supplies, and investor distrust had taken their toll. "The mining stock market has achieved the impossible," asserted one cynic. "It was actually duller this week than ever before." Another skeptic knew of a broker who owned mining stock printed with par values totalling almost $267,000,000, and who was willing to sell the lot for $1.72. "At this writing," concluded the storyteller, the broker "has been unable to find a victim. But he has not lost all hope yet."[11]

The Bodie Consolidated Mining Company struggled into 1895, hoisting ore that barely met expenses. In June, the company's New York office closed its doors amid progressively disheartening reports from the mine. That Bodie's entire economy was based on mining made it difficult for anyone living there to be very optimistic. Industry-wide, stock prices were lackluster, and one of the town's wealthiest companies was on the brink of collapse.

Still believing that the Bodie Mine could not have been worked out, optimists speculated that managers were hiding a cache of rich ore. To expose the alleged deceit, stockholders sent an expert, accompanied by an attorney, to examine the mine.[12] After a thorough investigation, the expert concluded that the Bodie Mine had been "exhausted" for some time.

His report was sobering. He had been "unable to locate any concealed ores, but found, on the contrary, that they were [already] stoped out."[13]

Early in 1896, a stock analyst made a rare disclosure that solidified the Bodie Company's ongoing difficulties. "So far as official advices go, there is not much of an encouraging character for shareholders." But he concluded with obligatory optimism, "an improvement may be reported any day."[14] Another San Francisco financial columnist assured investors that miners (presumably with firsthand knowledge) were looking forward to a revival during the coming year.[15] No revival came. Someone suggested that the Bodie Company might drive deeper if electricity were employed to pump out the Lent Shaft. The new form of power had been adopted by other western mines, including the Standard, but it was not applied at the Lent.[16]

The Bodie Company levied one last assessment in April 1896. Then, at a special meeting in October, stockholders ratified a proposal to sell the mine to the Standard Consolidated Mining Company. Owners of stock in the Mono Company followed suit. In January 1897, shareholders of the Bodie Consolidated Mining Company and the Mono Gold Mining Company were notified to surrender their stock. They received one share of Standard stock for two shares of Bodie stock. Holders of Mono stock received one share of Standard stock for every six of theirs. Shareholders of two other Bodie mines, the Bulwer and Summit, sold out on similar terms.[17]

With this sale, the Bodie Consolidated Mining Company and the Mono Gold Mining Company faded into obscurity. Over the years, Bodie Con. had paid its investors $1,677,572 in dividends, placing it second behind the Standard in total dividends paid. Its assessments totaled $716,490. The Mono Company, on the other hand, levied almost $700,000 in assessments and paid only one dividend, amounting to $12,500. How the Bodie and Mono mines fared under their new ownership cannot be determined, since their yield after 1897 was incorporated into fig-

ures for the Standard Company. Bringing Bodie's premium mines together under one management apparently benefited stockholders. The Standard would pay dividends for almost two more decades.

In 1903, six years after the Bodie and Mono mines had been taken over by the Standard Company, the machinery at the Lent Shaft was dismantled for scrap and sold to the Sacramento Pipe Works. William M. Lent, who outlived the two companies that sank the famous mine shaft bearing his name, died in San Francisco on October 17, 1904 at the age of 86. In 1917, lightning struck the buildings that remained at the mouth of the shaft, destroying them by fire.[18]

The Standard and Bulwer Mines

It appeared that Bodie's last hope had faded early in 1890, when the Bodie and Mono companies gave up deep-level pumping and prospecting at the Lent Shaft. Throughout the district, mining below the 700-foot level had repeatedly failed to expose another bonanza. Bullion production was at an ebb. Completing the worst year in its history, the region's preeminent mine, the Standard, was in debt and facing withering legal expenses.

On February 9 that year, another setback befell the district when Standard Company president and resident manager Augustus Pettibone died in San Francisco.[19] The town of Bodie held its collective breath, anticipating what adversity might come next. Concern became reality in March, when two more Bodie companies were struck from the San Francisco Stock and Exchange Board for non-payment of dues. Even though neither mine had been worked in years, removal of the Booker and Goodshaw from the list of trading securities was one more blow to the community's tottering pride.[20]

Faced with what appeared to be inevitable ruin, the Standard Consolidated Mining Company sought to settle its indebtedness by levying an emergency assessment of 25 cents per share and appealing to investors. "As there is urgent necessity for funds to pay pressing claims," read management's plea, "stock-holders are requested to pay at once without delay to the Farmer's Loan and Trust Company, No. 20 and 22, William Street, New York City." [21]

Unwilling to abdicate, Standard directors made a farsighted decision that set a course for the company that guaranteed the town's survival for the next quarter of a century. Departing from their usual practice of employing "practical" superintendents, they hired a 38-year-old, college-educated mining engineer. An 1875 graduate of the School of Mines at Columbia College in New York City, Arthur Macy was recognized as an able and innovative superintendent, who had successfully managed mines in North Carolina, Colorado, Idaho, and Arizona. He arrived in Bodie on April 29, 1890 to take charge of the "more or less wrecked property of the Standard Consolidated Mining Company." [22]

Macy imposed immediate changes. He saw that prolonged litigation between the Standard and Bulwer companies was a persistent drain on corporate finances and promptly ended it by negotiating "a mutual withdrawal of all complaints." [23] Next, based on engineering principles, carefully gathered data, and meticulous calculations, he determined that the biggest waste of company resources was the Bulwer-Standard mill, only half of which the Standard Company owned outright. Macy abandoned the mill, turning instead to the older, 20-stamp Standard mill, which had been inactive for six years except for occasional steamups to treat tailings.

The aerial cable tramway, the old mill's former delivery system, was dismantled. Rather than transporting ore down the hill from the main shaft, Macy had track laid from the mouth of the Bulwer Tunnel. Now ore loaded in mule-drawn cars exited the tunnel, then was pulled along the base of the hill to the mill. A snowshed covered the rails, allowing ore shipments to continue in foul weather. Often referred to as a "tramway," the track eliminated the cost of hoisting rock to the top of High Peak.

Inside the mill, Macy designed a more effective process for treating ore. He retained the stamps, but instead of employing the Washoe Pan Process, he had the mill refitted with a combination of plate amalgamation and mechanical concentration. To remove even more gold and silver from the ore, the old Washoe pans and settlers were rearranged sequentially into Boss's continuous process, an efficient method of treating low-grade ore that had been adopted years earlier by the Noonday. [24] An unusually large assessment of 50 cents financed the changes, and Standard stock slumped to 10 cents per share.

On July 23, 1890, the boilers were lit, and the "Old Reliable" Standard mill sprang back to life. "While not yet a matter for general rejoicing," pontificated the Bodie Evening Miner, "it is still a gratifying fact that the old Standard 20-stamp mill, which has been lying idle so long, was again started up last Wednesday for a short run. Let us pray that it may be for a long run and a prosperous run." [25] Macy's new combination process did the trick, reducing the cost of milling from $5.20 to $3.89 per ton, and increasing the mill's capacity by 20 tons per day. It also provided a better yield, recovering between 3% and 5% more gold and silver (known among millmen as "obtaining closer results"). By year's end, Bodie's leading mine was again on a paying basis, having produced $134,901. [26] In less than eight months, Macy had revived the Standard Company and returned it to preeminent status.

As the old mill clattered away, Bodie's residents overcame their disappointment with the Lent Shaft and its poor showings by shifting their enthusiasm to the Standard. Cheerfulness radiated across the region, where scattered inhabitants hoped that prosperity would spread. Mono County "has not been half prospected for its mineral wealth," locals asserted, "and many prominent mines have been idle for years awaiting a cheap system of ore reduction." [27]

Throughout 1891, the Standard mill hammered out more and more bullion. Its newly-fashioned milling process recovered more gold and silver from the ore and consumed less fuel than ever before, a perfect combination for Bodie, where thousands of tons of low-grade lay underground. Investors, most of

Figure 7-2: The Standard mill underwent several renovations during its long life. In this mid-1890s view, its cluttered interior sports a mixture of old and new machinery. After ore was crushed by the stamps, seen at upper left, it washed over amalgamating plates coated with quicksilver (mercury) to which particles of gold clung, forming an amalgam. Frue concentrators then removed heavy silver-bearing sulphurets from the mixture of crushed ore and water, after which a line of old amalgamating pans, arranged in the Boss continuous system, ground, heated, and stirred the mixture of crushed ore and water as quicksilver was added. Below the pans, a row of settlers separated the dense gold-and silver-bearing amalgam from the water and sand. The pans and settlers, remnants of the obsolete Washoe Pan Process, were abandoned in 1895, when cyanide supplanted their function. (*Cassier's Magazine* March 1895. Courtesy, Trustees of the Boston Public Library)

whom lived in New York City, were reassured as the mine blossomed. There were 70 Standard employees, many of whom were stoping ore on the 300-, 350-, 400-, 450-, 500-, and 550-foot levels.[28] The *Evening Miner* cheerfully noted:

> The mining outlook for Bodie at present is better than for years past. More men are employed, and there is a great deal of activity throughout the entire camp. A feeling of confidence prevails. . . . While Bodie will perhaps never again be as lively as it was ten or eleven years ago, there is every reason to believe that she will continue for many years to be one of the leading bullion-producing camps in the State.[29]

The Bulwer Company also resumed mining—and levying assessments. But, having abandoned the Bulwer-Standard mill, it was now hauling ore—with great difficulty—by wagon from the Standard hoisting works atop High Peak to the Bodie mill near the Lent Shaft. A letter to stockholders dated March 1, 1891 struck the usual positive chord, confirming that the stopes were "looking well, and yielding a good quality of ore."[30] The Bulwer removed enough ore from its 200-foot level to produce $31,227 in bullion before the long-disputed question of ownership re-emerged. Mining was suspended at the request of the Standard Company until a survey could determine which side of the boundary the ore body was on. Though short-lived, the ore shipments replenished the Bulwer's treasury and removed any immediate need for another assessment.[31]

Except for the Standard and the Bulwer, none of Bodie's mines showed real indications. The district's financial stability was also bridled by a nagging national depression that eroded investor confidence and drew capital away from the highly speculative market in mining shares. The brunt of the industry's problems, first felt on the San Francisco exchanges, had spread to the country's great financial center, New York City.

Despite overriding national financial difficulties and the public's disinterest in mining stocks, the Standard Company battled its way back from the brink of ruin. A 10-cent dividend was declared in October 1891. It was the company's first dividend in three years, spawning praise. "Through all the gloom attendant upon a dull and dispirited market," wrote one New York financial columnist, "there is one ray of brightness. Standard Consolidated was the feature of the week."[32] Quarterly dividends, even though they were just 10 cents per share, became almost regular.

Macy had placed the Standard Company on solid footing, a recovery that went beyond investors. Driven by layoffs elsewhere, men were wandering into Bodie in search of work—many more than the fragile economy could support. "There are from 75 to 100 idle men there, with no prospect of being put to work," reported the Hawthorne paper. "It is said that able bodied men, who are willing and anxious to work, are forced to beg for food about town. Lundy is also overrun with men. In view of these facts it would be well for miners to steer clear of the Bodie country for the present."[33]

Macy sought to further reduce milling costs by powering the Standard mill's machinery with electricity, a new energy form that was developing into an economical replacement for steam, especially where the expense of fuel was high. Unfortunately, he did not live to see his idea implemented. Suffering from ill health throughout his adult life, Arthur Macy died on April 14, 1891, while traveling to San Rafael, California. The task of developing electric power at Bodie fell upon his equally qualified and enterprising successor, Thomas H. Leggett.[34]

Leggett, like Macy, was an alumnus of the Co-lumbia School of Mines and shared a keen interest in the latest scientific developments. After graduating in 1879, he assumed the superintendency of mines in Mexico, Honduras, Columbia, and Colorado. At Bodie, he sought to improve the Standard Company's economic condition by focusing on milling expenses. Cordwood to fuel the mill cost the company $22,000 per year. Leggett recognized that by running the machinery with electric power, he could substantially reduce this figure. Initially, he hoped that decreasing energy costs would broaden his choice of milling processes to include some that would improve the mill's rate of recovery. Early in 1892, he reported:

> Most probably, roasting with sulphur and salt by either the Platner or Barrel Process [two chlorination processes], would give a much higher percentage of extraction, but with wood, at Bodie, costing $10 per cord, laborers wages . . . and freight rates . . . (the latter necessary to take into consideration on account of the chemicals essential for either process) it would be impossible to figure a profit.[35]

Leggett chose not to introduce a more complex treatment method. Instead, he retained the process engineered by Macy, but adapted it to electric power.

Two more quarterly dividends had been paid by the Standard Company during the first half of 1892, when the momentous decision was made to construct an electric generating plant to furnish cheap power for the mill.[36] This event was accompanied by the fire that swept away a substantial part of the business district in July 1892, transforming Bodie's outward appearance as much as electricity would transform its economics. Although electricity was well established as an energy source in America by 1892, it mostly ran urban streetcars and lighted building interiors in metropolitan centers, where generating machinery was driven by steam engines in neighborhood power stations. The type of electricity most often produced by these plants, direct current (DC), suited these situations, where transmission distances rarely exceeded three or four miles.

Because Leggett intended to avoid the high cost of producing steam, he looked to water power as a source of cheap energy to generate electricity for the Standard mill. Hydroelectric power had been growing in popularity in the mining West, where mountain streams were plentiful. Unfortunately, none of them flowed through Bodie. Reliable water sources were a dozen or so miles away in the Sierra foothills. How to transmit electricity over such a distance at reasonable cost was a problem that perplexed even the experts. When Leggett approached General Electric, the descendant of Thomas A. Edison's pioneering company, engineers were still working to overcome the difficulties of transmitting DC electricity over extended distances. Leggett and his consultant had reservations about GE's proposal, and they decided that the Westinghouse Electric Company's alternating current (AC) system was more likely to succeed.

In August 1892, just as Bodie was being connected for the first time to Hawthorne and points beyond by telephone,[37] construction began on the Standard Company's system of electric power. To generate electricity for the Standard mill, Leggett selected Green Creek, a mountain stream with adequate fall that coursed some 12½ miles from Bodie. Seven miles due south of Bridgeport on the northern slope of Castle (now Dunderberg) Peak, an old ditch left over from intermittent mining was repaired to divert water from Green Creek 4,570 feet across the face of the mountain to a point directly above the site for the proposed generating plant.

Enlarging and clearing the ditch at Green Creek, fabricating the penstock, pipe, water gates, and weirs, and erecting a powerhouse were all accomplished between August and October 1892. The Bulwer-Standard mill, neglected by the Standard Company since 1890 and abandoned by the Bulwer Company in 1891, was torn down for materials. Formerly recognized as the district's "model quartz mill," it furnished parts to fabricate the penstock and high-pressure receiver tank for the Green Creek generating station. The mill's salt shed was moved to become the powerhouse.[38]

Water wheels were put in place in November. Meanwhile, a transmission line was constructed that traversed the hills between Green Creek and Bodie. To conduct the electricity, two copper wires were suspended on wooden poles spaced 100 feet apart.[39] The power line entered Bodie from the hill above the cemetery, crossed Main Street just south of the brick post office, then passed diagonally across an open field. It turned northward near Green Street, following Wood into the mill. A telephone line traced existing roads to provide communication between the mill and powerhouse.[40]

After the system became operational, water from Green Creek would be diverted into the ditch, from which it would enter the penstock and plunge 1,571 feet through an 18-inch diameter pipe to the powerhouse.[41] Eight nozzles would then shoot high-pressure water against four Pelton water wheels spinning on a common axle with a Westinghouse 120-kilowatt AC generator. Spent water was to be discharged into the creek bed, eventually joining the East Walker River. The generator would produce 3,530 volts of AC power that was conducted 12.46 miles over rugged terrain to Bodie. After losing some potential in transmission, the 3,100 volts arriving at the mill would power a 120-horsepower motor that turned the belts, shafts, and gears that ran 20 stamps, 4 concentrators, 8 pans, 3 settlers, and 1 agitator at the Standard mill. Electric current, after being reduced to 100 volts, would also light the mill's interior and adjoining offices.[42]

The Standard Company's new hydroelectric plant was near completion at the end of 1892, when the mine reported the year's production at $237,996. Four quarterly 10-cent dividends had been paid, a remarkable achievement considering the outlay of capital for new technology. Of the Bodie stocks still trading on major exchanges, Standard was selling for $1.75, Bodie $1, Mono 75 cents, and Bulwer 25 cents.

While the Standard developed its new power system, the Bulwer had resumed hauling ore to the Bodie mill

Figure 7-3: The hydroelectric plant at Green Creek was key to the Standard Company's success with long-distance electric power transmission. Operational by the fall of 1893, the powerhouse generated electricity which was conducted over copper wires 12½ miles to run the Standard mill at Bodie. (Emil Billeb collection. Courtesy, Vickie Daniels)

in January 1892, after the boundary dispute and a threatened lawsuit by the Standard were resolved.[43] Except for occasional interruptions when the Bodie and Mono companies employed the mill, the 10 stamps ran on Bulwer ore throughout the year. The rock earned the company $65,117 and paid a 10-cent dividend in April and a 5-cent dividend in October. These were the Bulwer's first dividends since 1884, good reason for San Francisco's premier mining journal to spill some optimistic ink. "After such a long period a dividend . . . refutes any statement that the camp is played out. There is no reason to doubt that the company will declare many more in the future."[44]

Dividends and electric power were not all that Bodieites welcomed in late 1892. Another improvement was aimed at keeping their spirits high. "There are only nine saloons in Bodie at present," observed the Hawthorne newspaper, "and as there are not thought to be enough, another will open soon. Bodie is a great camp in some ways."[45]

Innovative building projects rarely go as planned, and the Standard Company's long-distance transmission of electrical power was no exception. Originally scheduled for startup on December 1, 1892, it was not completed when extreme weather gripped the area during the winter of 1892-93. Expecting to be under electric power, the Standard mill had not purchased its usual supply of cordwood before the railroad's winter shutdown. Insufficient fuel halted milling several times, until roads were cleared of snow and wagon deliveries resumed. Harsh weather also hampered work on the electrical system and delayed the arrival of key components. After months of setbacks that extended into the summer of 1893, the contractor finally completed the installation in July, and the Standard mill was turned over to electric power.[46] "Everything is working smoothly and satisfactorily," observed the *Bodie Evening Miner* on July 15, 1893. "The familiar toot of the Standard mill whistle is no longer heard and many a miner will miss its sound in the morning and will have to rely upon other means of waking up in time for work."[47]

Despite accolades, problems persisted. One major concern was safeguarding the equipment from lightning strikes along the exposed transmission wires. Also annoying were critics. In September a leading electrical engineering publication concluded that the project was a flop. "The transmission of power electrically over long distances in California was a failure," announced *Electrical World*. "Today the superintendent of the mine in which the installation was made in eastern California is looking at his burned-out field coils after the generator has been in operation for less than thirteen days."[48] By the time magazines reached newsstands, however, the machinery at Bodie had nearly completed a required 30-day continuous test run. Trials concluded late in August, upon which the mill's steam engine and boilers were disconnected, and Leggett's vision became reality.[49]

It had cost the company $37,000 to build an electric system that promised to save $22,000 annually. So far, the Standard mill was the only facility in Bodie with electricity. Because AC motors were unsuited for the varying loads and changing speeds required by hoisting, the Standard works atop the hill continued to operate under steam at a cost of $11,000 per year for fuel. Likewise, other companies operating mines and mills in the district, such as the Bulwer, Bodie, and a few of sporadic character like the Mono and Syndicate, were not furnished with electricity and managed as best they could with their old steam engines. Nor were any of the town's dwellings or businesses connected to the new form of energy.

To America's clique of mining stock speculators, Bodie's 1893 success with electricity was about the only good news. Although it was a defining moment for Bodie, the Standard's new power system was overshadowed by national economic worries.[50] Congress, seeking to end the country's depression, had repealed the Sherman Silver Purchase Act, which had subsidized silver mining for the past three years by requiring the federal government to purchase 4,500,000 ounces of silver monthly. Adopted in 1890, the act had come under immediate attack by critics, who considered it responsible for widespread economic problems by depleting the federal treasury of its gold reserve. Many businessmen felt that gold was the only reliable currency, and they lost confidence when the government's gold supply eroded to levels insufficient to redeem silver coin and paper money. Responding to their pleas, President Grover Cleveland successfully argued in a special session of Congress for the act's repeal to stop the drain on the nation's gold reserve and restore economic strength.

The 1893 repeal had some beneficial effects, but it did not bring about economic revival. Without government support, the price of silver tumbled to half its earlier level, devastating mining in the West. Mines, mills, and smelters shut down, and thousands were left jobless. Banks failed, and the crisis nearly paralyzed stock exchanges on both coasts in what became known as the "Silver Panic of 1893." A New York analyst reported, "The public takes no interest in mining stocks, and the continued depression in the silver market . . . tend[s] to maintain the 'masterly inactivity' in the mining stock market which has prevailed for months past."[51] The outlook was slightly more positive in San Francisco, where it was hoped that the closing of so many silver mines would give California gold mining a boost.[52]

The Standard Company's new hydroelectric system possessed some interesting quirks. The generator producing the power at Green Creek determined the speed of the motor at the mill, and early AC motors could not start by themselves. Three well-trained men were required to put the milling machinery into motion: two at the mill, who communicated by telephone with a third 12½ miles away at the powerhouse.

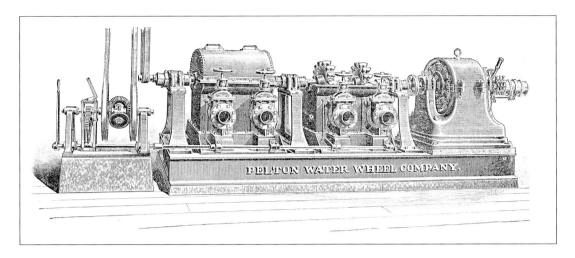

Figure 7-4: The principal machine inside Green Creek's powerhouse was an assembly manufactured in San Francisco by the Pelton Water Wheel Company. Water from Green Creek plunged 1,571 feet downhill (a 355-foot vertical drop) through an 18-inch diameter pipe to a receiver tank in the powerhouse. Individual pipe connections, at center, directed high-pressure water at four 21-inch water wheels, causing them to spin at 870 rpm. Two of the water wheels are shown with their cover removed. Turning on a common axle with the water wheels, a Westinghouse AC generator, at right, produced 3,530 volts of electricity for transmission to Bodie. Sensing the load, a governor, at left, automatically controled the volume of water turning the Pelton wheels. (*Engineering and Mining Journal* 17 June 1893. Courtesy, Engineering and Mining Journal)

Figure 7-5: Generating machinery inside the Green Creek powerhouse was photographed in 1895 for Thomas Leggett's widely distributed report describing Bodie's long-distance transmission of electric power. (*Transactions of the American Institute of Mining Engineers*, Vol. 24. Courtesy, Society for Mining, Metallurgy, and Exploration)

Figure 7-6: At the Standard mill, a motor room was built to house the 120-horsepower AC motor that turned the milling machinery. Also shown in this 1894 view is the drive belt that transferred power to the mill, and a small starting motor used to bring the large motor up to operating speed. After the steam-powered hoisting works atop the main shaft burned down in 1894, the large motor was belted to a dynamo that sent DC power to an electric hoist inside the Bulwer Tunnel. (*Transactions of the American Institute of Mining Engineers*, Vol. 24. Courtesy, Society for Mining, Metallurgy, and Exploration)

Figure 7-7: The Standard Company was about to begin a new era based on electric power when this wintry snapshot captured Bodie with its principal mine dominating the skyline. Although the northern part of town had been destroyed by a recent fire, the Standard, Bulwer, Bodie, and Mono mines were still operating. Looming on the hill above town, the Standard's hoisting works brings gold- and silver-bearing ore with a value of $20,000 to the surface every month. Entering the scene from the left, the yet-to-be-energized power line from Green Creek passes south of commercial buildings on Main Street before angling toward the Standard mill. (Courtesy, Bancroft Library, University of California, Berkeley)

When the mill was ready, water aimed at the wheels at Green Creek spun the generator, and electricity began passing through the wires to Bodie. A small, hand-started, electric motor at the mill received the current and brought the main motor up to operating speed. One man engaged the motors while the other watched the switchboard's flashing lights and meters. When the large motor was spinning and synchronized with the distant generator, the small motor was disengaged and the main power switch was thrown. If the operators reacted correctly, the big motor began running on electricity; otherwise the process had to be repeated. "There is therefore but a fraction of a second during which the jaw-switch should be closed," stressed Leggett, recalling

the intricacies of the procedure. "It will be seen that the operation of starting the motor is one requiring considerable practice."[53]

Once the big motor was running, a clutch engaged the cumbersome milling machinery. Thereafter, the mill's operating speed was controlled from the powerhouse, where a mechanical governor sensed the load, then automatically adjusted the electrical output by controlling the volume of water shot against the wheels.

During 1893, the Standard Company paid two more 10-cent dividends from a yield of $239,382, and its stock sold for 85 cents per share at year's end. The Bulwer's good fortune faded when the Bodie mill produced only $32,246, half the 1892 yield, after running almost all year on Bulwer ore. Thereafter, ore shipments became sporadic, and no more dividends were declared. A share of Bulwer stock sold for five cents. Stock in the Bodie Company was selling at 25 cents, Mono 15 cents, and the Bodie Tunnel and Mining Company had been dropped from the San Francisco stock exchange for nonpayment of dues.[54]

A decade of operating trains had not brought the Bodie and Benton Railway and Commercial Company's tracks any closer to Benton than they were in 1882. Nor had the company paid down an 1881 loan of $300,000 that funded construction of the railroad and sawmill. The mortgage holder, William J. Menzies, foreclosed in 1893 and formed the Bodie Railway and Lumber Company. Adopting the railroad's original name, the new corporate entity announced plans to finish the tracks to Benton, from which the Carson & Colorado Railroad would con-

vey Bodie's lumber products into Inyo County. Bodieites applauded the proposal, and looked forward to a railroad to replace horse-drawn stage and freighting lines. But, as in 1882, the extension was never built and operation of the main line between Bodie and Mono Mills was turned over to a lessee.[55]

The Standard Consolidated Mining Company began 1894 by introducing more improvements. Leggett, his eyes set on the future, defied public indifference toward his industry with three innovations. The first was using cyanide to recover more gold and silver. Since its 1890 introduction as the MacArthur-Forrest Process, the cyanide method had swept the mining world after proving successful in New Zealand, Australia, and South Africa.[56] By simply soaking finely-ground ore in a weak solution of potassium cyanide and water, a high percentage of precious metals could be recovered. All that were needed were some large wooden vats, inexpensive chemicals, a few

Figure 7-8: When the Standard mill was built in 1877, its machinery came from an abandoned mill in Aurora. Replacement mortars were cast locally in 1879 from patterns made for the Bulwer-Standard mill (raised letters read: "Bodie Foundry"). Screens have been removed from one battery to reveal the stamps. Recalling the mill's 1893 modernization, a light bulb dangles from a gnarled electric wire. Because electricity from the power station on Green Creek proved unreliable, a trusty oil lamp was hung nearby. (*Engineering and Mining Journal* 27 June 1896. Courtesy, Engineering and Mining Journal)

Figure 7-9: Known simply as Tailings Plant No. 1, the Standard Company's first cyanide plant was completed in September 1894. It was located on the dump at the mouth of the Bulwer Tunnel, immediately above the company's tailings ponds. The building contained four large leaching vats, where a diluted solution of potassium cyanide percolated through tailings to dissolve gold and silver. (Courtesy, Russ and Anne Johnson)

Figure 7-10: Mine cars at Standard Tailings Plant No. 1 convey excavated tailings to cyanide leaching vats inside. (Courtesy, Gregory Bock)

small pumps, and yards of canvas from which to make filters. Leggett had first considered the process in 1892 for use in treating old tailings. A two-ton sample of the waste material was sent to Denver, Colorado, where it was tested by MacArthur-Forrest's U.S. representative, the Gold and Silver Extraction Company of America. The results were poor, and Leggett dropped the idea. Then, in 1893, encouraged by experiments underway elsewhere in California and spurred by solicitations from MacArthur-Forrest and promotions by rival cyanide processes, Leggett had more Bodie tailings tested. Laboratory trials performed in San Francisco by Alexis Janin and Charles Merrill showed that cyanide recovered 80 to 90 percent of the sample's assay value. Leggett invited Merrill to Bodie, where large-scale tests were conducted. The outcome was the construction of a cyanide plant to treat tailings just below the Standard mill.[57]

The cyanide plant stood on top of the huge waste dump at the Bulwer Tunnel's entrance, conveniently above the Standard and Bulwer-Standard mills' tailings ponds. Construction began in June 1894 and was completed in September. In the absence of an official name, the new plant was simply called the "Standard Tailings Plant." Its capacity was 75 tons of tailings per day, handled by four large cyanide-leaching vats, each measuring 20 feet in diameter and seven feet in height, with false bottoms covered by canvas. After tailings had soaked in a cyanide solution, the liquid, now rich in dissolved gold and silver, was collected by allowing it to percolate through the canvas. Soaking and filtering were repeated several times over four days, while three strong-solution zinc boxes and four weak-solution boxes precipitated the precious metals from the liquid. By the time freezing weather shut down the digging of tailings in December, the plant had paid for itself.[58]

A disaster on August 19, 1894 inspired Leggett's second innovation of the year. It happened on a Sunday afternoon, as six employees worked at the big hoisting works on the hill. The blacksmith, at the

forge with his helper, was the first to notice flames and gave the alarm. Several men started a steam pump, sending water streaming against the fire while smoke billowed toward the main building. Fanned by a brisk breeze from the southeast, flames suddenly leaped to the hoisting works. The engineer grabbed a fire hose and battled the fire from inside, but the rapidly spreading flames soon enveloped the building. At one o'clock in the afternoon, sharp toots from the steam whistle alerted the town that the Standard hoisting works was on fire. Bodie's fire engine was hitched to a team of horses that had just arrived with a fruit wagon from Sonora, and the animals charged up the hill toward the mine. The apparatus, however, was of little use against the inferno. At the same time, the engineer lowered a man into the mine, where he alerted those working below of the danger. All 26 hands escaped through the Bulwer Tunnel before a sudden downdraft filled the dark passages with deadly smoke and poisonous gas. The engineer remained at his post as long as possible, barely escaping the flames by scrambling through a window.[59]

One awestruck and dismayed observer recorded the grand building's final moments.

In a few minutes the side and roof were gone, and one by one the heavy timbers gave way, leaving the big gallows frame till the last. Its supports burned away and finally it toppled over, leaving nothing but a lot of smouldering ruins to mark the place where formerly stood the big works of Bodie's star mine.

Finally, the hoisting cables broke, and the cages went "tearing down the shaft" into eternity.[60] There they remain to this day, submerged at the bottom of the mine.

Fortunately, no lives were lost, but the fire destroyed the works that had dominated Bodie's eastern skyline since 1881. The hoisting and pumping machinery were ruined, and timbering was charred 20 feet down the shaft. The railroad's nearby trestlework and tracks were reduced to ashes along with about 440 cords of stacked wood.[61] It was thought that the hoisting works was worth $100,000, although the company had insured it for only $30,000.

A nearby hoist house and some old equipment were purchased and quickly moved from the defunct Consolidated Pacific Mine. But instead of building another steam-powered hoisting works, Leggett decided to install an electric hoist underground.

Possessing quick starting and stopping capabilities, DC motors were superior to AC motors for handling the irregular loads demanded by hoisting. To obtain DC electricity in a district that was supplied only with AC, the big alternating current motor at the mill was belted to a 90-kilowatt, 500-volt dynamo. Copper wires conducted direct current 1,200 feet from the mill's motor room to the mouth of the Bulwer Tunnel, then 1,800 feet through the tunnel to power the hoist at the intersection of the tunnel and the Standard shaft. From there, wires ran 500 feet down the shaft to an electric motor that drove a plunger pump and worked iron rods connected to a sinking pump placed at water level 40 feet below. The sinking pump lifted water to the plunger pump, which pushed it up to the tunnel, through which it was delivered to the Standard mill and cyanide plant. Because of insufficient electric power, however, pumping and hoisting could not be carried on simultaneously.

Branching northward from the tunnel's mouth, wires also delivered DC power to the cyanide plant, where an electric motor replaced a small steam engine and boiler. A second motor winched mine cars loaded with tailings up an inclined track into the plant. Electricity also illuminated the mine, mill, and cyanide plant, though the light bulbs tended to flicker and dim when the hoist was running. Construction of the subterranean hoisting works, begun in January 1895, was completed in July. Thus, alternating current arriving from Green Creek ran the Standard mill, and generated direct current for hoisting, pumping, cyaniding, and lighting.

Deep inside High Peak, the new electric hoist raised a single cage no higher than the 250-foot level. Since cages no longer reached the surface, all rock, men, and supplies entered or exited the mine through the Bulwer Tunnel.[62]

The Standard Company's third major innovation arose from a need for a steady power source to run its scattered array of motors. Because Green Creek froze in winter and ran dry in summer, the Standard mill kept its old steam engine and an ample supply of cordwood ready for occasions when water volume was insufficient for generating. Winters were particularly troublesome, as explained by the superintendent. "There was a considerable length of ditch to be kept open, and, as the stream is small . . . any freezing night may stop the whole flow of water."[63] Leggett's solution was one that had been employed by millers for centuries. He would build a dam and store enough water behind it to keep the mill running for several days.[64]

The dam, located 3,875 feet upstream from the power plant,[65] was made of "logs, cribbed up in squares of about 12 feet, ballasted with earth and rock, and sheathed on the water-face with 3-inch plank."[66] It measured 235 feet along its top edge, was 42 feet tall, and 60 feet thick at the base, sloping upward to a thickness of 15 feet. The dam, equipped with a spillway and fish ladder, impounded 24,000,000 gallons of water. Work started in October 1894 and required a full year to complete, keeping the sawmills near Bridgeport busy until October 1895. The reservoir, later named "Dynamo Pond," would enable Leggett to abandon the problem-prone ditch and penstock, and replace them with a 24-inch diameter buried iron pipe, which, tapering to 18 inches, conveyed high-pressure water to the wheels.[67]

The fire at the hoisting works in August restricted the Standard's 1894 production to only $171,536 in bullion, most of which came from cyaniding tailings. The company did pay four quarterly dividends of 10 cents each, despite the outlay of funds for various building projects. Standard stock traded at $2.25 per share, while Bodie stock sold for 81 cents and Mono 25 cents. Bulwer shares sold for a dime apiece.

Illustrating the rapid success of working old tailings with cyanide, Bodie sported three plants by the

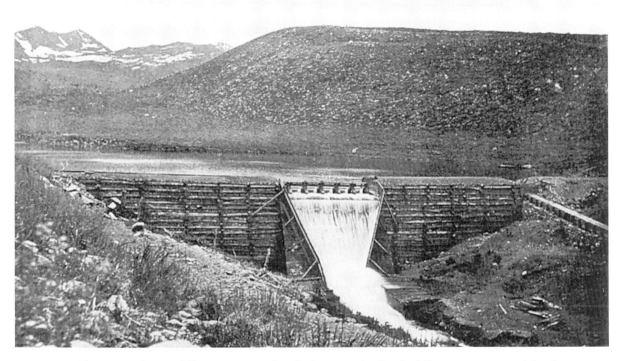

Figure 7-11: After a year of successfully running its mill with electricity, the Standard Company constructed this dam on Green Creek to store water for power generation. Finished in October 1895, the dam was built of logs cribbed in earth-filled squares, and measured 235 feet in length and 42 feet in height. A buried pipe pierced the dam below the spillway to carry high-pressure water to the power plant three-quarters of a mile downstream (a vertical drop of 343 feet). A fish ladder, at right, was required by state law. The reservoir behind the dam became known as Dynamo Pond. (*Transactions of the American Institute of Mining Engineers*, Vol. 26. Courtesy, Society for Mining, Metallurgy, and Exploration)

end of 1894: one at the Bodie Tunnel mill (presumably Bodie's first), the Standard Tailings Plant, and another down the canyon near the Syndicate mill. The Syndicate property had been operated the last four years by lessees John F. Parr and Sam Tyack. Parr had been a member of the work force sent by the Syndicate Company in 1876 to recondition the old Empire mill after the neighboring Bullion Mine began showing profitable ore. In the 1880s, he had been foreman of the Syndicate Mine and mill. During the early 1890s, he and Tyack employed about 10 men in their mining and milling operation, building Bodie's third cyanide plant in 1894 near the mill, a site abundant in rich tailings. Some of these tailings were the residue of bonanza ore milled during the boom years, and were worth up to $183 per ton.[68]

Around town there were other signs of revival. After demonstrating a lack of faith by closing its Bodie office the year before, Wells, Fargo & Company re-opened in July 1894. "Without exaggerating in the least," exhorted the *Bodie Evening Miner*, "it can be said that Bodie's outlook is brighter than for years past, and the old camp will continue to produce bullion in large quantities for years to come."[69]

A new chapter in Bodie's history had begun, though in a dismal financial climate. The morbid scene inside a New York mining exchange tells the tale.

All the mining brokers—they are but few, nowadays—grumble at the dull times and lament the lack of interest shown by the public in what once was a favorite pursuit. . . . It appears, therefore, that although three or four of the "old timers" still meet every day and buy or sell a few hundred shares, the mining stock market has been given up as a hopeless case by the majority. It is safe to say that not more than 15% of the mining securities listed . . . are traded in, and yet the entire lot is still kept on the list and their names are called three times per day and two or three—and sometimes as many as four—brokers stand about the rostrum listening conscientiously to the sonorous and commanding voice of the chairman, who automatically reads the long list to the bitter end. Everybody knows that two-thirds of the stocks listed are worthless.[70]

Early in 1895, the eastern exchanges witnessed a brief rise of interest brought about by a mining boom at Cripple Creek, Colorado, and during April and May stock in the Standard Company strengthened to $3 per share. The San Francisco market, however, remained stagnant. Of the stocks listed there, most "have not been traded in for years past, because the original companies . . . no longer exist, or are hopelessly bankrupt, or the mines have closed down permanently, or been sold by the sheriff for taxes, or because they are worth less than nothing, which is all that some of them were worth anyway."[71]

After completing the task of modernizing the Standard Company's facilities, Thomas Leggett resigned in July 1895 to accept employment with a British mining corporation operating in Johannesburg, South Africa.[72] He was replaced by Robert Gilman Brown, a mine superintendent from Butte City, Montana. Brown wrote extensively about the Standard's new technology, first as mine superintendent, then as general manager.

Based largely on new cyanide plants, old tailings, and ample quantities of low-grade ore, Bodie was said to be the "liveliest town" in California. Nevertheless, four of its five remaining stamp mills — the Bodie, Syndicate, Bodie Tunnel, and Miners — ran only seasonally, or when someone spent enough money to reopen one of the mines. Bodie's newspaper reflected upon the economic weakness elsewhere. "Strangers are flocking to this place every day and cannot get work. Beds are scarce, and in some instances, men have been obliged to sit up all night in saloons."[73] The Standard Consolidated Mining Com-

Figure 7-12: Based on new technology, Bodie experienced a comeback, despite a downtown fire in 1892. This view looks toward the south end, where the crest of Silver Hill is highlighted against distant hills. In 1894, Bodie banker and businessman James S. Cain began purchasing mines on Silver Hill, where the recently built Addenda and Oro hoisting works can be seen on the ridge above the Catholic church. (Courtesy, California Department of Parks and Recreation)

pany did its part to support the local economy by hiring swarms of men to construct its dam on Green Creek. When it was completed in October, the future of the Standard looked bright.[74] One Bay Area reporter speculated that Bodie's mines would be sunk deeper. "Taking the situation on the different lodes as a whole," he argued, "there is much encouragement to look forward to for good things in the future, but at present it does not warrant venturing in on a legitimate investment proposition."[75]

On the exchanges, Bodie stocks were treated with the same contempt accorded to other mining shares, and the cautious public avoided them. It did not help the district's standing when the Standard Company missed paying two quarterly dividends in 1895, and the two dividends that were declared continued a trend established five years earlier, in 1891, paying only 10 cents per share. At year's end, Standard Con. sold for less than $1.75. Wallowing in successive disappointments, the Bodie Company also saw its stock slide to 40 cents, and Mono had softened to 7 cents per share. Bulwer advanced from 10 to 13 cents. Meanwhile, another Bodie company, Tioga Consolidated Mining, was struck from the San Francisco stock board.

The tailings ponds were still frozen in the spring of 1896 when building materials began arriving for the Standard Company's second cyanide plant. A little more than three miles below town, the Standard had purchased several placer claims, and the newly acquired real estate included tailings deposited along the banks of Bodie Creek. Across a meadow fronting the road to Hawthorne, a flat area was gouged out of a hillside to support four cyanide vats. The site was near the ruins of the old Wagner and Gillespie tailings mill, at a bend in the canyon where large quantities of discarded tailings had accumulated. So that no one would confuse the company's two plants, the new facility was known prosaically as Tailings Plant No. 2, its predecessor as Tailings Plant No. 1.[76]

Tailings Plant No. 2 was just about completed when the company was beset by another disastrous fire, this one deep inside the Standard Mine. Nothing is feared more by miners than an underground fire. There are forests of timber and very few escape routes. Thick clouds of black smoke displace life-sustaining oxygen, quickly extinguishing candles. Men must grope their way to the shaft in utter darkness, praying that they will be delivered to the surface alive. Otherwise they languish until suffocated. When a fire starts, heroic attempts are made to rescue anyone below, then passageways are sealed, smothering the fire and dooming anyone trapped inside.

The inferno against which all others in the region were measured occurred in 1869 on the Comstock. That fire, on the 800-foot level of the Yellow Jacket, Crown Point, and Kentuck mines, claimed 34 lives and burned in one confined area for more than a year. Bodie's worst mine fire, and its third-deadliest industrial accident, had taken place in November 1880, when the Goodshaw hoisting works burned down. Even though flames did not reach more that a few feet below the shaft's collar, four miners on the 600-foot level were asphyxiated.[77]

Now Bodie faced another mine fire. At three o'clock Saturday morning, April 25, 1896, the Standard's night shift departed through the Bulwer Tunnel, unaware that anything was wrong. As the next group of workers started for the mine at 6:30 A.M., dawn lit the horizon to reveal smoke spewing from the shaft on the hill. It was quickly determined that no workers were in the mine.[78] Approaching the shaft through the tunnel, men ventured to within 100 feet of the hoisting station before they were driven back by smoke and gas.

"There was a nest of old timbers . . . where the fire could lurk for months," recalled superintendent Brown describing conditions inside the mine.[79] As rapidly as possible, all openings except the Bulwer Tunnel and the main Standard shaft were closed. By leaving the two passageways open, it was hoped that an updraft would be created to clear smoke from the tunnel, allowing men to move closer. The plan worked. Within two hours an underground hand-to-hand fight against the flames had commenced. Fran-

THE STANDARD MULE'S GHOST

A ghost town needs a good ghost story, and the Standard Mine's 1896 fire gave rise to one: a spooky tale about a company-owned mule named Jerry.

Mules were often required to work inside mines, where they pulled ore cars through long passageways. At the Standard, however, everything taken above or below Bulwer Tunnel level had to fit inside the shaft. Mature mules were too large, so the company purchased a half-grown mule named Jerry, then lowered him to the 500-foot level on the cage. Jerry lived there in a specially-built underground stall, where he received regular deliveries of feed and water brought down to him.

Before long, Jerry had grown too big to leave the mine. Residing in his dingy, subterranean world, the luckless beast of burden toiled until the day the shaft caught fire. All of the miners escaped, but they left poor Jerry to his fate—asphyxiation from smoke and gas.

One hundred and fifty feet above the trapped creature, determined men fought a four-day battle against the fire. After the flames were extinguished and the hoist and shaft had been repaired, miners returned to the lower levels, where they found Jerry dead in his stall. He was buried at the bottom of an incline known as Mule Canyon.

Miners are traditionally superstitious, and they enjoy swapping scary stories. When one of them was killed the day after he reported seeing a white mule roaming the dimly lit underground, the frightful tale spread until all who heard it feared that they too might see the deadly apparition.[1]

Bodie's hills cloak many mysteries, but the strangest tale ever told warns of a ghostly mule that haunts the Standard Mine. Decades after the fire, folks still talk about the district's restless spirit. "I worked in the Standard," recalled Robert Bell. "I never saw the white mule, but I sure heard him plenty of times. You could hear him walking around down there in the dark. Those iron shoes make a hell of a clatter, and you'd think he was headed right toward you."[2]

ervoir to a hose attached near the flames. Meanwhile, from atop the hill, water pumped from a neighboring mine was channeled through a hose and sprayed down the shaft. The men fought valiantly for four days before the flames were extinguished.[80]

Damage to the Standard Mine was concentrated at the intersection of the shaft and Bulwer Tunnel. The hoisting station and shaft were caved, the electric machinery was destroyed, and the ore bins were ruined. The cage, after jamming in the shaft, prevented fire from spreading downward, while water streaming from above saved the upper 200 feet of timbering. The company deemed itself quite fortunate considering the horrid possibilities. Within a week, miners resumed work in the upper levels, dropping ore through chutes to the tunnel. A month later they had retimbered the shaft and were raising ore with a makeshift hoist. The underground electric hoisting works, considered a stunning success, was replaced exactly.[81]

As Tailings Plant No. 2 neared completion, the Hawthorne press acknowledged Bodie's expanding economy. "Large quantities of freight are being shipped to Bodie," the paper reported. "Cyanide tanks, machinery and whisky are the main articles."[82] The Standard's new cyanide plant, up and running in midsummer, was similar to Tailings Plant No. 1, with four leaching vats capable of handling 75 tons of tailings per day, though its layout was considerably different.

tic men ransacked drugstores and assay offices for acid and soda to recharge spent fire extinguishers. They also battled the fire with water brought through the tunnel in barrels, directing it at the flames with hand pumps. On the second day, an electric pump was connected to the discharge pipe that coursed through the Bulwer Tunnel, forcing water from a nearby res-

Figure 7-13: Completed in 1896, Standard Tailings Plant No. 2 was built near the site of an old tailings mill about three miles below Bodie, where tailings tended to collect at a bend in Bodie Creek. Horse-drawn wagons traversed a timber bridge, from which they dumped tailings into the plant's leaching vats. A large tank on the hill held 8,000 gallons of water for washing tailings and flushing the vats. A shed, at right, housed zinc precipitation boxes, pumps, and a "hit-and-miss" gasoline engine that ran the plant. (Courtesy, Russ and Anne Johnson)

Its vats were 18 feet in diameter and eight feet deep. There were four zinc precipitation boxes for the strong solution, and two for the weak solution. Several pumps were employed: a vacuum pump, a centrifugal pump, and a rotary pump that raised wash water from a reservoir to an 8,000-gallon storage tank on the ridge above. An eight-horsepower internal combustion gasoline engine, manufactured by the Union Gas Engine Company of San Francisco, furnished motive power.[83]

During the last half of 1896, managers negotiated terms under which the Standard would absorb four major companies with mines on High Peak: the Bodie Consolidated Mining Company, the Mono Gold Mining Company, the Summit Gold Mining Company, and the Bulwer Consolidated Mining Company.[84] With the signing of this agreement, in September 1896, the Standard Company took control of the Bulwer property and the three other adjoining mines. Holders of Bulwer stock received one share of Standard stock for three of theirs.[85] While these negotiations were underway, stock in the subject companies rallied as investors positioned themselves to take advantage of the mergers. Bodie Company stock reached 65 cents per share, Bulwer 40 cents, and Mono sold for 23 cents. Stock in Standard Consolidated, with the merger finalized, finished the year at $1.25.

Even though the Standard's mine and tailings ponds yielded $234,618, the company paid no divi-

Figure 7-14: This tailings wagon, displayed at Bodie State Historic Park, once hauled tailings for the Standard Consolidated Mining Company. The wagon's box is constructed with transverse planks that were pried out one by one to dump the load through the running gear into cyanide vats. (Photograph by the author)

Figure 7-15: A four-horse team pulls a load of tailings onto the grated bridge above Tailings Plant No. 2. Although the Standard Company kept a stable of horses and mules for work in the mine, tailings were usually hauled by private contractors. In the distance, the road from Aurora and Hawthorne winds through the canyon toward Bodie. (Courtesy, California Department of Parks and Recreation)

Figure 7-16: After dissolving gold and silver, the cyanide solution was drained from the leaching vats and pumped through zinc precipitation boxes. Baffles in the boxes forced the liquid to pass through perforated trays holding zinc shavings. When the clear cyanide solution came in contact with the zinc, particles of gold and silver precipitated, then dropped to the bottom of the boxes. Periodically, the precipitate was collected, cleaned, dried, and melted into bars of bullion. Zinc precipitation boxes in Standard Tailings Plant No. 2 are seen here, with the strong-solution boxes in the foreground. (*Practical Notes on the Cyanide Process*. Courtesy, Engineering and Mining Journal)

dends during 1896. But acquiring three former dividend-paying mines (and one that had never paid a dividend) added significantly to Standard holdings and placed it in a strong position for an extended life. The merger also increased the number of Standard stockholders. To accommodate its new owners, many of whom lived in the West, the company paid $300 in back dues and was reinstated on the San Francisco Stock and Exchange Board and the Pacific Stock Exchange. Once again, "Standard Con." was called in San Francisco.[86]

While Bodie expected that consolidating its best properties under one management would prove beneficial, the district's pay rate of $4 per day for miners continued to come under fire. Throughout the 1880s, the scale had been repeatedly blamed in San Francisco for faltering profits and infrequent dividends. Arguments against the rate were also voiced locally. "One thing that is against working our low [-grade] ores," Bulwer superintendent John Kelly complained in 1888, "is the high price of labor. Bodie and Virginia City are the only mining towns in this section of the coast that are paying $4 a day. If we could get the work done for $3 to $3.50, a number of other mines would be worked."[87]

Elsewhere in the West, pressure to reduce wages during the 1880s had been intense, provoking worker dissatisfaction when mining companies tried to impose lower pay rates. Unions fought long, bitter fights against cuts, but suffered crippling blows when mining companies received support from armed forces at

Leadville, Colorado, in 1880; Tombstone, Arizona, in 1884; Wood River, Idaho, and Eureka, Nevada, in 1885; and Grass Valley and Nevada City, California, in 1887.[88]

By the mid-1890s, workers in silver camps were suffering most from layoffs and wage reductions, as managers faced plummeting silver prices and declining profit margins. At Bodie, however, miners still received $4 for a 10-hour day, generous in a doubtful economy. "Bodie is the only $4 camp in the State," noted the *Mining and Scientific Press* in 1897."[89] By comparison, miners' wages in most other western districts, including California's Mother Lode, ranged between $2.50 and $3.50 per day. Although Bodie's relatively high pay scale was cause for concern to some, it also enabled the district to avoid violent confrontations, such as those at Coeur d'Alene, Idaho, in 1892, and Leadville, Colorado, in 1896. These skirmishes, and the earlier conflicts throughout the western mining areas, had fueled a national labor movement that gave birth to the Western Federation of Miners in 1893.[90]

Insulated against such disruptive wage disputes, the Standard Company maintained peaceful relations

Figure 7-17: The town of Bodie is shown in 1897, about the time the Standard Consolidated Mining Company took control of the Bodie and Mono mines. The Bodie Mine, famous for two bonanzas, is on the ridge slightly to the right of center, where its hoisting works, ore bin, and dump are contrasted above the schoolhouse. Right and slightly lower on the hill, the Mono Mine, from which the hoisting works was removed in 1880 to provide machinery to sink the Lent Shaft. Above the Mono's dump, the Lent Shaft's distant smokestacks jut above the horizon. Silhouetted at far right, the Bodie Railway and Lumber Company's office. Commanding the center, the electrified Standard mill, and, in the left foreground, the Protestant church, which displays a dazzling coat of white paint. (Courtesy, California Department of Parks and Recreation)

with the local union and enjoyed uninterrupted production. It also improved its ore treatment process in February 1897 by constructing a flume to carry tailings directly from the Standard mill to Tailings Plant No. 1. After the mill had crushed the ore and removed gold and silver particles readily recovered by amalgamation and concentration, a bucket elevator raised tailings above the mill's roof for gravity flow through the flume to the cyanide plant 1,800 feet away. This system of treating tailings without first depositing them into the ponds was known as "direct treatment." Combining milling and cyaniding into one process, it eliminated the cost of excavating tailings and transporting them to the cyanide plant, and overcame winter shutdowns when the ponds froze.[91]

By the end of 1897, the Standard Company was prospering. The year's production was valued at $294,279. Its stockholders had two more 10-cent dividends in their pockets, and stock in the company was selling for $1.50 per share. In contrast, the Comstock's best performing stock, Con. Virginia and California, sold for only about $1 per share.

The Alaska gold rush of 1897 had done little to revive faith in western mining stocks as avenues to quick riches. Instead, the few hardened speculators who dealt in metal mines were drawn to copper, an emerging industry essential to America's rapid acceptance of electricity. Other traders expressed no interest whatsoever in mining shares. To a bold new generation of investors, railroads, petroleum, and steel were the "gold mines" of the future, and the names of tired old mining camps, once identified with high finance, were displaced by those of eastern industrialists, such as Rockefeller, Carnegie, and Morgan.

Already unpopular, speculation in gold and silver mining shares was utterly demoralized in July 1898, when the Federal government imposed two taxes on the market to finance its war with Spain. The first was a two-cent sales tax on every $100 of stock, based on par value instead of actual selling price. Most mining stock certificates, printed during earlier excitements, displayed par values of $100 per share. By 1898, few of these stocks were selling for more than 25 cents per share, and many were worth no more than a nickel.

The second tax imposed was a $50 demand upon every broker. A financial editor in New York described the plight:

This is discouraging, but the same condition prevails in the West. There we hear the Board of Trade Mining Exchange at Colorado Springs has adjourned indefinitely, while the Gold Mining Exchange of Cripple Creek has closed. At Denver the Mining Exchange reports a dull business. . . . In the Comstock shares matters are dejected, and stocks continue to fall. Consolidated California & Virginia reached 12¢ in San Francisco.[92]

Comstock mining stocks received a tepid response when a plan was announced to generate and transmit electric power from the Truckee River, some 35 miles north of Virginia City. According to the proposal, electricity would be used to pump out the mines and inaugurate an assault on poor-grade ore lying in the lower levels. Instead of developing interest, it appeared to wary investors as an excuse for another round of assessments. Thus, by default, Bodie's Standard Con., at $1.70 per share in mid-1898, was the most valuable mining stock in California and Nevada. The old town of Bodie, where mining companies had employed nearly 2,000 men two

Figure 7-18: The Standard Company attempted to treat tailings directly in 1897 by conveying them from the stamp mill through a 1,800-foot flume to Tailings Plant No. 1. The following year, a cyanide plant, seen here, was built adjacent to the 20-stamp mill to eliminate the problem-plagued flume, which tended to clog with sand. Leaching vats and storage tanks were photographed during the plant's construction. Months later, the Standard mill, at right, was destroyed by fire. Although the cyanide plant survived, it was dismantled in 1902 to furnish parts to increase the capacity of Tailings Plant No. 1. (*Practical Notes on the Cyanide Process*. Courtesy, Engineering and Mining Journal)

Figure 7-19: A charred battery of 20 stamps towers above the wreckage of the Standard mill. Destroyed by fire on October 4, 1898, the old reliable mill had served Bodie since 1877. (Emil Billeb collection. Courtesy, Vickie Daniels)

decades earlier, still received recognition.

> From a perusal of last week's *Miner Index* a person not familiar with the facts would think that Bodie was a very dull camp. Any camp where 100 or more miners are employed at $4 a day is not dead. There are between 20 and 40 stamps dropping here continuously that turn out a steady stream of bullion that requires the services of a shotgun messenger twice a month when it is shipped.[93]

In the fall of 1898, the Standard Company began construction of its third cyanide plant. By locating it adjacent to the Standard mill, tailings could be cyanided as they emerged from the mill, a version of direct treatment that no longer required the flume to Tailings Plant No. 1. After cyaniding, tailings entered the ponds, where they were stored, excavated with older tailings, and cyanided a second time at Tailings Plant No. 1.[94]

Construction of the new cyanide plant was well underway when, on October 4, another disastrous fire struck the Standard Company, its third fire in four years. This time it was the "Old Reliable" Standard mill that burned. Its boilers were carrying a small head of steam for heating while the hydroelectric plant at Green Creek was shut down for repairs. About 3:00 A.M. fire broke out in the mill's boiler room. Flames raced to devour tinder-dry timbering and wooden siding. Soon the entire structure was ablaze. Within minutes, little more than smoldering ashes surrounded a heap of charred and mangled machinery. Company officials were relieved when the adjoining office buildings and cyanide plant were spared.[95] The mill had been adequately insured, and rebuilding began immediately after the debris was cleared.

At the close of 1898, the timber frame for a new mill was erect.[96] Replacement machinery had arrived, and the Standard Company reported the year's production at $261,750—respectable, considering that no ore had been milled after the October fire and no DC power was generated for hoisting and cyaniding. Stockholders had been paid two more dividends of 10 cents each before fire stopped production. Stock in the company ended the year at $1.90 per share.

In January 1899, new stamp batteries were placed in position while badly needed repairs were made to the leaking dam and pipe at Green Creek. The hydroelectric power plant was renovated and a third wire added to the 12½ -mile transmission line. Stock in the company advanced to $3 per share when a shiny new Standard mill, roofed and sided with fireproof corrugated iron, started up on February 9, 1899.[97] Like its predecessor, this combination mill sported 20 stamps and used amalgamating plates and concentrators to extract gold and silver from ore. Obsolete Washoe pans and settlers, once key elements in milling, were omitted in favor of the cyanide process. The Standard Company powered its new mill with a state-of-the-art, polyphase AC induction motor. To overcome occasional water shortages at Green Creek, the mill was equipped with an auxiliary steam engine and boiler.[98]

Galvanized iron shimmered in the sunlight as the Standard Company's new mill pounded rock during the final 10 months of 1899. The results were amazing. Stockholders received three more 10-cent dividends from a gratifying annual production of $445,180, the highest yield since 1884. Accordingly, stock in Standard Consolidated climbed to a healthy $3.20 per share.

---

1. California State Mining Bureau, *Eighth Annual Report of the State Mineralogist, for the Year Ending October 1, 1888* (Sacramento, CA: Superintendent of State Printing, 1888), 392.

2. *Engineering and Mining Journal* 11 January 1890, 66; 22 February 1890, 231. Large scale pumping at Bodie was not attempted again until 1928, when electric pumps were used in the 870-foot deep Red Cloud shaft.

3. *Engineering and Mining Journal* 22 March 1890, 342.

4. *Mining and Scientific Press* 11 October 1890, 235.

5. *Engineering and Mining Journal* 18 October 1890, 464.

6. California State Mining Bureau, *Tenth Annual Report of the State Mineralogist, for the Year Ending December 1, 1890* (Sacramento, CA: Superintendent of State Printing, 1890), 336-338.

7. *Mining and Scientific Press* 25 January 1890, 59; *Engineering and Mining Journal* 11 June 1892, 623.

8. *Chronicle-Union* 30 July 1892; Russ and Anne Johnson, *The Ghost Town of Bodie As Reported in the Newspapers of the Day* (Bishop, CA: Chalfant Press, 1967), 113-116; U.S. Department of the Interior, "Population," *Eleventh Census of the United States, 1890*, part 1 (Washington, DC: Government Printing Office, 1892), 72.

9. California, *Tenth Annual Report*, 337.

10. *Daily Territorial Enterprise* 7 January 1894.

11. *Engineering and Mining Journal* 28 July 1894, 93.

12. *Chronicle-Union* 22 June 1895; *Engineering and Mining Journal* 22 June 1895, 588.

13. *Chronicle-Union* 20 July 1895.

14. *Mining and Scientific Press* 25 April 1896, 350.

15. *Mining and Scientific Press* 23 November 1895, 350.

16. *Mining and Scientific Press* 25 July 1896, 82.

17. *Engineering and Mining Journal* 26 September 1896, 309; 3 October 1896, 353; 24 October 1896, 404-405; 31 October 1896, 429; 9 January 1897, 57.

18. *Walker Lake Bulletin* 28 August 1903; 21 July 1917; *Mining and Scientific Press* 22 October 1904.

19. *Engineering and Mining Journal* 22 February 1890, 230.

20. The Booker had been reinstated by the board when the mine was reopened briefly in 1887.

21. *Financial and Mining Record* 22 March 1890, 183.

22. Arthur Macy (1852-1891). *Engineering and Mining Journal* 9 May 1891, 561. Early in the development of industrialized western mining, investors wishing to optimize profits sought competent engineers to apply science toward mine operation and management. When Columbia opened its School of Mines in 1864, the New York *Evening Post* noted that the college fulfilled "a want which every capitalist in the country has felt." (Sears, *Mining Stock Exchanges*, 16)

23. *Engineering and Mining Journal* 14 June 1890, 686.

24. *Engineering and Mining Journal* 27 September 1890, 369; *Financial and Mining Record* 20 December 1890, 393; *Pioche Weekly Record* 27 December 1890; California, *Tenth Annual Report*, 337.

25. *Mining and Scientific Press* 9 August 1890, 86.

26. Charles W. Chesterman, Rodger H. Chapman, and Cliffton H. Gray, Jr, *Geology and Ore Deposits of the Bodie Mining District, Mono County, California (Bulletin 206)* (Sacramento, CA: Division of Mines and Geology, 1986), 32, 33.

27. *Mining and Scientific Press* 16 August 1890, 105.

28. *Engineering and Mining Journal* 6 June 1891, 662.

29. *Mining and Scientific Press* 27 June 1891, 404.

30. *Financial and Mining Record* 14 March 1891, 180.

31. *Financial and Mining Record* 11 April 1891, 254.

32. *Engineering and Mining Journal* 3 October 1891, 397.

33. *Walker Lake Bulletin* 25 May 25 1892.

34. Thomas Haight Leggett (1859-1935).

35. *Mining and Scientific Press* 30 April 1892, 315.

36. *Engineering and Mining Journal* 8 October 1892, 353; *Mining and Scientific Press* 12 November 1892, 325.

37. *Walker Lake Bulletin* 22 June 1892; 6 July 1892; 3 August 1892; 19 October 1892. Low-voltage telegraph and telephone transmissions did not suffer from the same long-distance problems associated with high voltages needed to power machinery. Successful long distance telegraph and telephone systems had been in existence since 1851 and 1855, respectively. By 1892 Bodie was well acquainted with telephones. In 1879 a telephone line provided voice communication between the Standard Mine and mill. Later that year the Standard mill and the Bodie hoisting works were connected, linking the town to its two principal mines on the hill. In 1881 the Bodie Railway and Lumber Company installed a line between its offices at Bodie and Mono Mills, placing telephones along the route. In 1882 a telephone line on Main Street served several subscribing stores. (*Daily Bodie Standard* 4 February 1879; *Weekly Bodie Standard* 8 February 1879; 22 February 1879; *Daily Free Press* 8 January 1882; *Bodie Evening Miner* 7 August 1882)

38. The Bulwer-Standard mill was dismantled and divided between various local entities. The Bulwer half of the mill was purchased in August 1892 by James S. Cain and Alexander J. McCone. The Bodie Company bought some of the mill's pans and settlers, and in June 1892 installed them in the Bodie mill. The Standard Company, aside from salvaging building materials for the hydroelectric plant, used the mill's timbers in its mine. No photographs have been found depicting the 30-stamp Bulwer-Standard mill, the district's preeminent milling facility between 1884 and 1890, when the Standard mill was idle. (California State Archives. "Bill of Sale: Bulwer Consolidated Mining Co. to J. S. Cain and A. J. McCone." Bodie Collection, linknum 4078: 22 August 1892; *Engineering and Mining Journal* 11 June 1892, 623; 13 May 1893, 439-440; *Mining and Scientific Press* 17 June 1893, 370; *Daily Territorial Enterprise* 10 January 1895)

39. *Engineering and Mining Journal* 13 May 1893, 439-440; *Mining and Scientific Press* 17 June 1893, 370; Thomas Haight Leggett, "A Twelve-Mile Transmission of Power by Electricity," *Transactions of the American Institute of Mining Engineers,* 24 (New York, NY: A. I. M. E., 1895), 315-338. Local folklore asserts that the transmission line had to be "absolutely straight, no angles, no curves, which might cause the power to jump off into space." (Cain, *Story of Bodie*, 49) This delightful anecdote is not upheld by technical literature of the period, nor does it account for vertical curves (hills and valleys) that the line traversed. "The line crosses extremely rough country," wrote Leggett in his paper to the American Institute of Mining Engineers, "not 500 yards of which is level

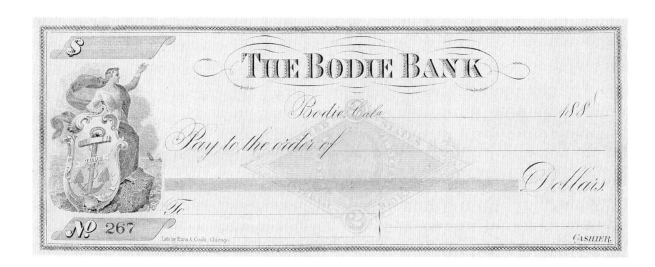

beyond the town-limits. Most of the ground is very rocky, over 500 pounds of dynamite being used in blasting the pole-holes." (Leggett, "A Twelve-Mile Transmission of Power by Electricity," 328)

40. The Mono County seat was linked to Bodie by telephone in 1894, when A. F. Bryant connected a telephone in his Bridgeport store to the Standard Company's line at Green Creek. This link provided his customers with voice communications to Bodie, Hawthorne, and the rest of the world. Aurora was not connected by telephone until its 1903 revival. (*Chronicle-Union* 7 July 1894; 14 July 1894; 21 July 1894; *Walker Lake Bulletin* 5 July 1903)

41. A vertical drop of 355 feet.

42. *Engineering and Mining Journal* 13 May 1893, 439-440; *Mining and Scientific Press* 17 June 1893, 370; Leggett, "A Twelve-Mile Transmission of Power," 315-338.

43. *Mining and Scientific Press* 9 January 1892, 20.

44. *Mining and Scientific Press* 30 April 1892, 318.

45. *Walker Lake Bulletin* 21 December 1892.

46. *Mining and Scientific Press* 12 November 1892, 325; 6 May 1893, 285; 1 July 1893, 13; 29 July 1893, 77.

47. *Mining and Scientific Press* 22 July 1893, 61.

48. *Electrical World* 9 September 1893, 197.

49. *Inyo Register* 12 October 1893.

50. Bodie's success with electricity was also obscured by a rapid succession of power transmissions over increasingly greater distances during the three years following 1890. In his autobiographical sketch for *Who's Who in Engineering* (1925), Leggett held that he had erected "the first long-distance electric transmission for power purposes in [the] US," an assertion that ignores greater distances achieved in Europe and longer distances transmitted in the US to light cities. Occupying the nation's attention in 1893 was ongoing construction of a monumental hydroelectric plant at Niagara Falls, New York (11,000 volts to be transmitted 26 miles) that gained recognition as a milestone in power engineering. Even widespread distribution of a paper written by Leggett to advance the Standard's success with electricity failed to earn the feat lasting distinction. Leggett's articles include: Thomas Haight Leggett, "A Twelve-Mile Transmission of Power by Electricity," *Transactions of the American Institute of Mining Engineers*, 24 (New York, NY: A. I. M. E., 1895): 315-338; "Electric Power Transmission Plants and the Use of Electricity in Mining Operations," *Twelfth Report of the State Mineralogist, Two Years Ending September 15, 1894* (Sacramento, CA: Superintendent of State Printing, 1894): 413-435; *Electric Power Transmission Plants and the Use of Electricity in Mining Operations* (Sacramento, CA: Superintendent of State Printing, 1894); "An Electric Power Transmissions Installation—In the Mining District of Bodie, in California," *Practical Engineer* (London), 2 November 1894; "Electric Power Transmission," *Mining and Scientific Press* (San Francisco, CA), Part 1, 30 March 1895: 196-197; Part 2, 6 April 1895: 212-213; "A Twelve-Mile Transmission of Power by Electricity,"

Cassier's Magazine (New York, NY), 7, no. 5 (March 1895): 355-368; "A Twelve-Mile Transmission of Power by Electricity," *Engineering News and Railway Journal* (New York, NY), 26 July 1895: 74-77.

51. *Engineering and Mining Journal* 12 August 1893, 175.

52. *Engineering and Mining Journal* 5 August 1893, 149.

53. Leggett, "A Twelve-Mile Transmission," 332, 336.

54. *Engineering and Mining Journal* 11 March 1893, 233.

55. *Inyo Register* 12 October 1893; 19 October 1893; *Mining and Scientific Press* 14 October 1893, 253; Karen Colbourne McAbeer, "The Bodie Railroad" (Master of Arts Thesis, California State College, Sonoma, CA, 1973), 53-56.

56. *Mining and Scientific Press* 2 July 1892, 3-13; *Engineering and Mining Journal* 14 November 1896, 460.

57. T. A. Rickard, *Interviews With Mining Engineers* (San Francisco, CA: Mining and Scientific Press, 1922), 261-262.

58. California State Mining Bureau, *Thirteenth Report of the State Mineralogist, for the Two Years Ending September 15, 1896* (Sacramento, CA: Superintendent of State Printing, 1896), 231; Francis L. Bosqui, *Practical Notes on the Cyanide Process* (New York, NY: Scientific Publishing Co., 1899), 44; Rickard, *Interviews*, 261-262. According to local tradition, the first cyanide plant at Bodie was built by James S. Cain, the town's banker, and Alex J. McCone, a well-known Virginia City mill and foundry owner. "They hired an expert from New Zealand, who was familiar with the process, to build the first plant and work the tailings." (Cain, *Story of Bodie*, 82-83) Interviewed in 1937, John F. Parr recalled that, ". . . curious Bodie mining men on many occasions (during the secret construction of Bodie's first cyanide plant) slipped out at night to glue their eyes to a handy knothole or a crack in the siding, to try and see what in thunder was going on behind the locked doors." (Loose, *Bodie Bonanza*, 211) Unfortunately, these sources reveal neither the date nor location of this landmark endeavor. Research has disclosed little about Bodie's first cyanide plant, but scattered clues indicate that it was built at the Bodie Tunnel mill and that it operated for only four years. Leggett's entry in *Who's Who in Engineering* (1925) left room for Cain's achievement while embellishing his own by stating that he had "erected the first successful large cyanide plant on [the] Pacific Coast . . . ." (Leonard, *Who's Who in Engineering*, 1244)

59. Johnson, *The Ghost Town of Bodie*, 66; *Inyo Register* 30 August 1894.

60. *Inyo Register* 30 August 1894; *Walker Lake Bulletin* 22 August 1894.

61. *Walker Lake Bulletin* 22 August 1894; *Inyo Register* 23 August 1894; 30 August 1894; *Chronicle-Union* 25 August 1894.

62. Robert Gilman Brown, "Additions to the Power-Plant of the Standard Consolidated Mining Company," *Transactions of the American Institute of Mining Engineers*, 26 (New York, NY: A. I. M. E., 1897), 331-339; *Engineering and Mining Journal* 3 November 1894, 420; *Mining and Scientific Press* 16

February 1895, 110; *Cassier's Magazine* March 1895, 368. It is unclear to what degree the mine was lighted by electricity. Most likely, only the Bulwer Tunnel and selected stations along the shaft were illuminated. Records indicate miners still used candles in their daily work. Equally ambiguous is the history of the surviving brick structure in Bodie known as the "Hydro Building." Though clearly adapted for high voltage electric power, records and photographs indicate it played no part in the transmission of power from Green Creek during the system's early years.

63. Brown, "Additions to the Power-Plant," 319.

64. *Chronicle-Union* 29 September 1894; 13 October 1894; *Mining and Scientific Press* 13 October 1894, 227.

65. A difference in elevation of 343 feet.

66. Brown, "Additions to the Power-Plant," 319.

67. For more information on the Standard's subterranean hoist and the dam on Green Creek, see Robert Gilman Brown, "Additions to the Power-Plant of the Standard Consolidated Mining Company," *Transactions of the American Institute of Mining Engineers*, 26 (New York, NY: A. I. M. E., 1897), 319-339.

68. *Engineering and Mining Journal* 16 September 1893, 299; *Mining Record* 30 September 1882, 320.

69. *Mining and Scientific Press* 20 October 1894, 250.

70. *Engineering and Mining Journal* 14 April 1894, 357.

71. *Engineering and Mining Journal* 19 January 1895, 56.

72. After serving in South Africa (1895-1904), Leggett earned recognition as a consulting engineer, first in London (1904-1907), then in New York (1907-1915). He also served as vice president and director of the American Institute of Mining and Metallurgical Engineers (1912-1914), and was president of the Mining and Metallurgical Society of America (1924). (Leonard, *Who's Who in Engineering*, 1244)

73. *Virginia Evening Chronicle* 19 June 1895.

74. *Mining and Scientific Press* 7 December 1895, 374; *Chronicle-Union* 12 October 1895.

75. *Mining and Scientific Press* 30 November 1895, 366.

76. *Mining and Scientific Press* 18 January 1896, 48-50; *Engineering and Mining Journal* 4 April 1896, 332.

77. Eliot Lord, *Comstock Mining and Miners* (1883; reprint, San Diego, CA: Howell-North Books, 1980), 269-277; Dan De Quille [William Wright], *The Big Bonanza* (1876; reprint, Las Vegas, NV: Nevada Publications, 1982), 125-131, 143; *Daily Free Press* 9 November 1880; 10 November 1880; 11 November 1880; 16 November 1880.

78. *Chronicle-Union* 25 April 1896; *Walker Lake Bulletin* 29 April 1896.

79. Robert Gilman Brown, "Note on a Shaft-Fire and its Lesson," *Transactions of the American Institute of Mining Engineers*, 26 (New York, NY: A. I. M. E., 1897), 316.

80. Brown, "Note on a Shaft-Fire," 315-319; *Engineering and Mining Journal* 19 September 1896, 269.

81. Recalling 1908, Emil Billeb noted that, "High on the hill above the lumber yard was the Standard Mine hoist. Lumber and heavy timber for the mine had to be hauled on wagons with four-horse teams, up a heavy grade, . . ." (Billeb, *Mining Camp Days*, 84) The date when hoisting operations were relocated from within the Bulwer Tunnel to the top of the shaft remains unknown, but scant information indicates that it occurred about 1903.

82. *Walker Lake Bulletin* 6 May 1896.

83. Bosqui, *Notes on the Cyanide Process*, 44, 56-57.

84. Since 1890, when it split from the Standard, the Bulwer had been aligned with the Bodie and Mono companies, and their mines were run under the mutual supervision of John W. Kelly. The Bulwer Mine, a frequent disappointment to investors, had yielded enough pay ore in 1892 to declare a 10-cent dividend, followed by one of 5 cents. Assessments ensued, usually one per year, of 10 cents each as ore shipments declined in 1894 and ceased in 1895.

85. *Engineering and Mining Journal* 24 October 1896, 404; 31 October 1896, 429; 19 December 1896, 588; 7 January 1897, 57; *Mining and Scientific Press* 9 January 1897, 34.

86. *Mining and Scientific Press* 31 October 1896, 370; *Engineering and Mining Journal* 7 November 1896, 453.

87. *Mining and Scientific Press* 28 January 1888, 56.

88. Richard E. Lingenfelter, *The Hardrock Miners: A History of the Mining Labor Movement in the American West, 1863-1893* (Berkeley, CA: University of California Press, 1974), 157-181; Mark Wyman, *Hard Rock Epic: Western Miners and the Industrial Revolution, 1860-1910* (Berkeley, CA: University of California Press, 1979), 35-37, 151-165; *Bodie Standard* 9 January 1878. Armed "forces" could be federal troops, state militias, local police, hired gunmen, vigilance committees, or a combination of the above.

89. *Mining and Scientific Press* 27 November 1897, 506.

90. Wyman, *Hard Rock Epic*, 166-174.

91. *Mining and Scientific Press* 20 February 1897, 151; Bosqui, *Notes on the Cyanide Process*, 88-91. Despite cyanide's advantages, it did not replace milling. The Standard mill still crushed the ore, then its amalgamating plates removed coarse gold that would have taken too long to dissolve in the cyanide solution. Concentrators removed silver sulphurets, which were later subjected to lengthy treatment in a specialized amalgamating pan that contained an extraordinaily strong cyanide solution.

92. *Engineering and Mining Journal* 9 July 1898, 55.

93. *Chronicle-Union* 19 March 1898.

94. *Bodie Miner-Index* 3 September 1898; Bosqui, *Notes on the Cyanide Process*, 88-91. The fate of Tailings Plant No. 2, the Standard's cyanide plant located several miles below town in Bodie Canyon, is uncertain. Its parts were probably used in 1898 to build the cyanide plant adjoining the Standard mill. Whether the new cyanide plant was placed in op-

eration before fire destroyed the adjacent Standard mill is also unclear.

95. *Chronicle-Union* 8 October 1898; *Engineering and Mining Journal* 15 October 1898, 475.

96. *Engineering and Mining Journal* 10 December 1898, 714; 31 December 1898, 795; *Mining and Scientific Press* 17 December 1898, 611.

97. *Mining and Scientific Press* 11 February 1899, 155; *Engineering and Mining Journal* 11 February 1899, 190.

98. *Engineering and Mining Journal* 6 March 1909, 487. Although not specifically stated in historic documents, the addition of a third wire to the transmission line, and the adoption of a polyphase induction motor, indicates that the motor placed in the new mill was self-starting and that a rotary converter replaced the belted dynamo to change AC to DC power for distribution to the motors in the mine and cyanide plant.

The Standard Mule's Ghost

1. Ella M. Cain, *The Story of Bodie* (San Francisco, CA: Fearon Publishers, 1956), 174-175; *Walker Lake Bulletin* 29 April 1896.

2. Robert T. Bell, telephone interview by author, 17 February 2001.

THREE PANORAMIC VIEWS

Three panoramic views from nearly the same vantage point depict Bodie at noteworthy times in its history.

View 1: A reputation for fabulous gold mines and ferocious characters was well established at Bodie in 1880, when a photographer climbed High Peak and captured the booming town of about 8,000 inhabitants. Main Street was said to be a mile long and the district had seven stamp mills with two more about to be built. The Standard Company's 20-stamp mill and tailings ponds dominate the foreground. (Courtesy, California History Room, California State Library, Sacramento, California)

View 2: Fifteen years later, in 1895, Bodie had declined after enduring a sudden drop in population, followed by a decade of diminishing ore values and a devastating fire in 1892. Five stamp mills are operational, but only the Standard is running full time. Still, the town of about 800 is enjoying something of a comeback after the Standard mill was upgraded with innovative machinery and powered by electricity. Adding to the town's economic growth, cyanide plants are springing up outside of town. (Courtesy, California Department of Parks and Recreation)

View 3: A decade later, the Standard Company has become the town's principal employer, but the population remains steady at about 800. This 1906 view shows a new 20-stamp mill, where cyanide has become integral to the milling process. (A. A. Forbes photograph. Courtesy, Seaver Center for Western History Research)

View 1: 1880

View 2: 1895

View 3: 1906

Figure 8-1: Bodie entered the twentieth century with a shiny new 20-stamp mill sheathed in corrugated galvanized iron. Although electrically powered, it was equipped with a steam engine to overcome Green Creek's chronic deficiencies in power generation. Like its predecessor, the mill extracted gold and silver from crushed ore using a combination of plate amalgamation and mechanical concentration. Completed in 1899, Bodie District's most notable landmark appears about 1927 in an image by visiting Pomona photographer, Burton Frasher, showing the huge Standard Mine dump on the hill, where waste rock would become the subject of an intense but short-lived revival a year later. (Burton Frasher photograph. Author's collection)

CHAPTER EIGHT

"THE ORE WAS MINED AT AN ACTUAL LOSS" 1900-1915

The Chronicle-Union *complains because the mail to Bodie and Bridgeport, via Hawthorne, is not received every day, and suggests that the mail be sent by stage from Carson, via Wellington.*
      —Walker Lake Bulletin (Hawthorne), September 4, 1903

The Standard is not only the most important company at Bodie, but the most productive in Mono County. It pays higher wages than any other company in California for its miners and helpers.
      —Engineering and Mining Journal, October 26, 1907

The Noonday and Red Cloud Mines

It seemed certain that once their buildings were removed in 1888, the Noonday and Red Cloud mines had rendezvoused with oblivion. Nevertheless, rumors persisted that there was still plenty of ore deep inside Silver Hill—a notion not so farfetched, considering that the Noonday companies had collapsed before the mine was depleted. A decade after the Noonday's 1882 closure, E. L. Reese, Archie Graham, James A. Kelly, and Andy P. Cameron, a Miners Union official, tested the premise by leasing the property and erecting a gallows frame and steam hoist. The extent of their work and the degree of their success is uncertain. Beginning in 1893, they worked the old mine about four years, sending ore through the canyon to the Bodie Tunnel mill. They never mined more than 100 tons per year, the equivalent of a single day's shipment by the former Noonday companies.[1]

Pinning hopes on an unprofitable gold mine might seem foolhardy, but Robert Bell explains how lessees, or "leasers," made money by small-scale mining.

> Leasers would go down in the mines and take out "stringers." All the big ledges were already gone—but there were still stringers, maybe an inch or so wide, of high-grade rock still there. Some of those old guys made a lot of money mining stringers. They would take it out by hand with a pick or a picky-poke bar, then break down the waste rock with powder [dynamite] to give them room to work. . . . If you keep a bar sharp, it will dig like hell. . . . Most of the ore in Bodie was soft enough to dig out with hand tools.[2]

About this time, Bodie's able banker, businessman, and mythmaker, James Stuart Cain, began buying claims in the south end.[3] In 1894, he purchased a group of abandoned mines that formed a

Figure 8-2: As part of J. S. Cain's development strategy, the South End Tailings Company built this cyanide plant in 1895 to process tailings that had accumulated behind the dam seen at right. The dam, built fifteen years earlier across Booker Flat, impounded a hundred acres of tailings from the Noonday, Spaulding, and Silver Hill mills—three south end mills that operated only a few years during Bodie's mining boom. (Courtesy, California Department of Parks and Recreation)

continuous chain from the crest of Silver Hill southward to Queen Bee Hill. His acquisitions included the Addenda, Oro, Concordia, White Cloud, East Noonday, Queen Bee, and Governor Stanford claims.

After building a hoisting works over its shaft, Cain reopened the Addenda Mine in June. Then the Oro received new hoisting machinery. Associated with these projects were several familiar Bodie figures: August Soderling, a well-known assayer; John W. Kelly, superintendent of the Bulwer, Bodie, and Mono mines; and Alex J. McCone, a Virginia City foundry and mill owner who had recently been elected state senator from Storey County, Nevada.[4]

The success of the cyanide process in the early 1890s also prompted Cain, who would become the driving force behind Bodie's survival into the mid-twentieth century, to organize the South End Tailings Company and build a cyanide plant at the base of Silver Hill. Erected in 1895 on the site of the former Silver Hill mill, it was Bodie's fourth cyanide plant.

The South End plant, as it came to be known, was designed to process tailings from the short-lived and long-since dismantled Noonday, Spaulding, and Silver Hill mills. Their tailings, ignored for more than a decade, covered 100 acres behind the dam on Booker Flat and reached depths of five feet in places. The South End Tailings Company's plant was said to be the largest in the state, capable of processing 100 tons per day. It worked tailings for the next three or four years. Although no figures are available, the owners were reported to have profited handsomely.[5]

The South End cyanide plant proved so efficient at extracting gold and silver that Cain decided to apply the treatment to the low-grade ore still lying below ground in the old south end mines. In 1900, he and his Bodie associates incorporated the Southern Consolidated Mining Company, and purchased the Red Cloud, Noonday, North Noonday, and a dozen other contiguous claims. A year later the company built a hoisting works over the Red Cloud's great

Figure 8-3: The South End Cyanide Plant, built on the site of the former Silver Hill mill, was capable of processing 100 tons of tailings per day. Pictured in 1897, it was Bodie's fourth cyanide plant, and was reported to be the largest one in California. (Courtesy, California Department of Parks and Recreation)

Figure 8-4: In 1901, J. S. Cain's Southern Consolidated Mining Company built this hoisting works over the Red Cloud shaft to access numerous south end mines. Because the building contained no pumping machinery, underground exploration was limited to levels above the water line. The enterprise operated sporadically under steam for the next 10 years. This photograph was taken several years after the venture was abandoned in 1911. The dump, extending to the left, provides some evidence of a vast underground workings that were expanded after 1880, when the centrally-located Red Cloud became crucial to south end mining. (Emil Billeb collection. Courtesy, Vickie Daniels)

Figure 8-5: Endeavoring to reopen the south end and encourage mining at the Red Cloud, Cain built a 15-stamp mill in 1901 to treat ore from leasers. Located immediately off the road to Mono Lake, near the South End Cyanide Plant, the mill was equipped with secondhand machinery purchased at Mammoth. Three batteries were arranged so that any combination of 5, 10, or 15 stamps could be run, depending on the quantity of ore. The mill's ruins were photographed in 1947, long after mining had ceased. (Courtesy, California Department of Parks and Recreation)

shaft. Powered by steam, the works was substantial enough to sustain extensive production but lacked pumping machinery, a deficiency that limited mining to areas above water standing at the 490-foot level. Capital was again furnished by James Haggin, a principal backer of the mine in the 1880s. The second major stockholder was the estate of Senator George Hearst.[6] Like Haggin, Hearst had become wealthy as a western mining industrialist. The syndicate that these two men headed owned the famous Homestake gold mine in Lead, South Dakota, and the enormous Anaconda copper mine in Butte City, Montana.

Through the Red Cloud's central shaft, the Southern Consolidated Mining Company began hoisting ore from several south end mines, most of which had been quiet since that fateful day in December 1882, when Silver Hill's three principal mines—the Noonday, North Noonday, and Red Cloud—abruptly closed. Since ore taken from underground had to be crushed prior to cyaniding, a 15-stamp mill was built near the South End plant. Mining continued sporadically over the next 10 years. No great profits were made public, and no reliable figures document production. The venture does not appear to have met expectations, for leasers operated the mine during at least two of the years, 1905 and 1906.[7]

In anticipation of the availability of commercially generated electric power, the Red Cloud shaft was prepared in 1910 to receive electric pumps so that the lower levels could be worked. Electricity reached the area the following year, but no pumps were installed. The only recorded use of electricity at the mine was to run a makeshift air compressor in 1911, which served pneumatic drills.[8] After the enterprise closed that winter, the Red Cloud and Noonday mines disappeared from the record for the next 16 years.

The Standard Mine

The federal census at the turn of the century recorded Bodie's population at 965—an increase in the number of inhabitants since 1890. Growth resulted largely from the Standard Company's success with cyanide, electric power, and advanced milling technologies.[9] (The census enumerator also noted that 118 "Indians" lived in town.) Employing 115 Bodie residents, the Standard was the largest employer in the region, and, like clockwork, its shareholders collected 10-cent dividends every quarter. Company stock reached $5.76 per share in October 1900—by far the highest-priced mining stock in California and Nevada. Its new mill and cyanide plants produced $425,614 during 1900, and the company purchased the prop-

Figure 8-6: After September 1879, when the Standard shaft was connected to the Bulwer Tunnel, the tunnel became the principal entryway into the Standard Mine. Posing about the turn of the century with dinner pails and candles, Standard employees gather at the mine's entrance. A utility pole, at right, supports wires that brought electricity to a subterranean hoist and pump, located deep inside the tunnel. (Courtesy, Gil Schmidtmann)

Figure 8-7: Emerging from the Bulwer Tunnel, a pair of mules pull mine cars loaded with rock destined for the dump. Waste rock not used as fill in the old stopes was pushed to the dump in cars holding only a half ton, which one man could handle. (Courtesy, Gregory Bock)

erty of the former Bodie Tunnel and Mining Company, which included a 15-stamp mill and a tunnel into Bodie Bluff.

In an unusually detailed annual report, the Standard's superintendent noted that, during 1900, the company had consumed 35,975 pounds of dynamite, 952 boxes of blasting caps, 271,900 feet of fuse, and (even in an age of electricity) 17,840 pounds of candles. The average assay value of the ore was $26.06 per ton, $24.30 of which was gold, the rest silver. Tailings were averaging $8.48 a ton.[10]

The old town caught a few moments of excitement that recalled something of its former wicked reputation. Early on Monday morning, June 17, 1901, gunfire broke out when night watchman Joe Beck surprised a band of robbers in the Standard mill's retort building. The burglars had nabbed a bar of bullion valued at $3,000, and were pilfering a second retort, when Beck discovered them at about 8:00 A.M. Beck received a bullet in the shoulder during the ensuing shootout.

The bandits escaped without their plunder, but the Standard Company offered a $500 reward for their capture and conviction. Ten days later a man named Scotty Burns was taken into custody in Hawthorne on suspicion of involvement in the robbery attempt. He was transported to Bridgeport, then held for trial in September. The jury deadlocked, with a vote of nine to three for acquittal. Burns was retried the following June and acquitted. Not wishing to press his luck, he hastily departed Mono County and headed for Nevada.[11]

The armed robbery attempt failed to disrupt production at the Standard's mine and tailings ponds, allowing the company to pay four more quarterly dividends of 10 cents each during 1901. It produced $351,804, approximately $100,000 less than the previous year, and its stock reflected the decline, slumping to about $4 per share. Since its incorporation more than 20 years earlier, the Standard had paid $3,999,780 in dividends, equal to nearly 225% of its currently issued capital stock of $1,783,940. This rate of return ranked the Standard among the nation's best-paying gold mines.[12]

In May 1902, the cyanide plant adjacent to the Standard mill was torn down. Manager Brown explained why it no longer paid to cyanide tailings as they left the mill, and then again in Tailings Plant

No. 1. "This double treatment of the sands had proved itself fully worthwhile when dealing with high-grade tailings; that is, the extra cost of $2 per ton was more than offset by the increased [yield]. When, however, the grade of our mill ore was lowered, resulting in a lowered tenor for the tailings, the value of this treatment was lessened."[13] Since all tailings would now be processed in Tailings Plant No. 1, its capacity was increased with parts from the dismantled structure. The remodeled and enlarged plant was ready in August,[14] and quickly became known as the "Standard cyanide plant." To gather tailings from the ponds, an experimental, electric-powered scraper was installed. It was expected to replace 12 horses and drag tailings from areas too soft for horse-drawn wagons.[15]

By the time 1902 came to a close, milled ore and cyanided tailings had yielded $360,775, funding four more quarterly dividends of 10 cents. Because investors held on to their shares, stock in the company rarely traded. When someone did sell, the price was firm at $3.50.

Nevada's economy had been withering under a mining depression since the mid-1870s, when the Comstock's decline began. During this 25-year slump, undaunted prospectors faced self-imposed hardships and incalculable odds searching desert wastelands and mountain ranges for the next bonanza. One wanderer's dreams came true in 1900, when he found silver- and gold-bearing ore about 100 miles due east of Bodie. Shortly thereafter, southwestern Nevada entered a seven-year period of sequential mining booms. Thousands rushed to Tonopah, then to Goldfield, Rhyolite, and other camps, most of which sprang into existence, produced briefly, then took rapid journeys to oblivion. Even nearby Aurora enjoyed a resurgence. Death Valley, and the southeastern California counties of Inyo, Kern, and San Bernardino were caught up in the excitement, too. Gold,

silver, and copper strikes across the region stirred mining men into a frenzy reminiscent of earlier rushes. The speculating public, which for years had given little thought to western mining stocks, was suddenly captivated by the market. As mining shares regained much of their former popularity, many new, unproven corporations were hastily listed on the San Francisco exchanges, where they displaced famous but forlorn Bodie and Comstock companies.[16]

To the east and south of Bodie, mineral strikes became destinations for anyone seeking quick riches. Prospectors, miners, businessmen, scoundrels, and others so motivated rode the Carson & Colorado Railroad (purchased in 1900 by the Southern Pacific) to Sodaville or Candelaria, where they secured passage aboard connecting stagecoaches to the booming camps. Hordes traveled the C&C, but few passengers debarked at Hawthorne, where a dusty, lonely road led to Bodie.

Although many impatient, sometimes desper-

Figure 8-8: The only known photograph of Bodie's underground was taken in the Standard Mine, near the shaft. The men stand on an unidentified level where a cage has been landed and a mine car is ready to be hoisted. (Emil Billeb collection. Courtesy, Vickie Daniels)

Figure 8-9: A mule exiting the 1,860-foot long Bulwer Tunnel pulls a string of "end-dump" mine cars, each of which holds more than a ton of ore. The cars have been loaded from two huge underground bins at the intersection of the tunnel and the Standard shaft. From the tunnel's mouth, nearly a quarter mile of snowshed-covered tracks lead south, where the cars will be winched one at a time up an incline and dumped inside the mill. (A. A. Forbes photograph. Courtesy, Seaver Center for Western History Research)

Figure 8-10: Excavating tailings in 1903. (Courtesy, Gregory Bock)

Figure 8-11: The Standard mill's furnace, where gold and silver were melted and turned into bullion. A worker is shown pouring the liquid metal from a crucible into a mold. (A.A. Forbes photograph. Courtesy, Seaver Center for Western History Research)

Figure 8-12: Mill workers proudly display a shipment of bullion. (Courtesy, Russ and Anne Johnson)

Figure 8-13: After Standard Tailings Plant No. 1 was enlarged in 1902, it was commonly referred to as the Standard cyanide plant. Two years later, Theodore Hoover oversaw a rebuild that incorporated the Moore Slimes Process. Thereafter, the plant was sometimes called the Standard slimes plant. The plant is depicted about 1906 in a view by visiting Bishop photographer, A. A. Forbes, looking southward toward Bodie. The road from Aurora and Hawthorne bends around tailings ponds and an immense dump that extends from the Bulwer Tunnel. This huge pile of rock, discarded from the Standard Mine, would play a key role in Bodie's survival into the 1940s. Beyond the tailings ponds lie the Standard mill and the town of Bodie, with a population of about 800. On the crest of Silver Hill, in the distance, a hoisting works that Cain built for the Addenda Mine in 1896, when he began reopening the south end mines. (Detail, A. A. Forbes photograph. Courtesy, Seaver Center for Western History Research)

ate travelers disregarded Bodie, the aging town defied moribund status by welcoming another college-educated mining engineer. The 31-year-old Theodore J. Hoover, a 1901 graduate of Stanford University, arrived on June 3, 1903, after accepting the assistant manager's position with the Standard Company.[17] Hoover brought his family to Bodie, where they occupied the company's house near the mill. He later recalled living near the pounding stamps. "In time we got to like the roar."[18]

Hoover entertained no illusions regarding the district's financial state. Stock in the Standard Company had softened to $2 a share as production tumbled by $50,000 to $309,426 in 1903. "It was evident that the Bodie mines had seen their best days," remembered Hoover, adding that they "had no very bright future ahead."[19]

The Standard skipped its third-quarter dividend, but Hoover understood where future profits lay.

Dividends at that time had been suspended. The chief reason for my selection as assistant manager was that I might begin a careful study of the accumulated slime dumps, to determine whether they could be turned to account. It was thought, rightly, that the mine would probably continue to yield sufficient ore to pay running expenses only for several years, but that the shareholders must look to the values locked up in the old tailings or slime dumps for further profits.[20]

Slimes in tailings, the very fine particles that defied treatment even by the cyanide process, had been largely ignored since the 1870s. There were roughly 40,000 tons of them gathered in certain areas of the ponds. At $4 per ton, slimes were quite valuable— if someone could find a method of profiting from them. They confounded Bodie's cyanide plants, where only granular particles, coarse enough to allow the timely percolation of cyanide solution, could be treated. The tiny particles also plugged the canvas filters covering the bottoms of the leaching vats, halting the recovery of gold- and silver-carrying liquid. Hoover later recalled: "I say without hesitation that the Bodie slimes were the most difficult that any metallurgist has ever had to handle. They were composed of about equal portions of pure limonite [iron oxide] and pure kaolin [clay], and a settled layer of them one sixty-fourth of an inch thick was as impervious as a sheet of rubber."[21]

Inspired by an article in the *Engineering and Mining Journal*, Hoover decided to try a new filtering system designed by George Moore. Marketed as the "Moore Slimes Process," it employed suction pumps and self-cleaning hanging filters to draw clear cyanide solution from a slurry containing particles so small that they would clog an ordinary filter. A small experimental plant was set up at Bodie, and throughout the winter of 1903-04 Hoover tested the process on Standard tailings. The results were encouraging, and in May he recommended that the recently enlarged Standard cyanide plant be rebuilt again, this time with Moore filters.[22]

Modifications were undertaken in mid-1904. The new filters promised to handle slimes and tailings without difficulty. When treating freshly crushed ore, the filters' principal advantage was that they al-

lowed rock to be ground extremely fine, exposing more gold and silver to the cyanide. To grind the sandy portion of the tailings to the consistency of slimes, a cylindrical device of modern design called a "tube mill" was installed. Hoover also added an 1,800-foot flume to carry tailings from the Standard mill to the cyanide plant, thus reintroducing "direct treatment." Tailings containing slimes from the mill would enter the plant through the flume, and be processed along with tailings and slimes excavated from the ponds.[23]

Because ongoing modifications to the cyanide plant halted the treatment of tailings during the last half of 1904, Standard Company production for the year decreased to $221,870, most of which came from mined ore. The extensive remodeling project consumed capital, and no dividends were paid that year. Company stock slid to $1.70 per share.

The discovery of gold about 12 miles northwest of Bodie in 1904 caused a small rush of humanity to pass through town on its way to Masonic. Bodie's lumber-hauling railroad gained new customers who needed wood products with which to build a town and develop their mines. The railroad's Bodie yard became the staging point from which wagons transported the commodity to the budding district. Wagons traveling in the opposite direction brought ore, causing some long-idled Bodie stamp mills to start

Figure 8-14: A 16-animal team hauls a new Allis-Chalmers tube mill toward Bodie, where it will be introduced as a component of the Moore Slimes Process during the Standard cyanide plant's 1904 renovations. Very hard flint pebbles, crashing about inside the revolving cylinder, caused an abrading action that ground crushed ore and tailings to the consistency of slime. Said to have been the nation's first tube mill, its interior lining proved inadequate, so the Standard Company's blacksmith substituted iron straps from old Cornish pump rods. (Emil Billeb collection. Courtesy, Vickie Daniels)

Figure 8-15: The interior of the Standard cyanide plant is shown about 1909, after it was converted to use the Moore Slimes Process. Crushed ore and tailings, ground in the tube mill to the consistency of slimes, were cyanided in large vats, where specially-designed vacuum filters extracted liquid containing dissolved gold and silver. A row of cyanide vats fades into the distance, where one of the plant's two filter baskets hangs from a gantry crane. A truss surmounting the vats supports the crane as it travels from vat to vat. (*Report 15 of the State Mineralogist*. Courtesy, California Division of Mines and Geology)

Figure 8-16: This side view of a Moore filter basket illustrates one of the 5-foot by 16-foot canvas filter plates caked with a thin layer of slimes. Parallel stitching created hollow channels between two canvas sheets into which a vacuum drew gold- and silver-enriched liquid through the fabric while holding caked solids on the surface. (*Report 15 of the State Mineralogist*. Courtesy, California Division of Mines and Geology)

Figure 8-17: Another view from about 1909 shows the end of a Moore filter basket that contains 49 hanging filter plates. The basket has been raised from a slurry containing cyanide solution and slimes after a vacuum drew liquid carrying dissolved gold and silver into the plates' hollow interiors and left the solids caked on the exterior surfaces. The basket will be transported to a vat of wash water, where suction will remove more cyanide solution from the saturated cakes. At a discharge hopper, air pressure will be reversed to dislodge the solids. Meanwhile, the filtered liquid is being piped to zinc precipitation boxes, where the precious metals are removed. (*Report 15 of the State Mineralogist*. Courtesy, California Division of Mines and Geology)

crushing again.

The Standard cyanide plant was ready to begin trial runs on January 1, 1905, after six months of renovations. With minor alterations, everything was running smoothly by the end of March and the Moore Slimes Process was a success. The system had cost the company $60,000, or the equivalent of three 10-cent dividends and no dividends were paid for the second consecutive year, but it handled previously untreatable slimes, recovering an additional 60 cents per ton from crushed ore. Although the first few months of the year were consumed in perfecting the new process, production for 1905 increased by about $50,000 to $273,049. Anticipating that dividends

would soon resume, traders drove Standard stock up to $4.50 at year's end.

Bodie's isolation from major rail lines, a constant irritation to its inhabitants, grew during 1905, when the long wagon road to the old Carson & Colorado railroad was extended. The route of the Nevada & California Railway (the name given to the C&C by the Southern Pacific) was moved to take advantage of the Tonopah and Goldfield trade. The N&C's new standard-gauge rails bypassed Hawthorne, where a locomotive fueling and servicing yard had long been Bodie's principal rail connection. The N&C built a replacement facility further east at Mina, closer to the intersection of the newly-built Tonopah & Goldfield Railroad, and a new train station was established at Thorne, six additional miles from Bodie by stagecoach.[24]

This inconvenience to Bodie residents was overshadowed by benefits achieved through the Standard's improved ore treatment technology, which made the company financially strong by January 1906, when Theodore Hoover left Bodie. He subsequently became a distinguished manager, director, and consulting engineer for numerous mining concerns worldwide. He returned to his alma mater as a professor of mining and metallurgy in 1919, and retired as dean of Stanford's School of Engineering in 1936. He wrote several important textbooks on mining and metallurgy. His younger brother, Herbert, also a mining engineer, became the nation's 31st president in 1929.

Mine ownership at Bodie by 1906 was configured much like the panels of a giant triptych. On Bodie Bluff, to the north, the former Syndicate group of properties was under the control of the Loose brothers, who had returned from Utah and organized the New Bodie Mining Company. The middle panel was represented by High Peak, now referred to as Standard Hill, where Bodie's richest and most productive ore bodies were owned by the Standard Company. To the south, the Southern Consolidated Mining Company, headed by James S. Cain, controlled nearly all the mines on Silver and Queen Bee hills. The Red Cloud, however, was the only south end mine operating in 1906, and it was worked by leasers.

Repetition and routine were the reality of mining town life in early twentieth-century Bodie, where children raced to the Bulwer Tunnel to greet their fathers as the men came off shift. "We'd hike in and press an ear against the car tracks to listen," recalled Lillian Ninnis. "When we heard the click of movement on the tracks, we'd peer into the distant dark-

Figure 8-18: Sometime around 1903, hoisting operations at the Standard's main shaft were returned to the top of High Peak (by then referred to as Standard Hill). The electric hoisting works is shown that year amid scattered relics of steam power days. (Courtesy, Gregory Bock)

Figure 8-19: Competing with Bodie's railroad, Chinese woodcutters packed cordwood from their camp among piñon pine groves near Nine Mile. A train of their burros is shown shortly after the turn of the century where the trail enters Bodie Canyon, just above the Syndicate mill. (Detail, A. A. Forbes photograph. Courtesy, Seaver Center for Western History Research)

ness. . . . If many twinkling lights bobbed about like fireflies in the blackness we'd soon hear miners talking, each bearing his candlestick."[25]

The month Hoover departed, a reporter from Bridgeport described how much Bodie had changed since 1880, when between 7,000 and 8,000 uneasy fortune seekers overran the place.

It now has a population of 800. It has good schools and procures the services of the best instructors that money can afford. Its water is the purest that naturally springs from the earth. It has several fraternal orders, principally among which may be mentioned the Bodie Miners Union, organized in 1877 and has maintained its standing up to the present time by its conservative and prudential business methods. It has two churches, a Catholic and Methodist Episcopal. Bodie people have the virtues of the west with few of its vices. They have no city government, yet the best of order is maintained.

They are generous and hospitable to visitors, progressive and independent. It is by no means a one horse town as more than one mining company is operating in its vicinity. Although the Standard Consolidated is the employer of most of the labor marketed here, it makes no attempt to regulate the morals, religion, or political views of its inhabitants. . . . Outside of its mining industries, [Bodie's] only industry is a brewery and a very good judge of good beer, boasts: "Have you seen our brewery? It makes the best beer in the State" and they prove their respect for it by drinking it almost exclusively.[26]

Perhaps reflecting the nation's changing views toward insobriety, the author neglected to mention the number of saloons, a highly esteemed Bodie statistic in previous times.

After the headquarters of the San Francisco Stock

THE BODIE MINERS UNION, 1904

Little is known about the day-to-day workings of Bodie's Miners Union. Only occasionally do bits of information surface that provide insight into the association that was central to town life. In 1903, Theodore Hoover arrived at Bodie to take a supervisory position with the Standard Consolidated Mining Company. These were difficult times. National economic problems and widespread strife in labor-management relations were influencing Bodie's workforce. Hoover's memoirs provide a rare glimpse into the organization whose meeting hall has survived as one of the prominent buildings on Main Street.

I gave employment of sorts to every university man who applied, and at one time had as many as thirty on the mine. I did this because I wanted loyalty in a disloyal camp, and also a check to agitation in the labour unions. These men all joined the unions and were a good sprinkling of conservatives to offset the radicals . . .

N. Westheimer, a director of the company, came up in May [1904]. He was a fussy, suspicious old man, and was quite a trial, but I endeavored to treat him tactfully, and succeeded in calming his many fears and complaints. He would listen to all the lurid tales of all the "soreheads" in town, and then be in a panic for fear the company was going to the dogs. I invited him to dinner one evening, and on his way up a very small and generally inoffensive town dog chased and bit him. He left the next day, chiefly, I think, because he was afraid the dog had rabies, and he wanted to be nearer civilization. . . .

In the course of time I had to make not a few changes in the personnel of the employees, and reluctantly had to discharge several who would not do a fair day's work. There was some loud talk in the streets with threats to kill the manager, and the matter was discussed at the union meetings. The conservative element in the union was able to make the point that a mine manager had a right to discharge men for almost any reason, or without reason. . . . The fact that these radicals [who had been discharged] had referred to me as "a blank of a blank who ought to be tarred and feathered and chased down the canyon," did not meet with any action on the part of the Union. . . . The members of the Bodie unions were a fairly level-headed lot, and I am glad to say we got along pretty well together. There was occasionally some incendiary talk by a few, and there were some acts of incendiarism, which I know were not approved by the majority of the local people.

One interesting matter in connection with the Bodie Miners' Union deserves mention. Miners' wages in Bodie had always been on a good scale, and the union itself was in a prosperous condition up to 1904. It had, I think, about thirty thousand dollars in the bank, and owned its own hall building, which brought in good rental. This was the period when Haywood and Moyer were making their ill-starred attempt through the Western Federation of Miners to tie up the industry. They had missionaries out in all the camps trying to get a universal movement started. One of these anarchists came to Bodie. I told several of the more sensible men that they would find that all he wanted was to get their money. But the silver tongue of the born agitator overcame their scruples, and they put their union into the federation. Naturally their cash assets and their property had to go in too. In addition, during the Colorado strike they paid large assessments in support of their brethren. When the Western Federation finally came to the ground with a sputter, Bodie Miners' Union had no cash balance; their hall had been mortgaged by the officials of the federation for thirty thousand dollars, and they had paid out thousands of dollars besides, in support of a war on an industry which has always treated its employees in a liberal manner. Altogether it must have cost the Bodie union not short of a hundred thousand dollars, a sum sufficient to have paid the whole membership a fair annuity for life. A peaceful-minded man does not mention in Bodie the name—Western Federation of Miners or Haywood and Moyer.[1]

and Exchange Board were destroyed in the great earthquake and fire of April 1906, its members embraced the promising but highly speculative companies of southwestern Nevada and southeastern California that suddenly appeared after the Tonopah and Goldfield booms. As up-to-date prospectors sped across vast deserts in automobiles, the speculating public's fascination with mining shares broadened. "There is more excitement in the mining-stock market in San Francisco than has been the case since the bonanza days of the Comstock," wrote a mining correspondent.

> The brokers are working double time without being able to catch up. Seats in the Stock Exchange have doubled in value within a few months. . . . The San Francisco papers publish columns daily about the developments in the new camps. . . . Any old stock in any old mine seems to find buyers, and little or no inquiry is made into the merits of the properties themselves.[27]

Mining shares were so popular that the camps of Tonopah, Goldfield, and Rhyolite had, or would soon have, their own stock exchanges. As might be expected, the outburst of reckless speculation encouraged swindlers. Maneuvering to profit from the frenzy, shady promoters resurrected schemes employed decades earlier against Comstock investors. Equally unscrupulous shenanigans employing advanced communication technology and modern get-rich-quick advertising campaigns victimized a whole new generation of eager investors.[28] The stocks, selling from 50 cents to $2.80 per share, were risky at best; most were little more than worthless. Only a few had actual merit.

Standard Con, even after slumping to $2.50, was "high-end" compared to most stock in mines at more raucous Nevada and California boomtowns. Upgrading the Standard cyanide plant had achieved the desired effects. In 1906, the company's yield increased by $50,000 for the second year. From its production of $323,069, the Standard declared three dividends: two at 10 cents per share and another at 15 cents.[29]

In late 1906, a syndicate of Tonopah mining men headed by Charles E. Knox purchased the Bodie Railway and Lumber Company, then renamed it the Mono Lake Railway and Lumber Company. Showing little faith in Bodie as a future market for lumber products, the new owners planned to extend their tracks into Nevada. The proposed branch would connect with the N&C near its junction with the T&G, a direct route to Tonopah and Goldfield, and provide Bodie's inhabitants with their long-awaited rail connection to the outside world. The new route, unlike earlier plans to build in a southeasterly direction toward Benton, would head northeast from Warm Springs on Mono Basin, and cross Whiskey Flat to Sodaville, where the N&C and T&G shared trackage over a 10-mile stretch between Mina and Tonopah Junction.

The intended 60-mile link was to be standard gauge, with a third rail between Mono Mills and Warm Springs to accommodate both narrow gauge and standard gauge equipment. Initial reports indicated that the branch line would be completed by November 1907, but it, too, failed to materialize. Bodie's lumber hauling railroad remained isolated, maintaining seasonal operations on the original line.[30]

Labor relations had long remained cordial in Bodie, where wages were high and the Miners Union hall was the center of social and theatrical events. Nevertheless, in 1903, when the Western Federation of Miners sent agitators across the West to build support for a national movement, the visiting organizers charmed Bodie's union members into joining the Federation and pledging financial assistance to labor strikes underway at Cripple Creek and Telluride, Colorado.[31]

Labor unrest crept closer to Bodie in mid-1906, when a series of Federation-organized strikes erupted at nearby Goldfield. Complicating matters and intensifying animosities was the sudden collapse, in January 1907, of the recent boom in mining stock speculation, which grew out of another nationwide

REGULATIONS OF STANDARD
CONSOLIDATED MINING COMPANY, 1907

POWDER must be thawed only in the appliances provided for that purpose. Powder fuse and caps always must be kept in boxes.

Miners are forbidden to use a tool of iron of any kind to load or tamp holes.

All missed holes must be reported to foreman or shift boss when miners are going off shift.

Holes shall be fired only at end of shift and just before meal hour, unless directions to the contrary are given by the foreman or shift bosses.

THE HEATING of lunches by means of candle snuffs [short candle ends] will only be permitted in places specially designated by the foreman or shift bosses.

Miners are specially cautioned against dropping lighted snuffs.

Positively no lights must be left burning upon departure of shift, or at any time when leaving working place.

WHEN WORK is discontinued at any working place, miners working there last are expected to report to the foreman or shift boss the leaving of tools or supplies at that point.

TIMBERS, tools, etc., must not be left in raises or manways.

Miners starting to ascend or descend manways, must give notice of their coming and wait for answer from those above or below, if there are any, before proceeding.

Throwing tools down manways or chutes is strictly forbidden.

ANY MINER discovering bad or dangerous places in this Company's mines, will at once notify the foreman or shift boss.

No miner will lose his position by declining to work in a dangerous place.

THE TUNNELS and workings of the mine are for the use of the Company and its employees only. People desiring to visit the same must apply at the office for a pass.

No employee shall take strangers underground without a pass.

Tunnel carmen and shift bosses are expected to report at once any violation of this rule.

LEAVE OF ABSENCE must be applied for the day before.

Where absence is unforeseen, as in case of sudden sickness, word must be sent to the foreman or shift boss before the shift is due.

BELL SIGNALS as posted must be strictly followed. The station tender only is authorized to handle the bell rope.

Miners must not ride in a loaded cage.

ALL EMPLOYEES ARE EXPECTED TO READ AND POST THEMSELVES UPON THESE RULES.
FAILURE TO COMPLY WITH THE ABOVE RULES WILL RESULT IN SUSPENSION FROM THE ROLL.[1]

economic downturn known as the Panic of 1907. Banks across the country closed their doors and alarm swept the nation when depressed stock prices and a scarcity of credit resulted in runs on several high-profile New York banks. To protect Nevada's financial institutions, the governor declared a three-day bank holiday in October 1907.[32]

Closely linked to these financial difficulties, labor problems inevitably reached Bodie, where the work force was represented by two unions: the Miners Union, now Local 61 of the Western Federation of Miners; and its affiliate, Local 99 of the American Labor Union. Both organizations were strongly influenced by the militant philosophy of the Industrial Workers of the World—the Wobblies—a socialist labor organization that controlled the Western Federation of Miners and had instigated the strife at Goldfield.

A primary objective of the national unions was the establishment of an eight-hour workday. The "eight-hour movement," as it came to be called, had appeared a generation earlier on the Comstock, where the eight-hour workday had been standardized by 1866. Elsewhere in the West, workdays were 10 to 12 hours. The movement gained considerable momentum during the ensuing years, before suffering a crushing defeat under martial law at Leadville, Colorado, in 1880. The issue continued to smolder throughout the 1890s, then became a flash point in the bitter labor struggles that brought armed forces to Cripple Creek and Telluride in 1903.[33]

The Standard Consolidated Mining Company at Bodie was noted for paying the highest wages of any mining company in California. Its miners received $4 for a 10-hour day. Sensing impending labor troubles, the company voluntarily reduced the workday of its miners to eight hours in August 1907, but other underground workers and surface hands continued working 10-hour shifts. In October, these employees, represented by the American Labor Union's local branch, demanded that their workday be reduced also.

Figure 8-20: Winters are harsh at Bodie, as illustrated by this icy 1908 view of the Standard mill. The assay and main office building survived the 1898 fire, which destroyed the previous mill. The Standard cannon, at lower left, was later placed on display at the Mono County Courthouse in Bridgeport. (Courtesy, Gregory Bock)

A labor strike was temporarily averted when union members agreed to turn their dispute over to arbitration. In November, the arbitrating committee found that anticipated profits from the Standard Mine did not warrant a shortening of hours.[34] In other words, the company could not afford to increase operating expenses. Elsewhere, disagreements between labor and management were not resolved so peacefully. In December, federal troops moved into Goldfield and restored order by breaking the union.

Pervasive revolutionary passions and difficult financial times no doubt sharpened emotions at Bodie, where, occasionally during 1907, the old mining camp seemed to revert to its boomtown ways. "There was a hot time in town this week owing to an over indulgence in booze which resulted in the blacking of eyes, the abrazing [sic] of heads, the discharge of firearms, and the rapid departure of five Irishmen."[35] News from the Standard Company at year's end was less exhilarating. Decreased earnings substantiated concerns about the mine's financial condition. From the $284,047 yield only two dividends were declared during 1907, each of 10 cents per share.

Labor dissatisfaction continued to simmer at Bodie, where many Standard hands still worked 10-hour shifts. During January 1908, threats of a strike returned after company managers in New York announced that work hours would not change, but wages would be reduced in accordance with the diminishing grade of ore. A wage scale effective the first of February called for miners to receive $3.50 per day, muckers $3, timbermen $4, and surfacemen $2.75. At special meetings held by the two unions, workers refused to accept the pay cuts.[36]

Management responded decisively. On Sunday evening, February 16, orders telegrammed from the East closed the mine, mill, and cyanide plant. The lockout "has thrown a pall upon Bodie for the present," reported the newspaper in Bridgeport. "A number of miners have left and many others are preparing to do so."[37] Complying with insurance regulations devised to foil saboteurs, the company positioned watchmen around its facilities. Meanwhile,

employees stiffened their opposition, and steadfastly rejected every alternative wage reduction proposed.

Shareholders ended the impasse by taking matters into their own hands on February 28. At the annual meeting they elected a new board of directors.[38] Within the week, Standard employees returned to work at their former wages under the same timetable as before. Miners worked eight-hour days and other hands 10-hours. Mono County breathed a sigh of relief when its principal employer resumed production. "The days of gloom have passed and once again the cheering rumble of the mill makes sweet music to our ears."[39] This notice appeared in local newspapers on the same day the last soldier departed Goldfield, leaving mine owners there firmly in control.

Because the national press reported extensively on the violence at Goldfield, Cripple Creek, and Telluride, the period has become known for militant unionism. Congenial compromises, however, took place quietly between labor and management in most western mining localities, including Bodie.[40]

Although no actual strike took place, the lockout at the Standard, which closed the mine for three weeks during 1908, reduced the company's production for the year by $30,000 to $253,252. Two dividends were paid, each of 10 cents per share. "Recently, the company has not done well," confessed Superintendent W. H. Landers, reporting the mine's condition and acknowledging the company's mounting financial problems. "The high cost [of mining] is explained by the price of labor and the small size of the veins, which vary in width from 1 to 4 inches."[41]

In the early months of 1909, California was the only western state without a protective eight-hour law for its mining men. The legislature rectified this in May by establishing an eight-hour workday for miners, other below-ground workers, and those employed in stamp mills or smelters. Its liberal coverage placed a great hardship upon owners of marginally-profitable properties, such as the Standard. Confronted by increased costs, many mines closed. Others, with the cooperation of unions, found amicable

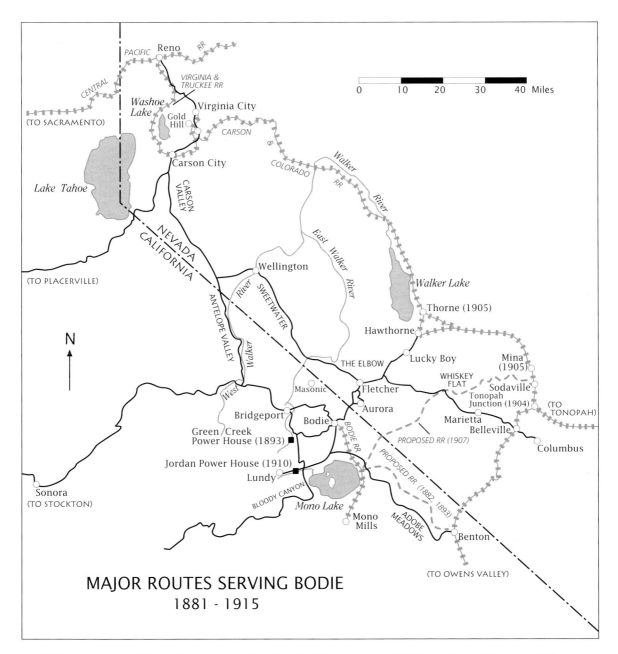

MAJOR ROUTES SERVING BODIE
1881 - 1915

Map 8: The narrow gauge Carson & Colorado Railroad reached the south end of Walker Lake in 1881, after which Hawthorne became the region's transportation hub. A wagon road built from there over Lucky Boy Pass, which bypassed Aurora by going through Del Monte Canyon, would serve as Bodie's primary route to the outside world for the next 25 years. Because this frequently used route to and from Bodie passed through Nevada, a peculiar disadvantage arose. Bodie's citizens resided in California, but a visit to their state capital at Sacramento usually required traveling through Carson City, the capital of Nevada.

The Bodie Railway and Lumber Company also completed its railroad in 1881, but the tracks never extended beyond the timberland south of Mono Lake. Proposals that would have connected the line with the Carson & Colorado at Benton by crossing Adobe Meadows failed in 1882 and 1893. In 1905, the Southern Pacific standard-gauged the Carson & Colorado as far south as its junction to the booming towns of Tonopah and Goldfield. The newly-named Nevada & California's tracks bypassed Hawthorne, and Bodie's closest railroad link was moved six miles further away to Thorne. Another unsuccessful proposal was made in 1907 for a branch line to connect Bodie's railroad to the N&C. By crossing Whiskey Flat to Sodaville, it might have encouraged lumber trade with Tonopah and Goldfield.

ways to comply with the law and still keep men working. A common compromise interpreted the law to mean that "eight hours of work shall be done at the face," so that travel to and from work stations was not on company time.

Trouble arose industry-wide when employers in some camps cut wages in proportion to the reduced hours, a trend that concerned Standard miners, who still received the daily rate of $4. Although mindful of the company's strained finances, the miners threatened to strike if their wages were decreased. Management heeded the warnings, retained the existing pay scale, and scheduled two eight-hour shifts per day. Daily wages were: foremen, $6; shift-bosses and engineers, $5; timbermen, $4.50; miners, cage-tenders, and carmen, $4; and watchmen, $3.[42]

After yet another year of diminishing yields, the Standard Company reported at the end of 1909 that its production had declined to $226,404, with no dividends paid. The company's poor condition was revealed in another discouraging report. "The year for this company . . . has been rather unsatisfactory," wrote Superintendent Landers, adding that "work carried on during the past thirty-one years has almost exhausted the ore-supply."[43]

Bodie's apparent obituary greeted the citizens of Mono County and the mining world at large on May 21, 1910. Quoting largely from the Standard superintendent's annual report, an article in the New York-based *Engineering and Mining Journal* titled "The Passing of Bodie, California" laid open the precarious state of the town's industry and seemed to sound a death knell for the Standard Company—and Bodie as well:

> We now find ourselves with little likely territory left to explore. Such as is left, containing many veins of very small size and only moderate value, cannot be counted on to furnish sufficient ore to keep the plant in full operation . . . later than the coming summer.

The article suggested that certain avenues might afford the company new opportunities.

> Some territory has been thrown open to leasers, and the only other hope of the company seems to be to open the mine to greater depth. . . . The question of pumping out the lower levels or of either sinking one of the shafts or driving a long tunnel is being seriously considered. While it is possible that there is but little ore of pay grade on the lower levels, it *might* be well for the company to take the mining chance and endeavor to open up new orebodies at greater depth.[44]

Challenged by an ore supply that was fast diminishing in size and grade and increasingly expensive to mine, the Standard's management considered augmenting the power output of the Green Creek plant to run electric pumps to drain the 1,000- and 1,200-foot levels.[45] It was common knowledge that most of the paying ore had been taken above the 500-foot level, but old-timers recalled "a good low-grade ledge" on the 1,000-foot level. "In those days," explained the *Bodie Miner*, "low-grade rock was what is now considered good milling ore."[46]

Pumping out the lower levels and sinking either the Lent or Standard shaft deeper would have been expensive and fraught with uncertainty, and was not adopted. One last effort, however, sought to forestall the inevitable. The company updated its cyanide plant in 1910 by replacing the Moore filters with automated Butters filters, a process that improved efficiency by increasing the rate of filtration for tailings containing larger quantities of clay.[47]

Even with this new technology, a decade into the new century, gratification was difficult to find at Bodie. One modern convenience, however, promised to ease the severity of life. With few exceptions, the town's 700 or so inhabitants did not have electricity in their homes. Bodie's pioneering power plant at Green Creek, designed to run the Standard's machinery, lit the dwellings of only a few high-level employees, and occasionally responded to pleas for creature comforts by lighting downtown streets during social gatherings at the Miners Union hall.[48] To the delight of most Bodie residents, a utility company now proposed constructing a hydroelectric plant in

Figure 8-21: Ice-skaters frolic on the Standard's frozen tailings pond in 1910. The enormous dump, surmounted by a row of mine cars from the Bulwer Tunnel, provides an imposing backdrop for the wintry scene. (Courtesy, Gregory Bock)

Figure 8-22: Seasoned by years of successes and disappointments, Bodie was sidelined by early twentieth-century mining excitements at Tonopah, Goldfield, Rawhide, and Rhyolite. This panorama from about 1909 looks southwest to reveal the old town reposing beyond several key elements of its economy. From left: the Standard mill, built in 1899; the flume and its supporting trestle, reintroduced in 1904, that convey crushed ore to the cyanide plant; the covered incline where mine cars are winched into the mill and dumped; a snowshed-covered track through which mules pull cars loaded with ore from the Bulwer Tunnel; and the tailings ponds that provide a large percentage of the Standard Company's revenue. (*Mines and Mineral Resources of Alpine, Inyo, and Mono Counties.* Courtesy, California Division of Mines and Geology)

Figure 8-23: On King Street, observed a visiting reporter in 1880, ". . . are located the Chinese with their opium dens, gambling houses, restaurants, josh houses, prostitutes, and the vilest smells and the filthiest sanitary conditions that can be experienced." Thirty years later, in 1911, Bodie's nearly-deserted Chinatown displays little of its former boomtown vitality. (Emil Billeb collection. Courtesy, Vickie Daniels)

the Sierra foothills and supplying electricity to homes in several area towns.

The upstart utility, championed by James S. Cain, was an alliance of four entities: the Pacific Power Company, the Central California Power Company, the Mono County Irrigation Company, and the California Hydro-Electric Company. Cain, serving as the Hydro-Electric Company's vice president, opened a Bodie office. The conglomerate's power generating plant was at Jordan, a nearly abandoned mining center on the flank of Copper Mountain, immediately north of Mill Creek about 16 miles southwest of Bodie. Named for the sawmills it had powered to supply lumber to Aurora in the 1860s, Mill Creek coursed through the Homer mining district, where it fed Lundy Lake before passing through the Jordan mining district and emptying into Mono Lake.

In addition to placer, hydraulic, and quartz mining of gold, Jordan District had been known for the high copper content in its ores. Copper mining in 1879 led to the construction of a small smelter there in 1882. Before work stopped the following year, the Detroit Copper Mining Company had yielded about $60,000. Later, in 1896, an immense 40-stamp mill was built, and a three-mile ditch was dug to bring water to it from Lundy Lake. Sustained mostly by stock promotions, the venture spent large sums of money that gave rise to the town of Jordan, consisting of two merchandise stores, two saloons, a large blacksmith shop, and a post office. By 1900, the mine was closed, and in 1903, the mill was moved to Esmeralda County, Nevada.[49]

The new hydroelectric plant, like the mill that preceded it, ran on water from Lundy Lake. A dam built by the utility company raised the lake 15 feet, nearly doubling its capacity. From the Jordan powerhouse, the transmission line passed through Bodie, but its townsfolk were not the primary customers. The

Figure 8-24: Festively dressed on July 4, 1909, a group of Paiute Indians crosses Main Street opposite the Occidental Hotel. Because Bodie's streets have always been treeless, saplings were hauled into town to furnish holiday trim. (Courtesy, Gregory Bock)

Figure 8-25: Built in the spring of 1878, the Miners Union hall was the center of Bodie's theatrical entertainment and social affairs. The old building is graced with patriotic observers attired for an early 1900s Independence Day celebration. (Courtesy, Gregory Bock)

Figure 8-26: Their mining industry was faltering, but Bodie's citizens enjoyed turning out on the Fourth of July. The scene looks south on Main Street, where a three-legged race is enjoyed by a crowd of enthusiastic onlookers. (Courtesy, Gregory Bock)

Figure 8-27: The U. S. Hotel, a prominent feature on Main Street, is shown in an undated view, looking northeast. (Courtesy, Gregory Bock)

real objective was to meet the industrial needs of numerous other mining localities farther away. The power line stretched 100 miles beyond Bodie to places such as Lucky Boy, Hawthorne, Rawhide, Fairview, and Wonder, where mining activity had spread during Nevada's recent boom. Aurora, where J. S. Cain had been encouraging a revival since 1905 by leasing out mines, also expected to benefit.[50]

The prospect of commercially available electricity was of interest to Bodie's inhabitants, but it did little to fortify their primary employer, which had benefited from cheap power since 1893. As residents welcomed the new energy source, the Standard Company's fading fortunes remained their primary concern. Most of its revenue during 1910 came from tailings, not from the mine. Excavated tailings and an improved cyanide plant increased the annual yield to $267,935, but funded only one 10-cent dividend. Furthermore, another pessimistic annual report expressed that the mine "has for the last three or four years been approaching the point of exhaustion."[51]

The hydroelectric plant at Jordan was completed in the summer of 1910. In what many thought would

be a climactic change, electricity became available to nearly everyone in Bodie on Christmas Day. The Jordan facility, often referred to as the "Mill Creek power plant," proved to be short-lived. The electricity lasted little more than two months before the line went dead, at five minutes to midnight on March 7, 1911, the final night of a two-week blizzard that blanketed Bodie with snow "as high as the roofs of the houses."[52] Telephone lines were down, and every attempt by power company employee Paul Greenleaf to contact the plant's operators at Jordan failed. As the storm abated during the morning hours, Greenleaf and another man set out on skis to trace the 16-mile transmission line and locate the source of the power outage. Not until they arrived at a Mono Lake ranch house did they learn that an avalanche had demolished the powerhouse a quarter of a mile away. The two men skied to the site, but found no sign of the buildings or their occupants.

Meanwhile, locals from the lakeshore community of Hammond's Station had organized a relief party to assist people stranded by the storm. After skiing through the low-lying fog that had enveloped

Mono Basin, the group arrived at Jordan, where they, too, saw no trace of the powerhouse and nearby buildings. Two men, dispatched to inform Bodie of the disaster, rowed across Mono Lake where they found a rancher's telephone that was open to Mono Mills. At about 3:00 in the afternoon, they called the caretaker, who spent the next 17 hours trying to telephone Bodie and relay the message about the disaster at Jordan and the missing inhabitants.

Unaware of the distant avalanche, folks at Bodie lit their homes with oil lamps and began digging out. The mines closed, allowing every able-bodied man to help clear roads until "there were about 70 men and 10 horses on the job."[53] After the caretaker's frantic call came in about 8:00 on the morning of March 9, a party was formed to convey Bodie's physician to Jordan, where rescuers were digging through 14 to 20 feet of snow to locate survivors and recover bodies.

The generating complex's reinforced concrete powerhouse and two cottages had been demolished, along with a barn and storage building. Several private cabins occupied by miners and some 30-year-old mill and smelter buildings were also destroyed. All eight residents were buried alive: three power company employees, the chief electrician's wife, and four miners. Only Agnes Mason survived. Pinned in bed beside her dead husband, she had been spared when a collapsing concrete slab caught on the iron bedstead and nearby furniture. Buried under eight feet of snow for more than 60 hours, she was pulled from the frozen wreckage on March 10, then transported on a sled crafted from sheet iron to the Conway ranch. When circulation failed to return to her right leg after several days of care, she was wrapped in blankets and placed back on the makeshift sled, which had been improved by the addition of a mattress for the trip to Bodie. Twelve men on skis pulled her cross-country to Bodie, from where she was taken by sleigh, then by automobile, to Thorne, then by rail to an Oakland hospital. There her right leg was amputated below the knee.[54]

The Jordan transmission line was connected to the Green Creek plant, and the Standard Company provided Bodie residents with electricity while damaged machinery was repaired. Early in May, Jordan began supplying power from a temporary building while a new powerhouse was under construction nearby. This time the plant was situated on a site that was "absolutely safe from snowslides."[55] After the new Jordan facility commenced supplying electricity to Bodie, two 55-foot masts were erected on Main Street to support arc lights, which illuminated downtown. Thereafter, the Standard's 18-year old plant at Green Creek returned to generating power for company operations.[56]

Backed by the Hydro-Electric Company's promise of cheap power, Cain hoped to induce an economic comeback for Bodie. The utility company's presence, however, had little effect where it mattered. The Standard's 1911 report stated that ore from the mine was "insufficient to keep the mill operating at full capacity" and several tailings ponds were "worked out during the year." Frustrated by shrinking profits, the superintendent explained that the remaining ore was difficult to mine and that clay in the tailings impeded cyaniding. "The total tonnage was much less than last year and the cost per ton higher."[57] When the figures were tallied, the company had produced only $235,477, a decrease of more than $30,000 from the previous year. Profits, mostly spent on exploring for more ore bodies, were so slight that dividends could not be paid.

Notwithstanding the difficulties facing the Standard, it was generally believed that commercially marketed electric power would be used to reopen other Bodie mines. Little occurred, except that the Red Cloud closed down, leaving the south end abandoned. In Aurora, however, the availability of electricity enhanced a revival already underway when a series of highly-financed mining companies moved in.

Aurora's success had no effect on its neighboring community, where the beleaguered Standard Company sought guidance from a respected former superintendent. Thomas H. Leggett arrived as a consultant to examine the property and determine the next course of action. His report, submitted in July 1912, starkly described the situation.

> [The Standard Mine] holds a network of veins, a few of them over 2 feet wide, but most of them narrower, often 6 to 10 inches wide. These veins become impoverished at 400 to 500 feet vertical depth. The wide veins were exhausted years ago. Only the narrow seams are left, and many of these are unprofitable, and the others scattered over a wide area connected by long cross-cuts which make their development and mining very costly. . . . By acquiring adjoining claims and by mining remnants of orebodies in the upper levels, the mine and mill have been kept in operation. The annual reports issued by the company have shown a decreasing tonnage, and an increasing cost for development, and they also show that the value of the ore treated at the present time is much lower than in former years. In the [fiscal] year ended February 28, 1912, an unusual amount of development resulted in a production of about one-half the tonnage produced in earlier years, and the ore was mined at an actual loss. . . . The resulting loss was offset by the yield from the [tailings ponds]. The amount of tailings remaining to be treated is estimated at 12,000 tons, and three-quarters of this amount will be exhausted by the close of the present season in November.[58]

Leggett advised against pumping the lower levels and thought it unwise to purchase the south end mines owned by J. S. Cain's Southern Consolidated Mining Company. He concluded that "while small orebodies may be discovered in the future, it is advisable to change the working of the mine into a leasing system as soon as possible." Even though Leggett's advice was followed closely, efforts to interest leasers were only marginally successful. Eight leases were issued on ground not actively worked by the company. By the end of the year three of them had been abandoned.

Another problem, one that had plagued the Standard for years, became acute in the spring of 1912. At the end of winter the snow pack in the Sierra should have been 10 to 12 feet deep. Instead, the mountains were almost bare, resulting in a shortage of water in Green Creek that made generating electricity agonizingly sporadic. During power outages, the company sidestepped the expense of purchasing wood or electricity from outside sources by simply shutting down and laying off employees. This procedure became commonplace, throwing financial affairs into a rapid decline since the mill and cyanide plant rarely ran. Only a small underground force continued developing the mine.[59]

Bodie's plight was described at year's end in Carson City. "Word comes from Bodie that there are at this time but twelve men working in the camp; the residents are rapidly leaving and before long the town will be practically deserted. There is no hotel running and it is said that the one butcher shop will soon close its doors."[60] Wells Fargo again removed its Bodie agency. The Standard's 1912 production was a scant $188,902. Only one 10-cent dividend had been declared, paid in January from revenue that the bookkeeper had carried over from the previous year.

By the time the last of the tailings were exhausted in September 1913, only "several hundred tons of ore" remained in the mine. What little was left consisted of narrow veins that fed the mill at only one-third of capacity. When the tailings ran out, the Standard Mine was closed. Of the five leasers who had been working Standard ground at the beginning of the year, all but one suspended operations before their terms were up.[61] The Standard Consolidated Mining Company paid its last dividend on November 17, 1913. Extravagant at 25 cents per share, it was the company's Last Hurrah.

For a few years thereafter, the primary force that kept Bodie alive was the Mono Lake Railway. Scattered eruptions in mining and construction provided the line with substantial trade after the Standard Company, its principal customer, ceased operations. Although its tracks never extended beyond the timberland at Mono Mills, the railroad fulfilled a demand for lumber growing out of booms at Masonic, Lucky Boy, and, especially, Aurora.

Efforts to develop Aurora's mines blossomed in June 1914, when a 3,000-foot-long drainage tunnel slicing through numerous old mining properties was completed, and work began on an immense, electric-powered, 40-stamp mill with an adjoining 500-ton-per-day cyanide plant. The venture was initiated by the Aurora Consolidated Mining Company, headed by Jesse Knight, a wealthy Utah mining magnate. The activity hastened Aurora's rejuvenation, which merited the opening of several saloons and a brothel. One local resident recalled that Aurora's dilapidated "stores, rooming houses, and especially saloons" were rebuilt.[62] Influenced by his Mormon convictions, Knight had a dry town built nearby, which he named after company secretary and treasurer, W. Lester Mangum. Located near the mill, the village of Mangum contained dwellings and bunkhouses for company employees, but no barrooms. Later that year, Knight's Aurora affairs were taken over by the Gold-field Consolidated Mining Company, which completed the ore-treating facilities, then ran the enterprise another three years.[63]

To furnish building materials required at Aurora, lumber from Mono Mills was delivered by train to the railroad yard above Bodie, where an electric planing mill was installed. Finished lumber was then transported by wagon and team into the surrounding region. "There were about sixty animals in daily use hauling to Aurora over the short haul of fourteen miles," recalled railroad employee Emil Billeb. Each team contained from 6 to 20 animals, depending on the size of the load. "The longer teams," he added, were driven by a "jerk-line."[64] Meanwhile, a couple of Bodie residents organized competing automobile mail and stage lines that replaced the horse- and mule-drawn stagecoaches between Bodie, Aurora, Hawthorne, and Thorne.[65]

Little more was heard of Bodie's premier min-

Figure 8-28: The slimes plant was photographed shortly before the Standard Company ceased operations in 1913. By then the plant had been refitted with Butters filters, an improvement over the Moore system. At upper right, an inclined track brings up mine cars loaded with tailings and slimes excavated from the ponds. Slightly below it, a flume conveys crushed ore directly from the Standard mill. Ruins of the Bulwer-Standard mill lie in the foreground, where debris surrounds several standing battery foundations. (A. A. Forbes photograph. Courtesy, Seaver Center for Western History Research)

Figure 8-29: The first time a motor car was driven into Bodie on June 12, 1905, recalled Emil Billeb, the event was considered historical. Years later, after Wells, Fargo & Co. closed its Bodie office in 1912, horse-drawn stagecoaches were replaced by local entrepreneurs who established automobile mail and stage lines. Autos of that era gather on Main Street, at the Occidental Hotel. (Courtesy, Gregory Bock)

ing company until early in 1915, when an item appeared in New York's *Engineering and Mining Journal.* "STANDARD (Bodie)—Property sold to J. S. Cain Co. in settlement of suit against Standard Consolidated Mining Co. for ore extracted from Midnight."[66]

The Midnight claim, owned by Cain, was situated on the summit of High Peak above the Standard. It had been located 10 years before Bodie's boom by area pioneer Judge J. G. McClinton, who named it the McClinton. Later, in 1877, it was among the district's earliest prospects to spawn an organized corporation. Owned by the McClinton Mining Company, the mine was one of the first to be equipped with a steam hoist, in 1878. During the few years it operated, its total production was a mere $1,064. It never paid any dividends and levied $123,000 in assessments. An 1881 description of the mine called its abandoned hoisting works, office, and dwelling houses a "noble monument" near the "flag staff on the summit of High Peak, which looms up from the city of Bodie like a mansion in the skies."[67] The mine was renamed the Midnight in 1884, following which it faded from the historic record.

Cain had acquired the Midnight by 1915. He also owned Bodie's only remaining bank, and was the principal owner of the dormant south end mines. Cain paid some men to sink an incline shaft on the Midnight. They followed the vein from its outcrop, confirming Cain's suspicions that the Standard had encroached on the property and removed Midnight ore. Robert Bell tells how Cain gained control of the Standard property.

He owned the Midnight and knew the Standard Company had been stoping outside their location line. Miners will follow a ledge all the way to the surface, but this time they stayed down about 100 feet so nobody would know they were working down there. Cain sunk a shaft into the Standard's stope. He had a crooked mining lawyer named Billy Metson. They took over the Standard by suing them—ended up owning the whole company. Another guy from San Francisco put up the money.[68]

Metson, in addition to his duties representing Cain, was an officer of the Standard Company.

Cain sued the Standard for $700,000 for ore taken from the Midnight. The company settled by selling their property to Cain for $25,000. The deed was recorded on February 23, 1915. Cain's acquisition included the mine, comprising 61 claims, the Bulwer Tunnel, the former Bodie Tunnel Company's tunnel, the 20-stamp Standard mill, cyanide plant, tailings ponds, offices, dwellings, water rights, horses, mules, and the power plant at Green Creek.[69] The transaction was reported without fanfare in *Poor's Manual of Industrials*.

STANDARD CONSOLIDATED MINING COMPANY—The Manual was officially informed July 21, 1915, that this company disposed of its property and the corporation was dissolved March 31, 1915. Distribution of assets amounted to 13½ cents per share.[70]

So ended the tale of the Standard Consolidated Mining Company. Gold and silver from its mine built one of the West's wildest boomtowns, then sustained a seasoned mining community into the twentieth century. Over a period of 38 years, the mine yielded $18,202,855 in bullion, enriching its investors with dividends totalling $5,264,407, while levying just three assessments.

1. *Mining and Scientific Press* 15 April 1893, 237; *Engineering and Mining Journal* 4 November 1893; 479; *Walker Lake Bulletin* 13 June 1894; 22 May 1895; California State Mining Bureau, *Thirteenth Report of the State Mineralogist, for the Two Years Ending September 15, 1896* (Sacramento, CA: Superintendent of State Printing, 1896), 230.

2. Robert T. Bell, interview by author, 7 June 1996, Nevada.

3. James Stuart Cain (1854-1938).

4. *Engineering and Mining Journal* 23 June 1894, 588; *Inyo Register* 14 June 1894; *Walker Lake Bulletin* 6 June 1894; 13 June 1894.

5. *Mining and Scientific Press* 3 August 1895, 78; 21 September 1895, 186; 23 May 1896, 422; *Virginia Evening Chronicle* 1 August 1895; California, *Thirteenth Report*, 226, 231; Francis L. Bosqui, *Practical Notes on the Cyanide Process* (New York, NY: Scientific Publishing Co., 1899), 45; Mono County, *Mining Deeds, Book V*, 137-142.

6. Senator George Hearst (1820-1891). *Engineering and Mining Journal* 7 April 1900, 417; 20 April 1901, 497; 27 April 1901, 204; 4 May 1901, 214; *Walker Lake Bulletin* 7 August 1901. Hearst was later noted for providing his son, William Randolph, with the means to become a newspaper tycoon.

7. *Mining and Scientific Press* 1 June 1901, 254; 20 July 1901, 28; *Engineering and Mining Journal* 14 December 1901, 798; *Chronicle-Union* 14 July 1906; 22 December 1906; Robert T. Bell, telephone interview by author, 5 July 1995.

8. *Chronicle-Union* 29 October 1910; 7 October 1911.

9. U.S. Department of the Interior, "Population," *Twelfth Census of the United States, 1900*, vol. 1 (Washington, DC: Government Printing Office, 1901), 77.

10. *Engineering and Mining Journal* 25 May 1901, 665.

11. *Walker Lake Bulletin* 19 June 1901; 18 September 1901; 27 June 1902.

12. *Engineering and Mining Journal* 27 July 1901, 125.

13. *Engineering and Mining Journal* 12 September 1903, 397.

14. *Engineering and Mining Journal* 12 September 1903, 397.

15. *Mining and Scientific Press* 17 May 1902, 274; 14 June 1902, 326; *Engineering and Mining Journal* 7 June 1902, 807.

16. Russell R. Elliott, *Nevada's Twentieth-Century Mining Boom: Tonopah, Goldfield, Ely* (Reno, NV: University of Nevada Press, 1966), 77-78, 82-98; George Graham Rice, *My Adventures With Your Money* (1913; reprint, Las Vegas, NV: Nevada Publications, 1986), 53-134.

17. Theodore J. Hoover (1871-1955).

18. Theodore J. Hoover, "Memoranda: Being a Statement by an Engineer, 1939" TMs [photocopy], Hoover Institution Archives, Stanford University, Stanford, CA, 129.

19. Hoover, "Memoranda," 129.

20. Hoover, "Memoranda," 129.

21. Hoover, "Memoranda," 129.

22. *Walker Lake Bulletin* 20 May 1904.

23. *Chronicle-Union* 21 October 1905; *Mining and Scientific Press* 23 September 1905, 214; 15 December 1906; 714-715; *Engineering and Mining Journal* 20 October 1906, 754.

24. David F. Myrick, "The Bodie & Benton Railway," chap. in *Railroads of Nevada and Eastern California*, Vol. 1 (Berkeley, CA: Howell-North Books, 1962), 202-205.

25. Lillian Ninnis, "Bodie Yesterday," *Desert: Magazine of the Outdoor Southwest* 23, no. 10 (October 1960): 19-21

26. *Chronicle-Union* 6 January 1906.

27. *Engineering and Mining Journal* 24 November 1906, 1003.

28. Elliott, *Nevada's Twentieth-Century Mining Boom*, 77-78, 82-98; Rice, *My Adventures With Your Money*, 53-134.

29. October 1906 was the last time Standard Consolidated was quoted by an exchange. The stock sold for $2.40 per share on the Consolidated Exchange in San Francisco. Sparse clues indicate that, thereafter, stock in the dividend-paying company was held by a few individuals, and not traded.

30. *Engineering and Mining Journal* 17 November 1906, 941; 16 March 1907, 540; Emil W. Billeb, *Mining Camp Days* (Berkeley, CA: Howell-North Books, 1968), 36-37, 46-50; Myrick, *Railroads of Nevada and Eastern California, Vol. 1*, 181, 202-203, 312-313; Karen Colbourne McAbeer, "The Bodie Railroad" (Master of Arts Thesis, California State College, Sonoma, CA, 1973), 56-60.

31. Hoover, "Memoranda," 132-133.

32. *Chronicle-Union* 26 October 1907; Elliott, *Nevada's Twentieth-Century Mining Boom*, 103-152.

33. Eliot Lord, *Comstock Mining and Miners* (1883; reprint, San Diego, CA: Howell-North Books, 1980), 224-225; Mark Wyman, *Hard Rock Epic: Western Miners and the Industrial Revolution, 1860-1910* (Berkeley, CA: University of California Press, 1979), 207-220.

34. *Chronicle-Union* 3 August 1907; *Engineering and Mining Journal* 26 October 1907, 800; *Mining and Scientific Press* 2 November 1907, 542.

35. *Chronicle-Union* 31 August 1907.

36. *Chronicle-Union* 1 February 1908; 15 February 1908.

37. *Chronicle-Union* 22 February 1908.

38. *Chronicle-Union* 29 February 1908.

39. *Chronicle-Union* 7 March 1908.

40. Wyman, *Hard Rock Epic*, 207-220; Elliott, *Nevada's Twentieth-Century Mining Boom*, 103-152.

41. *Mining and Scientific Press* 5 June 1909, 800.

42. *Engineering and Mining Journal* 22 May 1909, 1059; *Mining and Scientific Press* 31 May 1913, 809.

43. *Mining and Scientific Press* 14 May 1910, 699.

44. *Engineering and Mining Journal* 21 May 1910, 1051.

45. *Bodie Miner* 7 August 1909; *Engineering and Mining Journal* 4 September 1909, 477.

46. *Bodie Miner* 11 September 1909.

47. Department of the Interior, United States Geological Survey, *Mineral Resources of the United States* (Washington, DC: Government Printing Office, 1911), 489; California State Mining Bureau, *Report XV of the State Mineralogist* (Sacramento, CA: California State Printing Office, 1919), 154.

48. *Walker Lake Bulletin* 18 September 1895; 20 May 1896; *Bodie Miner* 9 May 1909; Billeb, *Mining Camp Days*, 152-154.

49. *Daily Free Press* 19 September 1882; *Chronicle-Union* 21 May 1910; *Engineering and Mining Journal* 7 May 1910, 981; Thomas C. Fletcher, *Paiute, Prospector, Pioneer: The Bodie-Mono Lake Area in the Nineteenth Century* (Lee Vining, CA: Artemisia Press, 1987), 55, 70-71, 91.

50. *Western Nevada Miner* 7 January 1911; Billeb, *Mining Camp Days*, 157; U.S. Department of Commerce, "Population," *Thirteenth Census of the United States, 1910*, vol. 2 (Washington, DC: Government Printing Office, 1913), 147.

51. *Engineering and Mining Journal* 25 March 1911, 600.

52. Billeb, *Mining Camp Days*, 158.

53. Billeb, *Mining Camp Days*, 159.

54. *Chronicle-Union* 18 March 1911; 22 April 1911; Russ and Anne Johnson, *The Ghost Town of Bodie As Reported in the Newspapers of the Day* (Bishop, CA: Chalfant Press, 1967), 94-97; Billeb, *Mining Camp Days*, 158-160. For Paul Greenleaf's recollection, see William A. Myers, *Iron Men and Copper Wires: A Centennial History of the Southern California Edison Company* (Glendale, CA: Trans-Anglo Press, 1983), 76. Researched accounts of avalanche victims are found in James Watson and Doug Brodie, *Big Bad Bodie: High Sierra Ghost Town* (Philadelphia, PA: Xlibris Corporation, 2000), 136-153.

55. *Chronicle-Union* 25 March 1911; 18 March 1911; 22 April 1911. The Jordan plant was linked in December 1913 to a consolidation of area power networks that supplied towns as far away as Bishop, Tonopah, and Goldfield. Bridgeport, the seat of Mono County, did not receive electricity until 1931, enduring until then with individually-owned generators. (*Western Nevada Miner* 13 December 1913; *Chronicle-Union* 22 August 1931; Myers, *Iron Men and Copper Wires*, 75-81.)

56. *Chronicle-Union* 7 October 1911; 18 November 1911.

57. *Engineering and Mining Journal* 11 May 1912, 951.

58. *Mining and Scientific Press* 17 August 1912, 209.

59. *Chronicle-Union* 17 February 1912; *Mining and Scientific Press* 2 March 1912, 354.

60. *Walker Lake Bulletin* 17 December 1912.

61. *Walker Lake Bulletin* 30 September 1913; *Mining and Scientific Press* 21 March 1914, 507; Department of the Interior, United States Geological Survey, *Mineral Resources of the United States* (Washington, DC: Government Printing Office, 1913), 488.

62. Billeb, *Mining Camp Days*, 86-88; *Western Nevada*

Miner 12 June 1915.

63. For more information on Aurora's early twentieth century revival, see Robert E. Stewart, *Aurora: Ghost City of the Dawn* (Las Vegas, NV: Nevada Publications, 1996), 34-40; "The New Aurora Mill," *Mining and Scientific Press* 11 July 1914, 57-59; "Mining and Milling Methods at the Aurora Consolidated Mines," *Western Nevada Miner* 28 November 1914. Excellent photographs are reproduced in Billeb, *Mining Camp Days*, 105-112.

64. Emil W. Billeb, "Bodie's Railroad That Was," *The Pony Express* 24 (June 1957): 6. Also see, Michael H. Piatt, "Hauling Freight Into the 20th Century by Jerk Line," *Journal of the West* 36, no. 1 (January 1997): 82-91.

65. Billeb, *Mining Camp Days*, 179, 188.

66. *Engineering and Mining Journal* 27 March 1915, 592.

67. *Mining Record* 25 June 25 1881, 608.

68. Robert T. Bell, telephone interview by author, 6 June 1997; 12 August 2002. For another version, see Ella M. Cain, *The Story of Bodie* (San Francisco, CA: Fearon Publishers, 1956, 86.

69. California State Archives. "Deed: Standard Consolidated Mining Company to J. S. Cain." Bodie Collection, linknum 4078: 23 February 1915; *Chronicle-Union* 6 March 1915; *Walker Lake Bulletin* 6 March 1915.

70. *Poor's Manual of Industrials* (1915), 1553.

The Bodie Miners Union, 1904

1. Theodore J. Hoover, "Memoranda: Being a Statement by an Engineer, 1939" TMs [photocopy], Hoover Institution Archives, Stanford University, Stanford, CA, 132-133.

Regulations of Standard Consolidated Mining Company

1. *Mining and Scientific Press* 19 October 1907.

Figure 9-1: Leasers are pictured working the old Bodie Mine after J. S. Cain took over the Standard's properties. Leasers (actually lessees) contracted to pay a specified percentage of their bullion in exchange for the right to work a mine. Leasers usually ran makeshift operations, scrounging material from abandoned mines nearby. If they made any money at all, recalled Robert Bell, they "pretty much had to pay it all back to Cain for the lease plus the $6 per ton for milling." Because pumping expenses were enormous, miners, as shown in this 1921 photograph, restricted their work to areas above the flooded lower levels. In the foreground, a granite block foundation that supported steam-powered machinery during Bodie's more prosperous days. (Emil Billeb collection. Courtesy, Vickie Daniels)

Figure 9-2: Viewed from nearly the same angle as figure 6-3, the *Mono* pauses at the Bodie end of the line. Although large-scale mining had disappeared from Bodie by the end of 1913, the railroad kept operating until 1917, hauling lumber to the Bodie yard, where it was loaded onto wagons destined for outlying towns such as Masonic, Aurora, and Lucky Boy. Dominating the background, the dump at the abandoned Lent Shaft stands against the encroaching sagebrush. (Emil Billeb collection. Courtesy, Vickie Daniels)

CHAPTER NINE

LEASERS WORK THE MINES
1915-1942

A visit to Bodie last Saturday revealed the fact that there is a little activity in the famous old mining camp these days, and the citizens of that place are looking forward to better times. In quite a number of instances leasers are working in the old properties and are using the Standard mill for reducing and extracting gold and silver values.
    —Bridgeport Chronicle-Union, *November 19, 1932*

When Planning Your Weekend Recreation, Don't Forget The Dance That Will Be Held In Bodie This Saturday Night, July 15. The old Mining Camp is noted for the good time that is had at its dances and it is promised that this one will be more enjoyable than ever with the Rainbow Orchestra of Bishop furnishing the music.
    —Bridgeport Chronicle-Union, *July 12, 1939*

The Cain Properties

Through both development and purchase, the Standard Company had amassed approximately 60 miles of underground workings accessed through 12 shafts and two tunnels. In 1915 most of these were caving.[1] Few of the shafts had hoisting works, and everything below the 540-foot level was under water. Rather than endure the difficulties of overseeing a large-scale mining operation, owner James S. Cain opened the properties to leasers. The leasing system had been popular among the early claim owners of Tonopah and Goldfield, where it proved effective for rapidly developing the mines. Cain, too, had embraced leasing as a convenient way of capitalizing on his properties at Aurora and at Bodie's south end. The method placed most of the responsibilities and risks on the leaser, and was favored by owners who had little expendable cash and no stomach for managing a mine—especially one like the expansive, rundown, and decidedly worked-out Standard.

Except for the Syndicate group of mines on the northern slope of Bodie Bluff, the entire district was effectively owned by Cain. Anyone interested in mining had to sign a lease with him, and he made sure he received his share of the yield through lease agreements containing specific language.

LESSEES shall pay to LESSOR as rental or royalty, FIFTEEN PER CENT (15%) of the gross proceeds from all ores, tailings, concentrates, bullion, and other mill products recovered. The term "gross proceeds" used in the preceding sentence shall be deemed to mean the gross sale price

Figure 9-3: A big team leaves the Bodie railroad yard pulling two wagons loaded with lumber. (Emil Billeb collection. Courtesy, Vickie Daniels.

of all ores, tailings, concentrates, bullion and other mill products, without deduction for any milling, reduction or other treatment charges, transportation, or other costs or charges whatsoever.[2]

Not coincidentally, Cain also owned the Standard mill, the only stamp mill in the area that was in working order, and he charged for milling.

During the early years of Cain's ownership, leasers were often former Standard employees, who knew where to find profitable ore in the old workings. Because of these miners and their families, Bodie maintained its population of about 250 for a few years after the demise of its primary employer. The 20-stamp mill and cyanide plant ran regularly, and the railroad supplied necessary timbering. Leasers brought out enough gold- and silver-bearing ore during 1916 and 1917 that the district's overall production actually increased from that of the Standard's final years.[3]

Among the first to work one of Cain's newly acquired properties was a drifter who spent as much time in jail as he did in the mines. "Hobo Matt" Kelly

was known in many mining camps for his custom of working a few days, spending his wages on drink, then leaving town for another job. Kelly, a nephew of former mine superintendent Captain John Kelly, had been raised in Bodie, where, as a youth, he had worked in the Bodie Mine. It was said that he knew "every twist and turn" of the mine's underground, including the location of some very rich ore. Kelly brought his wife and children to Bodie in 1915, then he and a partner recovered a small fortune from the Bodie Mine. "In Bodie," reported the regional mining newspaper, "they claim that the share of 'Hobo Mat' will be in excess of fifty thousand dollars."[4]

At the same time, a Utah-based company considered spending several hundred thousand dollars to drive a three-mile drainage tunnel from Mono Basin to Bodie's 1,500-foot level. With modern mining and milling techniques, the planners felt that low-grade ore from the lower levels might be profitable and anticipated that the project would revive Bodie.[5] Except for the application of advanced technology, the idea was essentially the same as one proposed in

1888, after pumping in the Lent Shaft proved exorbitant. Like the earlier plan, nothing came of it.

The Mono Lake Railway operated seasonally, supplying Bodie's leasers with timbers, until the mining company in Aurora stopped work in 1917. Late in the year, the line, which included three remaining locomotives, rolling stock, rails, spikes, spur tracks, turntables, machine shops, and the big sawmill at Mono Mills, was sold for scrap. The equipment was dismantled in 1918, and its salvageable parts, mostly rails, were hauled from Mono Basin in motortrucks to Benton. There the salvage was loaded onto the Southern Pacific's Nevada & California Railway for delivery overseas.[6]

Interest in leasing at Bodie waned within five years of Cain's acquisition of the Standard. The 1920 census taker counted only 110 people.[7] "We were always poor," recalled Robert Bell. "Just scraped around to make some money." Bell's family and their neighbors, barely forming a community, occupied a few dwellings among hundreds of vacant structures. "In the 1920s, Bodie had been pretty dead for a long time," Bell remembered of his youth.

When the Standard shut down, there was nothing going on, but there were lots of leasers around town. The population was about 50 or 75, maybe 100. It varied from year to year. My dad, granddad, and uncles all had leases. The leasers were mostly two- or three-man operations.

Cain had a store—the old Boone store. George Langrell had a saloon down on the corner—the Sawdust Corner Saloon. He used to sell candy. Us kids weren't supposed to go in there, but he had the best candy in town. You could buy a candy bar for five cents. He had a player piano. When you put a nickel in the slot it would play you a hell of a tune. His mother ran the U.S. Hotel across the street. The Occidental Hotel was open, too. You could get a meal at the hotels. Some people lived in the hotels. You could rent a room and live there, or just stay overnight—either way.

There were a lot of vacant buildings in Bodie. The whole street was vacant. Most of the buildings on both sides of the street were locked up. Most of the houses were locked up, too—the people moved out. The church was vacant. . . . . We still had school though. Me and another kid had to stay after school an awful lot. They taught grades one through seven. There were only two classrooms, one up [stairs] and one down, but they only had us in one. Ella Cain was a teacher for a while. So was her daughter Helen Cain. Both taught school there.

There was no civic government in town as far as I can remember, just a justice of the peace—but he could put you in jail. The road through town is a county road. There were a few guys in Bodie who worked for the county to maintain the road. They kept a grader in town and hired a few guys. There was also a post office. . . . . Most people had cars, but a few still had horses, especially if they had to move anything heavy. My uncle had a cow. Some people left town for the winter, but most stayed around.[8]

Cain hired a local man to operate the pioneering power plant at Green Creek, where electricity was still generated for the mill and cyanide plant, though they seldom ran after 1917. Excess electricity was sold to the Southern Sierras Power Company, a network based at Bishop, of which Jordan's hydroelectric plant had been a part since 1913. Cain also provided electricity for the few inhabitants of Bodie until 1923, when he sold the Green Creek power plant. The plant's purchaser, the Mono Mines Company, built a new transmission line to its Silverado Mine near Bridgeport, leaving Bodie in the dark.

Denied electricity, the stalwart residents of Bodie reverted to kerosene lamps and gasoline lanterns to light their homes. The mill and cyanide plant, having also lost their power source, were connected to the commercial power network. Now Southern Sierras supplied electricity for treating ore on the few occasions when it was needed.[9]

Bodie was as close to being a ghost town as a place could be and still have occupants. Its overgrown streets were lined with weathered storefronts dating from an era long-romanticized by magazines, pulp fic-

Figure 9-4: Bodie showed the effects of neglect in the 1920s. Decaying buildings with peeling paint line overgrown streets, where trade with remaining inhabitants kept only a few businesses open. (Emil Billeb collection. Courtesy, Vickie Daniels)

Figure 9-5: Bodie was nearly abandoned in 1927, when a visiting photographer captured this ghostly scene on Main Street. (Burton Frasher photograph. Courtesy, Bancroft Library, University of California, Berkeley)

tion, and Wild West shows. Motion pictures now thrilled audiences with dramatizations that glamorized America's vanishing frontier. Enamored of western themes and heroes, sightseers motored to Bodie from great distances to experience a genuine relic of the Old West. "Tourists have been making themselves obnoxious," complained locals. "They have entered homes and have attempted to carry off other peoples goods as souvenirs. One lad attempted to carry off the lanterns belonging to the fire department, but was stopped from so doing. A few arrests would put an end to this kind of a thing."[10]

The years wore on, until only an occasional leaser, after a lot of hard work, would bring a few truckloads of ore to the Standard mill for crushing. Lester L. Bell was in charge of the mill, which was described by his son Robert.

We ran the mill for J. S. Cain in the late '20s and early '30s. The leasers were charged a flat fee per ton to mill their ore. We did the complete process, turning the bar of bullion over to Cain, who shipped it to the U.S. Mint in San Francisco. When the check arrived from the mint, Cain would keep his cut, pay us our wages, and give whatever was left to the leasers. Sometimes there wasn't much left for the leasers—if their ore was poor.

Usually we ran 10, 20, maybe 30 tons—three or four days' run at the most. A couple of times we ran 50 or 60 tons. More if it was low-grade. But it usually didn't make much of a showing on the plates. If there was only a ton or two, we only ran five stamps. I never ran more than ten of the stamps. We were stealing parts from two of the batteries to keep the other two running.

We got about 80% [of the assay value] with amalgamation alone. Didn't use the concentrators. We got as much gold by cleaning up the batteries as was on the plates. The scrapings from the amalgamation tables was squeezed through a flannel rag. We couldn't afford a chamois, so we used a piece of that real thick flannel, the kind you can't tear. . . . This reduced the amount of mercury with the gold. Then we retorted what was left.

We built a wood fire out in the street and had a retort that used a water-jacketed pipe to condense the mercury vapors. We built the fire in a 100-gallon barrel we had. We put the retort down in that. The end of the pipe stuck into a bucket of water to condense any vapors that came out the end. That way we didn't lose any mercury. The bottom of the retort was red hot and vaporized the quick[silver]. The water came from a garden hose.

Once the quick is boiled out, you have to melt the bullion in a crucible. We used the old company furnace across from the mill. They'd left about half a ton of coke in one of the buildings up there. You've got to have a coke fire with a draft or it won't get hot enough to melt the gold. We added some flux—borax and soda. . . . You couldn't get close to that crucible or it would set your clothes on fire. There was a great big pair of tongs to pick it up with. They hung from a tong drop. The slag would run around like hell and you'd have to keep your feet out of the way. The company used 1,000-ounce molds, but they had all sizes there. The bars they poured were great big old buggers. The bars of bullion we shipped were usually 10 pounds or less, and we shipped them by the U.S. Post Office, registered mail.[11]

Bell explained that the Standard cyanide plant also ran during these years.

Cain owned the cyanide plant then, and most of the tailings around town. Whenever he milled any ore for leasers, Cain would assay the tailings and give them some small amount for their value. A lot of times he got the tailings for nothing. Sometimes the tailings sat around for a couple of years. After enough tailings built up and dried out, Cain hired some men to run them through the plant. Cain made a lot of money on tailings.[12]

Individuals also brought tailings dug from deposits along Bodie Creek and abandoned mill sites, near and far. By this time the plant's high capacity filtering system had been dismantled, and four serviceable vats had been retrofitted with crude canvas filter-bottoms (reminiscent of Bodie's early plants) to treat tailings in small batches by percolation.

People would . . . get enough tailings to fill a tank or two. My Dad did it a few times. They'd find some old mill tailings someplace and run them through. The old Standard plant was still there then. It took 80 tons to fill a tank, but you didn't have to have that much. You could just put 20 tons or so in a tank and you'd get whatever gold was in it.[13]

Bell recalled a story about the Bodie Mine during this period.

One time a guy named Harwood and another guy took out a lease on the Bodie Mine where the Fortuna vein came across the shaft on the 400-foot level. The Bodie shaft went right through the Fortuna. The company left a big hunk of the vein there to support the shaft. All the rest of the vein had been stoped out, but nobody wanted to take out that last pillar because the ground would settle. Those two guys got a lease and went down there and got it. They took out about 25 tons of high-grade ore. We milled it for them and got a great big bar of bullion that weighed about 75 pounds and was worth $7,500. That was *bullion* — not pure gold. Bullion is a mixture of gold and silver. It was what

Figure 9-6: A massive gallows frame surmounts the Red Cloud shaft inside the abandoned hoisting works, where snow has invaded in 1922. One cage is poised at the surface while the other dangles below (hoisting cables were counter-wound to balance the load). Protecting the open shaft, a safety bonnet covers the right compartment, while the bonnet, at left, is perched atop the cage. Flat wire rope cables suspend the cages in the 870-foot shaft. At left, one of the locomotive-type headlights used to furnish interior and exterior lighting. (Emil Billeb collection. Courtesy, Vickie Daniels)

that of hired laborers performing the minimum amount of work required each year to retain ownership of a mining claim. Bell continued:

When I was a kid, my father and grandfather would take me up to the Red Cloud while they did the assessment work. They fired up the old boiler with a bunch of wood scraps they found laying around town. There was a spring over there on the hill that they used to fill the boiler. It was high enough above the mine that all you had to do was turn on a valve in the pipe to get water into the boiler. They didn't get a full head of steam, just 50 pounds [psi] or so. That was enough to operate the hoist. One of them would stay on top to run the hoist while a crew of men went down in the mine. They hoisted carload after carload of muck out of the mine and pushed it all out to the dump. Tons of muck went over the side of the dump. I was too young to run the hoist, so I just hung around and watched. It takes a lot of skill to run a steam hoist like that.[15]

After almost two decades of near-solitude, Bodie's south end suddenly became central to a new era of mining in 1928, when a newly organized corporation moved in. Promoted by showman and huckster Charles Courtney Julian, the Old Gold Mining Company leased the Red Cloud, Noonday, and other south end claims.[16]

Julian had achieved celebrity status during the 1920s for his relentless petroleum stock schemes, later known as the "Great Los Angeles Swindle." Familiar as C. C. Julian, he abandoned oil promotions in 1926 to choreograph a spectacular fleecing of investors

you call low-grade bullion—lots of silver in it. . . .

They wanted to ship it to the San Francisco mint by mail but found out the maximum size allowed was 50 pounds per package. They took a big cold chisel and a sledge hammer and busted it into three pieces. Took them all day, but they finally got it done.

After they took out all that rock, the ground down there settled and the shaft became all crooked. You've got to keep a shaft straight or the cage will hang up. There was some rich rock down there. That old Fortuna was tremendous.[14]

Cain did not have nearly as much luck leasing his south end properties, where the only activity was with an unprofitable Death Valley silver-bearing lead mine. "Lets go, folks, on 'WESTERN LEAD,' because it's time to twist her tail," read one of Julian's zany ads in the *Los Angeles Times*. "And every day you postpone placing your 'BUY' order is costing you money." [17] With the subtlety of a carnival barker, Julian razzle-dazzled gullible investors, until the California Corporation Commission announced an investigation into Western Lead.

Hounded by scandalous accusations, indictments, and a string of lawsuits, Julian arrived at Bodie in March 1928 to try mining gold for a change. He concluded that the relatively unexplored ground below Silver Hill was a likely place to start digging, and resolved to pump out the Red Cloud shaft and reach its lower levels. Old Gold repaired the shaft's timbering, replaced the steam-powered hoisting engine with an electric hoist, and installed a big 200-horsepower submersible electric pump. [18] Julian's need for abundant electricity reestablished power to the community, furnished by the region's network, Southern Sierras, and Bodie's inhabitants enjoyed electric lighting once again.

Pumping 500 gallons per minute, Old Gold's managers believed that the mine would be free of water in a month or two. They were still pumping nearly a year later, when the company gave up in May 1929 and forfeited its 10-year lease. The Bridgeport newspaper observed, "The job required eight months of uninterrupted pumping which drained forty-two miles of underground workings, extending to the Standard and Syndicate mines at the north end." [19] Although Old Gold had drained nearly every mine in Bodie, water in the Red Cloud was only down to the 726-foot level. Tired of the pitfalls and setbacks that complicated gold mining, Julian headed

Figure 9-7: Bodie was showing its age in 1928, when workers of several well-financed mining companies began arriving to revitalize the district. The weather-beaten and neglected town, captured on film by Palm Springs photographer Stephen Willard, greets Old Gold, Clinton-West, and Treadwell-Yukon employees with a display of mining camp spirit that reveals a taste for whiskey. (Stephen Willard photograph. Author's collection)

for Oklahoma and returned to petroleum speculation. He would be on the lam and evading creditors five years later, when he took his own life.[20]

Five months after Julian withdrew from Bodie, his lease was taken over, in September 1929, by the well-financed Treadwell-Yukon Company, Ltd. This prospecting entity had been formed in 1928 by two mining giants: the Bunker Hill and Sullivan Mining and Concentrating Company of Idaho, and the Alaska Juneau Gold Mining Company of Alaska. The latter was a consolidation of Alaska Treadwell Gold Mining Company, Alaska Mexican Gold Mining Company, and Alaska United Gold Mining Company.[21]

Organized specifically to discover new ore bodies that would perpetuate its parent companies, Treadwell-Yukon held rights to explore properties in Ontario, British Columbia, the Yukon, Nevada, Idaho, and Bodie. Its Bodie venture received substantial cash advances from the Hearst estate through the Homestake Gold Mining Company of South Dakota.[22]

Treadwell-Yukon began work at the Red Cloud by installing a second 200-horsepower submersible pump in the shaft. Raising 1,000 gallons per minute, the pumping continued for another year, costing $4,500 per month in power bills.[23] Robert Bell recounted some of the difficulties encountered.

They had a hand crank to lower the pumps as the water level went down. It worked fine going down, but it was too slow coming up. The electric pump motors had to stay above the water. Every once in a while some old workings would let go and the water in the shaft would rise about fifteen feet. The hand crank was too slow and the motors would go under water.[24]

Success was finally in sight in May 1930, when a Reno mining journal reported: "The water is practically all out of the Red Cloud shaft, which has been reclaimed to a depth of 850 feet, within 50 feet of

Figure 9-8: The south end came alive in 1929, when Treadwell-Yukon took over operations at the Red Cloud. Employing electric pumps, the company drained the shaft, then reopened the mine. The hoisting works, built in 1901, is shown amid newly-stockpiled lumber that will be used to support underground operations, where a battery-powered locomotive did away with mules for pulling mine cars through the extensive workings. (Courtesy, California Department of Parks and Recreation)

Figure 9-9: All adjacent mines were accessible from the Red Cloud shaft, where Treadwell-Yukon set up operations between 1929 and 1931. By this time, Bodie's lumber-hauling railroad had not operated in more than a decade, so trucks were used to deliver timbers needed to repair the shaft and support 22,000 linear feet of underground workings. (Courtesy, California Department of Parks and Recreation)

the bottom. This part of the shaft is filled with muck, old water columns and other debris which slows down the work."[25] A sinking pump was installed, and the shaft was drained to its bottom. Nearly a half century had passed since anyone had seen the 870-foot level of the mine.

Miners returned to the depths below Silver Hill, where they sought the Concordia, Noonday, Red Cloud, Oro, and Booker vein systems. To recover gold and silver from the ore, Treadwell-Yukon repaired the Standard mill. A bin was built on the hill behind to receive the rock, and a new wooden trestle conveyed the ore in mine cars into the mill. The company also added Union concentrators to handle the difficult south-end ore. Bell described the operation.

The Red Cloud ore was "sulfide rock" and would not amalgamate. It had to be concentrated, dried, sacked, and shipped to a smelter. All the ore from the Red Cloud went through the old Standard mill. They had two dump trucks that hauled from the ore bin at the Red Cloud dump to the mill, where they dumped it into a bin. They had a guy that ran back and forth from the chute to the mill pushing a mine car over the trestle. Treadwell fixed up the mill by putting concrete foundations under the stamps and adding those concentrators. . . . My father had an assay office in town where he did assaying for leasers. Then he went to work for Treadwell-Yukon. Up there they were running 100 samples a day. Two or three crews did nothing but take samples. . . . My father did assaying for them, then went to work operating the hoist at the Red Cloud.[26]

Treadwell-Yukon's Bodie operation took place during the Great Depression, while unpretentious locals carried on their usual livelihoods of leasing

ground in old mines or prospecting for new ones. Ed Gray, George Langrell, and Jack Holmes worked Gray's Blue Point Mine high on Standard Hill, crushing their ore in a 7-stamp mill they built in late 1927 on the site of the former Bodie Company's first mill. Powered by a Diesel engine, their little rock-pounding affair employed amalgamation and flotation. During the next four years, the partners milled about 100 tons of ore, which they trucked down the hill's eastern slope through Taylor Gulch.[27] "That mill

Figure 9-10: Bristling with carbide lamps, a Treadwell-Yukon miner poses outside the Red Cloud hoisting works. Pipes stacked in the foreground are casings for oil wells, brought in by C. C. Julian to use as water columns during his failed 1928 attempt to pump out the mine. Two miners were seriously injured underground in May 1931, when the round of holes they had drilled and loaded with explosives detonated before the men retreated to safety. (Francis H. Frederick collection. Courtesy, California Division of Mines and Geology)

could make you some good money crushing high-grade rock—if you had any," remarked Bell, stressing that gold mining at Bodie did not always produce riches.[28] In later years, leasers Carl Bloom and George Gunnerson took over Gray's operation.

Toiling in the big company's shadow, other locals also eked out their livings. Robert Bell and his father secured a six-month lease on a block of ground inside the Standard Mine, where the Bulwer Tunnel intersects the main shaft. Robert recalled the 1930 effort.

We worked a ledge in the Bulwer Tunnel 2,000 feet in—behind the Standard shaft. The ledge was about four feet wide and had a stringer about four inches wide between it and the hanging wall. It was above the big Bulwer Station. The company had left it because it supported the station above. . . . The stringer was real high-grade, about $200 or $300 a ton. The rest of the ledge was just $10 rock. We dumped that. Cain was charging us $6 a ton to mill, so with Cain's percentage and our labor figured in, my Dad decided [the low-grade ore] wasn't worth monkeying with. . . .

We didn't use powder. The ledge was so soft we could break it out with a picky poke bar. We broke it down from the hanging wall. There was a lamination between the ledge and the hanging wall and foot wall, and it broke off clean. We dumped the $10 rock down the old Ralston stope. You could really hear those rocks clattering around down there in the dark. It was a real job pushing the loaded cars uphill to dump them. We didn't bother running an air line because we were so far back in the mine. Didn't do any drilling anyway. . . . I was about 16 then. The Bulwer Tunnel level had caved into the shaft a long time before we started working in there. Most of the high-grade ore in that ledge—about 90% of it—went down the shaft. There were some timbers there that held some of it back. That is where we worked. We only got out about $2,000. We would have gotten $20,000 if we could have gotten it all. . . . That was the last time anybody worked in the Standard Mine.[29]

Bodie's gold- and silver-bearing ore had been its primary source of wealth, and Treadwell-Yukon was intent on exploiting that fact. But the resource that sustained the town through the late 1930s and into the early 1940s was not its mines, nor its placer gravels, nor even in its tailings ponds. It was precious metals contained in two enormous piles of waste rock discarded years earlier from the Standard Mine. Like giant hands with extended fingers, these massive man-made mountains of dumped rock reached outward from the mine's two main entrances. Stretching from the mouth of the Standard shaft, one pile overspread the south slope of High Peak. The other, extending from the mouth of the Bulwer Tunnel, almost blocked Bodie Canyon. These two dumps represented what miners call "development work," the material removed while sinking shafts, driving tunnels, crosscutting, and drifting. In other words, it was the rock they had blasted out of the way to reach the silver- and gold-laden quartz veins. The two dumps held an estimated 400,000 tons of nearly barren broken rock, assaying at most $5 per ton, with an average value of about $3 per ton.[30]

Recovering gold and silver from such low-grade rock, and returning a profit, required an exceptional treatment process. The first attempt had been in 1918, shortly after the railroad was dismantled. Emil Billeb, George Denham, and J. S. Cain's son, Victor, secured a lease on the piles of discarded rock, and built an electric-powered cyanide plant just below the Standard dump on the hill. They tore down the South End cyanide plant and used its parts to construct the new facility, which used the percolation method of cyaniding that had been introduced nearly a quarter of a century earlier. Six leaching vats, four solution tanks, and four zinc precipitation boxes headed its list of equipment. Instead of stamps, two sets of rolls, 14 by 24 inches and 14 by 36 inches, crushed the rock. Employing eight men, the operation ran on a small scale for a couple of years. It was unprofitable largely because the waste rock contained clay, which clogged the primitive canvas filter-bottoms. When the dumps proved unworkable, the idea of treating them was dropped for another decade. Al-

Figure 9-11: Three years after the J. S. Cain Company took over the Standard's property, a group of locals attempted to recover gold and silver from the mine's dump. Using parts from the South End Cyanide Plant, this electric-powered plant was built in 1918, below the huge mountain of waste rock stretching outward from the Standard shaft. An unfinished side reveals one of six cyanide vats. (Emil Billeb collection. Courtesy, Vickie Daniels)

though the plant was intended to process waste rock, it was reopened briefly in 1921 to cyanide tailings hauled by truck from Masonic. Otherwise, it sat idle.[31]

In the fall of 1928, while Julian was struggling to pump out the Red Cloud shaft, E. J. Clinton, the owner of a chain of San Francisco cafeterias, and W. D. "Billy" West, a mining man with Klondike experience, headed the second attempt to work Bodie's waste rock. Clinton-West Company, Inc. built a treatment plant on top of the Standard dump. It was an odd-looking pyramidal affair, sometimes referred to as a "dry-land dredge" because, when an area was worked out, it moved under its own power to a new spot. A drag line with a two-cubic-yard bucket fanned out, scooping up rocks and pulling them into the machinery. Inside, modern equipment consisting of a cone crusher and a tube mill ground the rocks to sand, after which amalgamation and mechanical concentration recovered the gold and silver.[32]

When it was learned that the Clinton-West plant only recovered 60% of the assay value, testing showed that extraction could be increased to 95% by using flotation, a method of concentration that isolated metallic particles in a froth of bubbles. Equipment modifications were begun in August 1929. The plant's crushers were altered to grind the rock finer, and flotation cells were installed to recover particles of gold and silver sulphurets. The process required large quantities of water. Since Bodie's municipal water system had sufficient pressure to keep the reservoir full, but not enough to reach the plant surmounting the dump on High Peak, Clinton built a water tank that resembled those used by railroads. Treadwell-Yukon, having taken over pumping in the south end, kept it filled by sending water from the Red Cloud through a four-inch pipe. By mid-November 1929, Clinton had all the parts assembled, and his dredge began scratching away at the Standard dump.[33]

"E. J.," as Clinton was called, made himself at home in Bodie. He enrolled his three children in school and set up housekeeping in the abandoned

Figure 9-12: Late in 1928, this metallurgical monstrosity was assembled atop the Standard dump by the Clinton-West Company to treat waste rock that had been discarded during 38 years of underground mining. Known as a "dry land dredge," it moved from place to place under its own power, while a drag line, partially shown at right, pulled bucket loads of broken rock into the machinery. After two years of tinkering, the plant was abandoned and stripped for parts. (Emil Billeb collection. Courtesy, Vickie Daniels)

he shut the plant down for Sunday and all the pipes froze. It was two or three weeks before they got it running again."[34]

The families of Clinton-West's 20-man crew and Treadwell-Yukon's 150-man force swelled Bodie's population from 30 to about 400. The schoolhouse received a fresh coat of paint to welcome a throng of pupils, and previously unoccupied stores and restaurants opened to new customers. Overall, the town presented "quite a busy appearance" as its streets became congested with automobiles.[35] Traffic was further snarled by tourists, who drove into town to glean a sense of nostalgia from a living legend of the Old West. To accommodate popular modes of transportation, Cain opened gasoline pumps at the Boone store on Main Street. "When Treadwell moved in," added Bell, "about 20 saloons opened up."

That was Prohibition. You weren't supposed to have booze, but Bodie still had saloons. Hell, I guess they had saloons! The whole street was full of them. There were a lot of people in town then—lots of kids too. . . . Everywhere was gambling. They had all kinds of it, even roulette wheels and a few other things that took your money. There were a lot of gambling joints there. The '30s was when things were really wheeling and dealing. The lights were on all night, I'll tell ya.[36]

It seems that some things never change. Bell remembered another aspect of Bodie's twentieth-century boom that recalled earlier bonanza days.

railroad office on the hill. By installing indoor plumbing, he turned the old train station into something of a mansion, at least by Bodie standards. His new plumbing fixtures used water supplied by the nearby tank. Clinton also extended his influence among the few remaining Bodieites and the families of his workers and those employed by Treadwell-Yukon. He renovated the Protestant church, and with his wife's help began delivering Sunday sermons. "Clinton was so religious that he wouldn't work on Sunday," recalled Bell. "He used to hold services every week in the old church. He was a pretty good preacher. One winter

Figure 9-13: During Bodie's brief but intense 1928 to 1931 revival, old, venerable Main Street establishments enjoyed increased trade, and other businesses opened to accommodate an influx of miners and their families. Several boomtown vices returned as well, invited by a scarcity of law enforcement officials. Still, Bodie's remote location provided little protection for lawbreakers in September 1930, when federal prohibition officers raided the town and arrested about 15 local entrepreneurs for selling liquor in violation of the Eighteenth Amendment. (Stephen Willard photograph. Courtesy Gregory Bock)

Figure 9-14: "Big Dance at Bodie," reads an announcement painted on a makeshift panel truck. Dances at the Miners Union hall were all-night, intemperate celebrations that drew ballroom cavorters from Bridgeport, Lee Vining, Hawthorne, Yerington, and Bishop. Briefly repopulated, Main Street is shown in 1930. Two years later, the large mining companies had departed, and Bodie was nearly deserted when fire swept this section of town. (Courtesy, Gregory Bock)

Figure 9-15: Bodieites were never far from their gold mining heritage. A gathering at the Protestant church socializes in sight of distant hills, where Clinton-West's failed plant pierces the skyline. (Burton Frasher photograph. Author's collection)

There were three or four places that were running gals. They were in Chinatown and a few other places around town. Sam Leon, the Chinaman, had two or three girls in the U.S. Hotel. He brought them up from San Francisco. One of them was known around town as the "Pink Rabbit." She was just about as good looking as a woman can get. They were in town to make money. That's a mining town for ya! If they haven't got booze and women, everybody will leave.[37]

The dry-land dredge processed about 300 tons of rock daily. The concentrates it developed were shipped via Thorne to the Selby smelter in central California, where they were treated and reduced to bullion. In the end, however, the plant frustrated every attempt to make it profitable. Beset by shutdowns, it ran only 35 days during 1930.[38] Clinton forfeited his lease on the Standard dumps and left town in September. "The going of the Clintons," fretted the Bridgeport paper, "is regretted by many of the Bodie people, who wish them better luck in their new undertakings than they experienced at Bodie."[39]

Clinton-West had labored on High Peak for nearly two years. At the time it gave up, Treadwell-Yukon had drained the Red Cloud and was pressing its search for profitable ore below Silver Hill. Although its main interest was underground mining, Treadwell-Yukon decided to try treating rock from the Standard dumps. The Clinton-West lease was purchased, and, for an extra $25,000, the dry-land dredge was thrown into the deal. The plant was stripped of its usable parts, including its sheet metal skin, and for a number of years its skeletal ruins remained perched atop the dump on High Peak. Visible from town, the rusting triangular framework loomed on the horizon as a peculiar kind of memorial to failed twentieth-century technology. Treadwell-Yukon used the salvaged equipment to remodel the Billeb/Denham/Cain cyanide plant, where its engineers performed experiments to develop a large-scale process for treating Bodie's mine dumps.

High on the hill, Treadwell-Yukon's power shovel dug into the Standard dump, and two 7-ton dump trucks hauled the rock to the new test plant. The first trial run was completed on Christmas Eve, 1930. By using a combination of cyaniding and flotation, managers hoped that 400 tons could be handled per day. Throughout most of 1931, adjustments were made, equipment was modified, and machines were tried.[40]

Meanwhile, miners working the Red Cloud a mile to the south were piercing the darkness below Silver Hill with a 3,000-foot crosscut. From the 700-foot level, they drove southeastward, hoping to intersect extensions of the great bonanza veins to the north. They found a high-grade streak that produced

Figure 9-16 and 9-17: Treadwell-Yukon purchased Clinton-West's lease in late 1930, expecting to find an inexpensive method to process low-grade waste rock from Bodie's dumps. Forming the lower portion of Treadwell's test facility, the Billeb/Denham/Cain cyanide plant (figure 9-11) was fitted with parts salvaged from Clinton-West's dry-land dredge. When no satisfactory combination of cyaniding and flotation could be found, the experiments were abandoned after less than a year. (Emil Billeb collection. Courtesy, Vickie Daniels)

Treadwell-Yukon's first bullion in January 1931. Its size, however, was insufficient to overcome the formidable cost of pumping and make the Red Cloud a paying proposition.

After exhausting the vein, Treadwell-Yukon terminated its underground operations at Bodie in October 1931. Working slightly more than two years, the company had opened about 22,000 lineal feet of new and old tunneling, looking for an ore body that would sustain its industry. It had invested about $1,000,000 dollars, but recovered only $90,771. The south end was abandoned again, concluding the last significant underground mining at Bodie.[41]

When Treadwell-Yukon quit the Red Cloud, 35 of its employees were kept on to run the test plant at the Standard dump. Mono County residents were confident that when the technical problems were solved, Bodie would become a large-scale producer again. Experiments were given up two months later. Company experts revealed that they could not recover more than 60 cents from each ton of rock.[42] "The past week saw about the last of the Treadwell-Yukon Company's operations at Bodie," lamented the Bridgeport newspaper. "It is . . . regretted that this company, after expending so much money in its efforts to extract the gold values from the dumps was unable to do so at a profit, for their stay in Mono County added very materially in the employment of a number of men, all of whom were paid good wages."[43]

Bodie's mines were worked out and flooded. Its tailings ponds were depleted, and every attempt to recover gold and silver from its waste rock had failed. The recent four-year assault by heavily financed companies had produced little more than a brief population surge and a spasm of interest. Except for a few steadfast locals, the town was nearly deserted again. Yet faith was not totally lost. The newspaper editor in Bridgeport believed that the district could still come back.

> It might be noted that even though the Treadwell people failed to extract the gold . . . it does not mean that the values are not there; it is acknowledged that they are there, but that the methods used were not of a character to successfully get results of extraction in paying quantities. . . . It is hoped . . . that in the near future, some company will come in and be successful in extracting the gold values from the big Standard Hill mine dumps.[44]

Five months later, on Thursday afternoon, June 23, 1932, a second disastrous fire swept away about 75% of Bodie's business district. The blaze was believed to have been started by a boy playing with matches.[45] Flames spread rapidly from a vacant building behind the Sawdust Corner Saloon. The few remaining inhabitants dragged out leaky fire hoses to fight the flames. When the hydrants were opened, rocks came through the neglected screens at the reservoir and clogged the nozzles. Any hope of controlling the flames was dashed. From one side of Main Street to the other, flames spread unchecked and familiar old buildings were reduced to ashes: the U.S. Hotel, Occidental Hotel, Masonic hall, and J. S. Cain's bank. Also destroyed were the barrooms: the Sawdust Corner, Bodie Club, Butterfly Resort, and others.[46] "The hotels were gone, the bank was gone, the stores were gone—nothing much was left," recalled Bell. "Most of the people had to leave because they had nothing left. They all got burned out. The population was maybe 20 or 30—just a few leasers and their families."[47]

In September, Bell's father and grandfather leased a block of ground in the Noonday Mine. At age 18, Robert helped set up a makeshift hoist at the old Noonday shaft.

> My dad and granddad got a lease from Cain to work on the 200-foot level of the Noonday. They knew where there was some high-grade rock that the company didn't get. It was a stringer, a little bitty old thing. We didn't get much out of it—only about a ton or two—but it was all high-grade. . . . We used bars to dig out the ore, then broke the wall rock down with powder. Had to do all the drilling by hand. We were in too far for [compressed] air. . . . The shaft was . . . already

beginning to cave. It still had the old gallows frame and sheaves—built heavy enough to handle cages. We rigged it up with an ore bucket and used a Model T Ford engine for a hoist. Set it up right there in the hoist house next to the old boiler.[48]

They climbed to and from the 200-foot level on rickety ladders left behind by earlier miners, and used their dump truck to haul ore to the Standard mill, where they ran it through the stamps. Bell continued:

We worked out there quite a while—about a month. Didn't get much, only about $1,200. We were the only ones working out there back then. The shaft caved right after that—took the gallows frame down with it.[49]

One could reasonably assume that the pickings were mighty poor at Bodie. Even its venerable Bodie Mine, worked for nearly 40 years, was stoped out. Yet legendary gold mines have a way of overcoming good sense, and hope persisted that some rich ore, perhaps even a long-sought segment of the Fortuna lode, might be found. Late in April 1933, headlines in Bridgeport cried out, "Big Strike Made At Bodie."

From the famous old mining camp of Bodie, comes the good word of another of those big strikes for which the camp was famous in its better days. Working from the 400 foot level of the old Bodie mine, Bert Davis, Sam Leon and Joe Mosier, struck what is believed to be the old Fortuna vein, famous in its day for its richness. . . . It is said that the rock being brought out from the mine is rich in high gold values, and will yield upwards of $1,000 per ton of this much sought valuable mineral. Lester Bell, who from long experience in the Bodie mine, states that there is little doubt in his mind but that the men have struck the famous Fortuna Vein, for he says it bears all the peculiar characteristics of the same.[50]

Everybody in Mono County scrutinized the article and wondered if Bodie would boom again. Robert Bell recalled that any optimism was exaggerated.

Those guys were my neighbors. Sam Leon was a Chinaman. He owned a bar and restaurant—a real businessman. Sam put up the money to eat on while they were working the Bodie Mine. The mine had already been stoped out. They went down in those old stopes and pulled down some good specimens, but not much worth milling. Just a few small stringers and little pieces of high-grade rock that the company left behind. Those guys didn't make much money on it. My dad made it sound like they made a big discovery, but all they were doing was scratching around in those old stopes. The big ore body was already gone. You can find high-grade down there, but you have to pick through the rocks like a chicken.[51]

During the Great Depression, the federal government contributed to the revival of gold mining in 1933 by raising the price of gold from $20.67 an ounce (where it had been essentially fixed since 1837) to $25.56. The figure was increased to $34.95 the following year, then to $35 in 1935.[52] Unemployed and destitute miners returned to many of the old camps to prospect or eke out a living by leasing. Such was not the case at Bodie, where the last two underground leases were worked in 1935. "That was the last rock that ever went through that old mill," affirmed Bell.[53]

Cain left Bodie that year, clinging to his belief that there was still gold in the hills. All it would take, he thought, was someone with sufficient capital to exploit it. From his home in San Francisco, he continued promoting the district, often saying, "Bodie can and will come back as a good producing camp."[54]

Expecting profits if Bodie ever boomed again, Cain had purchased numerous abandoned buildings that could be rented to newcomers. To safeguard his investment, a watchman was hired to protect what was left of the nearly deserted town from sightseers who were tempted to break into unoccupied buildings and steal the contents. This single act probably saved Bodie from being thoroughly ransacked and hauled away by souvenir hunters, a fate that ultimately befell nearby Aurora and other western ghost towns.

Figure 9-18 and 9-19: In 1936 the Roseklip Mines
Company built this plant to treat waste rock from the
Standard dumps. During the next six years, 346,000 tons of
rock disappeared through its cyanide vats, changing Bodie's
skyline forever. The operation closed in 1942, when
restrictions during World War II made it impossible to get
materials essential to recovering precious metals. (Emil
Billeb collection. Courtesy, Vickie Daniels)

Bodie's revival seemed imminent in 1936, when Jack Rosecrans and Henry Klipstein enlisted the Western-Knapp Engineering Company to design a state-of-the-art cyanide plant for processing the waste rock in the Standard dumps. They built a modern treatment complex on the hill where Treadwell-Yukon's failed test plant once stood, and constructed a dam to impound tailings in Taylor Gulch. On Saturday night, October 10, 1936, Bodie held a dance

Figure 9-20: Treadwell-Yukon, followed by Roseklip, changed the face of mining at Bodie by employing power shovels and dump trucks to recover mineral wealth from low-grade rock. (Emil Billeb collection. Courtesy, Vickie Daniels)

to celebrate the start of the 250-ton-per-day Roseklip plant. Expecting an influx of workers and their scholarly offspring, the schoolhouse was reopened. But a population boom never came. The company's 35 employees and their families brought the number of residents to only 113. Instead of rebuilding the town, newcomers found lodging among decaying dwellings that had survived the fire. James S. Cain died in San Francisco on October 28, 1938. He had lived just long enough to see the Roseklip Mines Company begin the last large-scale recovery operation in Bodie.[55]

Even to those living in a virtual ghost town, the Miners Union hall was the center for social gatherings. The venerable old building had not witnessed a union meeting since the Standard Company failed more than a quarter of a century earlier, but, during the late 1930s, it became the site for impromptu dances. Its wooden floor, which had supported dancers for decades, was in good condition, and chairs lined the walls. An upright piano, played by one of the housewives, would often be accompanied by a workman or two with a banjo, fiddle, or guitar. Except for the shift on duty at the plant, "Everyone came," a former Roseklip employee recalled, "even children."[56]

Roseklip's plant utilized sophisticated equipment manufactured by leaders in the field of mineral extraction: a crusher by Traylor, a tube mill, scrubber, and hydro-separator by Hardinge, two Kraut flotation cells, two Dorr classifiers, diatomaceous-earth filters, and a Merrill-Crowe precipitation system. This thoughtfully engineered combination of machines efficiently exploited Bodie's mine dumps. Producing a yearly average that was slightly less than $188,000, the plant succeeded where its three predecessors had failed.[57] For the next three years, the huge, man-made mountain of broken rock atop High Peak slowly disappeared as it fell victim to a power shovel and a couple of 10-ton dump trucks. The work continued until the entire rock pile, a monument to 80 years of underground mining, was ground to dust and fed through the cyanide vats. In 1940, the plant was enlarged to handle 500 tons per day, and the trucks started hauling away the dump at the mouth of the Bulwer Tunnel. Once the cyanide plant had consumed that mound, the big shovel started digging above the Standard Mine, gouging out small quartz veins immediately below the surface. By 1942, 346,000 tons of dumped rock and 55,000 tons of ore from surface cuts

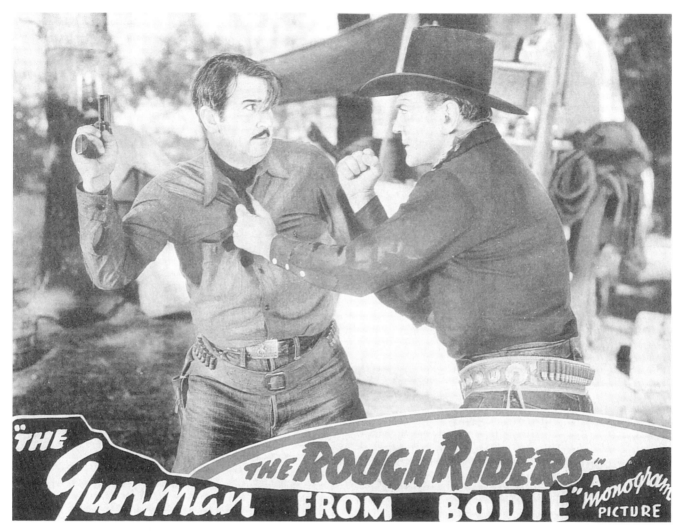

Figure 9-21: By the time Roseklip set up Bodie's last large-scale recovery operation, popular forms of entertainment had elevated cowboys to mythical status in western lore. Bodie, rich in gold mining history, was incorrectly linked to cowboys when the 1941 motion picture, *The Gunman From Bodie* featured a trio of celluloid heroes known as the "Rough Riders." Ignoring Bodie's true past, the film starred Buck Jones, at right, in the title role as a federal marshal disguised as a cattle-rustling ranch boss. (Monogram Pictures Corporation. Author's collection)

had gone through the plant.[58]

While Roseklip's trucks were hauling away Bodie's hillsides, the town was unexpectedly recognized in Hollywood, where references to the West's colorful past lent credence to imaginary story lines. The 1941 motion picture *The Gunman From Bodie* starred Buck Jones playing a federal marshal posing as a corrupt cattleman. The town was not featured in the film, which contained dialogue that upheld the cinematic tradition of contradicting history.

"Have you ever been around Bodie?" asks a land-grabbing lawyer, worried that the hardened rustler has recognized him.

"Yeah, why?" the black-clad, gunslinging range boss responds forcefully.

"Ever see me before?" the nervous attorney inquires.

"Yeah," replies the cunning lawman, preserving his rustler disguise. "It was up on the Bar T Ranch. I was one of the hands when you pulled that deal."[59]

Moviegoers across the country watched spellbound as fast-shooting cowboys galloped back and forth on the silver screen, but few in the audience were aware, or even cared, that Bodie was a *mining* town, not a *cattle* town.

Hollywood's disregard for historical facts was irrelevant at Bodie, where little remained of its gilt edge. When World War II broke out, the Roseklip Company was classified as a producer of nonstrategic metals, a priority rating so low that it could not obtain essential supplies. It closed in April 1942. Soon thereafter the War Production Board issued Limitation Order No. L-208 to release manpower for producing copper, lead, zinc, and other metals vital to the war effort. The order ended most gold mining across the country for the duration of hostilities.[60] The loss of Bodie's last significant employer ended another phase in its history. School opened that fall with an enrollment of only five children. "With mining activity in the old camp dwindling rapidly," observed a Bridgeport reporter, "it is doubtful if sufficient pupils will remain in Bodie to keep the school open during the entire term."[61]

Epilogue: 1942-Present

Any hopes that J. S. Cain might have held of preserving Bodie intact had been dashed by the 1932 fire. The mining district was next to suffer large-scale destruction, when outmoded machinery was hauled away during World War II in patriotic response to scrap metal drives. "In the town of Bodie alone is enough scrap iron to keep several trucks busy hauling for some time," reported the Bridgeport newspaper. "The majority of the scrap has been laying in the same place for the past twenty years or longer." Historic preservation was not a consideration as people focused on more urgent goals. "The purpose of this drive is to get all this junk and scrap gathered up and at central points in the communities where it can be loaded onto trucks and shipped to the foundries."[62] As early as November 1942, Bodie had shipped 120 tons of scrap metal, and the county chairman estimated that approximately 500 tons were still scattered around town awaiting removal.[63]

When gold mining was permitted to resume in 1945, Sierra Mines, Inc., secured a lease from the J. S. Cain Company to continue where Roseklip had left off. In April 1946, workers were repairing and enlarging the plant when it caught fire and burned to the ground.[64]

There must have been something touchingly pathetic about the end of the industry that had fueled Bodie's spirit. Still, the old town remained a link to the Old West. To minimize plundering of historic artifacts by thoughtless visitors, the Cain Company's watchman remained on duty. Even under his watchful eye, thieves were sometimes successful. "It is beyond understanding what people will do," Billeb wrote, lamenting the theft of children's caskets from the building used as a mortuary.[65] Cemeteries were desecrated, headstones were taken, and even the firehouse bell was stolen (and recovered) twice.

Rumors of undiscovered bonanzas buried within the hills continued to find believers, and miners, usually former residents, drifted back to Bodie from time to time to prospect or work their claims. None of them unearthed anything of value, and the Standard mill never ran again.[66] In July 1954, the Standard cyanide plant was destroyed by a spectacular fire that some believe was ignited by careless tourists.[67]

The vigilant watchman continued to patrol the town's lonely streets, pausing occasionally to indulge tourists by telling a story or two about Bodie's past. The caretaker who filled the position in the 1950s routinely drove his beat in a Model A Ford with a 12-gauge shotgun and a bottle of wine by his side. "That crazy old fool," remembered Bell. "He was half drunk all the time, and you couldn't trust him with that shotgun." By the early 1960s, a more restrained watchman wore a silver star inscribed "DEPUTY SHERIFF, MONO COUNTY."[68]

During these quiet years, Victor and Ella Cain of Bridgeport acquired more Bodie properties on behalf of the J. S. Cain Company, intending to ensure the town's preservation. Foremost among their acquisitions was the schoolhouse where Ella had taught. Instead of watching it razed for scrap lumber, they bought the old building after the county put it up for sale. The Cains also opened a museum in the Miners Union hall, where they displayed a collection of historic Bodie artifacts.[69]

Figure 9-22: Two mid-twentieth century fires nearly swept the district of its few remaining industrial buildings. When the Roseklip plant burned down in the first fire, on April 3, 1946, plans to resume large-scale recovery operations ended. The building had been undergoing repairs after World War II in anticipation of treating low grade rock from mine dumps. (Courtesy, California Department of Parks and Recreation)

Figure 9-23: Except for a hired watchman and his wife, a miner or two, and a family that kept a café in the old brick post office, Bodie was deserted when a second mid-twentieth-century fire destroyed the Standard slimes plant in July 1954. In less than a decade the old mining town would become a California state historic park. (Emil Billeb collection. Courtesy, Vickie Daniels)

Figure 9-24

Figure 9-25

Figure 9-26

Figure 9-27

Figure 9-28

Figure 9-24: Silent and overgrown with sagebrush, the abandoned Red Cloud was the district's only remaining hoisting works in 1962, when Bodie was designated a California state park. The smokestack stands as a reminder of the use of steam for power when the works was built in 1901. A nearby sub-station provided electricity for pumping and hoisting between 1928 and 1931, when trucks, loaded from the bin at right, hauled ore to the Standard mill. (Courtesy, California Department of Parks and Recreation)

Figure 9-25: A 1970 view looks south along the lonely road that winds through the district's south end, where the abandoned Red Cloud stands in eerie silence. A corrugated iron building, built by Treadwell-Yukon, contains a carpenter shop for framing mine timbers and a blacksmith shop, in which air-powered drills were sharpened. The Noonday Mine is visible in the distance. (Photograph by the author)

Figure 9-26: Haunting stillness and ghostly desolation recall the sadness of unfulfilled hope. Viewed from the dump in 1970, the Red Cloud Mine is strewn with discarded pieces of equipment. The gallows frame stood over the shaft at this end of the building. The attached shed housed two reels used to raise and lower the 200-horsepower electric pumps installed in 1928 and 1929. A wooden storage building stands to the left. (Photograph by the author)

Figure 9-27: The Noonday Mine produced more than $1 million in gold and silver during Bodie's boom years, but the Noonday and Red Cloud companies went out of existence heavily in debt. This 1969 view reveals nothing of the magnificent Noonday hoisting works that once symbolized the giddy delusion of gold fever. A humble hoist house, left behind by leasers, contains a small steam hoist and integral boiler. (Courtesy, David E. Shell)

Figure 9-28: The diminutive hoist house at the Noonday shaft is seen in 1970, three years before its machinery was moved to Bodie State Historic Park. Absent from the scene is the gallows frame, which was swallowed by the shaft when it caved shortly after the mine was last worked in 1932. (Photograph by the author)

Figure 9-29: Preserved at Bodie State Historic Park, the steam-powered double-drum hoisting engine from the Noonday hoist house (raised letters read: "Prescott Scott & Co, Builders, San Francisco, Cal, 1878"). The hoist and integral boiler give little hint of the mine's former glory. Silver Hill and the district's south end dominate the background. (Photograph by the author)

Figure 9-30: Exhibited at Bodie State Historic Park, the electric hoist used at the Red Cloud Mine by Treadwell-Yukon during its short-lived attempt to mine the south end. (Photograph by the author)

Figure 9-31: Representing many time periods, equipment from the Red Cloud Mine is on display at Bodie State Historic Park. From left: an air compressor with a Pelton-type water wheel that was adapted in 1911 to run by electric motor (raised letters read: "Risdon Iron Works 1896"); a double-reel steam hoisting engine with flat wire rope cables that was installed when the hoisting works was built in 1901 (raised letters read: "Prescott, Scott & Co. 1880"); the mine's gallows frame and sheaves; the boiler (raised letters read: "Prescott & Scott 1880"); and two geared reels which raised and lowered the 200-horsepower electric pumps used between 1928 and 1931. In the distance, Bodie Bluff and High Peak, where Bodie's most profitable mines were located. (Photograph by the author)

Seeking relief from the expense of protecting the town, the J. S. Cain Company had, since about 1954, been exploring ways of turning its Bodie holdings over to the State of California. The Division of Beaches and Parks, concerned with potentially high restoration and maintenance costs, declined all offers until officials realized that Bodie should be preserved as a ghost town and not restored.

The famous old town was watched over by a park ranger after 1962, when it became a California State Historic Park under the Department of Parks and Recreation. Land added to the park between then and 1967 comprised 324 acres acquired from the Cain Company, the Bell and Loose families, the Roman Catholic Church, Mono County, and others. In 1982, an additional 132 acres were purchased from the Cain Company, and the 40-acre cemetery was obtained from the U.S. Bureau of Land Management.[70]

The town's surviving structures and the 495 or so acres on which they sit were now safeguarded. The mining district, however, remained in the hands of private owners, many of whom were descendants of Cain. This group, which controlled the J. S. Cain Company and the mineral claims it owned, continued pursuing ways to profit from leasing the properties. Phelps Dodge Corporation, the American Smelting and Refining Company, and the Homestake Mining Company considered terms that would allow the resumption of a large-scale recovery operation. Those interested in preserving Bodie were relieved when none of these companies found reason to begin a modern-day mining process that would certainly have displaced enough earth to reduce the famous hills to nubs. Meanwhile, the south end's abandoned Red Cloud hoisting works was partially destroyed by fire. The works and adjacent structures, along with those of the Noonday, were judged a safety hazard and torn down. In 1973, their machines were moved to the state park where they are displayed as static exhibits.

The most recent threat to Bodie's legendary hills came in 1988, when Galactic Resources, Ltd. began exploratory drilling on Bodie Bluff and High Peak. Their probes determined that the hills contained between 1,000,000 and 40,000,000 ounces of gold, requiring an open-pit process to recover it. Despite Galactic's promises to the contrary, the wholesale destruction of landscape behind the Standard mill would have ruined Bodie's historic setting. The very thought of earth-moving equipment taking away the hills was gut-wrenching to everyone who cherished the old town, no matter how many ounces of gold might be recovered.

Galactic was confronted by a committee of the California State Park Ranger Association called SAVE BODIE! and a grassroots movement named the Eastern Sierra Citizens for the Protection of Bodie. Joining the protest were the National Trust for Historic Preservation and the Wilderness Society. Meanwhile, the National Park Service identified Bodie as an endangered National Historic Landmark in its annual report to Congress. While California used existing laws and regulations to check Galactic's progress, the company suffered financial difficulties stemming from environmental violations elsewhere that delayed the destruction long enough for Congress to pass the Bodie Protection Act of 1994. This legislation discouraged further mineral exploitation by prohibiting new mining claims and subjecting work on old claims to stringent requirements intended to prevent adverse effects on the Bodie townsite. In the summer of 1997, the hills that comprise the mining district became immune to further development when 564 acres east of town were purchased by the state and added to Bodie State Historic Park.[71]

Those who visit Bodie are struck by the stark landscape and weathered structures, which merely hint at the events that took place years ago. Mining at Bodie began in 1859 with the arrival of a small band of adventurous prospectors and ended nearly a century later with the departure of a few solitary miners and their families. In the interim, the belief that opportunity was within grasp lured thousands to Bodie, where buried riches once caused a mining sensation.

The excitement was short-lived. In retrospect,

Bodie's mines never came close to fulfilling the expectations of fortune seekers and enthusiastic stockbrokers, who believed that its hills concealed another Comstock Lode. To the generation that experienced America during the 1870s, the Comstock was the most prodigious mining district ever seen, eventually producing about $380,000,000.[72] By comparison, Bodie's total bullion production was meager at $34,000,000.

For a few years, while the West was wild, Bodie had a fearsome reputation for deadly mayhem that rivaled all other contemporary boomtowns. Stories about its wickedness were widespread, but to those who lived there, Bodie's style of danger was merely a sideshow. What really mattered to them and the world outside was its industry. The fact is, most people came to Bodie with no greater expectation than to earn a living.

Bodie's mines no longer provide for it, and we must experience the old town in its afterglow. Bodie belongs to the West, a place that is still young, yet we walk along its silent streets and sense that the chance for opportunity has already passed. Perhaps we gaze upon a vacant house and feel the spirit of people who lived and worked in this desolate place.

The Old West died a long time ago. What remains is frequently masked by a make-believe West crafted in disregard of historical fact. Today, efforts in preservation and restoration are saving many buildings and relics, while persistent research is correcting the errors of writers, showmen, and filmmakers who freely distorted and embellished the past. Other historic western towns ensconce themselves in popular history for the entertainment of tourists, but Bodie stays true to its mining heritage and displays it for all to see. The town and its mining district are authentic. They symbolize the real West. Although what remains is a shadow of the past, the longer and closer we look at Bodie, the more vividly its golden hue returns. This once-vibrant place, where hope, determination, and courage met, survives as one of the best-preserved ghost towns in the American West.

Bodie has fought time to a standstill, and remains an enduring, if fragile, monument to the nation's heritage and the West that was.

---

1. Department of the Interior, United States Geological Survey, *Mineral Resources of the United States* (Washington, DC: Government Printing Office, 1911), 489.

2. California State Archives. "Lease and Agreement: J. S. Cain to Earl W. Bell and E. G. Wiley." Bodie Collection, linknum 4247: 15 February 1935.

3. *Western Nevada Miner* 15 January 1916; Francis M. Guido, "Bodie & Benton Railway, Cain vs. Mono Lumber Co.," *The Western Railroader for the Western Railfan* 37, Issue 411 (August/September 1974): 3; Charles W. Chesterman, Rodger H. Chapman, and Cliffton H. Gray, Jr, *Geology and Ore Deposits of the Bodie Mining District, Mono County, California (Bulletin 206)* (Sacramento, CA: Division of Mines and Geology, 1986), 32.

4. *Western Nevada Miner* 15 January 1916; *Walker Lake Bulletin* 29 January 1916.

5. *Western Nevada Miner* 12 June 1915.

6. *Walker Lake Bulletin* 21 July 1917; Emil W. Billeb, *Mining Camp Days* (Berkeley, CA: Howell-North Books, 1968), 199-200, 212-213.

7. U.S. Department of Commerce, "Population," *Fourteenth Census of the United States, 1920*, vol. 1 (Washington, DC: Government Printing Office, 1921), 355.

8. Robert T. Bell, telephone interview by author, 5 April 1997; 1 March 1997.

9. *Chronicle-Union* 6 March 1915; 27 April 1921; 7 March 1924; Bell, telephone interview by author, 6 November 1999.

10. *Chronicle-Union* 8 August 1923.

11. Bell, telephone interview by author, 27 January 1995; 14 July 1996; 23 May 1999; Bell interview by author, 11 June 1995; 9 June 1995, Nevada.

12. Bell, telephone interview by author, 16 January 1996.

13. Bell, telephone interview by author, 1 January 1997.

14. Bell, interview by author, 11 June 1995, Nevada.

15. Bell, telephone interview by author, 27 February 1995.

16. Charles Courtney Julian (1885-1934).

17. Richard E. Lingenfelter, *Death Valley & the Amargosa: A Land of Illusion* (Berkeley, CA: University of California Press, 1986), 428.

18. Lenox H. Rand and Edward B. Sturgis, *The Mines*

Handbook (Suffern, NY: Mines Information Bureau, 1931), 634; *Chronicle-Union* 4 February 1928.

19. *Chronicle-Union* 12 October 1929.

20. For more stories about C. C. Julian and his zany stock promotions, see Jules Tygiel, *The Great Los Angeles Swindle: Oil, Stocks and Scandal During the Roaring Twenties* (New York, NY: Oxford University Press, 1994); Richard E. Lingenfelter, "The Last Hurrah," chap. in *Death Valley and the Amargosa: A Land of Illusion* (Berkeley, CA: University of California Press, 1986), 421-440; Walter V. Woehlke, "The Great Julian Pete Swindle," *Sunset Magazine*, September 1927, 12-15, 69, 80-81, October 1927, 16-19, 78-82, November 1927, 18-20, 66-68, 81-83.

21. Rand, *The Mines Handbook* (1931), 200.

22. Rand, *The Mines Handbook* (1931), 2656-2657; *Engineering and Mining Journal* 24 April 1930, 422.

23. Bell, letter to author, 24 April 1993; *Nevada Mining Press* 13 September 1929; *Chronicle-Union* 12 October 1929.

24. Bell, telephone interview by author, 20 November 1995.

25. *Nevada Mining Press* 9 May 1930.

26. Bell, telephone interview by author, 4 May 1995; Bell, interview by author, 10 June 1995, Nevada.

27. *Chronicle-Union* 15 October 1927; 29 October 1927; 4 February 1928; 8 October 1932.

28. Bell, telephone interview by author, 1 January 1997.

29. Bell, interview by author, 9 June 1995, Nevada.

30. *Mines Register* (New York, NY: Mines Publications, 1937), 808; *Engineering and Mining Journal* January 1932, 56; California State Mining Bureau, *Report XXIII of the State Mineralogist* (Sacramento, CA: California State Printing Office, 1927), 417.

31. Billeb, *Mining Camp Days*, 101, 200, 214; *Walker Lake Bulletin* 21 June 1919; 30 August 1919; *Chronicle-Union* 26 October 1921; California State Archives. "Inventory: J. S. Cain." Bodie Collection, linknum 1308: 21 May 1923.

32. *Los Angeles Times* 26 November 1928; Rand, *The Mines Handbook* (1931), 528-529.

33. *Chronicle-Union* 10 August 1929; 9 November 1929; 16 November 1929.

34. Bell, interview by author, 7 June 1996, Nevada.

35. *Chronicle-Union* 29 November 1930.

36. Bell, telephone interview by author, 1 March 1997; 17 February 2001.

37. Bell, telephone interview by author, 6 February 2000.

38. Bell, telephone interview by author, 26 April 1995; 26 July 1998; *Chronicle-Union* 20 November 1929; Department of the Interior, United States Geological Survey, *Mineral Resources of the United States* (Washington, DC: Government Printing Office, 1930), 999.

39. *Chronicle-Union* 13 September 1930.

40. California State Mining Bureau. "Field Report: Property of Standard Consolidated Mining Co." 31 July 1931; *Chronicle-Union* 3 January 1931; 20 September 1930.

41. *Chronicle-Union* 30 May 1931; *Engineering and Mining Journal* 26 January 1931, 79; 27 April 1931, 383; 26 October 1931, 376; 23 November 1931, 465; Warren Loose, "Bodie: Archangel of the Mining Camps," *True West* 23, no. 2 (November/December 1975): 8-13, 30, 44-47.

42. *Engineering and Mining Journal* 26 October 1931, 376; *Chronicle-Union* 26 December 1931.

43. *Chronicle-Union* 30 January 1932.

44. *Chronicle-Union* 30 January 1932.

45. Eyewitness accounts of the 1932 fire and a biographical sketch of William Godward, Bodie's 2½ year-old firebug, are found in James Watson and Doug Brodie, *Big Bad Bodie: High Sierra Ghost Town* (Philadelphia, PA: Xlibris Corporation, 2000), 77-99.

46. *Chronicle-Union* 25 June 1932.

47. Bell, telephone interview by author, 1 March 1997.

48. Bell, telephone interview by author, 6 July 1996; Bell, interview by author, 7 June 1996, Nevada.

49. Bell, telephone interview by author, 14 July 1996; 6 July 1996.

50. *Chronicle-Union* 29 April 1933.

51. Bell, telephone interview by author, 14 March 1996.

52. Edwin Walter Kemmerer, *Gold and the Gold Standard: The Story of Gold Money, Past, Present, and Future* (New York, NY: McGraw-Hill Book Co., 1944), 76, 103; Jack R. Wagner, *Gold Mines of California* (Berkeley, CA: Howell-North Books, 1970), 13.

53. Bell, telephone interview by author, 11 September 1996.

54. *Chronicle-Union* 15 October 1936.

55. *Engineering and Mining Journal* June 1936, 305; *Chronicle-Union* 15 October 1936; 3 November 1938; *Mines Register* (1940), 464.

56. Zady Kriel, "Letter to Jack Shipley from Mr. Zady Kriel." *Friends of Bodie Newsletter* 9, Issue 1 (Spring 1999): 9.

57. California Division of Mines, *State Mineralogist's Report XXXVI* (San Francisco, CA: State Division of Mines, 1940), 138; Chesterman, *Geology and Ore Deposits*, 32.

58. *Chronicle-Union* 25 July 1940; 5 September 1940; Chesterman, *Geology and Ore Deposits*, 31-33.

59. Scott R. Dunlap, *The Gunman From Bodie*. Monogram Pictures Corp., 1941. It's not surprising that Hollywood confused mining and ranching. Popular entertainment forms had muddled western history for decades. Even before 1880, novelists, biographers, and playwrights misrepresented actual events to exploit the eastern public's deep and uncritical enthusiasm for portrayals of life in the West. Mixing fact and fiction, they expanded upon America's frontier myth with

thrilling stories that had lasting influence on American ideology.

After the mid-1880s, traveling shows competed with dime novels, both embellishing profitable story lines. Setting their scenarios on the Great Plains, Buffalo Bill Cody, Pawnee Bill, the Miller brothers, and other showmen staged performances that were promoted as accurate depictions of historic events. Narratives devised for grandstand audiences presented episodes such as Custer's Last Stand (the most remarkable version featured Buffalo Bill Cody, who arrived moments too late to save the 7th Cavalry), Pony Express riding, buffalo hunts with live animals, and Indian attacks on westbound emigrant wagon trains and settlers' cabins. These and similar exciting dramas were punctuated by demonstrations of trick shooting and exhibitions of cowboy skills such as roping and bronco riding. The shows delivered a particular interpretation of western culture that ignored the fact that a good part of the West existed in commercial, agricultural, and industrial settings.

Perhaps the closest reference to mining in Buffalo Bill's Wild West was the popular "Attack Upon the Deadwood Mail Coach." The act featured an authentic mule-drawn stagecoach from the Cheyenne & Black Hills Stage Line, which was chased about the arena by mounted Native American performers in war paint. Around and around the coach careened as its occupants and their whooping pursuers exchanged gunfire, until a cast of dashing cowboys, lead by Buffalo Bill himself, galloped in and drove away the Indians in a climactic battle that sent surviving savages fleeing for their lives. Such spectacles of drama and skill set pulses racing and led audiences to believe that they had witnessed an accurate portrayal of the American West.

Based on the popularity of adventure stories starring cowboy heroes, motion pictures later depicted cattle driving as if it were the West's highest calling. By 1941, herding beef had permanently overshadowed mining and all other frontier occupations in American mythology, and cowboys are remembered as the leading figures in western history. Even Virginia City, rich in Comstock mining lore, has been strangely contorted for the enjoyment of tourists into the television haunt of Ponderosa ranchmen. (Paul Reddin, *Wild West Shows* (Chicago, IL: University of Illinois Press, 1999), 53-123; Joseph G. Rosa and Robin May, *Buffalo Bill and His Wild West: A Pictorial Biography* (Lawrence, KS: University Press of Kansas, 1989), 65-137; Richard Slotkin, *Gunfighter Nation: The Myth of the Frontier in Twentieth-Century America* (New York, NY: Harper Perennial, 1992), 29-228.)

60. *Chronicle-Union* 2 April 1942; 15 October 1942; Wagner, *Gold Mines of California*, 13-14.

61. *Chronicle-Union* 17 September 1942.

62. *Chronicle-Union* 27 August 1942.

63. *Chronicle-Union* 19 November 1942; Billeb, *Mining Camp Days*, 207.

64. *Mining and Industrial News* July 1946, 19.

65. Billeb, *Mining Camp Days*, 209.

66. Michael H. Piatt, "Sinking the Bell Lode Shaft," *Narrow Gauge and Short Line Gazette* 27, no. 4 (September/October 2001): 36-41.

67. Billeb, *Mining Camp Days*, 207.

68. Bell, telephone interview by author, 13 April 2000, 26 August 2001; Colin Fletcher, *The Thousand-Mile Summer* (Berkeley, CA: Howell-North Books, 1964), 149.

69. Nell Murbarger, "Bodie Today," *Desert: Magazine of the Outdoor Southwest* 23, no. 10 (October 1960): 12-17.

70. Noah Tilghman, letter to author, 27 July 2001.

71. *Los Angeles Times* 1 July 1992, E1, E5; J. Brad Sturdivant, "Executive Secretary's Message; Newsflash: The Bodie Protection Act Passed." *Friends of Bodie Newsletter* 1, Issue 1 (Spring 1994): 1, 3-4; J. Brad Sturdivant, "Executive Secretary's Message." *Friends of Bodie Newsletter* 8, Issue 1 (Spring 1998): 2; Ann Huston and B. Noah Tilghman, "Bodie, California: Preserving a Historic Mining Landscape." *Cultural Resource Management* 20, no. 9 (1997): 41-45.

72. This yield was later surpassed by Cripple Creek, Colorado, at $433,000,000, and Homestake, South Dakota, with $494,000,000. Vardis Fisher and Opal Laurel Holmes, *Gold Rushes and Mining Camps of the Early American West* (Caldwell, ID: Claxton Printers, 1990), 26.

THE TECHNOLOGY
OF MINING GOLD

Geology

Most of those who rushed to California in 1849 sought gold that could be found quickly, usually in the gravel of streambeds. The techniques they used, known as "placer mining," yielded gold dust and nuggets. Gold also exists deep inside the earth, but it tends to be in small particles, often invisible to the naked eye, imbedded in rock. Reaching this gold requires excavating into formations, where geological events deposited it millions of years ago. While placer miners worked on the surface, others blasted their way deep into the earth to reach gold-bearing minerals. This involved driving tunnels and sinking shafts. Because subterranean mineral deposits containing gold are usually composed of quartz, the underground mining of gold was called "quartz mining."

The 49ers were quick to find gold-laden quartz deposits, and California's first quartz mine was started in Mariposa County in 1849. Even the discovery of gold in other rock types failed to change the use of the term, and "quartz mining" continued to describe underground gold mining regardless of the chemical composition of the surrounding rock. When silver was discovered in quartz on the Comstock in 1859, the term expanded to include the underground mining of silver as well as gold.[1] More recently, descriptive terms such as "lode" or "hard rock" mining have been applied to underground gold and silver mining, but during the late-nineteenth century, the term "quartz mining" was universally used. The meaning of the word "quartz" was also broader then, implying much more than the conventional mineral. At the height of Bodie's mining boom, quartz was defined as "any hard gold or silver ore, as distinguished from gravel or earth."[2]

Driving tunnels and sinking shafts were expensive endeavors that could not be sustained for long by individual prospectors. Companies were needed to raise capital, and, even though the odds were against striking it rich, people across the country were eager to invest. During the last third of the 1800s, speculation in gold and silver mines was a popular pastime, something akin to playing today's lotteries. The spirited reception of western mining stocks encouraged a proliferation of unregulated companies, many of which scandalously misused investors' money. Corruption was widespread and quickly brought discredit to the industry. Among unwary investors who had been fleeced, "quartz mining" became synonymous with "swindle."

The mining companies that operated at Bodie intended to exploit quartz veins that bore enough mineral wealth to make mining profitable. Reaching the ore bodies, however, involved considerable effort. Surrounding Bodie's veins was a yellowish volcanic rock that mining men called "porphyry," known to geologists as "andesite." Miners had to burrow through it, and tons of worthless rock were removed, then dumped at the entrances to mines.

Bodie has long been known as a gold mining town, yet along with the gold came silver. Based on value, bullion produced from Bodie's ore during the early 1880s averaged 70% gold and 30% silver. Because silver was far less valuable than gold, an average 100-pound bar of the district's bullion would have contained about 73 pounds of silver and only 27 pounds of gold. This high silver content made Bodie's bullion very pale in color with little, if any, discernible golden hue.[3]

There were two major sources of silver in Bodie's ore. The first was the gold itself. Pure gold rarely occurs in nature. Gold is almost always mixed, or alloyed, with silver and sometimes other metals, such as iron and copper. Gold can contain enough silver to significantly reduce its value, as was noted by the early placer miners at Washoe, who grew concerned when their gold was lighter in color than the California gold to which they were accustomed. In his history of the Comstock Lode, Dan De Quille explained the unwelcome characteristics: "The gold dug in the placer-mines of California is worth from $16 to $19 per ounce, whereas the gold taken from the croppings of the Comstock was worth no more than $11 or $12 per ounce."[4] The concept that a piece of gold can be diluted in value was recognized by Grant Smith, who recalled Bodie: "All of the gold in the district was heavily alloyed with silver and was rarely worth more than $12 per ounce. In some of the shallow placer diggings, at the south end of the ridge, the gold was worth only from $3 to $8 per ounce."[5] In discussing mining at Bodie, the term "gold" always assumes a certain silver content.

Bodie's ore also contained large quantities of silver that were chemically combined with other elements, notably sulfur. Several such alloys were known collectively as "sulphurets," a mining term for any gold- or silver-bearing ore possessing sulfides. The sulphuret ores at Bodie included tetrahedrite, stephanite, argentite (known on the Comstock as "blasted blue stuff"), galena, pyrargyrite, chalcopyrite, and pyrite. Each type of sulphuret ore presented a distinct degree of difficulty in its treatment. While the silver was combined with sulfur, very often the real value of sulphurets was in miniscule particles of embedded metallic gold.[6]

Silver was occasionally found at Bodie in other forms, such as silver chloride, or "horn silver." Also rare at Bodie was metallic silver. Known among mining men as "native silver," it occurred deep underground where it escaped the corrosive effects of the atmosphere. When discovered, native silver attracted extraordinary attention and enhanced a mine's allure by presumably legitimizing claims of wealth.

Drilling and Blasting at Bodie

Sinking shafts and driving tunnels through rock required explosives, and the following sequence was used in blasting out a passageway: drilling a pattern of holes in the rock, loading the holes with explosives, blasting, removing the broken rock, trimming the opening to form, installing timber supports, then drilling the next group of holes.

Until the early 1870s, holes were drilled in rock using hand tools comprising a hand-held hammer and a drill consisting of a chisel-tipped steel rod. The miner held the drill against the rock with one hand, then struck the drill repeatedly with a short-handled, four-pound hammer clutched in the other hand. With each blow, the drill was rotated a fraction of turn. Drills of progressively greater lengths were used until the hole was about three feet deep.

The hammer had to be swung at drills angled in all directions—upward, downward, horizontal, and every conceivable angle in between. Horizontal and downward holes were the easiest to drill, but rock dust had to be removed periodically with a long thin spoon. Cuttings fell out of holes directed upward, but these were the most difficult to drill. As the drills dulled quickly, they had to be changed frequently. On the surface, the company blacksmith kept busy forging, heat-treating, and sharpening drills. Hand drilling could also be performed by two men working together, a tradition brought to this country by Cornish miners. One man

held, turned, and changed the drill, while his teammate wielded an eight-pound sledgehammer. Though impressive for its human dynamics, the economy of this method is doubtful, and it was only employed where labor unions were strong enough to enforce its use.

Depending on the measurements of the passageway, the hardness of the rock, the size to which the rock pieces were to be broken, and the strength and amount of explosives used, six or more holes were drilled into the rock in the direction the passageway was to be advanced. The group of drilled holes was known as a "round of holes." Major passageways often required more than 30 holes. The miners were keen to save labor, so the holes were directed and arranged to take advantage of natural flaws in the rock. The holes were loaded with explosives, usually in the form of cartridges, which were pushed in with a long wooden stick called a "tamping rod." Several cartridges filled each hole. When the explosives were detonated, the holes exploded in a particular sequence controlled by the lengths of the fuses. The middle holes exploded first, relieving the ground by blowing out a core from the center. In driving a tunnel, the top holes detonated next, forcing the debris downward into the void created by the first explosion. The final blast at the bottom lifted the broken rocks and dumped them onto iron sheets placed in the work area to make shoveling, or "mucking," easier. To sink a shaft, the first explosions relieved the ground in the center, radiating outward to the corners. The sequence of explosions made it possible for the miners, listening from a safe distance, to tell when a charge did not detonate. These were called "missed holes" or "misses." Missed holes were extremely dangerous and had to be discovered and detonated before work continued.

Given that most of Bodie's gold and silver lay encased in rock, it is a wonder that anybody expected to gain by mining there. Anticipating large profits, however, was something at which western mining men excelled. Their penchant for optimism was nourished by an epic transformation taking place in nineteenth-century America: the Industrial Revolution. Beginning in the early 1860s, the industrialization of underground mining reached the western frontier and vastly improved the odds of profiting from quartz mining. Foremost among the technological developments were two inventions that eased the formidable task of reaching, then removing, gold- and silver-bearing ore. Bodie's major mining companies took advantage of both.

Dynamite. During the early days of underground mining in the West, blasting was accomplished with blasting powder, a cheap form of gunpowder, otherwise known as "black powder." Not until Alfred Nobel of

Sweden discovered a reliable packaging for nitroglycerine was the superior power of "high explosives" tamed for practical use. In 1868 he received a U.S. patent for dynamite.[7] By combining nitroglycerine with an inert absorbent filler, his product produced nearly the power of liquid nitroglycerine but was much safer and easier to manage. For convenience, it was manufactured in paper cartridges.[8] At Bodie, as in most western mining camps of that era, dynamite was generally known as "Giant powder," a name taken from its first licensed U.S. manufacturer, the California-based Giant Powder Company, which began producing dynamite in 1868.[9]

Driven as much by a desire to circumvent Nobel's patents as to improve upon the properties of Giant powder, numerous American companies sprang up to produce competing brands. Aside from simple changes in the proportions of principal ingredients, the main difference between products was the material used for the absorbent base. By choosing fillers, such as saltpeter or blasting powder, that actively enhanced the explosion, dynamite could be produced with varying explosive characteristics. By 1874 it was available under the names of Giant, Judson (a second line manufactured by the Giant Powder Company named for a company founder, Egbert Judson), Hercules (manufactured by the California Powder Works until 1876, when its plant was purchased by Du Pont of New Jersey, the country's largest black powder manufacturer), and Vulcan. Agents for the companies advertised conspicuously in Bodie newspapers. "GIANT POWDER," proclaimed one ad. "The company manufactures three different grades—Nos. 1, 2 and 3—and sells the same as low [in price] as any of the infringing powders under the names of Vulcan or Hercules Powders."[10] Merchants selling competing products also advertised vigorously. "Hercules—Nos. 1 & 2. The best mining powder in use. Prices as low as any in the market."[11] Until mid-1879 Giant, Hercules, and Vulcan brands were distributed to Bodie's mining companies from a magazine centrally located near the Standard Mine. In July the magazine accidentally blew up, killing seven men and demolishing one of the Standard Company's hoisting works.

Air-Powered Machine Drills. It was estimated that hand drilling holes for blasting represented 75% of the cost of mining. The powerful demand for an apparatus that could do the job more cheaply resulted in machine drills, the second technological development that revolutionized underground mining. When a hole is drilled into rock by hand, striking a steel drill with a hand-held hammer, the hole progresses about a foot per hour. An early air-powered machine drill struck the rock between 200 and 300 times per minute, increasing the rate of drilling to about a foot every two minutes. (These figures vary considerably depending on the hardness of the rock and the diameter of the hole.)

Following a string of inventors starting in about 1838 (including Isaac Singer of later sewing machine fame), Charles Burleigh developed the first successful air-powered rock drill in 1866-67.[12] Burleigh introduced his drill to the western mining world in 1870, when he drove a tunnel into Sherman Mountain at Georgetown, Colorado. At times the tunnel advanced through solid rock at speeds that were six times the rate accomplished by hand drilling. A demonstration in Idaho garnered such approval that one witness exclaimed, "If hell is below, it wouldn't take long to go there."[13] The Comstock's acceptance of Burleigh's rock drill was described two years before Bodie boomed. "It is, without doubt, one of the greatest successes ever known. . . . It combines simplicity, strength, lightness and compactness to a remarkable degree, and is convenient, easily handled and not liable to get out of order."[14]

Competing manufacturers quickly challenged the Burleigh Rock-Drill Company. As early as 1874, a multitude of drills was available. The four most practical were judged by one expert to be the Burleigh, Rand, Ingersoll, and Waring.[15]

The superior power of high explosives allowed holes to be drilled much deeper into rock than holes intended for black powder. Machine-drills accomplished this, furnishing holes that were also larger in diameter and held more explosives than hand-drilled holes. Spurred by the destructive force of high explosives, deeper and larger holes, and drilling speeds allowed by machine drills, miners opened passageways at tremendous rates. This was demonstrated in 1879 at the Noonday Mine, where sinking and timbering the company's three-compartment vertical shaft proceeded at five feet per day.

Machine drills greatly improved the economics of large-scale mining at Bodie, but for various reasons they were not employed universally. The drills were powered by compressed air, which required machinery on the surface and extensive piping underground. During the first 15 years of Bodie's industrial development, machinery that compressed air was powered by steam. Additional boilers were required in the mine's hoisting works, which increased fuel consumption considerably. Because the machinery was costly, air-powered drills were usually employed only in mines that were worthy of the investment. Even then, their use was carefully considered, and the machines were often reserved for "development work," or the opening of major passageways and shafts. In isolated areas of a mine, where air pipes did not extend, hand drilling prevailed.

Bodie's ore deposits also tended to be narrow, and machine setups were impossible in confined spaces. Whether by pick, pry bar, or hand drill and dynamite, the necessity to take ore selectively also meant that its extraction was a hand process. Drilling by hand per-

sisted in the Standard Mine until it closed in 1913. The practice continued in Bodie into the 1930s, when small-time operators, working leased ground in old mines, were often well beyond the reach of air hoses from diesel-powered compressors on the surface.[16]

1. Sinking shafts and driving tunnels were feats also undertaken in coal and iron mining, but quartz mining's western setting and glamorous metals made it more prestigious than the others.

2. Rossiter W. Raymond, "A Glossary of Mining and Metallurgical Terms." In *Transactions of the American Institute of Mining Engineers* 9, Easton, PA: Institute of Mining Engineers, 1881: 99-192.

3. These figures are based on the district's overall production for the year 1881, the height of Bodie's mining boom, when the value of gold was $20.6718 per troy ounce, silver $1.2929 per troy ounce. Calculations using these prices indicate that gold made up 87% of the value of bullion produced from mines in the northern part of the district — Bodie Bluff and High Peak, whereas it made up only 47% of the value of bullion from the south end — Silver and Queen Bee hills.

4. Dan De Quille [William Wright], *The Big Bonanza* (1876; reprint, Las Vegas, NY: Nevada Publications, 1982), 24.

5. Grant H. Smith, "Bodie, Last of the Old Time Mining Camps," *California Historical Quarterly* 4 (1925), 76.

6. For a comprehensive explanation of Bodie's geology, see Charles W. Chesterman, Rodger H. Chapman, and Cliffton H. Gray, Jr., *Geology and Ore Deposits of the Bodie Mining District, Mono County, California—Bulletin 206* (Sacramento, CA: Division of Mines and Geology, 1986), 25-29.

7. From "dynamis," the Greek word for power.

8. As a liquid, nitroglycerine was difficult to use. It probably reached its highest degree of perfection in 1867, during construction of a 4¾ mile railroad tunnel in Massachusetts. While driving the Hoosac Tunnel, nitroglycerine was manufactured on site, but transporting the temperamental liquid to the work area at the tunnel's face remained a dangerous proposition until a mishap demonstrated that nitroglycerine was much safer when frozen. One bitterly cold day, the engineer transporting the liquid-filled cartridges to the tunnel was surprised to learn that he was still in one piece after his sleigh toppled over a snow bank. His investigation revealed that the nitroglycerine had frozen solid. From then on, the car-tridges were frozen and packed in ice for transportation, then thawed prior to use. See Carl R. Byron, *A Pinprick of Light: The Troy and Greenfield Railroad and Its Hoosac Tunnel* (Shelburne, VT: The New England Press, 1995).

9. The term "Giant powder" differentiated dynamite from blasting powder, then known simply as "powder." After the use of dynamite became universal, miners referred to it as "powder" too, applying the term to any explosive.

10. *Bodie Weekly Standard* 6 November 1878.

11. *Daily Bodie Standard* 7 July 1879.

12. The Hoosac Tunnel became something of a proving ground for several inventions that were later adapted to western mining. Burleigh's air-powered rock drill proved superior to every mechanical drilling contrivance tried at Hoosac, where the competing machines broke down so frequently that the tunnel was said to be always crowded with people carrying spare parts and tools for repairs. See, Rossiter W. Raymond, *Statistics of Mines and Mining in the States and Territories West of the Rocky Mountains* (Washington DC: Government Printing Office, 1870), 503-512.

13. Mark Wyman, *Hard Rock Epic: Western Miners and the Industrial Revolution, 1860-1910* (Berkeley, CA: University of California Press, 1979), 85.

14. *Gold Hill Daily News* 2 October 1875.

15. *Engineering and Mining Journal* 22 August 1874, 113.

16. For more information on drilling and blasting, see: Larry C. Hoffman, "The Rock Drill and Civilization," *American Heritage of Invention & Technology* 15, no. 1 (Summer 1999): 56-63; Rossiter W. Raymond, "Machines for Drilling Rocks," in *Statistics of Mines and Mining in the States and Territories West of the Rocky Mountains* (Washington, DC: Government Printing Office, 1870), 503-512; E. Gybbon Spilsbury, "Rock-Drilling Machinery" in *Transactions of the American Institute of Mining Engineers* 3, (Easton, PA: A. I. M. E., 1874), 144-150; Barbara Stack, *Handbook of Mining and Tunnelling Machinery* (New York, NY: John Wiley & Sons, 1982); Eric Twitty, *Blown to Bits in the Mine: A History of Mining and Explosives in the United States* (Ouray, CO: Western Reflections Publishing, 2001).

BIBLIOGRAPHY

Interviews

Bell, Robert T. "Bobby". Prospector, miner, mill operator, and former resident of Bodie. Personal interviews. 27-30 August 1994, 9-11 June 1995, and 7-8 June 1996. Telephone interviews. 27 February 1995—4 November 2002.

Sturdivant, J. Brad. Supervising ranger, Bodie State Historic Park, California Department of Parks and Recreation. Personal interview, 27 August 1994.

Books

Balch, William R. Mines, *Miners, and Mining Interests of the United States in 1882*. Philadelphia, PA: The Mining Industrial Publishing Bureau, 1882.

Billeb, Emil W. *Mining Camp Days*. Berkeley, CA: Howell-North Books, 1968.

Browne, John Ross. *Adventures in the Apache Country: A Tour Through Arizona and Sonora, With Notes on the Silver Regions of Nevada*. 1871 ed. New York, NY: Harper & Brothers Publishers, 1869. [Note: The same material appears with minor additions in "A Trip to Bodie Bluff and the Dead Sea of the West." *Harper's New Monthly Magazine* Part 1, 31, no. 183 (August 1865): 274-284; Part 2, 31, no. 184 (September 1865): 411-419.]

Bosqui, Francis L. *Practical Notes on the Cyanide Process*. New York, NY: Scientific Publishing Co., 1899.

Cain, Ella M. *The Story of Bodie*. San Francisco, CA: Fearon Publishers, 1956.

Coleman, Charles M. *P. G. and E. of California: The Centennial Story of Pacific Gas and Electric Company, 1852-1952*. New York, NY: McGraw-Hill Book Co., 1952.

De Quille, Dan [William Wright]. *The Big Bonanza*. 1876. Reprint, Las Vegas, NV: Nevada Publications, 1982.

Elliott, Russell R. *Nevada's Twentieth-Century Mining Boom*. Reno, NV: University of Nevada Press, 1966.

Fisher, Vardis, and Opal Laurel Holmes. *Gold Rushes and Mining Camps of the Early American West*. Caldwell, ID: Claxton Printers, 1990.

Fitch, Henry S. *Pacific Coast Annual Mining Review and Stock Ledger Containing Detailed Official Reports of the Principal Gold and Silver Mines of Nevada, California, Arizona, Utah, New Mexico, and Idaho; A History and Description of Mining and Stock Dealing on This Coast, With Biographical Sketches of 100 of the Principal Men Engaged Therein; and a Series of Finance Articles*. San Francisco, CA: Francis & Valentine, 1878.

Fletcher, Thomas C. *Paiute, Prospector, Pioneer: The Bodie-Mono Lake Area in the Nineteenth Century*. Lee Vining, CA: Artemisia Press, 1987.

Glass, Mary Ellen. *Silver and Politics in Nevada: 1892-1902*. Reno, NV: University of Nevada Press, 1969.

Goodson, D. V. *Mining Laws of Bodie Mining District Compiled from the Original Records*. Bodie, CA: Bodie Standard Printing House, 1878.

Harpending, Asbury. *The Great Diamond Hoax and Other Stirring Incidents in the Life of Asbury Harpending*. Norman, OK: University of Oklahoma Press, 1958.

Hunter, Louis C. and Lynwood Bryant. *A History of Industral Power in the United States, 1780-1930, Vol. 3: The Transmission of Power*. Cambridge, MA: M I T Press, 1991.

Johnson, Russ, and Anne Johnson. *The Ghost Town of Bodie: As Reported in the Newspapers of the Day*. Bishop, CA: Chalfant Press, 1967.

Leggett, Thomas Haight. *Electric Power Transmission Plants and the Use of Electricity in Mining Operations*. Sacramento, CA: Superintendent of State Printing, 1894.

Leonard, John William. *Who's Who in Engineering: A Biographical Dictionary of Contemporaries*. New York, NY: Who's Who Publications, Inc., 1925.

Lingenfelter, Richard E. *The Hardrock Miners: A History of the Mining Labor Movement in the American West, 1863-1893*. Berkeley, CA: University of California Press, 1974.

_____, and Karen Rix Gash. *The Newspapers of Nevada: A History and Bibliography, 1854-1979*. Reno, NV: University of Nevada Press, 1984.

_____. *Death Valley & the Amargosa: A Land of Illusion*. Berkeley, CA: University of California Press, 1986.

Loose, Warren. *Bodie Bonanza: The True Story of a Flamboyant Past*. Las Vegas, NV: Nevada Publications, 1979.

Lord, Eliot. *Comstock Mining and Miners*. Washington, DC: Government Printing Office, 1883.

Merrell, Bill with David Carle. *Bodie's Last Bonanza: The Frontier Odyssey of Constable John F. Kirgan*. Reno, NV: Nevada Publications, 2003.

McGrath, Roger D. *Gunfighters, Highwaymen, and Vigilantes: Violence on the Frontier*. Berkeley, CA: University of California Press, 1984.

McIntosh, F. W. *Mono County California: The Land of Promise for the Man of Industry*. Reno, NV: Presses of Gazette Publishing, 1908.

Moore, Joseph, and George W. Dickie. *Pumping and Hoist-*

ing Works for Gold and Silver Mines. San Francisco, CA: A. L. Bancroft & Company, 1877.

Myers, William A. Iron Men and Copper Wires: A Centennial History of the Southern California Edison Company. Glendale, CA: Trans-Anglo Press, 1983.

Myrick, David F. Railroads of Nevada and Eastern California: Volume One—The Northern Roads. Berkeley, CA: Howell-North Books, 1962.

Passer, Harold C. The Electrical Manufacturers, 1875-1900: A Study in Competition, Entrepreneurship, Technical Change, and Economic Growth. Cambridge, MA: Harvard University Press, 1953.

Patera, Alan H. Lundy. Lake Grove, OR: Western Places, 2000.

Rand, Lenox H. and Edward B. Sturgis. The Mines Handbook. Suffern, NY: Mines Information Bureau, 1931.

Rickard, T. A. Interviews With Mining Engineers. San Francisco, CA: Mining and Scientific Press, 1922.

Sears, Marian V. Mining Stock Exchanges, 1860-1930: An Historical Survey. Missoula, MT: University of Montana Press, 1973.

Tygiel, Jules. The Great Los Angeles Swindle: Oil, Stocks and Scandal During the Roaring Twenties. New York, NY: Oxford University Press, 1994.

Wasson, Joseph. Bodie and Esmeralda: An Account of the Revival of the Affairs in Two Singularly Interesting and Important Mining Districts, Including Something of their Past History, and the Gist of the Reports of Profs. Benj. Silliman and Wm. P. Blake, the late J. Ross Browne, and State Mineralogist R. H. Stretch and H. R. Whitehill—Also, Detailed Description of Mines Most Developed, Tunnels, Mills, etc.—Also, General Resources of Mono and Esmeralda Counties—With Maps and Illustrations. San Francisco, CA: Spaulding, Barto & Co., 1878.

_____. Complete Guide to the Mono County Mines: Description of Bodie, Esmeralda, Indian, Lake, Laurel Hill, Prescott, and Other Mining Districts—With Maps and Illustrations. San Francisco, CA. Spaulding, Barto & Co., 1879.

Watson, James, and Doug Brodie. Big Bad Bodie: High Sierra Ghost Town. Philadelphia, PA: Xlibris Corporation, 2000.

Wedertz, Frank S. Bodie 1859-1900. Bishop, CA: Chalfant Press, 1969.

Williams, George J., III. Rosa May: The Search for a Mining Camp Legend. Dayton, NV: Tree By The River Publishing, 1979.

Williams, James C. Energy and the Making of Modern California. Akron, OH: University of Akron Press, 1997.

Wyman, Mark. Hard Rock Epic: Western Miners and the Industrial Revolution, 1860-1910. Berkeley, CA: University of California Press, 1979.

Articles in Periodicals

Billeb, Emil W. "Bodie's Railroad That Was." The Pony Express 24 (June 1957): 1-12.

Brown, Robert Gilman. "Additions to the Power-Plant of the Standard Consolidated Mining Company." Transactions of the American Institute of Mining Engineers 26, New York, NY: A. I. M. E., 1897: 319-339.

_____. "Note on a Shaft-Fire and its Lesson." Transactions of the American Institute of Mining Engineers 26, New York, NY: A. I. M. E., 1897: 315-319.

_____. "Cyanide Practice With the Moore Filter." Mining and Scientific Press (San Francisco, CA), Part 1, 1 September 1906: 261-262; Part 2, 8 September 1906: 292-295.

_____. "The Vein-System of the Standard Mine, Bodie, Cal." Transactions of the American Institute of Mining Engineers 38, New York, NY: A. I. M. E., 1908: 343-357.

Browne, John Ross. "A Trip to Bodie Bluff and the Dead Sea of the West." Harper's New Monthly Magazine Part 1, 31, no. 183 (August 1865): 274-284; Part 2, 31, no. 184 (September 1865): 411-419.

Hasson, W. F. C. "Electric Transmission of Power Long Distances." Transactions of the Technical Society of the Pacific Coast 10, no. 4 (May 1893): 49-72.

Kersten, Earl W. Jr. "The Early Settlement of Aurora, Nevada, and Nearby Mining Camps." Annals of the Association of American Geographers 54, no. 4 (December 1964): 490-507.

Leggett, Thomas Haight. "An Electric Power Transmissions Installation—In the Mining District of Bodie, in California." Practical Engineer (London), 2 November 1894.

_____. "Electric Power Transmission." Mining and Scientific Press (San Francisco, CA), Part 1, 30 March 1895: 196-197; Part 2, 6 April 1895: 212-213.

_____. "A Twelve-Mile Transmission of Power by Electricity." Cassier's Magazine (New York, NY), 7, no. 5 (March 1895): 355-368.

_____. "A Twelve-Mile Transmission of Power by Electricity." Engineering News and Railway Journal (New York, NY), 26 July 1895: 74-77.

_____. "A Twelve-Mile Transmission of Power by Electricity." Transactions of the American Institute of Mining Engineers, 24, New York, NY: A. I. M. E., 1895: 315-338.

Loose, Warren. "Bodie—Archangel of the Mining Camps." True West 23, no. 2 (November/December 1975): 8-13, 30, 44-47.

MacDuff, Rod. "Prescott & Scott—A Short History of the Builders of BR&LC Locomotives #2 and #3." Link & Pin by the Friends of Bodie Railway & Lumber Co., Inc. (Spring 1998): 2.

Murbarger, Nell. "Bodie Today." Desert: Magazine of the Outdoor Southwest 23, no. 10 October 1960): 12-17.

Ninnin, Lillian. "Bodie Yesterday." *Desert: Magazine of the Outdoor Southwest* 23, no. 10 October 1960): 19-21.

Parr, John F. "Reminiscences of the Bodie Strike." *Yosemite Nature Notes* 7, no. 5 (May 1928): 33-38.

Piatt, Michael H. "The Red Cloud Mine of Bodie, California." *Narrow Gauge and Short Line Gazette* 22, no. 1 (March/April 1996): 38-44.

_____. "Hauling Freight Into the 20th Century by Jerk Line." *Journal of the West* 36, no. 1 (January 1997): 82-91.

_____. "Sinking the Bell Lode Shaft, Bodie, California." *Narrow Gauge and Short Line Gazette* 27, no. 4 (September/October 2001): 36-41.

Ransom, Jay Ellis. "Old Timer Relives Days When Railroad Was Built In the Sky." *The California Highway Patrolman* 13 (September 1949): 16-17, 121, 124, 128-130.

Rickard, T. A. "The Great Diamond Hoax: How a Colorado Desert Was Salted With Gems in 1872." *Engineering and Mining Journal* 119, no. 22 (30 May 1925): 884-888.

Smith, Grant H. "Bodie, Last of the Old Time Mining Camps." *California Historical Quarterly* 4 (1925): 64-80.

Spiller, Chris. "Mrs. Hoover Returns to Bodie." *Friends of Bodie Newsletter* 8, no. 1 (Spring 1998): 11-13.

Newspapers

Alpine Chronicle (Silver Mountain, CA) 23 April 1870—19 October 1878. *Mono Alpine Chronicle* (Bodie, CA) 28 December 1878—3 May 1879. *Bodie Chronicle* (Bodie, CA) 10 May 1879—23 October 1880. *Chronicle-Union* (Bridgeport, CA) 6 November 1880—19 November 1942. [No references for Bodie found between 3 February 1883 and 20 October 1888]

Bodie Evening Miner (Bodie, CA) 9 May 1882—7 November 1884.

Bodie Miner (Bodie, CA) 5 December 1908—24 November 1910.

Bodie Morning News (Bodie, CA) 14 March 1879—23 May 1880. *Bodie Daily News* (Bodie, CA) 24 May 1880—20 July 1880. *Bodie Standard-News* (Bodie, CA) 21 July 1880—11 December 1880.

Bodie Standard (Bodie, CA) 7 November 1877—8 May 1878. *Bodie Weekly Standard* (Bodie, CA) 15 May 1878—25 December 1878. *Weekly Bodie Standard* (Bodie, CA) 4 January 1879—5 April 1879. *Weekly Standard-News* (Bodie, CA) 4 September 1880—2 August 1882.

Daily Bodie Standard (Bodie, CA) 10 December 1878—20 July 1880.

Daily Free Press (Bodie, CA) 3 November 1879—22 April 1883.

Engineering and Mining Journal (New York, NY) 15 February 1870—June 1936.

Esmeralda Union (Aurora, NV) 23 March 1864 15 March 1865, 23 November 1867—3 October 1868.

Inyo Independent (Independence, CA) 2 January 1875—29 December 1877.

Mining and Scientific Press (San Francisco, CA) 27 August 1864—25 December 1915.

Mining Record (New York, NY) 28 November 1878—4 April 1885. *Financial and Mining Record* (New York, NY) 11 April 1885—8 October 1892.

Walker Lake Bulletin (Hawthorne, NV) 13 January 1886—29 December 1905. 21 March 1911—14 May 1924.

Western Nevada Miner (Mina, NV) 19 September 1908—16 March 1918.

Corporate and Government Publications

Browne, John Ross. *The Bodie Bluff Mines Located in Mono County, California, Belonging to the Empire Gold & Silver Mining Co. of New York*. New York, NY: Clark & Maynard, 1865.

_____, and James W. Taylor. *Reports upon the Mineral Resources of the United States*. Washington, DC: Government Printing Office, 1867: 21-77.

_____. *Report of J. Ross Browne on the Mineral Resources of the States and Territories West of the Rocky Mountains*. Washington, DC: Government Printing Office, 1868: 177-179.

California Division of Mines. *Report XXVII of the State Mineralogist covering Activities of the Division of Mines including the Geologic Branch*. Sacramento, CA: State Printing Office, 1931.

California State Mining Bureau. *Eighth Annual Report of the State Mineralogist, for the Year Ending October 1, 1888*. Sacramento, CA: Superintendent of State Printing, 1888: 382-401.

_____. *Tenth Annual Report of the State Mineralogist, for the Year Ending December 1, 1890*. Sacramento, CA: Superintendent of State Printing, 1890: 336-338.

_____. *Twelfth Report of the State Mineralogist, Two Years Ending September 15, 1894*. Sacramento, CA: Superintendent of State Printing, 1894: 177-184.

_____. *Thirteenth Report of the State Mineralogist, for the Two Years Ending September 15, 1896*. Sacramento, CA: Superintendent of State Printing, 1896: 226-233.

_____. *Report XV of the State Mineralogist: Mines and Mineral Resources of Portions of California, Biennial Period 1915-1916*. Sacramento, CA: State Printing Office, 1919: 143-160.

Chesterman, Charles W., Rodger H. Chapman, and Cliffton H. Gray, Jr. *Geology and Ore Deposits of the Bodie Mining District, Mono County, California (Bulletin 206)*. Sacramento, CA: Division of Mines and Geology, 1986.

Irwin, William. "Superintendent's Report." *First Annual Report of the Standard Consolidated Mining Co. for the Year End-*

ing February 1, 1880. San Francisco, CA: Bunker & Hiester, 1880: 7-12.

_____. "Superintendent's Report." *Second Annual Report of the Standard Consolidated Mining Company for the Year Ending February 1, 1881.* San Francisco, CA: Bunker & Hiester, 1881: 35-42 and sketches.

_____. "Superintendent's Report." *Fourth Annual Report of the Standard Consolidated Mining Company for the Year Ending February 1, 1883.* San Francisco, CA: W. T. Galloway & Co., 1883: 31-33.

_____. "Superintendent's Report." *Fifth Annual Report of the Standard Consolidated Mining Company for the Year Ending February 1, 1884.* San Francisco, CA: W. T. Galloway & Co., 1884: 32-34.

Leggett, Thomas Haight. "Electric Power Transmission Plants and the Use of Electricity in Mining Operations." *Twelfth Report of the State Mineralogist, Two Years Ending September 15, 1894.* Sacramento, CA: Superintendent of State Printing, 1894: 413-435.

Scheidel, A. "The Cyanide Process: Its Practical Application and Economic Results." *California State Mining Bureau Bulletin No. 5, October 1894,* Sacramento, CA: Superintendent of State Printing, 1894.

Silliman, Benjamin, Jr. and William P. Blake. *Prospectus of the Empire Gold & Silver Mining Co. of New York.* New York, NY: William H. Arthur, 1864.

Smith, Grant H. "The History of the Comstock Lode 1850-1920." *University of Nevada Bulletin* Volume 37, No. 3, 1 July 1943, Reno, NV: Nevada Bureau of Mines and Geology, 1980.

U. S. Bureau of the Mint. *Report of the Director of the Mint upon the Statistics of the Production of the Precious Metals in the United States [for 1880].* Washington, DC: Government Printing Office, 1881.

_____. *Report of the Director of the Mint upon the Statistics of the Production of the Precious Metals in the United States [for 1881].* Washington, DC: Government Printing Office, 1882.

_____. *Report of the Director of the Mint upon the Statistics of the Production of the Precious Metals in the United States [for 1882].* Washington, DC: Government Printing Office, 1883.

_____. *Report of the Director of the Mint upon the Production of the Precious Metals in the United States During the Calendar Year 1883.* Washington, DC: Government Printing Office, 1884.

_____. *Report of the Director of the Mint upon the Production of the Precious Metals in the United States During the Calendar Year 1884.* Washington, DC: Government Printing Office, 1885.

_____. *Report of the Director of the Mint upon the Production of the Precious Metals in the United States During the Calendar Year 1885.* Washington, DC: Government Printing Office, 1886.

_____. *Report of the Director of the Mint upon the Production of the Precious Metals in the United States During the Calendar Year 1886.* Washington, DC: Government Printing Office, 1887.

_____. *Report of the Director of the Mint upon the Production of the Precious Metals in the United States During the Calendar Year 1887.* Washington, DC: Government Printing Office, 1888.

_____. *Report of the Director of the Mint upon the Production of the Precious Metals in the United States During the Calendar Year 1891.* Washington, DC: Government Printing Office, 1892.

U. S. Department of Commerce. Bureau of Mines. *Mineral Resources of the United States, 1929, Part 1 - Metals.* Washington, DC: Government Printing Office, 1932.

_____. Bureau of Mines. *Mineral Resources of the United States, 1930, Part 1 - Metals.* Washington, DC: Government Printing Office, 1933.

Maps

Anderson, C. L. *Map of the Bodie Mining District, Mono County, California.* San Francisco, CA: Edward Eysen, 1880.

Sanford, H. F. *Map of the Bodie Mining District: A Birdseye View of the Mining District and the Town of Bodie, Mono County, California.* San Francisco, CA: Daily Stock Report, 1879.

Motion Pictures

Dunlap, Scott R. *The Gunman From Bodie.* Directed by Spencer Gordon Bennet. Monogram Pictures Corp., 1941.

Unpublished Material

Bell, Robert T. Letter to author, 24 April 1993.

California State Archives. "Deed: Haggin/Hearst to Southern Consolidated Mining Company." Bodie Collection, LINKNUM 4078: 27 May 1908.

_____. "Inventory." Bodie Collection, LINKNUM 1308: 21 May 1923.

_____. "Deed: Standard Consolidated Mining Company to J. S. Cain." Bodie Collection, LINKNUM 4078: 23 February 1915.

_____. "Lease: Southern Consolidated Mining Company to Treadwell Yukon Company, Ltd." Bodie Collection, LINKNUM 4078: 21 September 1929.

_____. "Lease: Cain/Billeb to Bell/Bell/Bell." Bodie Collection, LINKNUM 113: 10 September 1932.

_____. "Lease and Agreement: Cain to Bell/Wiley"

Bodie Collection, LINKNUM 4247: 15 February 1935.

_____. "Supplemental Agreement: Treadwell-Yukon Co. Ltd. and J. S. Cain." Bodie Collection, LINKNUM 4241: 1930.

_____. "Bill of Sale: Bulwer Consolidated Mining Co. to J. S. Cain and A. J. McCone." Bodie Collection, LINKNUM 4078: 22 August 1892.

_____. "Legal Agreement: Bulwer Consolidated Mining Co. and Standard Consolidated Mining Co." Bodie Collection, LINKNUM 1078: 14 April 1880.

_____. "Legal Suit: Bulwer Consolidated Mining Company vs Standard Consolidated Mining Co." Bodie Collection, LINKNUM 1079: 6 June 1888.

California. State Mining Bureau. *Field Report No. 8, Southern Consolidated Group of Mines, Mono County*: 29 July 1931.

Docken, Robert. "The Standard Consolidated Mine and Mill at Bodie State Historic Park" (Typescript) Cultural Heritage Section, California Department of Parks and Recreation, 1979.

Hoover, Theodore J. "Memoranda: Being a Statement by an Engineer" (Typescript) Hoover Institution Archives, Stanford University, 1939.

McAbeer, Karen Colbourne. "The Bodie Railroad." Master of Arts Thesis, California State College, Sonoma, CA, 1973.

Mono County. "Deed: Noonday to A. E. Davis." *Mining Deeds Book S*, Pages 570-573. 19 November 1883. Recorder's Vault, Bridgeport, CA.

_____. "Deed: Peter Eshington and Louis Lockberg to John F. Boyd." *Mining Records, Book L*, Page 586. 9 September 1876. Recorder's Vault, Bridgeport, CA.

_____. "Deed: Red Cloud to A. E. Davis." *Mining Deeds Book S*, Pages 574-578. 19 November 1883. Recorder's Vault, Bridgeport, CA.

_____. "Lien: Noonday and North Noonday Companies." *Liens Book B*, Pages 37-74. December 1882. Recorder's Vault, Bridgeport, CA.

_____. "Lien: Red Cloud Company." *Liens Book A*, Pages 417-481. December 1882. Recorder's Vault, Bridgeport, CA.

_____. "Notice of Location: Bunker Hill Lode." *Bodie Mining Records, Book A*, Page 63. 17 June 1861. Recorder's Vault, Bridgeport, CA.

_____. "Notice of Location: Bunker Hill Lode." *Mining Locations, Book A*, Page 90. 10 June 1875. Recorder's Vault, Bridgeport, CA.

_____. "Notice of Location: Bullion Lode." *Bodie Mining Records, Book D*, Page 91. 11 June 1875. Recorder's Vault, Bridgeport, CA.

_____. "Notice of Location: Fortuna Lode." *Mine Locations Book G*, Pages 28-29. 17 January 1880. Recorder's Vault, Bridgeport, CA.

_____. "Notice of Location: Red Cloud Lode." *Bodie Records Book A*, Page 163. 5 October 1876. Recorder's Vault, Bridgeport, CA.

_____. "Notice of Relocation: Noonday." *Bodie Records Book A*, Page 388. 13 November 1876. Recorder's Vault, Bridgeport, CA.

Smith, Herbert L. "The Bodie Era: The Chronicles of the Last Old Time Mining Camp," [1934] TMs (photocopy).

GLOSSARY OF MINING TERMS
(AS USED AT BODIE)

agitator n. A circular vat about 8 or 9 feet in diameter by 2 to 6 feet deep used in a stamp mill to recover gold and silver from crushed ore. A mixture of sand, water, gold, and silver (pulp), to which quicksilver (mercury) has been added, discharged from the settlers, is slowly (12 rpm) stirred by horizontal rotating arms (mullers), allowing the quicksilver, gold, and silver (amalgam) to separate from the sand and water. The denser amalgam settles to the bottom, where it is collected for further treatment. Water and lighter particles rise, to be wasted as tailings. Agitators are very similar to settlers, except that the pulp flows through them instead of being treated in batches.

amalgamation n. The process that employs quicksilver (mercury) to extract minute gold and silver particles from pulverized ore. Liquid mercury adheres to gold and silver, but it rejects water and sand. The denser mixture of quicksilver, gold, and silver, called an amalgam, separates from the lighter waste materials and is saved for further treatment.

amalgamating pan, also **pan** n. A circular vat about 4 or 5 feet in diameter by approximately 3 feet deep used in a stamp mill to recover gold and silver from crushed ore by fine grinding, heating, and amalgamating. Ore initially crushed by the stamps is mixed with water and heated in the pan, while horizontal rotating arms (mullers) further grind the ore against the cast iron bottom (about 75 rpm). Amalgamation takes place when quicksilver (mercury) is added to the finely ground ore, and the particles of precious metal adhere to the quicksilver. Pans used at Bodie were known as "Washoe pans."

arrastra, also **arrastre** n. A circular pit paved with rock, in which heavy stones are dragged to grind ore. The drag stones are attached to horizontal arms, which are pulled around a central post. Draft animals usually supplied motive power, but water power was also employed. Quicksilver (mercury) added to the arrastra during grinding forms an amalgam with the gold and silver. The denser amalgam settles to the bottom, where it is collected for further treatment. Water and lighter particles rise, to be wasted as tailings.

assay n. A chemical test that determines the concentration, and therefore the value, of gold, silver, and other metals in an ore sample. A laboratory analysis that ascertains the commercial value of a rock specimen. — v. To test a sample of ore for certain metals and determine its value.

assessment n. A sum of money demanded by a company to raise capital from its stockholders. Assessments forced stockholders, as part owners of a company, to share in its financial burdens as well as its profits. Suited to the speculative nature of precious metals mining, assessments enabled a company to raise additional capital as it was needed to sustain the search for ore bodies. Assessments also gave shareholders opportunities to reevaluate a company's prospects before investing more money. If the company's future looked promising, stockholders paid assessments. Investors who saw little merit in the venture forfeited their stock by not paying assessments. Forfeited shares could be resold by the company.

bailing tank n. A watertight container that is hoisted through a mine shaft to remove water. Bailing tanks automatically fill when lowered into the water, then self-dump at the surface. Variations include as "tanks," "bailers," and "bailing buckets." Some are free swinging in the shaft while others ride on guides or tracks.

battery n. **1.** A group of stamps, usually five in a row, dropping in a mortar to crush ore. Principal components include: bossheads, shoes, stems, tappets, cams, dies, mortar, camshaft, and a timber frame that supports the assembly. **2.** All the stamps operating in a stamp mill.

bullion n. Gold and silver, recovered from ore by a stamp mill, that has been melted and poured into a mold in the shape of a bar. Because of the high silver content in Bodie's ore, a 100 pound bar of bullion contained 73 pounds of silver and only 27 pounds of gold. Gold, however, was 16 times more valuable than silver in 1880. During Bodie's boom, the yellow metal comprised 70% of the value of the district's bullion.

cage n. An iron frame having one or more platforms that is hoisted through a vertical mine shaft to transport mine cars and/or personnel between the surface and different underground levels. Cages slide on guides inside a shaft.

chute n. **1.** An inclined trough through which ore falls from one level of a mine into a receptacle below. Chutes also provide temporary storage when equipped with gates to control or stop the flow of rocks. **2.** A gate at the bottom of an ore bin that controls or stops the flow of rocks.

collar n. Timbers framing the opening at the top of a mine shaft. The point where a shaft opens to the surface. Also called the shaft's "mouth."

Cornish pump n. A series of pumps positioned in a mine shaft, through which a reciprocating rod delivers power. A steam engine mounted on the surface moves the rod up and down. Pumps placed approximately 200 feet apart in the shaft push water upward, from one pump to the next, until it is discharged at the surface.

crosscut n. A horizontal underground passageway that crosses a vein, usually providing access from a mine shaft. — v. To tunnel from a shaft toward a vein with the intent of intersecting it.

dip *n.* See **pitch**.

donkey hoist *n.* A steam-powered hoisting engine, usually with an integral upright boiler, used to raise and lower an ore bucket, cage, skip, or bailing tank in a mine shaft. Characterized by an uncomplicated design, donkey hoists were easily transported, assembled, and operated.

drift *n.* A horizontal underground passageway that is parallel to a vein, usually beginning at the intersection of a crosscut and the vein. — *v.* To tunnel horizontally following a vein.

dump *n.* A pile of rock discarded from a mine. The place at the mouth of a mine shaft or tunnel where waste rock is discarded.

face *n.* The rock surface at the extreme end of a tunnel, crosscut, drift, or stope, where drilling and blasting take place to extract ore or to advance the passageway. The surface exposed by blasting or excavating. The work area in a mine where drilling and blasting take place.

gallows frame *n.* The heavy structural framework rising from the surface that supports sheaves above a mine shaft. The sheaves must be positioned high enough above the shaft's mouth so that ore buckets, cages, skips, bailing tanks, or a combination of these, will clear the shaft's collar. Known as a "headframe" in other mining regions. Pronounced "gallus."

giraffe *n.* A container that is hoisted through an incline shaft to lift waste rock, ore, and personnel out of a mine. Very large rear wheels allow the car to remain level. "It is capable of carrying eight tons of ore—more than eight ordinary carloads… [and] has in front and on the 'outside' two seats, facing each other, on which six passengers can ride very comfortably." (De Quille, *The Big Bonanza*, 236-237.)

horse *n.* **1.** A deposit of barren rock within a gold- and silver-bearing formation. **2.** Worthless rock lying between two ore bodies or between branches of an ore body.

horse whim, also **whim** *n.* A horse-powered hoisting machine used to raise and lower an ore bucket in a mine shaft. Small capacity and low speed limit its application to prospect shafts and shallow mines.

incline, also **incline shaft** *n.* A mine shaft sunk at an angle, usually following a mineral deposit from its outcrop at the surface.

lead *n.* A rock formation that constitutes a valuable mineral deposit. Frequently used as a synonym for vein or ledge. Pronounced "leed."

leaser *n.* Miner's slang for a lessee. One who obtains a lease to work a mine. Leasers, who conduct mining operations ranging in size from a few individuals to well-staffed corporations, usually pay a percentage of their yield to the mine owner in return for the privilege of removing minerals from the ground.

ledge *n.* A rock formation that constitutes a valuable mineral deposit. Frequently used as a synonym for vein or lead.

levels *n.* Interconnected underground passageways, made up of stations, crosscuts, and drifts, that form a horizontal plane. Mine workings that are at the same approximate elevation. Levels are spaced vertically at intervals, and are accessible through a mine shaft. They are identified by their distance from the surface.

locate *v.* To mark the boundaries of a mining claim and record it. To stake a claim.

location *n.* A legal mining claim.

lode *n.* A system of ore deposits, generally characterizing an entire district (as in the Comstock Lode.) "A lode is more general than a vein, and there may be a number of veins in a lode, while a 'vein' cannot contain a 'lode.'" (*Inyo Register* 12 November 1896)

miner's inch *n.* A unit measuring the flow of water, the value of which depends on local definition. In 19th century Bodie, a miner's inch was equal to 17,000 gallons per 24 hours. (*Daily Free Press* 01 February 1880) In 1901, an act of the California legislature standardized a miner's inch in that state at 1.5 cubic feet per minute (16,159 gallons per 24 hours).

mine shaft *n.* See **shaft**.

pan *n.* See **amalgamating pan**.

pitch, also **dip** *n.* The inclination of a gold- and silver-bearing formation. The angle at which a ledge or vein inclines below the surface, measured from horizontal. — *v.* To slope into the earth at an angle measured from the horizontal.

quicksilver, also **quick** *n.* Mercury. A dense metal that is liquid at room temperature. It has an affinity for gold and silver, but rejects sand and water. After mercury has adhered to the precious metals during ore milling, its density allows it to be separated from the waste materials.

retort *n.* An airtight furnace that removes mercury from an amalgam, then saves it for reuse. The mercury is vaporized by boiling, leaving behind the gold and silver, then it is condensed back to liquid form. Remaining gold and silver are later melted in a crucible, then poured into bars of bullion. — *v.* To remove mercury from an amalgam in a retort.

settler *n.* A circular vat about 8 or 9 feet in diameter by approximately 2 feet deep used in a stamp mill to recover gold and silver from crushed ore. A mixture of sand, water, gold, and silver (pulp), to which quicksilver (mercury) has been added, discharged from the amalgamating pans, is slowly (12 to 15 rpm) stirred in a settler by horizontal rotating arms (mullers), allowing the quicksilver, gold, and silver (amalgam) to separate from the sand and water. The denser amalgam settles to the bottom, where it is collected for further treatment. Water and lighter particles rise, to be wasted as tailings.

shaft, also **mine shaft** *n.* A vertical or inclined passageway excavated from the surface to reach a mineral deposit and provide a path through which the minerals can be removed. Shafts, providing access to the underground workings of a mine, can be used for hoisting, ventilating, and/or pumping.

sheave *n.* A grooved wheel over which the hoisting cable passes from the hoist to an ore bucket, cage, skip, giraffe, or bailing tank riding in the shaft. Pronounced "shiv."

skip *n.* A container that is hoisted through either a vertical or incline shaft to carry waste rock or ore out of a mine. Skips usually self-dump at the surface. They may also be equipped to raise water out of a mine. Skips ride on guides or tracks inside the shaft.

slimes *n.* Extremely small particles of gold and silver that are washed away with the tailings. Because the particles remain suspended in water and do not settle by gravity, they escape capture by amalgamation.

station *n.* An underground space excavated adjacent to a mine shaft, usually at the intersection of a level. Stations serve as staging areas for mine cars, timbers, supplies, and personnel waiting to be sent to the surface, transported to other levels, or conveyed to the place of work. Specialized stations, such as "pump-stations," "bob-stations," and "tank-stations" receive pumping machinery.

steam pump *n.* A steam-powered pump, characterized by a steam cylinder and an aligned pumping cylinder connected by a piston rod. These self-contained, versatile pumps were also known as direct-acting steam pumps, direct-driven reciprocating pumps, or Worthington pumps. They could be placed in remote areas of a mine, and were often used to remove water from winzes. When installed along the shaft at intervals of about 200 feet, steam pumps could drain a mine by pumping water to the surface in stages.

stope *n.* An underground excavation from which ore has been or is being extracted. — *v.* To excavate ore, usually in a series of horizontal steps.

strike *n.* The direction of an imaginary horizontal line drawn through a gold- and silver-bearing formation. The direction of a straight line that connects two points of equal elevation in a ledge or vein.

tailings *n.* The waste material discharged from a mill or cyanide plant, consisting of water and crushed rock from which the precious metals have been removed. Although a large percentage of the gold and silver has been recovered, tailings are often rich enough to justify further treatment.

tunnel *n.* A horizontal passageway driven into the side of a hill to reach an ore body. Tunnels provide access to the underground workings of a mine and can be intended for drainage, ventilation, and/or haulage. Known as an "adit" in other mining regions.

upraise *n.* **1.** A mine shaft that starts in an underground passageway away from the main shaft, which is excavated upward. **2.** A vertical connection between two levels.

vein *n.* A rock formation that constitutes a valuable mineral deposit. Frequently used as a synonym for ledge or lead.

whim *n.* See **horse whim**.

windlass *n.* A hand-cranked hoisting machine used to raise and lower an ore bucket in a mine shaft. Small capacity and low speed limit its application to prospect shafts, shallow mines, winzes (isolated deep inside a mine, where horse or steam power are not available), and the first few feet excavated when sinking deep shafts.

winze *n.* **1.** A mine shaft that starts in an underground passageway, away from the main shaft. Frequently a vertical connection between two levels. A winze is often sunk to explore an ore body below a mine's lowest level. **2.** A vertical connection between two levels.

INDEX

ABOUT THE AUTHOR

A native of California, Michael H. Piatt first visited the ghost town of Bodie in 1968. This initial visit has influenced his research, writing and way of life for more than three decades. In 1969 and 1970, he served as a Park Aide at Bodie State Historic Park. In 1981 he set aside his career as a civil engineer to study traditional blacksmithing in New Mexico. From 1982 to 1994, he worked at Old Sturbridge Village in Massachussetts, demonstrating the craft of fashioning tools and hardware in the manner of early American blacksmiths. The author of articles on western mining and transportation, he lives in central Massachusetts.

THE FRIENDS OF BODIE

The Friends of Bodie is a group dedicated to the preservation of the gold mining ghost town of Bodie. It is a chapter of the Sierra State Parks Foundation, a volunteer, non-profit organization that helps preserve and interpret state parks in the Sierra District of the California State Department of Parks and Recreation.

The Friends of Bodie raises funds and provides volunteer support to assure that Bodie is properly preserved. Their financial support and volunteer work are vital in preserving this historic treasure. Should you wish to participate in their efforts, please contact:

The Friends of Bodie
Post Office Box 515
Bridgeport, CA 93517